Southern Womanhood and Slavery

T0307769

Southern Womanhood and Slavery

*A Biography of
Louisa S. McCord,
1810–1879*

Leigh Fought

UNIVERSITY OF MISSOURI PRESS
COLUMBIA

Copyright © 2003 by
The Curators of the University of Missouri
University of Missouri Press, Columbia, Missouri 65211
Printed and bound in the United States of America
All rights reserved
First paperback printing, 2018

ISBN 978-0-8262-2171-1 (paperback : alk. paper)

Library of Congress Cataloging-in-Publication Data

Fought, Leigh, 1967–
    Southern womanhood and slavery : a biography of Louisa S. McCord,
1810–1879 / Leigh Fought.
            p.   cm.
Includes bibliographical references and index.
        ISBN 0-8262-1470-3 (hardcover : alk. paper)
        1. McCord, Louisa Susanna Cheves, 1810–1879.   2. Women and
literature—Southern States—History—19th century.   3. Women plantation
owners—South Carolina—Biography.   4. Women—Southern
States—History—19th century.   5. Authors, American—19th
century—Biography.   6. South Carolina—Intellectual life.
7. Plantation life—South Carolina.   8. Slavery—Southern States.
I. Title.
        PS2355.M6 Z67 2003
        818'.309—dc21   2003003714

♾™ This paper meets the requirements of the
American National Standard for Permanence of Paper
for Printed Library Materials, Z39.48, 1984.

Typeface: Adobe Caslon

FOR THOSE UNREPENTANT SOUTHERN WOMEN:

Velma T. Kemp,
Glenna K. Fought,
and Catherine McKenzie.

Without you . . .

Contents

Acknowledgments ix
Genealogical Tables xi

Introduction: Louisa McCord and Her History 1

1. The Cheves Family 14

2. Behind the Parlor Door 25

3. "Equality Is No Thought nor Creation of God" 43

4. "Submissive Bow, and *Be Content*" 66

5. "Inferiority Is Not a Curse" 101

6. "The Most Disastrous One to Me in Every Way" 127

7. "Mother of the Gracchi" 149

8. "At Rest" 177

Bibliography 187
Index 203

Acknowledgments

I once read an article about Alex Haley in which he said that he kept over his desk a drawing of a turtle on top of a fence post. The moral of the drawing was that the turtle could not have climbed to the top of the post by himself. By hanging it over his work place, Haley reminded himself that he had not become so successful without help. While I can only dream of becoming as successful as Haley, I do realize that any major task can be completed only with the help of many people. This project has taken up five years of my life, and most of my sanity. The fact that I did not go completely bonkers is due to the support of the following people.

First, Dr. Richard Blackett guided the first version of this book, as a dissertation, to its completion. When I told him that I would have problems reconstructing McCord's life because most of her documentation was destroyed, he said that there are some people in the past who do not have fully documented lives, but that does not preclude them from being subjects of study. I knew then that he would be the perfect advisor, and he has not proven me wrong. Eric Walther, Landon Storrs, and Elizabeth Gregory all read my dissertation and offered valuable comments for revising it into a book. John R. McKivigan, my editor at the Frederick Douglass Papers, deserves my gratitude for understanding the stress of coordinating the responsibilities of a full-time job with the duties of revising a manuscript. Babu Srinivasan and Dwight Watson, two incredible critics and friends, both helped to clarify many of my arguments.

The staff at the archives and libraries I visited were all quite helpful, especially at the Lancaster County Historical Society and the South Carolina Historical Society, where I spent most of my research time. In South Carolina, the two librarians kindly carried out box after box of the Langdon Cheves Papers, both documents and microfiche, and helped guide me through the routines of the archive. I thank them for every dusty pound that they lugged into the reading room. I also must not forget the interlibrary loan staff of both the University of Houston and Indiana University–Purdue University at Indianapolis. At the University of Missouri Press, Beverly Jarrett and Jane Lago held the hand of a terrified writer through the revisions and publication process. Gary Kass carefully read and cleaned up my prose, the one function that a writer finds unbearable to perform on her own work.

On the home front, Glenna K. Fought, Louis J. Fought, Karl Fought, Keith Fought, Velma T. Kemp, Fred Varela, Eliscia Jinkins, Amy Blackwell, and Farnoush Safavi all believed that I could finish this book, even when I did not. Unfortunately, Orland O. Fought and Cecil G. Kemp did not live to see the completion of this project, but supported me until their ends. Above all, my dear aunt, Catherine McKenzie, prodded me from the beginning, insisting that I pursue publication. One does not refuse her insistence!

My deepest gratitude goes to everyone who was part and parcel of the creation of this book. May the next require less of them.

Heatly–Dulles–Cheves Family Tree[*]

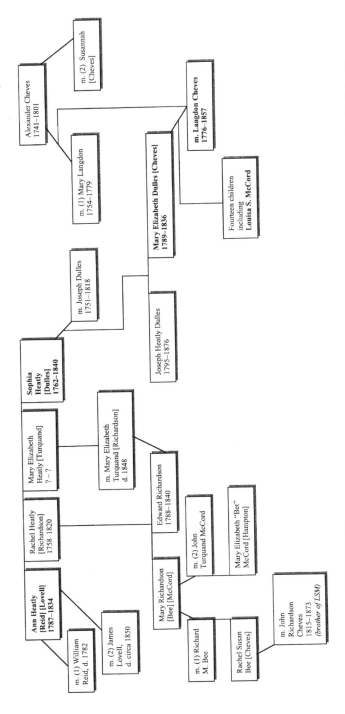

* This chart is not exhaustive, including only figures and relationships that appear in this biography. More extensive genealogies can be found in Richard C. Lounsbury, ed., *Louisa S. McCord: Political and Social Essays* (Charlottesville: University Press of Virginia, 1995) and *Louisa S. McCord: Poems, Drama, Biographies, Letters* (Charlottesville: University Press of Virginia, 1996).

Cheves Family Tree

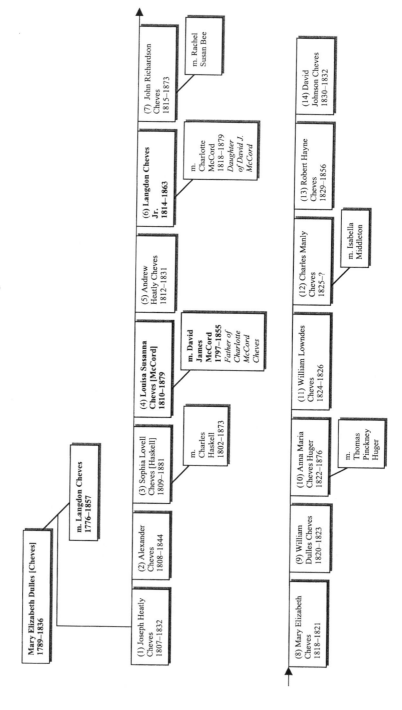

Mary Elizabeth Dulles [Cheves] 1789–1836

m. Langdon Cheves 1776–1857

(1) Joseph Heatly Cheves 1807–1832

(2) Alexander Cheves 1808–1844

(3) Sophia Lovell Cheves [Haskell] 1809–1881
m. Charles Haskell 1802–1873

(4) Louisa Susanna Cheves [McCord] 1810–1879
m. David James McCord 1797–1855 Father of Charlotte McCord Cheves

(5) Andrew Heatly Cheves 1812–1831

(6) Langdon Cheves Jr. 1814–1863
m. Charlotte McCord 1818–1879 Daughter of David J. McCord

(7) John Richardson Cheves 1815–1873
m. Rachel Susan Bee

(8) Mary Elizabeth Cheves 1818–1821

(9) William Dulles Cheves 1820–1823

(10) Anna Maria Cheves Huger 1822–1876
m. Thomas Pinckney Huger

(11) William Lowndes Cheves 1824–1826

(12) Charles Manly Cheves 1825–?
m. Isabella Middleton

(13) Robert Hayne Cheves 1829–1856

(14) David Johnson Cheves 1830–1832

David James McCord Progeny

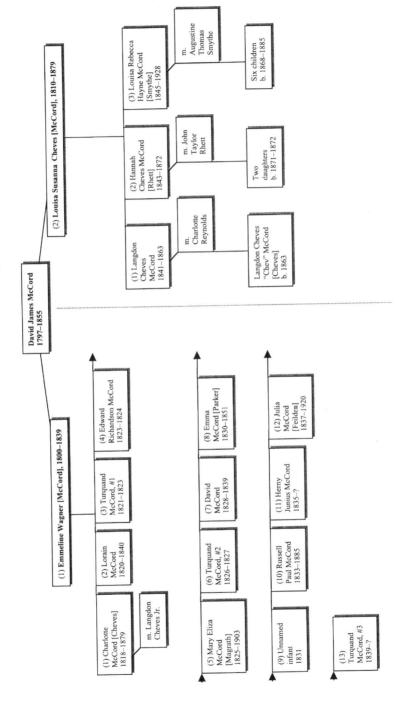

Cheves-McCord-Bee Connection

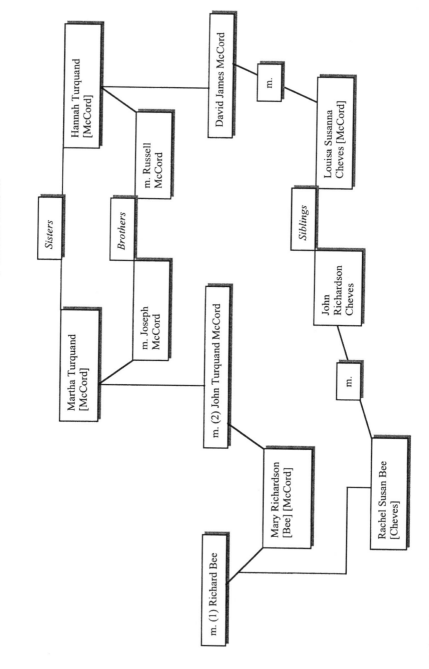

Southern Womanhood and Slavery

Introduction

Louisa McCord and Her History

During the Civil War, Mary Chesnut wrote in her prodigious diary of "the many larger brained women a kind Providence has thrown in my way—such as Mrs. McCord, daughter of Judge Cheves." Chesnut wrote: "She has the intellect of a man and the perseverance and endurance of a woman." "All Doric," strong and unadorned, Jesse Melville Fraser wrote of McCord, her thesis subject, in 1919. As historian Michael O'Brien has described her, "she did not equivocate, she did not excuse, she did not retreat a single inch, and she would be heard." "Vigor, living force of mind, energy," writes literary critic Richard C. Lounsbury, "Louisa McCord seems to have valued these characteristics, not always by these names." She did not comment upon herself. To do so would have violated her belief that "[w]oman was made for *duty*, not for *fame*" and therefore degraded and debased her.[1]

In her time, Louisa McCord was most famous for her play, *Caius Gracchus: A Tragedy in Five Acts.* Some knew her for her single volume of poetry or for her essays in which she advocated political economy and defended slavery and the submission of women. Others knew her as the matron of the hospital set up on the campus of South Carolina College during the Civil War. If asked what she thought was her greatest achievement, she probably would have echoed the Roman matron Cornelia and replied, "My son." For most of her life, McCord identified herself with her father: the statesman, lawyer, judge, planter, and one-time president of the Bank of the United

---

1. C. Vann Woodward, ed., *Mary Chesnut's Civil War* (hereinafter "Chesnut diary"), 733, 677; Jesse Melville Fraser, "Louisa C. McCord," 5; Michael O'Brien, introduction to *Louisa S. McCord: Political and Social Essays*, ed. Richard C. Lounsbury, 1; Richard C. Lounsbury, ed., afterword to *Louisa S. McCord: Poems, Drama, Biography, Letters*, 422; Louisa S. McCord (hereinafter LSM), "Woman and Her Needs," 131–32.

States, Langdon Cheves. Through him, through her husband, attorney David James McCord, and through her own intellectual prowess, she navigated the high political, social, and intellectual circles that included not only the Chesnuts but also the Middletons, the Prestons, the Hugers, Thomas Smyth, William Porcher Miles, William Gilmore Simms, and Francis Lieber, among many others.

Much of Louisa McCord's life reads like an exciting historical novel. Born in Charleston, South Carolina, in 1810, the young Louisa jostled from South Carolina to Washington, D.C., to Pennsylvania, to Rhode Island and back, as her family followed Langdon Cheves's political career. In 1829, the Cheveses permanently returned to South Carolina, where Langdon acquired several plantations. Although Louisa's sister, older by slightly more than a year, married, Louisa remained single for a decade. When she did marry, the plantation and slaves that she brought to the union remained in her name. Her husband died fifteen years later and Louisa took up management of the establishment herself. Meanwhile, she maintained an active intellectual life, publishing essays and associating with the faculty of South Carolina College (now the University of South Carolina).

During the 1850s, in the midst of the country's impending sectional divisions, McCord articulated a defense of slavery and paternalism comparable to that of her male counterparts, the "fire-eaters." When the Civil War came, she threw all of her resources into the secession movement and the defense of the Confederacy. She donated horses, slave labor, needlework, and time, serving as matron of the hospital set up on the college campus. Most of the men in her extended family, including her brothers and only son, died for the "Cause." The Union army marched into her Columbia home and seized it for the headquarters of General O. O. Howard, while Louisa forcibly blocked the staircase to protect the women hiding on the second floor. Her strength of character in the face of adversity both shamed and inspired Mary Chesnut, who would become the most famous southern woman of the era.

After the war ended, that strength nearly failed her, and McCord sank into a deep depression that she attempted to escape through a visit to relatives in Canada. Upon her return, she took upon herself the task of commemorating her father and, through him, the era prior to the national tragedy that had caused her so much personal pain. In the midst of this renewed vigor, she fell ill with "gout in the stomach" and died.

Although the events of Louisa McCord's life alone provide a page-turning narrative that rivals *Gone with the Wind,* they take on greater significance as a background to an intellectual life that makes an equally compelling story. McCord's delayed marriage and continued ownership of her plantation after marriage stand in stark contrast to her ideas on the submission of women, and on marriage and motherhood as the ideal state for women. Similarly, her choice of the essay form as a medium for her ideas and her decision to actively pursue their publication contradict the content of those essays in which she chastises women who seek fame or public recognition. Finally, her residence in northern, nonslaveholding states places her outside the realm of most southern women of the planter class who grew up with the institution of slavery. Louisa had known a life both with and without slavery, and concluded that slavery was the more ideal arrangement. Herein lay the drama of Louisa McCord herself.

Despite the absorbing narrative of her life, despite her status as the only female essayist in the antebellum South, and despite the regard in which others held her during her lifetime, Louisa McCord received little recognition in the century following her death. In the late nineteenth and early twentieth centuries, she was included in several dictionaries of southern writers, but she otherwise virtually disappeared from record, with two exceptions. In 1919, Jesse Melville Fraser chose McCord as the subject for her master's thesis at the University of South Carolina, and Margaret Farrand Thorp included her in *Female Persuasion: Six Strong-Minded Women,* a collection of short biographies of women from the antebellum era that appeared in 1949. Fraser had the benefit of interviewing McCord descendants who remembered Louisa, but she did not have the methodological tools that later historians possessed. Hence, her paper focused primarily on McCord's poetry and other literary contributions.[2] Thorp included

2. Jesse Melville Fraser, "Louisa C. McCord." Fraser made several errors, the most obvious of which was her reference to her subject as Louisa Cheves McCord. Louisa herself might have preferred Fraser's mistake out of her admiration for her father, but he, in fact, put "Louisa Susanna McCord" on all of her legal documents after she married, and that remained her name. Also, Fraser did not investigate many of the descendants' stories. As a result, she says that David McCord had his wife's work published when Louisa's letters clearly indicate that she herself actively pursued publication.

McCord in her book as a counterpoint to five northern women who contributed to the women's movement; she offered a straightforward narrative of Louisa's life as an accomplished, energetic, and individualistic woman. Aside from these studies, even as the fields of Southern history and women's history developed, McCord faded from view until the late 1980s.

Her disappearance might have been due to the odd place that she occupied. As a woman, she was left out of many studies of southern intellectuals, which, until the 1980s, tended to consider the ideas only of influential men. At the same time, women's historians overlooked McCord because she left behind few letters and no diaries, the two crucial types of documents necessary to reconstructing the experiences of women. Neither subdiscipline had yet found a means to incorporate McCord into their theories, and their exclusion of her was a consideration in the writing of this biography.

Then, in the late 1980s and early 1990s, Louisa McCord once more became a force to be reckoned with. Women's history had made a dramatic impact upon our understanding of American society, breaking down the notion of "separate spheres" that theoretically kept the lives and ideas of women segregated from those of men. Moreover, class and race analysis helped historians describe different groups of women in contrast to one another. In the process, women's ideas about their world became ever more important in accurately describing that world; and women who clearly articulated those ideas became a boon to historians. In the midst of these developments, Elizabeth Fox-Genovese's work on the relations between plantation mistresses and their female slaves, *Within the Plantation Household: Black and White Women of the Old South,* appeared in 1988 and reintroduced Louisa McCord.

In her book, Fox-Genovese responded to the work of Anne Firor Scott, author of the first comprehensive study of southern women, *The Southern Lady: From Pedestal to Politics, 1830–1930* (published in 1970), and Catherine Clinton, author of *The Plantation Mistress: Woman's World in the Old South* (1982). Scott argued that the mundane nature of plantation life frustrated the mistresses, and that the Civil War released them from the patriarchy dictated by slavery and allowed them to venture into the public world through women's associations. Similarly, Clinton argued that the mistresses' frustrations came from the feeling that the slaves actually multiplied their work because, in addition to participating in household production, mistresses also had to supervise the other workers on the plantation. The main question in these two books revolved around the relationship between elite women and slavery, and the conclusion echoed Mary Chesnut's sentiment that the mistresses were no better off than their chattel.[3]

Fox-Genovese took issue with this interpretation of the lives of southern slaveholding women. Reconstructing the everyday lives and imaginative worlds of these women, Fox-Genovese described a hierarchical society that extended beyond the boundaries of individual plantations. This hierarchy was based upon economic relationships in which slavery was understood as a class system and women as actors in their respective classes. Mistresses enjoyed the prestige of their position even though they complained about their work, which was predominantly supervisory. They and the enslaved women neither identified with nor had sympathy for one another as women, and identified more strongly instead with the men of their own class and race. The criticism that white women directed at the institution of slavery, Fox-Genovese argued, was merely the venting of frustration, and every slaveholding woman gladly defended slavery through the Civil War and into Reconstruction. In her chapter devoted to Louisa McCord, Fox-Genovese demonstrated that McCord, while clearly more educated than her peers, honestly articulated the ideas of such women.[4]

This biography owes a great deal to Fox-Genovese's work, not only for capturing my attention and imagination with her analysis of McCord, but also for providing the theoretical basis for understanding McCord's life. While Fox-Genovese describes McCord in order to explain antebellum plantation society, I attempt to explain McCord herself, to understand the ways in which McCord came to the conclusions expressed in her essays. The key to this understanding seems to lie in McCord's youth in Pennsylvania, away from supposedly

3. Chesnut diary, 15.
4. Elizabeth Fox-Genovese, "The Imaginative Worlds of Slaveholding Women: Louisa Susanna McCord and Her Countrywomen," chap. 5 in *Within the Plantation Household: Black and White Women of the Old South.*

"southern" institutions, and in her delayed marriage. Thus, this biography also diverges from Fox-Genovese's work by placing McCord in a national setting rather than in a purely southern setting. Finally, whereas Fox-Genovese discusses McCord's conception of herself as a member of a group, this biography explores McCord's definition of herself as an individual. Therefore, this narrative addresses the contradictions in McCord's life and explores her personal struggle to accept her position in the patriarchal society that she so strongly defended.

In considering these issues, my investigation has been informed by research that has emerged since the publication of *Within the Plantation Household*. Work that compares North and South, as well as that which focuses on particular issues in either region, has allowed an image of national class struggle to emerge. The elite classes of both regions struggled to cope with a white underclass and a multiracial working class that they considered a potential danger to social order. The elite classes also worried about radical factions that questioned, and thereby threatened, institutions of social order such as slavery and gender roles. As many historians recognize, McCord was not merely a witness to these struggles in both regions, but a participant in the debates, and she understood those debates to be a matter of national rather than sectional crisis. The competing factions in her arguments ultimately broke down into those who defended and those who threatened social order, which included slavery and the voluntary submission of women. Thus, as this biography shows, McCord was more than an articulate plantation mistress. She consciously participated in the public debates of the antebellum era, not only as a slaveholder, but as an intellectual and, more important, as a woman whose instincts might have led her to challenge the social order to pursue her intellectual ambitions, but whose commitment to that social order caused her to rein in those ambitions.

If this biography owes its inception and theoretical starting point to Elizabeth Fox-Genovese, it owes much of its direction and scope to Richard C. Lounsbury, a classical scholar. In 1995 and 1996, Lounsbury edited two volumes of McCord's letters, essays, poetry, and other writings.[5] His monumental efforts in locating, verifying, and

---

5. Lounsbury, ed., *Louisa S. McCord: Political and Social Essays* and *Louisa S. McCord: Poems, Drama, Biography, Letters.* Two years before the appearance of *Within the Planta-*

annotating these documents resulted in the most comprehensive compilation of McCord's essays, a detailed chronology of her life, and an extensive genealogy of her family, all of which provided historians with an invaluable research tool.

McCord's papers do not lie in a single collection or repository; Lounsbury's impressive work directed me to her known extant letters and to collections that contained documents that furthered my understanding of her life. For instance, I was led to discover the wonderful letters from McCord's sister, Sophia Cheves Haskell, to their childhood friend, Eleuthera DuPont. These letters helped me to reconstruct aspects of McCord's childhood and early adulthood that had been lost with McCord's own letters. Lounsbury's work also directed me toward letters from David McCord's first mother-in-law, which gave me some insight into his life before his marriage to Louisa and helped me to imagine him more as a man and less as a shadowy figure.

The final major contribution of Lounsbury's work was his verification of the memoirs of McCord's daughter, Louisa Smythe. Both he and I rely heavily upon this incredible document, which provides a window into McCord's personal life and behavior, albeit from a very biased source. Because this document is a typescript donated to the South Carolina Historical Society by Smythe's descendants (a copy of it is at the South Caroliniana Library at the University of South Carolina), its authenticity falls under suspicion. Passages in the document suggest that the memoir was originally handwritten, but such a manuscript has yet to be located. Lounsbury applied a critical eye to the typescript, compared it against extant letters from Louisa Smythe, and determined that Smythe herself indeed wrote the memoir. Although not trained as a literary analyst, I was able to retrace Lounsbury's steps through the letters of Smythe as well as those of other members of her extended kin, and came to the same conclusion. Perhaps a more critical eye, one that is not so invested in the document's authenticity, would find contradictory evidence. Until then, the memoir will serve as one of the primary resources in

---

tion Household, Lounsbury published his article *"Ludibria Rerum Mortalium:* Charlestonian Intellectuals and Their Classics," in which he discussed the influences of ancient Roman politics and literature upon southern ideology. He included McCord because she had based her notions of womanhood upon the concept of the Roman matron.

illuminating the private life of McCord. Understanding that criticism might arise from my use of a questionable source, however, I have provided corroborating evidence to bolster that supplied by the memoir wherever possible.

The contributions of Lounsbury's work are best understood in light of the paucity of McCord sources. The goal of this biography is to explain McCord as an individual and to explore the seeming contradictions in her character, and the most difficult obstacle to surmount was the lack of primary personal documents in her own hand. Ironically, McCord herself partially contributed to that very obstacle. Just before the Union occupation of Columbia, she and her daughters burned all of their personal papers to save them from falling into the hands of the enemy. Back on her plantation, in the jubilant aftermath of emancipation, the freedmen destroyed the plantation records, which were a clear symbol of their previous enslavement. Other personal effects must have met the same fate.

The result of this inferno of documents is that much personal information about McCord's life during the antebellum years must be recreated or surmised from other sources, such as the papers of her family or her contemporaries. The most abundant source of papers for the years 1810–1830 lie in the Langdon Cheves I Papers and Dulles-Cheves-McCord-Lovell Papers at the South Carolina Historical Society in Charleston. Letters from McCord's mother and father to one another, to friends, and to their business agents provide a surprising wealth of information about the slaves in the Cheves family in the years before 1820. Some exciting letters reporting the Denmark Vesey conspiracy as it unfolded in Charleston are also saved in these collections, as well as the story of Ann Lovell's disastrous second marriage and the letters from Sophia Haskell to Eleuthera DuPont. For this period, I also turned to the William Lowndes Papers, in the Southern Historical Collection of the University of North Carolina Library, which contain a handful of letters recording the family life of the Cheveses in Washington, D.C., and to papers in the Lancaster County Historical Society documenting the Cheves home, Abbeville, in Pennsylvania. The Langdon Cheves III Papers at the South Carolina Historical Society contain genealogical information and notes from Louisa McCord and Jesse Melville Fraser that fall into the category of "family stories" or "legend." Though the accuracy of such information, as with Smythe's memoirs, is suspect, it leads to an understanding of how the family collectively defined and mythologized its members. With the help of these sources, I was able to cobble together a portrait of the family in which McCord grew up.

For the years 1830–1860, I necessarily rely strongly upon the Langdon Cheves III Papers and the Smythe memoir. Some information can be gleaned from Sophia Haskell's letters, in which she occasionally mentions her younger sister. Probably the best series of sources in McCord's hand lie in the Langdon Cheves III Papers, which contain the letters that she wrote to her brother, Langdon Cheves Jr., as their father lay dying at her home.

The Civil War years provide some of the most complete documentation for McCord. The Smythe-Stoney-Adger Papers at the South Carolina Historical Society provide information on the growing friendship and romance between Louisa's youngest daughter, Louisa Rebecca, and Augustus Smythe, son of renowned Presbyterian minister Thomas Smythe. From these letters, McCord's activities during the war can be traced. Diaries of other women living in and around Columbia help to flesh out and verify the information contained in Louisa Smythe's memoir and letters to her fiancé.

Although I have relied as much as possible on primary material, sometimes the documentation simply does not exist. In these places, I have attempted to reconstruct a social environment typical of a particular time and place to suggest the influences that shaped McCord's life. Indeed, in my efforts to find McCord somewhere in the papers of her family members and my research on her society, I have relied heavily on psychological interpretation in the early chapters. She does not speak in her own voice until midway through this biography. My intention was that the sketch of her that emerges from my interpretations in the early chapters would merge seamlessly with the woman whose own words help construct the narrative of the latter chapters. Still, on the whole, large gaps remain, particularly in connection with some important questions about her private life. These questions circulate largely around three of the most important relationships in her life: with her husband, with her slaves, and with a divine being.

The decision to marry, I believe, was crucial to McCord's acceptance of her role in her society, as she defined her society. For

McCord, to marry meant to fully participate in society as an adult woman and to live her theories. To marry also meant to willingly subordinate herself to a man, who might not care for an intellectual wife, and to bear children and manage a household, which would detract from her intellectual pursuits. I use her poetry, which she wrote sometime in her young adulthood and which reveals a woman deeply torn, to explore the conflict between her personal ambition and her dedication to her duty as a woman to preserve social order in her conception of her world. Her marriage seemed the resolution of that conflict: she was able to have both a socially acceptable life and an intellectual life. Her choice of a husband, of course, was of the utmost importance. Yet very little documentation of their courtship and marriage has survived. Therefore, I examine their relationship with a rather cold and calculating eye, evaluating the union based upon mutual benefits, both social and economic, rather than upon love and sexual attraction.

It is also difficult to make judgments about McCord's abilities as plantation manager or as mistress to her slaves except in relation to those who appear in existing documents, such as letters to her brother during their father's final illness and her daughter's memoir. Her actions in these instances involved slaves who worked in her house in close proximity to her family. Anecdotes about African American life on her plantation have survived through the stories that served as a basis for the prize-winning novels of a subsequent resident of the McCord plantation, Julia Peterkin, and Louisa Smythe recorded some of the duties performed by her mother on the plantation. Aside from those instances, little remains with which to reconstruct even partially life on McCord's plantation. Much of her relationship to enslaved people must remain theoretical and in the realm of the social, rather than the personal.

In a related matter, McCord's financial status and abilities as a business manager of her plantation cannot be accurately verified. The same applies to her family's fortunes in her youth, though first her father and then McCord herself both seem to have followed an upwardly mobile economic path. The panics that plagued the antebellum world, particularly in 1819 and the late 1830s, apparently had little effect upon the Cheves family. Indeed, the 1819 panic had the opposite effect by earning Langdon Cheves the unenviable yet profitable position as the president of the Bank of the United States. That and his subsequent legal career in Pennsylvania paved the way financially for his entrance into the planter class in South Carolina. His eldest daughter, Sophia Haskell, and her family experienced some financial setbacks early in her marriage. The youngest daughter, Anna, made an unfortunate marriage to someone with less financial acumen than her father. Otherwise, the Cheves children who survived to adulthood, including Louisa McCord, seemed unaffected by severe financial difficulties until the Civil War. But this aspect of McCord's life is given little or no mention in this biography.

Another area that receives little attention is religious life. The Cheves family belonged to Presbyterian churches in South Carolina and in Pennsylvania. Louisa McCord also attended the Trinity Church in Columbia, South Carolina, as an adult, and believed Christianity to be a necessary component of civilization. Yet she did not leave any record of the emotional spiritual life led by most women in the first half of the nineteenth century. Even as the women in her extended family experienced religious conversion during the Civil War, McCord seemed cut off from that level of spirituality. Instead, in her essays and poetry, when she makes reference to a deity, she does so more in the language of biological determinism than in that of evangelical devotion. Her understanding of a divine being was intellectual rather than instinctual, and conformed to her suspicion of the individualism inherent in the evangelical experience. Thus, the issue of religion appears here only when McCord herself directly addresses the subject.

These limitations do not inhibit the reconstruction of a powerful story. Concentrating on the drama of McCord herself, this biography primarily traces two themes in her life: slavery and the role of women. Beginning with her childhood, I examine the encounters of her family with slave labor in South Carolina and free labor in Pennsylvania. During this period, between 1810 and 1829, the Cheveses both negotiated salaries and work conditions with wage laborers and dealt with a slave suing for his freedom as well as the news of Denmark Vesey's proposed uprising in Charleston. Since slavery was not central to the economic well-being of the family at this time, I consider this a period of experimentation with and evaluation of the two forms of labor. Later, after the return to South Carolina, slave labor did become central to the financial security and social status of the family. Mc-Cord herself became an active participant in the institution through the inheritance of slaves and a plantation, both of which remained legally hers even after marriage. This security provided her with an incentive to defend slavery and with the means to support herself regardless of marital status. She became a committed defender of the institution until its end.

Parallel to this acceptance of slavery, McCord developed a passion for philosophy and literature and an awareness of the ways in which her gender might interfere with these passions. Unable to receive the same formal education as her brothers, who trained for careers in law, McCord was fortunate in having a father who permitted her to educate herself. Yet her duties as a daughter required her to assist her mother with household management as the family grew by a member every two years. After her mother's death, Louisa became mistress of the household. The number of family members decreased through death or marriage. With fewer responsibilities as a mistress and surrogate mother to her siblings, and with more slaves to attend to the actual labor, Louisa probably found much more time to devote to her studies and creative efforts.

At this point, before her marriage, but after accepting the comforts of a slave society, Louisa found herself in a theoretical crisis. If slavery were necessary for security, and if it depended on a hierarchical social order in which everyone must accept the responsibilities of their position, her indulgence of her relative freedom well beyond an age when she should shoulder the responsibilities of a woman of her class served as a challenge to that social order. At the very least, her behavior meant that she shirked her full responsibilities to marry, raise children, and assume her position as wife within her own household. Yet marriage and children would tax her free time and health. I interpret this period of her life as one of crisis, in which her personal ambition and her responsibilities tugged her in opposite directions and in which her private crisis mirrored a national conundrum between the desire for a social order of hierarchical relationships and the desire for individual fulfillment.

Her marriage, as I have posited, was the resolution of this conflict. David McCord, for his own reasons, seems to have allowed his wife to keep the number of their children to a minimum, to hold legal title to her property, and to fulfill her ambitions as an intellectual. In fact, he seems to have encouraged her. In marriage, Louisa McCord could redefine herself as "Cornelia, Mother of the Gracchi," defender of the social order to the point of personal sacrifice, and incorporate her intellectual pursuits seamlessly into this definition, without contradiction. Moreover, I believe that this self-definition, with its inherent requirement of sacrifice, gave her the strength to imbue the tragedies of her later life with nobility and political purpose.

Finally, her relationship with her father bears note. McCord, by her own admission, worshipped her father. To her, he represented honor, nobility, and duty to nation and family. He permitted her to pursue studies beyond those permitted a girl, he created the contracts that allowed her to maintain legal control of her property, and he ensured that her property was well managed. She, in turn, managed his household after her mother's death and cared for him during his decline at the end of his life. This reversal of roles, well documented in her letters to her brother, was likely the most painful period of her life, testing her emotional strength and her capacity to interpret events in accord with her definition of herself as someone able to sacrifice for the greater good. Her last mission in life was to commemorate her father by making notes for his biography and urging a studio she had commissioned to complete work on his bust. In my opinion, one of the driving forces behind her personal conflict was the desire to imitate her father within the confines of her own gender.

The issues central to the nineteenth century—slavery, the "woman question," individualism, social order—were also central to the life of Louisa McCord. Well-placed socially and economically as a member of the upper class, which involved owning slaves in her case, she had opportunities for education and leisure not available to most people, let alone women, of her time. So rooted in privilege, she was also aware of its limits, particularly in regard to her gender. The ways in which she grappled with these issues and resolved these conflicts in her own life can illuminate the ways in which elite women rationalized and negotiated their position not only in a slave society, but within the nation as a whole.

I

The Cheves Family

On December 3, 1810, Louisa Cheves was born at 37 Meeting Street in Charleston, South Carolina, a city where residents claim that the Cooper and Ashley rivers join to form the Atlantic Ocean. In the first decade of the nineteenth century, that certainly seemed true to the planter class of South Carolina. The lucrative resources of their state, the products of their plantations, sailed down the two rivers to Charleston Harbor. There, the American South met the world on the wharves of the port, trading indigo and rice for manufactured goods and slaves. At the head of Broad Street, presiding over the throng, was the Customs House, where interstate and international trade permitted the accumulation of property. At the opposite end of Broad Street stood the courthouse, where the law defended the rights of those who owned that property. For the aristocracy of South Carolina, Charleston stood as the most cosmopolitan of southern cities and a citadel for their class.[1]

Louisa Cheves would one day belong to that planter class and share their views on slavery, paternalism, and the submission of women. Indeed, she would become the greatest female champion of those ideas. She did not arrive at such conclusions by simple fact of birth and environment, however. To understand her story, we must begin before her birth, with the lives of her parents, Langdon Cheves and Mary Dulles, and their own rise into the political, social, and economic elite. Their ambition and example would provide Louisa with the widest range of opportunities and choices available to a young woman in the early nineteenth century.

---

1. Walter J. Fraser Jr., *Charleston! Charleston!: The History of a Southern City*, 187–90; Robert Olwell, *Masters, Slaves, and Subjects: The Culture of Power in the South Carolina Low Country, 1740–1790*, 17–21.

Langdon Cheves and Mary Dulles met in Philadelphia five years before the birth of their most noted daughter. Cheves, a lawyer in Charleston, had just spent a season at Saratoga Springs in New York to recover his health after having exhausted himself by maintaining a grueling pace at his law practice. He was twenty-eight years old. Joseph Dulles, a merchant friend from Charleston, asked Cheves to escort his daughter home from school on his return journey. Cheves agreed. By the time the two arrived in Charleston, they had agreed to marry in the spring. The brevity of the courtship alarmed the bride's father, who preferred that the couple wait until his sixteen-year-old daughter's eighteenth birthday. He relented, however, when persuaded that a delay would be "ruinous" to the groom's "health and business to have his time and thoughts broke in upon by a long courtship."[2] At least, that was the story passed down to his grand-daughter, Sophia Cheves Haskell. Mary and Langdon married on May 16, 1806, two weeks before Mary's seventeenth birthday.

Marriage had entered a new era in which prospective spouses chose one another with little interference from their parents, and emotion played a stronger role in the partnership. Men and particularly women expected a marriage of reciprocal love and duty. The wife oversaw the functioning of the home and the care and upbringing of the children, while the husband ensured the safety and well-being of the household in relation to the world at large. Ideally, the family was a unit of survival, providing its members with economic and emotional stability. As such, the new role of romantic and sexual attraction did not overtake more practical considerations.[3]

Mary Dulles and Langdon Cheves obviously found one another attractive, given the brevity of their courtship and engagement. Yet both brought to the marriage ambitions of social mobility that the other could enhance. Langdon, a young and successful lawyer just beginning a political career, and Mary, the educated daughter of a

2. "Mrs. [Sophia Cheves] Haskell's account of his [Langdon Cheves's] early life," Langdon Cheves III Papers, South Carolina Historical Society (hereinafter LCIII).

3. For general discussions of marriage in nineteenth-century America, see Carl N. Degler, *At Odds: Women and the Family in America from the Revolution to the Present;* John Demos, *Past, Present, and Personal: The Family and the Life Course in American History;* Anya Jabour, *Marriage in the Early Republic: Elizabeth and William Wirt and the Companionate Ideal;* and Steven Mintz and Susan Kellogg, *Domestic Revolutions: A Social History of American Family Life.*

successful merchant who had ties to planters in the middle country, saw in one another an opportunity to rise into the political and social elite classes of the new nation.

Cheves's ambition stemmed from his early years in the backcountry during the American Revolution and the possibilities for upward mobility that he saw in his youth in Charleston. The son of a Scots immigrant trader and his Virginian wife, he was born in September 1776 into danger and a childhood of abandonment. The ravages of backcountry war between American rebels and the British army and its Loyalist allies, and between the white settlers and Native Americans, had driven the Cheves family and its neighbors into a blockhouse in the Ninety-six District. There, instead of on the family farm, Langdon Cheves first saw life.[4]

Langdon would suffer from both aspects of the war. Shortly after his birth, his mother's sister, Patty Langdon, disappeared in the forest surrounding the fort when she returned to the family farm to retrieve supplies for the new mother and child. Scouts later found her scalped body not far from the walls of the garrison. When the child was barely three years old, his mother, Mary Langdon Cheves, died, a memory that lingered with him. Decades later, Louisa McCord recalled that her father's "earliest recollection lasting him through as a vague and indistinct shadow to the end of his own career, was his mother's death." His eldest daughter, Sophia Haskell, noted that he even remembered the funeral.[5] At the age of six, Langdon also lost his father, Alexander Cheves. Alexander had wavered in his political convictions from the beginning of the War for Independence. In 1782, he resolved his wavering loyalties and professed sympathy with the Crown by leaving South Carolina and returning to Scotland. Before leaving, Alexander signed over his plantation in Abbeville to his son, and placed both the land and Langdon in the care of his brother's family.

According to family tradition, his father's political leanings and departure weighed heavily upon young Langdon. This bitterness per-

4. For further information on the American Revolution in the South Carolina backcountry, see Robert D. Bass, *Ninety Six: The Struggle for the South Carolina Back Country*, and Robert Stansbury Lambert, *South Carolina Loyalists in the American Revolution*.

5. LSM to Langdon Cheves III, May 4, 1876, LCIII; "Mrs. Haskell's account," LCIII.

sisted even after Alexander returned to South Carolina with a new wife, Susannah, in 1785. Langdon had no affection for his stepmother, and was reportedly ashamed of his father's Loyalist tendencies. Certainly this was true of the Cheves descendants. Almost a century later, Louisa McCord vehemently denied that Alexander was a Loyalist at all, stating: "very certainly 'honest Sandy Cheves' never was 'a noted Scotch Tory.'" She pointed to his earlier, brief service in the South Carolina militia to prove her point. As for Alexander's new and younger wife, Louisa insisted: "There was displeasure—no overt dispute between the boy (still a child in years) and his father. The step-mother must naturally have cared little for a child so long a stranger to her." Sophia Haskell added that the Cheves house "could never have been much of a home to him."[6]

The loss of both parents at so early an age probably affected Langdon profoundly, and might have been among the reasons that he insisted on keeping his own family close to him throughout his adulthood. His daughters' interpretation of the bitter relationship between Langdon and his father and stepmother, however, may have originated more in their desire to preserve their image of their father as the rootless American hero who created himself from the opportunities of a new nation. Tension might have existed between Langdon, Alexander, and Susannah, but little evidence other than family tradition remains to accurately characterize the boy's feelings for his family. Upon Alexander's return to South Carolina, Langdon moved into the home of his father and stepmother. Despite the fact that he had begun to earn his own living by his sixteenth year, an age at which most families encouraged their sons to seek independence, he remained under his father's roof until the age of twenty. As for his stepmother, if Langdon felt no affection toward Susannah Cheves, his animosity did not override his paternalist notions toward women. He disavowed his claim to his father's property upon Alexander's death in 1801, allowing Susannah to keep the whole of the estate.[7]

Alexander's decision to reunite with his son changed the course of Langdon's life. When the elder Cheves returned to South Carolina,

6. LSM, "Langdon Cheves: Review of 'Reminiscences of Public Men,'" 238; LSM to Langdon Cheves III, May 4, 1876, LCIII; "Mrs. Haskell's account," LCIII.
7. Langdon Cheves to Susannah Cheves, December 19, 1801, Langdon Cheves I Papers, South Carolina Historical Society (hereinafter LCI).

he chose not to resettle in the Ninety-six District. Although he had signed over his landholdings to his young son to prevent their seizure by the American rebels, he had perhaps lost too many friends in the area to the war and saw much greater opportunities in Charleston than he would find if he returned to the backcountry. Instead, he embarked upon a career as a merchant in the port city, and sent for his son to join him. In doing so, Alexander brought Langdon to the center of South Carolina's economic activity and political influence.

Langdon followed his father into trade, working for a Charleston merchant from 1788 until 1795. He proved a gifted clerk, and was often entrusted with more responsibility by creditors than they extended to his employer. Although he had ceased his scanty formal education at age twelve, he continued to study in his spare time. Lessons in Latin, French, and the social graces such as dancing all indicate an ambition above that of clerk, although Sophia Haskell noted that "he made no great proficiency in any." Nonetheless, according to Louisa, he continued his education "in the intervals of other and serious work," and "he read constantly and carefully; and he never forgot."[8]

Although entrusted with many duties as a merchant's clerk, he eventually turned his eye toward the legal profession. This was a common step for an ambitious young man with no significant fortune or family connections. Charleston society resembled a caste system, and the wealth and power of the state lay in the upper reaches. As a lawyer, a young man could collect large fees and ingratiate himself with this caste by defending its property rights in court. Thus, at the age of nineteen, Langdon began reading law with William Marshall, an attorney in Charleston. He ran errands, read cases, and studied law books late into the night. In 1797, at age twenty-one, he passed the bar examination, two years short of the usual four years of study. While many remembered his initial performance in court as less than outstanding, he soon gained a good reputation and an extensive clientele, beginning with the minister of the Scots Church, Reverend George Buist.[9]

8. "Mrs. Haskell's account," LCIII; LSM to Langdon Cheves III, May 4, 1876, LCIII.

9. Carl J. Vipperman, *William Lowndes and the Transition of Southern Politics, 1782–1822*, 27–28.

By 1801, Cheves had entered into a partnership with Joseph Pease, a lawyer educated in England. In the ensuing years, the firm of Pease and Cheves became involved in cases in nearly every court of South Carolina. Cheves acquired many students, including Thomas Grimke, brother to the future abolitionists Sarah and Angelina Grimke. When Pease announced his plan to retire to Philadelphia in 1808, Cheves contemplated a similar decision. His income exceeded $20,000 a year, a tidy fortune, and his public career now demanded more of his time.

Connections, such as his relationship with Dr. Buist at the church and those he had made as a merchant's clerk, had helped to expand the firm's business and the public life of Langdon Cheves. In the first few years of the new century he placed a foot squarely into the upper reaches of Charleston society by becoming a trustee of the Orphan House, secretary of the corporation of the Scots Church, and, in 1802, a member of the Charleston City Council. Later that same year, he won a seat in the South Carolina House of Representatives from the election district of Charleston, the Parish of St. Michael and St. Philip. Representing such a wealthy district was no small accomplishment for a twenty-five-year-old without a family legacy in politics, and it paved the way for greater influence in state matters. In 1806, the year of his marriage, he won reelection and also was appointed to the office of attorney general for South Carolina.

In the state legislature, Cheves's interests centered on matters involving both commerce and the legal and electoral processes. The committees that he served on included Contingent Accounts, Incorporations, Judiciary, Privileges and Elections, and Ways and Means. A Jeffersonian Republican, he supported the infamous Embargo Act of 1807, and as attorney general he made rulings on the state and federal powers over trade in South Carolina. In all of his actions, Cheves defended the interests of the propertied classes, which he saw as tied to the strength of government, particularly, at this time, the federal government.

Cheves could not have been as successful as he was in South Carolina politics, or politics elsewhere, had he not defended the rights of property. But he was driven by more than personal political ambition. He was part of the property-holding class of the state, and had been since an early age. When, before evacuating to Britain in 1782,

his father deeded his property in to Langdon, it was in order to protect it from seizure by the American forces. Alexander never reversed
the arrangement, and the Abbeville plantation, Long Canes, became
the cornerstone of Langdon's later extensive landholding. While that
property remained under the management of his uncle's family, and
while Langdon relinquished his two-thirds right to his father's intestate property in Abbeville in 1801, allowing his stepmother to claim
all, Langdon's ambitions at the time indicate that he had not given
up the desire to become one of the state's plantation elite. In fact,
his marriage to Mary Dulles sealed him through family obligation
to the Heatlys, planters in the Orangeburg District in central South
Carolina.

While Langdon brought his success as a lawyer and his rising political status to the marriage, Mary brought her charm and her ties to
the merchant and planter classes. Charm, of course, was a desirable
attribute in any mate, but more so for an aspiring politician. Social
success often relied upon the ability to provide a lovely and entertain-
ing companion for colleagues and their wives at balls and dinner parties. Most witnesses remembered that Mary excelled in this department. William Lowndes, a family friend and Langdon's colleague,
always delighted in her company. His wife and Mary became close
friends, and their letters to each other offer some of the few glimpses
we have into the home life of the Cheves family in the early decades
of the nineteenth century. The schoolmates of Mary's daughters are
said to have offered the girls their grudging respect after meeting
the fashionable and graceful Mrs. Cheves; and party guests at her
home in Lancaster, Pennsylvania, in the 1820s remembered her cool
head and good humor when a servant accidentally spilled soup in her
lap.[10] If the woman's charisma was at all evident in the sixteen-year-
old girl, then Langdon Cheves saw both an attractive companion and
one who could serve as an excellent hostess or guest in Charleston,
Columbia, or Washington society.

Mary also possessed an education that indicated her class upbringing and that enhanced and polished her natural social gifts. Educa-

10. The schoolmates are described in Mrs. Augustine T. Smythe, "Recollections of
Louisa Rebecca Hayne McCord," 100, South Caroliniana Library, University of South
Carolina; the soup incident appears in Anne Hollingsworth Wharton, *Salons Colonial
and Republican*, 228–30.

tion for girls had never been a high priority for any class or generation of Americans. Education for a son prepared him for a grander life. Education for a girl, it was believed, only ruined her for marriage. At best, girls could expect to learn little more than how to read and write, and most of those who did lived in the northern states. In the southern states, female literacy levels were abysmally low. Following the War for Independence, however, interest in educating girls increased nominally. If the most important duty of a woman was to raise the future citizens of the new nation, and if a mother was the first and sometimes only teacher a child knew, then the intellectual standards for women must rise. Of course, this new opportunity opened only for those who could afford tuition.[11] As the daughter of a merchant-planter, Mary benefited from the post-Revolutionary changes in female education.

Southern institutions, however, still lagged behind their northern counterparts. Hence, Mary was sent to a boarding school in Philadelphia, the leading city for girls' schools. Few records exist for her time there. She probably began attending at age thirteen, expecting to remain until age sixteen. In those three years, she would have learned the requisite needlework, penmanship, simple arithmetic, music to some proficiency, history for moral lessons, and perhaps elementary French. Paltry as this education might seem, it carried her further forward than her mother or aunts, and provided her with enough polish to ornament the correct suitor.[12] Later, she would pass these rudimentary lessons on to her children. She would expect her daughters to have at least as much education, a crucial factor in the life of her second daughter, Louisa.

More important than her winning demeanor, polished by her education, Mary Dulles's charms included her parents' prosperity and

11. Nancy F. Cott, "Education," chap. 3 in *The Bonds of Womanhood: "Woman's Sphere" in New England, 1780–1835*; Linda DePauw and Conover Hunt, *"Remember the Ladies": Women in America, 1750–1815*, 97; Linda K. Kerber, "'Why Should Girls Be Learned or Wise?': Education and Intellect in the Early Republic," chap. 7 in *Women of the Republic: Intellect and Ideology in Revolutionary America*.

12. Cott, *Bonds of Womanhood*, 112, 115; DePauw and Hunt, *"Remember the Ladies,"* 98–109; Christie Anne Farnham, *The Education of the Southern Belle: Higher Education and Student Socialization in the Antebellum South*, 2–4, 37–40; Jane H. Pease and William H. Pease, *Ladies, Women, and Wenches: Choice and Constraint in Antebellum Charleston and Boston*, 63–64, 78–79.

relations. Unlike her husband, Mary, who was born in Charleston on May 27, 1789, began life in relative comfort. Her father, Joseph Dulles, an Irish immigrant, owned a shop on East Bay Street near the wharves, where he catered to the upper echelon of Charleston society and provided a substantial living for his family.[13] Dulles's trade networks extended into the central part of South Carolina, bringing him into contact with the Heatly family of St. Matthews Parish in the Orangeburg District. In the 1780s, he married the youngest Heatly daughter, Sophia, and brought her to Charleston. Of their six children, only Mary and her brother Joseph survived to adulthood.

Sophia's family provided her daughter with the crucial connection to the planter classes. William Heatly and his wife, Marie Elise Courtonne, were among the first settlers in the Orangeburg District, and acquired extensive landholdings along the Santee River. They had three sons and four daughters. Three of the daughters, Sophia, Rachel, and Ann, would prove important both in maintaining the family prosperity and in the life of their granddaughter and grandniece Louisa. Sophia, obviously, had the most direct connection to the Cheves family as the mother of Mary Cheves. From their mother, both Mary Cheves and Joseph Heatly Dulles inherited land and slave property, as did their children. Sophia's sister, Rachel Heatly Richardson, had a granddaughter, Rachel Susan Bee, who would marry Langdon Cheves's brother, John Richardson Cheves. This union would lay to rest disputes over land inheritance among the Heatly descendants and Cheves family, including the title to Lang Syne, the plantation later owned by Louisa McCord. The eldest Heatly sister, Ann Heatly Reid Lovell, was among the first to experiment in the short-staple cotton that became the prime cash crop of the South. Lang Syne was her plantation. With no surviving children of her own, Ann became a benefactor to Louisa's father, who considered Ann to be like a mother to him, and who possibly hoped to become the heir to her estates.[14]

Each of these Heatly sisters, Sophia, Rachel, and Ann, outlived their husbands and eventually turned to Langdon Cheves, with his

13. Archie Vernon Huff Jr., *Langdon Cheves of South Carolina*, 35–37; Jonathan H. Poston, *The Buildings of Charleston: A Guide to the City's Architecture*, 106; Samuel Gaillard Stoney, *The Dulles Family in South Carolina*, 8–10.
14. Genealogical notes in LCI; Stoney, *Dulles Family*, 8–10.

political and legal influence, to protect their property. At the time of his marriage to Mary Dulles, they provided him with connections to a segment of the planter classes that was gradually gaining wealth and influence in relation to the established eastern planters. In fact, after the birth of his first son, Joseph, in 1807, Langdon planned to retire from law and embark upon a career as a planter himself. His public career took precedence, however, and he put off his plans for another two decades.

Land, however, was not the only form of property, and Cheves's property consisted of more than just land. By 1810, the year of Louisa McCord's birth, he also owned slaves. Langdon was no stranger to unfree labor. His father had owned one slave woman, Phoebe, to aid Langdon's stepmother, Susannah, in her housework, and also held the indentures to a number of servants. The exact number of people that Langdon held in bondage by 1810 cannot be ascertained from receipts, but by the 1820s he possessed at least six slaves: Anna, Nancy, Harry, Lewis, Pliny, and Stepney.[15] Although he may have had more, six "servants" were considered necessary for running an urban household.

The captive labor of black people was synonymous with property and white men's liberty, and conferred social and political status to their masters. Even if a household did not need the services of a particular slave, the income that the slave could procure through hiring out would contribute to that of his or her master. Thus, slaves were part and parcel of profit. Attacks on property and the commerce of South Carolina were attacks upon slavery, and vice versa. Cheves understood this. Given his planter-class ambitions and his income, Cheves probably did own a number of slaves in 1810. Even if he did not, his children would still have been born into an environment where whites readily accepted the bondage of black people as necessary to their own well-being.

When Louisa was born into the Cheves family on December 3, 1810, Langdon and Mary Cheves were emerging as members of the elite class through the combination of his political acumen and her

15. Bill of sale for "black cook Pliny," April 8, 1817, LCI; Ainsley Hall to Mary Cheves, April 7, 1819, LCI; Peter Esnaid [?] to Langdon Cheves, May 10, 1819, LCI; John Schnierle to Langdon Cheves, April 15, 1820, LCI.

familial connections. Her childhood and early adulthood would expose her to alternatives to some of the characteristic aspects of her class, particularly the institution of slavery and the inferior status of women. Yet Louisa would always retain the sense of social entitlement and superiority that accompanied her elite status.

2

Behind the Parlor Door

In 1852, Louisa McCord sat in the study of her home in Columbia, South Carolina, and wrote, "God, who has made every creature to its place, has, perhaps, not given to woman the most enviable position in his creation, but a most clearly defined position he *has* given her."[1] A matronly woman in her forties by that time, she had married, given birth to three children, and accepted her fate as wife and mother. Yet her acceptance also carried a strong note of resignation.

She was set on the path toward her adult attitudes on gender at an early age. In her youth Louisa demonstrated a love for intellectual pursuits beyond that expected of a girl. A family legend described her sitting behind the parlor door, secretly listening to her brothers' math lessons. Her father indulged his daughter's passion and allowed her to join in the boys' studies.[2] If Louisa harbored secret ambitions for a masculine career, however, she disciplined herself to accept a different fate. Louisa, like other elite and intelligent girls of the nineteenth century, faced a future entirely different from that of her brothers or her ambitions. The discovery of the limitations of her gender was the crucial lesson of her childhood and adolescence.

In the Cheves family, the peak of Langdon's political fame, Mary's childbearing years, and Louisa's formative education coincided, with important consequences for Louisa. Between 1811 and 1829, Langdon Cheves ran for or accepted a number of public positions that required him to change residence approximately every two years. With each move, he kept his growing family as close to him as possible. Thus, Louisa witnessed her father's career from as close a position as a little girl could expect. During those same years, Mary Cheves

1. LSM, "Enfranchisement of Woman," 108.
2. Jessie Melville Fraser, "Louisa C. McCord," 6–7.

not only readied the household for each move, but also gave birth to ten more children and began the education of those who survived infancy. Even as Louisa benefited from her mother's early tutelage, she learned from her the duties of a household mistress and witnessed her mother's fate as a woman. She soon learned the frustrations of a woman of ambitious intelligence, which, amid the constant upheaval in her home, taught her the difference between a man's importance and a woman's duty.

The life of the Cheves household and all of its members was dictated by Langdon Cheves's political career. By the time Louisa had celebrated her first birthday, Langdon had celebrated his election to the U.S. House of Representatives. He took his seat amid great national controversy. The Napoleonic Wars in Europe and British aggression toward the United States were drawing the country into the War of 1812. Cheves proved himself a dedicated Republican and war hawk, and supported American entry into the conflict against the British. His boardinghouse in Washington, D.C., filled with like-minded individuals, became known as the War Mess.[3]

Between 1811 and 1815, while Cheves served his term, his family lived with him in Washington, bouncing between boardinghouses, rented homes, and a summer retreat in Philadelphia. Luminaries such as Henry Clay, John C. Calhoun, James Monroe, banker Nicholas Biddle, and Pennsylvania Representative James Buchanan either boarded with the Cheves family or visited their home to heatedly discuss war strategy. The family narrowly missed the invasion of the capital by the British when Mary Cheves's impending confinement and Langdon's access to intelligence took the family to Mary's parents' home, which was now outside Philadelphia.

Langdon Cheves declined to run for office for another term and returned his family to South Carolina in 1815. The following year, he accepted the position of president of the Charleston branch of the Bank of the United States. For the next two years, the Cheves family enjoyed the winter social season in the South Carolina low country and escaped to Home Place, the plantation of Mary's aunt Ann Lovell, or to the upcountry during the sweltering summers.

3. Vipperman, *William Lowndes*, 44, 47, 51; James Sterling Young, *The Washington Community, 1800–1828*, 98–106.

When Cheves became a judge in the South Carolina state court in 1818, his duties took him both to the coast and to the far western reaches of the state. He therefore moved his family to Columbia, the state capital and a more centralized location, to which he could return when his circuit schedule permitted. Apparently, he expected to live out a life of luxury there, for he ordered a large home built.[4] Yet, before the carpenters could complete his new mansion, Cheves once again moved his family.

In 1819, the board of directors of the Bank of the United States appointed Cheves to its presidency, which required a move to the bank's headquarters in Philadelphia. "When first informed of my election as director it was my wish to resign," he wrote to his brother-in-law, Joseph Heatly Dulles. Despite his earlier association with the bank at the state level, Langdon shared his fellow South Carolinians' suspicion of any institution with federal authority. His business agent, John Potter, however, convinced him to take the position. "Mr. Potter told me I would disappoint the stockholders, who said I must go if but for a day," wrote Cheves, "and that unless I would serve, he did not think himself bound to do so, I therefore determined to serve."[5] Characteristically, Cheves threw himself into his work until his resignation in 1823.

After resigning from the bank, Cheves remained in Philadelphia, where he began a private law practice. If he continued to entertain dreams of becoming a planter, he had postponed them for the time being. Moreover, political life continued to beckon. From 1824 until 1827, he served on an international claims commission that was formed to settle disputes over property seized by the British during the War of 1812. In 1828, he was briefly considered as a running mate for Andrew Jackson.

When Cheves's career had taken him to Philadelphia, the Cheves family first stayed with Mary's mother, Sophia Dulles, a widow since 1818. Later, they rented a home in Germantown, a small but well-to-do village bordering the city. In 1820, Cheves bought a lot on Washington Square. There, in 1822, he began to build yet another mansion, which his family would occupy from 1823 until 1826. Summers were

4. William Hall to Langdon Cheves, July 24, 1819, and August 13, 1819, LCI.
5. Langdon Cheves to Joseph Heatly Dulles, February 4, 1819, LCI.

spent away from the city, in Newport, Rhode Island, "for a change of air" and "new health and vigor from the pure breezes of the ocean."[6]

In 1826, Cheves cast about for a new summer home closer to Philadelphia. He found a choice spot in Lancaster, sixty miles from the city. There, he purchased an eighty-acre farm on the Columbia Pike, just outside the city limits but before the tollgate. He named the farm Abbeville, after his childhood home. His daughter Sophia believed the house to be comfortable, but knew that her father would alter the structure to suit his own tastes.[7] Cheves added two wings to the already spacious house, which became the family's home for the next three years, although they did not spend many months at a time there. Newport continued to provide summer escape, and Mary Cheves escorted her daughters through the January and February social seasons in Washington, D.C. Louisa spent even less time in the Lancaster house because she boarded at her school in Philadelphia.

By 1829, the Cheves family numbered ten children, and Langdon pondered the future of this enormous brood. His oldest sons had attended college, and Sophia and Louisa had reached marriageable age. For all his monetary wealth, Cheves did not have sufficient property to ensure that his children would have socially and economically stable lives. With high property values and slim returns on farms in Pennsylvania, Cheves decided to return to South Carolina and establish himself as a planter. There, he began to amass land, still the mark of status in the nation, and slaves, a mark of wealth in the South. His landholdings would grow to include two plantations in South Carolina, two in Georgia, and a summer home in Pendleton, South Carolina, while his slaveholdings would rise to as high as three hundred. His public life as a statesman and his professional life as a lawyer drew to a close. He had attained that combination of wealth, public career, and social standing that defined the southern aristocracy.

6. Edward E. Law to Langdon Cheves, August 11, 1823, and Langdon Cheves to Ainsley Hall, June 1823, LCI.

7. Sophia Cheves to Eleuthera DuPont, August 11, 1826, LCIII. Information concerning the Abbeville farm in Lancaster can be found in the Dr. John L. Farmer Abbeville Collection, Lancaster County Historical Society (hereinafter LCHS), and in the *Lancaster Journal*, November 25, 1825.

In all of Langdon Cheves's movements, "became his wife always with him," Louisa McCord recalled, "unlike others."[8] Mary's following her husband was unusual among the wives of politicians in the early nineteenth century. Typically, politicians tended to affairs of state while leaving their wives at home to attend to the affairs of the household. This arrangement, also common among military wives and the wives of men in the maritime industries, was based upon the idea of "separate spheres" for each gender in the marital partnership. It also allowed the wives a certain level of independence, the ability to run a household without interruption, and a means of limiting their family's size through extended periods of sexual abstinence. On the other hand, if the partners desired sexual and romantic companionship, this arrangement caused loneliness and frustration that was hardly overcome by the frequent letter-writing that sustained such relationships.

At the opposite extreme from marriages of constant separation lay those of migrating families. The most typical migration pattern tended to be east to west, uprooting and transplanting the family into an unfamiliar and often rugged environment. Although the physical closeness of the marriage was preserved, the wife endured not only the hard labor required of the move, but also a severance of her ties to her circle of extended family and friends upon whom she relied for emotional support and communal labor. These marriages also did not benefit from the fact that the husbands unilaterally made the decision to move, often against the wishes of their wives.[9]

At the beginning of his political career, in an attempt to overcome the separation that his position in Washington would require, Langdon insisted that his family join him in the capital city. Mary would have liked to stay with her parents in Charleston, but deferred to her husband's wishes. Fortunately for her, the Dulleses themselves soon relocated to Germantown, where Mary could visit frequently. In fact, as mentioned, they proved a refuge during the British invasion of the capital in 1814. When Cheves's term expired and he returned

8. LSM's notes for a biography of her father, LCI (hereinafter "LSM notes, LCI").
9. For further discussion of migration and its impact upon families, see Joan E. Cashin, *A Family Venture: Men and Women on the Southern Frontier,* and John Mack Faragher, *Women and Men on the Overland Trail.*

the family to South Carolina, Mary again preferred to stay near her parents. The return south, however, proved less painful than the migration north because she returned to old friendships in Charleston and to her mother's family near Columbia. By the time that Cheves accepted the presidency of the Bank of the United States, he had learned to present the news to his wife in the most positive light, as indicated in her letter to her brother announcing her move to Philadelphia. "I am perfectly satisfied with the course things have taken," she wrote, "as it concerns our being in the same place, which really was the only object with my husband when he said yes!"[10] Later, Mary's mother suffered a stroke and joined the Cheves household, and Cheves could move the family back south without protest from his wife. Langdon and Mary Cheves had found a balance between the extremes of a marriage of separation and a marriage of migration.

One effect of constant companionship on the Cheves marriage was a large brood of children. Amid the frantic pace of changing residences, Mary gave birth to ten more children after Louisa, four of whom she buried.[11] When Louisa joined the family in 1810, two brothers, Joseph and Alexander, and a sister, Sophia, had greeted her. Within a year of Louisa's birth, Mary became pregnant with her fifth child, whom she carried through the move to Washington, D.C. There, on June 17, 1812, she gave birth to a boy, Andrew Heatly, named for one of his mother's uncles. Eighteen months later she conceived her sixth child. This one, a boy named after his father, entered the world on September 3, 1814, at his grandmother's home in Philadelphia as the British prepared to invade the capital city. Mary conceived her seventh child seven months later, and gave birth to John Richardson Cheves on December 27, 1815. Her eighth child, Mary Elizabeth, arrived on March 2, 1818, in Columbia.

From then until 1820, Mary managed to avoid pregnancy for the second longest period in her marriage. While she may have miscarried a child during this time, she may also have avoided conception by the mere fact that her husband traveled from home frequently in his duties as judge. Then, shortly after her return to Philadelphia, she

---

10. Mary Cheves to Joseph Heatly Dulles, January 27, 1819, LCI.

11. Lounsbury, ed., *Louisa S. McCord: Political and Social Essays*, 46–47; Susan Smythe Bennett, "The Cheves Family of South Carolina," 88–95.

conceived her ninth child. She gave birth to William Dulles Cheves in Germantown on December 2, 1820. A year later, a tenth child made its impending arrival known, and Anna Maria Cheves made her appearance on May 26, 1822. The next day, Mary Cheves turned thirty-three.

Childbirth and grief were close companions. New babies continued to arrive, but they did not safeguard against the loss of others. While Mary was pregnant with Anna Maria, her three-year-old daughter, Mary Elizabeth, died on October 9, 1821. Less than two years later, on May 2, 1823, William Dulles followed his sister to the grave. By 1824, Mary was expecting the arrival of her eleventh child. Two weeks before his mother's thirty-fifth birthday, William Lowndes Cheves made his appearance, named for a family friend and statesman who had recently died. At the age of one, little William followed his namesake.

The death of the infant William Dulles came so suddenly that Dr. Synge Physick, the family's physician, requested permission for an autopsy, "as the disease of my little patient was attended with uncommon obstinacy." He believed that the disease was whooping cough that had "seized upon the *Brain!*" According to his mother, William had demonstrated remarkable intelligence. "He had an accurate acquaintance into the general geography of the worlds as all the great divisions of the four quarters, his alphabet he knew well in Goldsmiths animated nature he was familiar with most of the prints and appeared constantly thirsting after information," she bragged. Tragically, diagnosed Dr. Physick, "such activity of mind naturally led the disease to the Brain so that the very object of our delight was the source of his death."[12] If Mary believed that assessment, she did not change her instruction of her other children, who continued to learn their first school lessons from her and from her eldest daughters, Sophia and Louisa.

To add to her sense of loss, Mary's father died in 1818, and her mother suffered a stroke in 1824, losing the use of one side of her body. A widow facing a long recovery, Sophia could not care for herself. The Cheves family took her in, providing Mary with the

12. S. L. Physick to Langdon Cheves, May 4, 1823, LCI; Mary Cheves to "My Dear Friend" [Mrs. William Lowndes], May 28, 1823, LCI.

companionship of her mother, but also increasing her responsibilities by adding an invalid to her care while her children continued to increase in number.[13] After her mother moved into the household, and before William Lowndes Cheves's death in 1825, Mary gave birth to her twelfth child, Charles Manly Cheves. Charles "made his debut August 12, 1825" in Newport, Rhode Island.[14]

For three years thereafter, until 1828, Mary escaped the rigors of childbearing. This was the longest period of her marriage, save for the final six years of her life, in which she was not in some stage of pregnancy. Again, she may have miscarried during this period, but no record of such an event survives. Then, in the fall of 1828, she learned that she would have a thirteenth child in the spring. She gave birth to Robert Hayne Cheves, named after her husband's favorite law student, on April 9, 1829.

Robert, known as Hayne, would not be Mary's last child. Shortly before the family returned to South Carolina in 1829, and approximately six months after the birth of Hayne, Mary conceived her fourteenth and final child. She gave birth to David Johnson in South Carolina on June 9, 1830. David died approximately two years later, in 1832. His death took place only a year after that of his older brother Andrew, who had died during the summer of 1831, and about the same time as the death of the eldest Cheves son, Joseph, now a young man. By the time she buried her eldest and youngest sons, Mary had weathered the physical trauma of fourteen pregnancies, mourned the deaths of six children, and oversaw six major household moves, not to mention the seasonal changes of residence.[15]

Growing up, Louisa witnessed her mother's pregnancies and declining health. She herself must have experienced a range of emotions with the impending arrival of each new brother or sister. A new sibling would have brought with it the thrill of watching a new life develop, and less supervision from her mother or nursery maid. At

13. Sophia Cheves to Rebecca Lowndes, August 12, 1824, LCIII.

14. Sophia Cheves to Eleuthera DuPont, August 30, 1825, LCIII.

15. Bennett, "Cheves Family of South Carolina," 88, 89, 92; Smythe, "Recollections," 95. The second eldest Cheves son, Alexander, after causing his family many years of pain through his neglect and taste for, in their opinion, unsavory company, died in 1844 after an extended illness related to a head injury. Langdon Cheves to Alexander Cheves, May 16, 1836, and Langdon Cheves to Langdon Cheves Jr., July 22, 1843, LCI; Smythe, "Recollections," 97.

the same time, with each child Louisa and her older sister, Sophia, took on new responsibilities in managing the household. "Carrying the keys" marked a higher stage in their apprenticeship as house-keepers, but also took them away from their own amusements. Their mother's confinement might also lead to the permanent assumption of her duties should she die in labor, not to mention the grief of losing a parent.

Furthermore, Mary did not seem able to control if or when she had a child. An intelligent girl such as Louisa would gradually have perceived the tyranny of female biology. As amazing as the idea of a new life emerging from a woman's body might be, a woman in labor was in extreme pain and danger. Her mother's body produced children, but the phenomenon of childbearing was something that happened to her. She was like the passive victim of some natural disaster, like a house in a hurricane. Louisa knew that the same fate awaited her. Childbearing, even disconnected from sexuality, under-scored her mother's and her own helplessness as women. Childbearing connected to sexuality might seem to be an act of violence against a woman.[16]

Girls in the nineteenth century might have remained naive about the intricacies of male-female relationships in the bedroom.[17] Extreme Victorian prudery, however, did not emerge in America until after Louisa's adolescence. Sexuality became taboo as a product of urbanization and the emergence of a middle class that sought to limit family size by limiting sexual intercourse. Prior to that development Americans were a rather bawdy lot, in the spirit of the democracy of the Jacksonian era. While upper-class families such as the Cheveses limited their daughters' knowledge of sexual behavior, they could not isolate them from some understanding of the consequences of sex. Mothers had babies, teenaged girls menstruated, the Bible listed *begat*s, animals mated on farms, and, in the cities, street actors put on

16. In *Woman of Valor: Margaret Sanger and the Birth Control Movement in America,* her biography of Margaret Sanger, Ellen Chessler argues that the sight of her mother suffering through six pregnancies moved Sanger to search for alternate options for women. While McCord did not go to such extremes, she seems to have recognized, as Sanger did, that childbirth limited female sexuality and opportunity.

17. Barbara Welter, *Dimity Convictions: The American Woman in the Nineteenth Century,* 13.

raunchy performances. If nothing else, girls understood that marriage meant pregnancy for the next twenty years of their lives.

In the nineteenth century, few questioned the belief that a woman's biological capabilities should define her economic, social, and political roles. Women were associated almost exclusively with pregnancy, breast-feeding, and child-rearing. As a result, they were tied to the household, particularly as industrialization took most production outside of the home. Only a few questioned the inevitability of this arrangement or the centrality of child-rearing to a woman's being.

Management of the household became the primary economic function of women, and child-rearing their central activity. The child-rearing role defined a woman socially, and gave her legitimacy as an adult. Women gave birth to future generations of Americans and inducted them into the social order. The production of children meant the production of a workforce for the working class and the perpetuation of property-holding and political power among the elite class. To ensure that girls were not seduced away from child-rearing and the reproduction of class, part of the mother's job was the perpetuation of gender roles. Child-rearing, then, was infused with political meaning, but not political power. Without political power, women could do little to change their social or economic roles, and remained in a dependent and inferior position relative to men. In fact, because of the accepted notion that childbearing defined a woman's purpose, few women questioned their fate, although many attempted to improve their status and the condition of their allotted role.[18]

In the nineteenth century, girls often entered an apprenticeship in housewifery under their mothers during their preteen and teen years. This served both as training for a girl's future in a similar capacity for her own husband and children and as a practical measure for the mother who found herself repeatedly preoccupied with the care of children under the age of two. By Louisa's teen years Mary had already inducted both Louisa and Sophia into "carrying the keys"

18. Nancy Chodorow, "Mothering, Male Dominance, and Capitalism," 96, 102; Simone DeBeauvoir, *The Second Sex*, 483; G. William Domhoff, *The Higher Circles: Governing Class in America*, 34; Hester Eisenstein, *Contemporary Feminist Thought*, 9, 11, 70–73, 88; Zillah R. Eisenstein, "Some Notes on the Relations of Capitalist Patriarchy," 44; Carroll Smith-Rosenberg, *Disorderly Conduct: Visions of Gender in Victorian America*, 65.

and management of the daily operations of the Cheves home. Sophia bragged to her friend Eleuthera DuPont: "I have been house keeper for the last fortnight, and have actually made such proficiency as to have made two puddings and superintend the making of some cake, and I can actually give out breakfast and even dinner without much prompting."[19] Louisa learned similar tasks, and took over for Sophia during the following two weeks.

Education of young children was also the province of the mother. "Mrs. Cheves seems I think to improve as a teacher," William Lowndes reported to his wife in 1814, "and her little school ones all uncommonly advanced for their age. Perhaps they learn too much but at least their memory and their power of attention are improved."[20] In her adulthood, Louisa credited her father with her own intellectual development. In fact, his influence affected her greatly. During Louisa's earliest years, however, it was probably Mary rather than Langdon who gave lessons to the bright little girl and first instilled in her a love of learning.

As with other household duties, however, Mary turned this task over to the elder children as part of their apprenticeship. Thus, when Sophia relinquished the keys to Louisa, she wrote to her friend: "I do not give up with them all of my dignity for I am school mistress besides." Sophia's pupils were her sister Anna, who was six, and a cousin of a younger age. She would listen to their lessons, "give them a little scolding, then a piece of gingerbread and then send them out to play." In the afternoon, she continued, she would "make them sew, give them a little more scolding, and get out of their way as soon as possible."[21] Although Sophia does not seem to have taken her teaching as seriously as her mother had, she passed along the skills her mother taught her.

For Louisa, however, education took on a much more important role in her life than as an appendage to her household training. She began her formal education in 1821 when she and Sophia

19. Sophia Cheves to Eleuthera DuPont, n.d., LCIII. For a discussion of girlhood in the nineteenth century, see Frances B. Cogan, *All-American Girl: The Ideal of Real Womanhood in Mid-Nineteenth-Century America*, and Welter, *Dimity Convictions*, 3–20.

20. William Lowndes to Elizabeth Lowndes, January 1, 1815, William Lowndes Papers, Southern Historical Collection, Manuscripts Division, University of North Carolina–Chapel Hill.

21. Sophia Cheves to Eleuthera DuPont, April 10, 1829, LCIII.

were enrolled at the Grimshaw School in Philadelphia. Their classmates came from the upper stations of Philadelphia society, and included Eleuthera and Sophie DuPont, the daughters of industrialist
Eleuthère Irénée DuPont. Presumably, then, the Cheves sisters received the best education afforded to the girls of their generation.
They learned to write proper letters and essays. They learned to con-
verse in French. Louisa also took lessons in bookkeeping and music.
Medals were offered in writing, grammar, composition, arithmetic,
history, and conduct.[22] Nevertheless, little substantial change in education for girls had taken place since Mary Dulles's school days.
Although more girls entered school by the 1820s, their education remained more decorative than practical. Lessons that served a purpose
in a woman's life, such as bookkeeping, were not meant to prepare
her for economic independence, but to make her a better and more
efficient housewife.[23] Louisa's desire for knowledge would not be
sated with mere polish or practicality.

Modeling herself after her father, Louisa began her own process
of intellectual exploration. The details of how she obtained this education, however, remain a mystery. The story of her hiding behind
the parlor door to eavesdrop on her brothers' math lessons is one
suggestive clue, yet no documentation exists to corroborate it. Like
many family legends, the tale represents a perceived truth more than
an actual event. Such stories reflect the lasting impression of an individual's personality or habits as remembered by their descendants.[24]
Louisa's dedication to intellectual pursuits outside of the classroom
became a hallmark of her work later in her life, and earned her the
adjective "masculine."[25]

The essays, poetry, and play written during her adult life indicated
the extent of her interests and reflected influences that extended back
to her childhood. She admitted to a talent for math and history. She
also maintained her fluency in French. In her adulthood her skilled
translation of *Sophismes Economiques* (Sophisms of the protective policy) by political economist Frédéric Bastiat made his prose more terse

22. Enrollment dates and Louisa's subjects: receipts in LCI; medals: Sophia Cheves
to Eleuthera DuPont, November 27 [1823], LCIII.
23. Cott, *Bonds of Womanhood*, 116–25; Farnham, *Education of the Southern Belle*, 1–4.
24. Elizabeth Stone, *Black Sheep and Kissing Cousins: How Our Family Stories Shape
Us*, 3–11.
25. Lounsbury, afterword to *Louisa S. McCord: Poems, Drama, Biography, Letters*, 416.

and powerful.[26] It was literature, however, that seems to have captured her youthful imagination. The command of language required by poetry impressed her, and moved her to copy the style of many eminent poets.

William Shakespeare and the English Romantic poets made a strong impression upon Louisa. Langdon Cheves was clearly responsible for her love of the Bard. In his early days as an attorney he recited Shakespeare as preparation to go to court, and he passed on this affection for the playwright to his daughter. Langdon may also have contributed to her love for the eighteenth-century poets, including the Romantics. She fondly remembered his reading of Robert Burns as a "treat."[27] Both Louisa's poetry and prose demonstrated that she shared these poets' love for the music of language. Through such poems as "The Village Churchyard," "The Dream of Life," "Ye're Born to Die," and "My Dead," among others, she also shared the melancholic fascination with death common in eighteenth-century poetry, a fascination that the frequent funerals in the Cheves home only heightened. Moreover, she often paid direct homage to earlier poets, opening her own volume of poetry, *My Dreams*, with a quote from Lord Byron's *Childe Harold*, and copying the style and subject matter of Oliver Goldsmith's "The Deserted Village" and Thomas Gray's "Elegy Written in a Country Churchyard" in her own "The Village Churchyard."

Whether Louisa absorbed the majority of these influences in her formative years or as an adult is uncertain. Her poetry, play, and essays did not see publication until she had reached her late thirties and early forties, but she clearly maintained a passion for the life of the mind that extended beyond her simple, practical, and polished formal education. Her pursuit of education would have interfered with her household duties at some point in her life. Indeed, many women of the time lamented that, as their family and responsibilities grew, their ability to maintain any intellectual life dwindled. An intelligent girl such as Louisa would have observed her mother's life and believed that her own would be the same: childbearing and childrearing constantly sapping her resources, preventing her from pursuing her intellectual interests. In Louisa's case the presence of her

26. Ibid., 423–24.
27. LSM notes, LCI.

brothers in her home, avidly pursuing an education that would take them beyond the home to a university, provided an additional reason for annoyance with the duties of the household.

Louisa saw that if she could have led the life of her father, she could have indulged her own intellectual ambitions. Furthermore, to Louisa, her father was the embodiment of power. He could supplant her mother's authority in the household, and he had control over his own destiny. Not only that, but he was also important to the nation. Fathers are important figures in all children's lives. In Louisa's case, however, her father also exercised authority outside her home, in the grand world of politics and finance. As an adult, Louisa insisted that she knew very little of her father's career, writing: "I need a history myself to learn it." She and her siblings grew up "in ignorance of the great man who stood among them."[28] Of course, small children seldom know of the great issues of their day. William Lowndes, a frequent visitor to the Cheves household in Washington, appreciated this fact. Despite Mary Cheves's "foolish prejudices against segars [sic] and billiard tables (the two best things at Washington)," he found much relief in his visits to the Cheves home, particularly in the childish prattle that filled the house and which reminded him of his own family left behind in Charleston. "Louisa and Sophia propose no projects of a bank," Lowndes wrote to his wife, "and Joseph has never started the subject of conscription."[29]

Nonetheless, national politics saturated the Cheves household, and the children became aware of national events sooner than most. Langdon "would discuss freely all subjects with his friends," Louisa remembered, lamenting, "What would I not now give to recall such conversations."[30] Her earliest memories of her father were of him surrounded by national luminaries, and he held the highest and most controversial financial office in the nation during her childhood.

Not only were the issues and events of the day discussed openly by her father and his visitors, but they also touched Louisa's life personally. As mentioned, Langdon Cheves had supported the War of 1812, which drove the family from their home as the British prepared

28. Ibid.
29. LSM notes, LCI.
30. Ibid.

to invade the capital in 1814. In her school days Louisa felt ostra-
cized by her classmates because her father headed the national bank.
While that persecution may have been minor and short-lived, given
the fickle nature of adolescent social life, Louisa distinctly remembered defending her father and the Bank of the United States against
her classmates' "jealousy of an honest outsider."[31] During the family's
stay at Lancaster, the city honored her father as a prominent member
of the community, twice bringing the public spectacle of Fourth of
July celebrations into the Cheveses' front yard. Although her child's
mind may not have grasped the nuances of adults' arguments or concerns, she was not insulated from the world of politics.

In fact, Louisa derived a sense of self-importance through her relationship to her father. She fondly remembered witnessing many of
his conversations with prominent men. Her father allowed her to sit
"upon his knee with any company often business," she wrote. "He
never repulsed me," she recalled, because she kept "quiet as a mouse
to be sure."[32] The child Louisa could not contribute to debates on
banks, conscription, or war, but merely being in the presence of such
men and such conversations, all involving her father, left a marked
impression upon her. Langdon Cheves baptized Louisa into a culture of politics and allowed her the vicarious experience of greatness.
Just as important, these moments on his knee were among the few
displays of warmth that he showed Louisa as a girl.

Louisa approached her father with awe, and in her poetry por-
trayed herself as a supplicant or a nonentity seeking vicarious experience. In "Dedication: To My Father," which prefaces *My Dreams,* she
presents herself as a humble, would-be poet, "o'ercome by my own
weakness." She continues: "I am built as one / amidst the crowd: an
atom in the sunbeam / Nothing more than all the triflers round me."
In offering her poems to the rest of the world, her hopes sink "Back,
back, upon myself and nothingness." Elsewhere in the volume, she
calls her poems "dreams" and "fancies, airy nothings" that she uses "to
be deceived" because "'tis sweet to deceive ourselves." She characterizes dreams and fancy as both teasing and comforting to us. Fancy

31. William Lowndes to Elizabeth Lowndes, November 30, 1814, William Lowndes
Papers.
32. Ibid.

cannot be taken seriously, despite the solace it may bring, because, ultimately, dreams and deceptions fade and turn into nothingness. As their creator, she is equally frivolous and also, finally, nothing. She will not be like the heroes in her poem "Who Dares to Say They Died?" whose spirits live on through the tales of their great deeds. Instead, at best she is an observer, sitting in a churchyard watching time pass, witnessing a great battle between good and evil, or simply loving "The First Star of the Evening," a metaphor for Langdon Cheves in his declining years.[33] She is the seemingly insignificant "nothing" in the shadow of great people, yet significant enough to witness their interactions. Louisa denied her own importance and in self-abnegation chose an acceptable feminine voice, finding identity through the subject of her observation, her father.[34]

Louisa's sole frustration with her father seems to have been his cold demeanor, which caused her to characterize him as an "Iron Man" even half a century later. "Undemonstrative, even as mounting to secretiveness of sorrow." "Momentary harshness at times, caused by effort to self-command." "The subdued passion within made his manner at times painfully undemonstrative . . . He was always coldly calm." These assessments, written in Louisa's old age as she prepared a biography of her father, suggest her conflict over his emotional distance.[35]

Fathers in the nineteenth century were not expected to do more than materially provide for the family. Yet Louisa seemed to long for more, and constantly apologized for Langdon's coldness. She insisted that he had "passions of the strongest," which might occasion-

33. Quotations are from "Dedication: To My Father," "Proem: Dreams," "The World of Dreams," "The Village Churchyard," "Combat of the Powers of Good and Evil," and "The First Star of the Evening," in *Louisa S. McCord: Poems, Drama, Biography, Letters,* ed. Richard C. Lounsbury, 41–42, 44–50, 103–7, and 137–44, respectively.

34. In *The Madwoman in the Attic: The Woman Writer and the Nineteenth-Century Literary Imagination,* their critique of female writers in the nineteenth century, Sandra M. Gilbert and Susan Gubar argue that Emily Dickinson used a similar tactic, seeming to nullify her own identity in her poetry (587–91). Joanne Dobson makes a comparable point in *Dickinson and the Strategies of Reticence: The Woman Writer in Nineteenth-Century America,* which delves into Dickinson's refusal to publish her poetry and into the persona that she adopted in her daily life. Dickinson, however, assumed the identity of a wry and ironic observer in her work, whereas McCord used her father as the conduit to her experience.

35. LSM notes, LCI.

ally seem "unreasonable passion." These displays, as well as the very lack of display that concealed emotional depth, she decided, came from his strong-willed self-control. She believed that he hid much grief, much "secretiveness of sorrow," although she did not seem to know the source of that sorrow, and she empathized with him rather than demanded his attention.[36]

Her empathy, however, was surpassed by her worship of her father. To her, Langdon Cheves represented nobility and honor in their highest forms. She found it "impossible to separate the man's private character from public acts." Wholly uncritical, her descriptions border on deification. "Does the greatest mind ever realize the vast stretch of its power?" she wrote of her father's humility. Of his advice, she wrote: "The oracle spoke plainly—never leaving a double sense to be divined." He did not run for vice president, according to Louisa, because "the tendency for things was toward corruption" and "he was too pure a man for such ambitions." She continued: "I have never known or read of any man equal for completeness of character . . . the very perfection was in its limitless usefulness. . . . This is the verdict I think not of a natural prejudice in his favor, but of my well-sifted reason."[37] This excessive admiration served as a backdrop for her other observations about her father in the notes she made for his biography.

Louisa grew to understand that her father was a man of importance in national politics. She also began to perceive his authority in her home. The mother is the first and seemingly absolute power in many children's lives. In the nineteenth century, as children grew, they learned that their father would supplant their mother as the arbiter of family life. In the Cheves household, Mary made the daily decisions. Langdon, however, set the context for those decisions, and sometimes defied them. Louisa gradually learned that the true source of power at home lay with her father. During the years in Washington, for example, Mary banned talk of politics from her parlor.[38] Nonetheless, Langdon regularly defied his wife's ban. This, of course,

36. Ibid.
37. Ibid.
38. William Lowndes to Elizabeth Lowndes, November 1814, William Lowndes Papers.

would not necessarily have shaped Louisa's perception of gender relations in her home without the larger context of her father's rule, which expressed itself in the constant moves and the growing size of the family.

Langdon Cheves spoke with the voice of authority in the world and in his home. Finally, and perhaps most important to Louisa, he possessed the power of self-determination in his own life. The legend of Cheves's rise from a poor, motherless infant in the backcountry of Carolina to a statesman, head of the national bank, and potential vice presidential candidate cast him as the rugged individualist who succeeded through hard work and determination. Such stories profoundly influence children by impressing upon them a family identity and a set of familial values.[39] Langdon Cheves made important decisions, lived an important life, and, according to family lore, created that life for himself. Louisa, on the other hand, was already learning that she faced a life of child-rearing and housekeeping regardless of her own proclivities.

Louisa associated power with politics, with the ability to make decisions concerning one's own life and the lives of others, and with masculinity. As she grew up, she learned the relationship of power to privilege. While privilege is not necessarily power, power certainly confers privilege. On her father's knee, Louisa learned that the closer she sat to power, the more privilege she gained. She came to understand her own privilege first in a material sense, represented by the luxuries of her homes, her entrance into society, and her education. Later, privilege took on a social connotation, as she acquired an elite class consciousness in relation to the working class represented most intimately by the slaves and servants in her own household.

39. Stone, "Family Ground Rules," chap. 1 in *Black Sheep and Kissing Cousins.*

3

"Equality Is No Thought
nor Creation of God"

Slavery was an ever-present phenomenon of Louisa Cheves's life from her birth through the Civil War. In her adulthood, she saw slavery as a necessity, not only for her own well-being and upkeep, but also for the improvement of people of African descent and for the maintenance of peaceful relations between classes and races. "The antagonism of races is working itself out, in every instance where two races are put in collision, by the quicker or slower extinction of the inferior and feebler race," she wrote in her essay "Negro-mania" in 1852. "The only exceptions to this rule which the world has ever seen are where the beneficent system of serfdom (i.e., slavery) has come to the rescue and protection of the weaker race . . ."[1] Her defense of slavery could easily be seen as a product of her immersion in a society that accepted not only slavery but also the inequality of the races, and as a product of her personal ownership of slaves, property that gave her financial autonomy.

In her formative years, however, slavery was not as prominent a feature in her social landscape. Her understanding of slavery developed first as a relationship of class, then as a relationship of race, and finally as a relationship of property. Experience in the changing market economy as well as the perceived betrayals and dangers of free servants led Louisa to believe that unfree labor was a practical system, at least for the master. Meanwhile, observation of the condition of free blacks in the North led her to the naive and unsophisticated conclusion that African Americans were incapable of advancing themselves without the structure of servitude that slavery

---

1. LSM, "Negro-mania," 239. The quotation in the title of this chapter is from the same essay, 241.

provided. When she herself provided that structure, the institution entitled her to property ownership that benefited her as a woman.

Louisa's first exposure to class relationships and systems of labor came in her own home through the domestic servants that her family used. When the Cheveses lived in South Carolina from 1815 to 1818, they owned slaves. From 1819 until 1829, the years in which they lived in Philadelphia and Lancaster, Pennsylvania, the question of labor became more complicated. While her father continued to own human property, he could not bring that property into Pennsylvania. That state had begun phasing slavery out of its labor system, declaring free all people born after March 1, 1780, regardless of race. Southerners residing in Pennsylvania could bring their slaves to the state for a period of only six months, after which, theoretically, the slaves would be manumitted by the state.[2] Slaves had comprised only one-twelfth of the population of Philadelphia during the peak of slavery in that city, and fewer had resided in rural areas. By 1820, the institution had all but disappeared from the Pennsylvania landscape, with the census recording only 211 slaves in the entire state.[3]

All forms of unfree labor had fallen into disuse in the North. White indentured servitude and bound apprenticeships, which had provided the bulk of labor during the colonial era and into the federal period, were also disappearing by the 1820s.[4] Instead, industrialization had led to the growth of a wage labor system. This system affected all areas of work, including domestic service. Thus, when the Cheves family moved to Pennsylvania, it had to adapt to a new labor environment. Despite the gossip in the Lancaster society pages that Langdon Cheves had erected an outbuilding next to his house in that town in order to house slaves, Cheves never brought "slaves" into Pennsylvania in the legal sense. Instead, all the workers in his house were "indentured servants," or, simply, servants.[5] Louisa, while

2. Gary B. Nash, *Forging Freedom: The Formation of Philadelphia's Black Community, 1720–1840*, 62–63.

3. Lottie M. Bausman, "General Position of Lancaster County on Negro Slavery"; Cheesman A. Herrick, *White Servitude in Pennsylvania: Indentured and Redemption Labor in Colony and Commonwealth*, 305; Gary B. Nash, "Slaves and Slave Owners in Colonial Philadelphia," 50.

4. Herrick, *White Servitude in Pennsylvania*, 265–66.

5. Clippings in the Dr. John L. Farmer Abbeville Collection, LCHS; letters in LCI and LCIII.

living in a slaveholding family and seeing slaves periodically, grew up in a household that did not directly employ slaves for most of her formative years.

Despite the supposed democratic spirit of wage labor, hierarchical social relationships persisted. By the 1830s, planters in slaveholding states had begun to formulate a defense of the plantation system that celebrated it as a paternalist model for all of society.[6] Slavery enforced paternalism upon the black working class. In non-slaveholding states, despite the move toward universal white male suffrage and despite rhetoric to the contrary, paternalism remained the norm in employer-employee relationships. The employer oversaw not only the work of the employee, but also the personal behavior and conduct of the employee. The employee was expected to see this as beneficial to his personal and social well-being, and to reward his employer with good work and loyalty. Nowhere was this more true than in domestic service, where a maid often lived beneath the roof of her mistress, and where the mistress often saw herself as providing her maid with exposure to necessary social skills, such as manners, dress, language, and religion. As Louisa described the relationship: "In more advanced stages of society, where mind asserts its supremacy, intellect makes the master; intellect is the true strength, and mere muscular power needs not only the guidance, but the protection, of that mighty power which man's intellect teaches him to sway."[7] In both northern and southern residences, Louisa Cheves grew up in households that regarded domestic servants as childlike dependents.

Louisa learned about being a mistress from both of her parents. Her mother managed the servants on a day-to-day basis, while her father had the final say in the financial matters of hiring, firing, and purchase or sale of indentures. Little documentation exists that reveals the behavior of Mary or Langdon Cheves toward their servants. The attitude of Langdon toward his slaves, however, appears in his

6. Fox-Genovese, *Plantation Household*, 31–35, 53–58; Eugene D. Genovese, *Roll, Jordan, Roll: The World the Slaves Made*, 4–7.

7. LSM, "Slavery and Political Economy," 442. For more on domestic service in the nineteenth century, see Faye E. Dudden, *Serving Women: Household Service in Nineteenth-Century America;* Daniel Sutherland, *Americans and Their Servants: Domestic Service in the United States from 1800 to 1920.*

business correspondence. Therefore, his attitude toward his servants, free or otherwise, can be extrapolated from his behavior toward his slaves both during and after his tenure in the North. In regard to his slaves, he saw himself as a loving patriarch who conceded to their wishes on occasion and within certain parameters.

From 1819 to 1829, when Cheves owned only a handful of slaves whom he hired out in South Carolina, he doled out acts of kindness. Most important to the slaves, he promised them eventual emancipation. "Nancy," he wrote, "was to be free when she please if laws will permit on paying back wages and charges of manumission." About another slave, Harry, he wrote: "I recollect him with kindness and my promise shall be faithfully kept to him and that he should be free in ten years from the time I left Carolina."[8] To a third slave, Lewis, he offered a different bargain. Lewis requested to move to Philadelphia with the Cheves family. Since Pennsylvania law would permit Cheves to hold Lewis as a slave for only six months, Cheves freed him on the condition that he "proceed to Philadelphia and as soon as he shall arrive at that place . . . bind himself according to the laws of Pennsylvania." In other words, Lewis would leave slavery, but enter a term of indentured servitude for "seven years from the first day of March 1819," after which he would be free.[9] But he only reluctantly brought Lewis into a non-slaveholding state and decided against bringing any more slaves to join him.

Cheves may have fully intended to manumit these slaves had he remained in Pennsylvania. He would have been unable to own them as slaves if he continued to reside in the North. Unlike some slaveholders, who lived most of the year in the North while their slaves worked plantations in the South, Cheves did not rely on his slaves as a major source of income. He could therefore afford to offer them their eventual freedom. Of course, he could also have sold his slaves; this would have brought him a profit, which emancipation would not. However, his relationship to his slaves was paternalist, which implies a personal as well as an economic relationship, and Cheves no doubt believed manumission to be the proper reward for these slaves' service to his family.

8. Cheves to John Kirkpatrick, August 7, 1822, and to William Jones, August 17, 1822, LCI.

9. Statement of Langdon Cheves, April 24, 1820, LCI.

Cheves also attempted to ensure the unity of slave families. When he returned to South Carolina in 1830, he called his slave Harry back to his service. "Having determined to live again in this state," Cheves wrote, his "relations to Harry have changed."[10] He intended to bring Harry to live with the Cheves family in Charleston and to purchase Harry's wife, Betty. Cheves withdrew his offer to free Harry, but he preserved Harry's marriage, probably believing that this ameliorated the broken promise.

Since 1822 Harry had been living in Georgia, hired out to Betty's master. Cheves did not want to "voluntarily separate him from his wife," so he offered to "either sell him . . . or buy his wife."[11] Betty's master, William Jones, sold her to Cheves. But Harry and Betty soon learned that they would not live in the same house when Cheves decided to send Betty straight to his summer home in Pendleton while keeping Harry in Charleston. The prospect of separation caused the couple much pain, and they agitated to be reunited as quickly as possible. Cheves, however, believed that he had done enough of a kindness in preserving the union by purchasing Betty. He had offered his benevolence, and expected obedience to his orders to separate the couple. He would not permit them to dictate his needs in regard to their labor. He refused their request, writing: "[I]t is entirely out of my power to send Harry [to Pendleton]. He is a House Servant and is daily in that employment and I have no substitute." He ordered Jones to "send the woman to Pendleton as soon as convenient where she is wanted to take care of a vacant house that I have hired." Harry went to the household in Charleston and Betty stayed in Pendleton, and they were reunited only when Cheves relocated his family to the upcountry several months later.[12]

As the number of his slaves grew after 1830, Cheves continued to advocate the preservation of enslaved families, at least those under his ownership or that of his immediate family. He upbraided his son-in-law for selling slaves that had been with the Cheveses for years,

10. Cheves to William Jones, June 7, 1830, LCI.

11. Cheves to William Jones, August 19, 1826, and June 7, 1830, LCI. Cheves's factor, Ainsley Hall, had originally employed Harry in Columbia. After Hall's death, Cheves briefly lost track of Harry, who turned up at the Jones household in Augusta, Georgia, where his wife was a slave.

12. Cheves to William Jones, December 16, 1830, and November 30, 1830, LCI.

and for separating many black families in the process. His daughter Anna Cheves had brought several slaves as dowry to her union with Thomas Pinckney Huger. Huger, however, fell on hard financial times. He wrote to Cheves for "approval and approbation" in "selling some of the Negroes that you gave me, enough to reduce my debt materially." Cheves replied: "The Negroes by the settlement are generally family Negroes, born in the family, have been the subject not of sale but of giver to the family and should be sacred from any but unavoidable sale." "Confounded" at the "lazy ways" of his son-in-law, he finished his letter with a lecture on the duties of a husband and master to his dependents.[13]

Enabling his slaves to maintain the semblance of family unity was one act of benevolence that could be bestowed by a master. A master who failed to do so, unless he was punishing his slaves, violated the paternalist relationship. Huger was a bad master, in Cheves's opinion. Cheves, however, believed himself to be a good master by ensuring that his slaves remained within his households, even if they did not live together. Louisa inherited from him a belief in the importance of preserving enslaved families. In a critique of the wage labor system, she wrote of slaves that "their family ties and social affections are respected and indulged in a greater degree than those of any laboring class in the world."[14]

Cheves felt that his benevolence fulfilled not only his end of the paternalist understanding, but also acted as a means of coercing good behavior out of his slaves. Yet, because he saw his slaves as children, he also used coercion to facilitate obedience. He kept them from "corrupting" influences, and dangled favors in front of them to ensure their obedience. Louisa wrote of "[t]his race . . . whom (considering the mutual social ties established between us) we regard it not only as a right, but as a sacred duty, to *protect* and *govern*."[15]

For instance, in 1826, Cheves considered bringing Harry north to Philadelphia, but decided against the idea.[16] Even at this early date he did not want to separate Harry from Betty, but another clue to

---

13. Thomas Pinckney Huger to Langdon Cheves, January 13, 1846; Cheves to Huger, January 16, 1846, LCI.
14. LSM, "British Philanthropy and American Slavery," 286.
15. LSM, "Diversity of the Races; Its Bearing upon Negro Slavery," 179.
16. Cheves to William Jones, August 19, 1826, LCI.

his decision may be found in his reluctance to bring his slave Lewis north. Cheves had hired out Lewis as a porter to the firm of Kirkpatrick, Douglas, and Hall in Charleston, but, as mentioned, Lewis requested to join the Cheves family in Pennsylvania. Cheves expressed reluctance, possibly because Lewis (or another slave with the same name) had run away during an earlier stay in Pennsylvania in 1814. His stated reason, however, was that he not only wished Lewis to stay with his own family, but also wanted to protect him from the evils of the northern city, where "he might be led into temptation." Louisa absorbed this attitude, writing: "[A]s the guiding and directing power, taking upon ourselves the responsibility in so far as we take the direction of his action, we should save him so far as in our power lies from the snares of the tempter."[17]

In the end, though, Cheves granted Lewis's request based upon his assessment that Lewis was "the most honest and faithful man of color I ever met." (That assessment does not rule out the possibility that this was the same Lewis who caused Cheves some trouble in 1914.) Likewise, Cheves's favors to Harry, such as the purchase of Betty, relied upon "the continuance of his good habits" and "that his habits and character are still good." As for Nancy, if South Carolina law did not permit her emancipation, Cheves would allow her a degree of freedom by permitting her "$20 per year set aside for her support in case of need" on the condition that she "pay one dollar per week clear wages" and "pay her taxes," as well as "superintend her daughter Anna's conduct."[18]

The experiences of these three slaves, Harry, Lewis, and Nancy, give some clues to Cheves's behavior as master and illustrate a dynamic aspect of the master-slave relationship. He would offer freedom, preserve families, and grant favors to his slaves on the condition that they performed their duties well. They were expected to exhibit good behavior and loyalty toward their master, to not attempt to run away, to take an interest in the master's family, and to accept their position as inferiors within the household.

17. Cheves to Kirkpatrick, Douglas, and Hall, August 26, 1820, LCI; LSM, "British Philanthropy," 297.
18. Cheves to Kirkpatrick, Douglas, and Hall, August 26, 1820, to William Jones, August 17, 1822, and May 20, 1824, and to John Kirkpatrick, August 7, 1822, LCI.

Although Cheves believed that he behaved kindly toward his slaves, the contradiction between his promises and their fulfillment betrays the inherent problem with paternalism. The master set the terms of the relationship. He determined good from bad behavior, and just rewards from unjust. The slave was not empowered to protect himself, nor to ensure that the master fulfilled his promises. Cheves never honored his promises to free Harry and Lewis. March 1826 passed, but Lewis remained the property of Langdon Cheves. His indenture ended, but he returned with the Cheves family to South Carolina and to slavery. When Cheves purchased Harry's wife, Betty, he kept the couple apart for several months. Other slave families that were owned by members of the Cheves family found themselves separated among several plantations between Savannah on the coast and Pendleton in the backcountry. Cheves's benevolence came not only with the condition of good behavior, but also with the understanding that his own needs overrode any promises made to his slaves.

Many servants, enslaved and free, refused to accept their lot with docility. Most resistance was mild, but took place on a daily basis. Mistresses tended to characterize their servants and slaves as lazy, prone to thievery, full of superstitions that frightened the children, and negligent, willful, or clumsy. Fanny Wright, a Scottish visitor to America and no friend to slavery, offered her own evaluations of the help, complete with ethnic stereotypes. The Irish and British immigrants proved "poor, dirty, and ignorant" in her estimation, and "the latter, discontented and insolent." These immigrant servants might "sometimes recover their good humor and good manners and become civil," she wrote, "though never again servile domestics." The Irish, she insisted, seemed particularly bent on their improvement as a class in America, making them "very indifferent household servants." As for the black servants, Wright wrote that "their faults are indolence and an occasional tendency to intemperance and petty dishonesty." As a rule, she advised, "those who employ negroes generally find it better to employ them exclusively."[19]

Much of this behavior may have stemmed from maids' rejection of their inferior position, or their displeasure with their mistresses'

19. Dudden, *Serving Women*, 65; Frances Wright, *Views of Society and Manners in America*, 238–39.

behavior, or from a desire to set their own work pace and to quietly defend their own concerns. In 1819, when Mary Cheves completed the process of packing the family home in Columbia for the move to Philadelphia, a recalcitrant "servant girl" refused to leave the city by boat. Instead she was sent by stagecoach with "five dollars to pay for her expenses."[20] This young woman may have had a very real fear of water. Just as likely, however, she merely wanted some time away from her mistress or other direct supervision. The longer stage drive would offer her that freedom.

Maids' rejection of their subservient position also extended beyond acts of household rebellion. Free white servants attempted to negotiate the terms of their service, and indentured servants and slaves frequently ran away. Sometimes, if conditions were harsh enough, resistance could reach the level of physical retaliation. In these instances, servants believed they were justified in attempting to improve their condition, and rejected the wholesale submission of their person. Masters and mistresses, on the other hand, interpreted any attempt at negotiation or level of resistance as a betrayal of the paternal relationship.

While living in Pennsylvania, the Cheveses probably employed free labor in their household. The Cheves family does not appear in the census for 1820 or 1830, possibly due to their constant change of residences during these years, so exact information on the number, gender, and age of their servants is unavailable. Sophia Dulles, the mother of Mary Cheves and grandmother of Louisa, and her son Joseph Dulles both appear in the 1820 census. Each had free black females living in their households. Sophia also had in her household a young woman between 16 and 26 years old. Most of her neighbors had between one and three free black females between the ages of 14 and 26 living in their households.[21] Presumably, all of these young women were employed as domestic servants. The Cheves family probably followed suit in their employment patterns, with the known exception of the indentured servant, Lewis.

By employing free servants, Mary Cheves would have experienced the bargaining power of her maids, a lesson that her daughter Louisa

20. Ainsley Hall to Langdon Cheves, April 7, 1819, LCI.
21. 1820 U.S. Census, Pennsylvania, Philadelphia, South Ward, Locust Ward.

also learned. A free servant working for wages had some latitude in negotiating for improved conditions. If a servant did not like her position, her wages, or her treatment in one household, she could always look elsewhere. The work itself would not improve, but the conditions might be more favorable. She could also use her ability to leave as a means of coercing better conditions at her current place of employment. Thus, among the mistresses, competition for good help became vicious as workingwomen vied for higher wages, more days off, and more freedom in their personal behavior. The maids embraced what independence the wage labor market offered.[22]

The mistresses, on the other hand, clung to the old ways. Believing that they offered their maids the fringe benefits of sharing in their own privileged lives, mistresses interpreted independent behavior as a subversion of the paternal relationship between mistress and servant. The implication of a potentially egalitarian relationship seemed, to mistresses, a personal betrayal of their own benevolence. A servant could run off to a better-paying position as soon as her mistress had trained her. No longer were the maids poor wretches from the streets in need of a mistress's guiding Christian hand. Instead, in their mistresses' eyes, they were hardened opportunists who cared only for wages and were unappreciative of their mistresses' charity. While the maids embraced a market economy in which they could use their ability to labor as a bargaining tool, the mistresses defended a system of deference.[23]

A slave or indentured servant could not bargain for better wages or working conditions. Instead, the temptations of liberty, with its potential for upward economic mobility, could cause a slave or indentured servant to challenge a master in more dramatic ways. Most commonly, they would merely seize the first opportunity to run away. Lancaster County, where the Cheves family lived from 1826 to 1829, received a number of these fugitives. Situated between two rivers, with its southern tip bordering the slave state of Maryland, Lancaster funneled runaways toward Philadelphia and points farther north.

22. Pease and Pease, *Ladies, Women, and Wenches*, 48–50.

23. The emergence of the wage labor market and the reaction of the upper classes to workers' bargaining are discussed in Charles Sellers, *The Market Revolution in Jacksonian America, 1815–1848*, and Harry L. Watson, *Liberty and Power: The Politics of Jacksonian America*.

Each spring Lancaster newspapers filled with advertisements offering rewards for the return of those who had seized the seasonal opportunity for escape, a daily reminder to the Cheves family of the risk their own household faced of losing domestic help.[24]

In 1814, during Langdon's term in Congress, the Cheves family had in fact experienced a bold bid for freedom when their slave Lewis sought to secure his emancipation through the court system. When the family relocated to Germantown, Pennsylvania, during the British invasion of Washington, Lewis "absconded from his service" and made his way to Philadelphia. There, he probably contacted one of the few abolitionist groups, such as the Quakers. He certainly made the acquaintance of people with legal connections. Rather than melt into free black society as a fugitive, Lewis sued for his freedom, becoming a test case for Pennsylvania's laws on bringing slaves into the state, and foreshadowing by several decades the Dred Scott case.[25]

Lewis argued that, because he had lived in a free state for longer than the six-month limit, he had earned his freedom. The Pennsylvania Supreme Court, however, disagreed. Presiding Chief Justice William Tilgham decided that the mitigating circumstance of the British invasion of Washington had forced the Cheveses to remain in the state for longer than six months. Because of the war, in Tilgham's opinion, Langdon Cheves could not leave Pennsylvania for a slaveholding state without threat to his life. The state could not force him to choose between his property and his own well-being. Therefore, Lewis remained a slave. As precedent, the court pointed to the slave-owning members of the Continental Congress who had kept slaves in Philadelphia for many years during the War for Independence and after the state's abolition law had been passed.[26] The fact that many southern congressmen still resided in Pennsylvania, when they could easily have given their business to Virginia or Maryland if they feared the emancipation of their "domestics," may also have swayed the court.

24. Marianna G. Brubaker, "The Underground Railroad," 99; *Lancaster Journal*, 1825–1828, LCHS.

25. W. U. Hensel, "Reminiscences of Langdon Cheves," 120–22; Helen Tunnicliff Catterall and James J. Hayden, eds., *Judicial Cases Concerning American Slavery and the Negro*, 4:249, 272–73.

26. Hensel, "Reminiscences of Langdon Cheves," 120–22.

The many apprentices, slaves, and indentured servants who ran from bondage performed one of the extreme acts of resistance available to unfree workers. Lewis, who may or may not have been the same person that Cheves described as "faithful" five years later, had a bit more sophistication and his act could have had more far-reaching consequences. In any case, however, masters perceived such escapes as similar to that of a free servant quitting, but more serious, because the unfree servant also broke a written contract and violated the privileges of property.

More extreme than escape was open, violent rebellion. Most often this took the form of poisoning or arson. While the Cheves family was living in Pennsylvania, news reached them of one of the most dramatic instances of slave rebellion. On a sweltering evening in June 1822, Charleston authorities supposedly uncovered plans for a slave insurrection. The leader of the plot was Denmark Vesey, a black minister and former slave who had won his freedom in a game of cards. His cohorts included other freedmen and slaves, some of whom had been fugitives from the slave revolution in St. Domingue.[27]

According to official reports, the co-conspirators had stockpiled weapons and ammunition and created a network of supporters throughout the black community of the city. House servants were to kill their masters in their beds, take over the city, then spread out into the countryside, liberating all slaves and eliminating all slaveowners. Indeed, the scope of the conspiracy frightened many of the slaves involved in the plot, who turned in Vesey and his cohorts. Captured at the home of one of his eight wives, Vesey stood trial and met his end at the gallows.

27. Walter J. Fraser Jr., *Charleston! Charleston!* 200–203; David Robertson, "Nothing Can Be Done without Fire," chap. 4 in *Denmark Vesey.* See also Michael P. Johnson, "Denmark Vesey and His Co-Conspirators" and "Reading Evidence." Through an insightful interpretation of the documents of the Vesey trials, Johnson argues against the veracity of the confessions of the co-conspirators because they were obtained through the use of torture. Johnson also argues that the conspiracy may not have actually existed at all, but that it was a fabrication created by the Charleston mayor in order to curry political favor with the elite planter classes. According to this theory, the mayor used the alleged conspiracy to play on fears of slave insurrection and to present himself as willing to aggressively protect Charleston's white citizens. While this interpretation has led to the qualifying adjectives in this section, the possibility that the plot did not truly exist does not change the fact that white people such as the Cheveses believed they were in danger.

Hysteria gripped the white population of Charleston. Rumors described the insurrection as "a scheme of guilt and murder to be intended, unparalleled even exceeding if possible the Demons of St. Domingo!!" Whites feared that Vesey had raised an army of nearly ten thousand black men. Even more alarming, suspicions grew that Vesey had formed alliances with St. Domingue as well as with European nations that had abolished slavery. John Potter, Cheves's factor in Charleston, wrote to him that he suspected "they were aided by the black missionaries from your city [Philadelphia]!"[28]

Not only did the potential revolutionaries, free or otherwise, pose a physical threat to the white population of Charleston, but they would also decrease the value of slaves. "As for negroes," wrote Potter, reporting on Cheves's investments, "I do not believe they would bring any price—at present." Cheves's slave Nancy, who was earning money to purchase her own freedom, reported that she could not get decent wages for her work. Like the other black citizens of Charleston, she faced suspicion and harassment. She "complains very much of the difficulties of the times," wrote another of Cheves's agents, "and I have but little doubt she finds them hard enough."[29] As heavily as the white Charleston population depended upon blacks for labor, after Denmark Vesey they suspected every black of complicity in his scheme.

Nancy's hardships represented only a small fraction of what black residents would soon face. Whites in the city began to arm themselves as if under siege. Patrols increased and the construction of a citadel was planned for the defense of the city against attackers. In addition, the legal fallout from the Vesey trials did not bode well for the black population of Charleston. Many blamed free blacks as the primary corrupting influence of the slave population. New ordinances were passed, such as the Negro Seamen's Act, designed to reduce if not eliminate the free black citizenship of the city by requiring every free black to have a guardian or be sold into slavery. Those who found sponsors were forced to wear metal tags, indicating their name and address and those of their guardian. The "Black Mariah"

28. John Potter to Langdon Cheves, June 19, 1822, LCI.
29. John Potter to Langdon Cheves, July 16, 1822; John Kirkpatrick to Langdon Cheves, July 29, 1822, LCI.

wagon carried to prison free black seamen whose ships had docked at Charleston's wharf. There they languished until their ships left port. If a ship disembarked without its black seamen, the city sold the black sailors into slavery.[30]

While the white residents of the city armed themselves against another revolt, most of them also worried about the threat posed by the slaves in their own homes. In a tone filled with horror, John Potter reported that "the trifling business of taking care of the [white] males would have fallen to other agents, with the servants of the family. Many of whom . . . I fear would have turned traitors on the Occasion." The governor himself "was to be the first victim by his favorite servant, Rolla." One of Vesey's partners, Gulla Jack, had approached a doctor's slave, asking him "to poison his master's well." Although the slave refused to do this particular deed, he expressed sympathy with the cause, and if Gulla Jack had made his request "sooner . . . the result probably would have been dreadful."[31] A sense of betrayal underlay every white response to the Vesey plot, which forced the white population to reevaluate their dependence upon slavery. Their conclusion was to enact a more repressive form of the institution in order to enforce loyalty where it could not be coerced, and to eliminate the influence of free blacks from a society that enslaved most of its black people. Years later, in her adulthood, the lessons of Denmark Vesey remained with Louisa McCord. She firmly believed that, in the absence of slavery, free blacks would become "brutish": "[T]here remains no road for their full exercise (unless the white man voluntarily retreats before him) but in the slaughter of his white master, and through that slaughter he strides (unless he himself be exterminated) to the full exercise of his native barbarity and savagism."[32]

In Pennsylvania during the years after the Vesey plot, where slavery was in the last stages of decline, the white population had no love for the free black citizens. The African American population of Philadelphia had grown in the first two decades of the nineteenth century, becoming one of the largest black populations in the urban North

---

30. Walter J. Fraser Jr., *Charleston! Charleston!* 202–3.
31. John Potter to Langdon Cheves, July 5, 1822; June 19, 1822; July 20, 1822, LCI.
32. LSM, "Negro-mania," 240.

by 1830. The black community thrived with churches, schools, and aid societies, a growing middle class, and the emergence of a black elite class. To many white Philadelphians, this upward mobility in the black community presented a social, an economic, and an ideological threat, belying all racial assumptions. In the opinion of white middle- and upper-class families such as the Cheveses, affluent black people had stepped outside of their place in the social hierarchy. In reaction, elite whites ensured that African Americans remained in low-wage jobs and found themselves segregated to the poorest sections of the city.

Because the majority of the black working class found themselves relegated to the poorest unskilled positions in industry, they became targets of ire for the white working class. Particularly to the growing Irish immigrant population, the black population represented competition for employment. Resentment developed through the 1820s, and erupted in a series of race riots beginning in 1834.[33]

The white population of Pennsylvania showed no compassion for the poverty that plagued the majority of African Americans. Instead, they blamed black citizens for their own deplorable conditions. White employers interpreted their workers' bargains for better wages and working conditions as inherent laziness, which they applied to the entire working class, particularly blacks. Louisa Cheves absorbed this stereotype. As an adult she maintained that the working class insisted upon "attaching to the word 'freedom' only the idea of *idleness*." The filthy living conditions of many blacks, featuring rats, poor sewage, dilapidated housing, and disease, was, in the minds of many whites, the result of poor morals, sloth, or the alleged backward culture of African Americans. Langdon Cheves himself came to such a conclusion when he wrote: "Many of the Blacks here are a wretched people."[34] Even when lack of individual and economic power led

33. Theodore Hershbert, "Free Blacks in Antebellum Philadelphia: A Study of Ex-Slaves, Freeborn, and Socioeconomic Decline," 126; Emma Jones Lapansky, " 'Since They Got Those Separate Churches': Afro-Americans and Racism in Jacksonian Philadelphia," 96, 99, 100, 102; Leon Litwack, *North of Slavery: The Negro in the Free States, 1790–1860*, 14–24, 154–68; Nash, *Forging Freedom*, 135, 173, 177, 182, 216–17, 223–27.

34. LSM, "Diversity of the Races," 184–85; Langdon Cheves to Kirkpatrick, Douglas and Hall, August 26, 1820, LCI.

black churches to form relief societies, thereby empowering themselves to improve their own conditions, the white population feared uprisings, violence, or some form of social chaos.[35]

The miseries of black life, blamed upon the black people, became a central point for drives to eliminate the African American population from the state. Despite the nascent abolitionist movement, even the most liberal white people generally did not believe in racial integration. In fact, many opposed slavery only because they hoped that abolition would end the flow of fugitives into the state. The *Lancaster Journal* expressed such an idea when reporting the arrival of "sixty-five manumitted slaves from Hanover County, Virginia." The editors wrote: "We are no friends to slavery, and should be rejoiced to see it gradually and totally abolished in this country; but we cannot, for a variety of reasons, think it altogether right to have the blacks of Virginia, or any other slave state, turned loose upon us by the hundred."[36]

Many Pennsylvanians and other northerners turned to the American Colonization Society. Formed in 1816, the society proposed to emancipate and relocate slaves to Africa. Only then, it argued, could African Americans achieve autonomy free from racial prejudice.[37] The society hoped to alleviate the condition of free black people without challenging the racism of whites. Louisa wrote of "the fast-perishing negro of our own free States, who, in the home of the agitator and the abolitionist, starves for want of a friend and a master."[38] The nation as a whole did not consider people of African descent worthy of American freedom. Southern states enslaved their black populations, while many northern states wished to bar their admission and deport them.

Growing up in Pennsylvania, away from the pervasive institution of slavery, did not shield Louisa Cheves from racist ideas. In fact, the conditions of both the wage labor market and the free black citizenry may have reinforced her belief that slavery was a good institution,

35. Arthur Brittan and Mary Maynard, *Sexism, Racism and Oppression,* 95–100; Lapansky, "'Since They Got Those Separate Churches,'" 96, 99, 100, 102; Litwack, *North of Slavery,* 67–70, 154–56, 168–70; Nash, *Forging Freedom,* 180–83.

36. *Lancaster Journal,* June 29, 1827, LCHS.

37. Litwack, *North of Slavery,* 22–24.

38. LSM, "Diversity of the Races," 178.

both for herself as a mistress and for those whom she would have enslaved. Wage or free labor only led to recalcitrant behavior on the part of the working class. Louisa insisted that free labor was imperfect, and "so new a thing that as yet it scarcely knows itself." In this emerging state, the working classes would insist not only upon political rights, but also economic equality. "The hitherto lower classes . . . see their rights and, knowing these withheld, fancy them greater than they are, and grasp beyond them," she argued. "Thus come the outcries for freedom of the soil, right to labor, communism, women's rights, fraternity, and equality, all men born free and equal, and all the divers follies of the day, which, like vaulting ambition, o'erleap their aim, 'to fall o' the other side.'" Advocates of such ideas might claim the authority of Christian morality and benevolence, but Louisa was not persuaded. "The angel form which we have gazed upon and worshipped as Christian charity and brotherly love," she wrote, "now starts forth, grinning upon us in hideous deformity of vice, and gibbering out its horrible obscenities of 'socialism' and 'communism,' drags along upon its track the shouting mob, who, in their ravings for 'negro abolition' and 'universal equality,' trample under foot at once God's law and man's law—virtue and decency." Moreover, she feared that, in "rushing from extreme to extreme, they forgot that liberty was but enfranchisement, and, with 'democracy' for their watchword, exercised a despotism much more fearful than that of the single tyrant, because its power, like its name, was 'legion.'"[39]

For the rest of her life Louisa remained convinced that all arguments for freedom were actually disguised attacks upon property by a lazy working class. She pointed to the condition of free blacks to support her argument. "Inconceivable to them the brain-workings and the heart-struggles of the white man," she insisted. "They think of liberty as of a long holiday, and would be surprised to find that hard work, scant pittance of food, sickness without help, rags for clothing, and shivering cold, without fire or house-room, are often the lot of the so-called freeman." What freedom really offered African Americans was poverty, she argued, because they were "without land,

39. LSM, "Slavery and Political Economy," 450; "Negro-mania," 225–26; "The Right to Labor," 81. Louisa's ideas mirrored those of other southern intellectuals, such as George Fitzhugh and James Henry Hammond, who published in the decades between 1830 and 1860.

without property of any kind, without habits of foresight and self-dependence, and without the capacity for attaining these things . . ." Only social disaster could result and, she wrote: "Only one door seems opened by nature to prevent such a catastrophe, and that is through the beneficent system of serfdom, or otherwise, slavery."[40]

Like the members of the American Colonization Society or even former President Thomas Jefferson, Louisa believed that the black and white races were inherently at odds. "Peaceable emancipation (could such a thing be) would consign the race to that gradual extinction which is already rapidly advancing upon that portion of it located in our Northern States," she wrote. No amicable coexistence was possible because one race would always attempt to eradicate the other. She pointed to the fate of the Native Americans as proof of her hypothesis. The specter of Denmark Vesey, compounded by Nat Turner's revolt in Virginia in 1831, probably reinforced her ideas. "The white and the black race can only exist together in their present relations," she insisted. "Abolition is the extinction of the one or the other."[41]

Slavery, according to Louisa, would raise African Americans from the poverty that seemed to plague them during freedom, and save them from annihilation by whites. The institution, she argued, was "a providential caring for the weak, and a refuge for the portion-less." Masters provided the necessities of life, and, more important, gave blacks a productive role in society. The black person, whom she described as "Nature's outcast, as for centuries he appeared to be, he—even from the dawning tradition, the homeless, houseless, useless negro," would "suddenly become one of the great levers of civilization."[42]

Louisa's first understanding of slavery developed from her socialization in a hierarchy of paternalism that seemed constantly under attack by the working class, be they free or enslaved. Workers attempted to subvert established paternalist relationships by refusing to accept their subservient position, sometimes to the point of rebellion. The poverty in which the working class lived, particularly that of

40. LSM, "Diversity of the Races," 184–85; "Negro-mania," 240.
41. LSM, "Diversity of the Races," 184–85; "Negro-mania," 228.
42. LSM, "Uncle Tom's Cabin," 279.

the free black population, seemed symptomatic of the breakdown of the paternal relationship and a prelude to anarchy. To Louisa, slavery was the most effective means of preserving this hierarchy and, thereby, also preserving social order. Yet slavery was not only an institution of social order. Just as important, it was also an institution of property. Until 1830, when Langdon Cheves returned his family to South Carolina and embarked upon the life of a planter, slaves and their labor provided only part, not all, of his wealth. They were merely one of his investments. It was from Louisa's extended family, especially her great-aunt Ann Lovell, that she came to understand that slaves and their labor could be the source of great wealth and also of independence.

The elder Cheves girls, Sophia and Louisa, frequently went with their mother to visit her family in the Orangeburg District, slightly southwest of Columbia in central South Carolina. In the 1810s and 1820s cotton production dominated the economy of Orangeburg. One of the first experimenters in this lucrative crop had been Mary Cheves's aunt, Ann Lovell. Planters in the district had long held slaves, employed primarily in the production of indigo; but the labor-intensive requirements of cotton planting increased the number of enslaved African Americans in the district. Ann Lovell was among the wealthiest Orangeburg planters, owning ninety slaves in 1810, a hundred in 1820, and over two hundred in 1830.[43]

Ann Lovell had an interesting history, one that must have impressed itself upon a strong and independent girl such as Louisa. Ann was an older sister of Sophia Dulles, Mary Cheves's mother. Born in 1757, she was the third daughter and sixth child of nine siblings. Her mother, Marie Elise Courtonne, had immigrated from France to the Carolinas at the age of thirteen, while her father, William Heatly, was "said to have been the first white child born on the Santee."[44]

Women knew that their financial security depended upon their choice of husband, but Ann learned the instability of such security.

43. Daniel Marchant Culler et al., eds., *Orangeburgh District, 1768–1868: History and Records*, 437–38, 594; Rachel N. Klein, *Unification of a Slave State: The Rise of the Planter Class in the South Carolina Backcountry, 1760–1808*, 28, 151, 246–47, 250; 1810, 1820, and 1830 U.S. Census, South Carolina, Orangeburg County.

44. Culler, *Orangeburgh District*, 2; notes concerning Cheves genealogy in LCI; notes in Ann Lovell Papers, Dulles-Cheves-McCord-Lovell Papers, SCHS.

Sometime before the War for Independence she married William Reid, with whom she had five children. In 1782, Reid, a member of the South Carolina militia fighting against the British, suffered a fatal wound at the hands of his own troops. As others remembered the story, he was testing the guard of his camp, who shot him for refusing to give the password. His widow took over the management of their plantation. Shortly after the war, James Lovell wandered into St. Matthews with tales of gallant bravery while serving as favorite secretary to General George Washington. In truth, he had served as ensign and adjutant in Lee's Battalion of Light Dragoons until March 1780. He was remembered as "not apparently too strict a follower of accuracy." Nonetheless, he won the hand and the property of the Widow Reid in 1788.[45]

The Lovell marriage proved turbulent. According to family legend, James took great liberties with Ann's wealth and "ran through it pretty soon, leaving her poor and with several children." How much of this is true is uncertain. Ann was among the larger landholders in Orangeburg, according to the U.S. Census, and her wealth and property seem to have increased between 1790 and 1810. Her seven children had all died by 1806, at which point Lovell took his final leave. According to another family story, "the plantation was flourishing and making good money for its owners." Lovell, however, "was not receiving as much benefit therefrom as he fancied, and was evidently not allowed any say so in managing the estate." Thus, "he left her for parts unknown," specifically, New Orleans.[46]

After her husband's departure, Ann kept a firm hand on all aspects of her plantation's business, which her descendants deemed a "wise" choice. Lovell reappeared on Ann's doorstep in early 1811. Time and distance had not improved the relationship. Ann would not relinquish any of her estate to her husband, even as she expanded her holdings. Instead, she placed her property in trust with her brother-in-law Edward Richardson, husband of her sister Rachel. In the agreement that created this trust, Lovell gave up all claim to his wife's property because "he did not contribute to her assistance and support," while she "acquired by her sole and separate industry and

45. Notes in Ann Lovell Papers.
46. Ibid.

economy and by inheritance devise or succession, considerable Real and Personal Estate." Ann could now operate her plantation free from her husband's interference.[47]

Such an arrangement was common in South Carolina, a state that was relatively liberal in its laws toward female property-holding. Women entered into trusts in order to protect their property from their husbands for their own security and for their children's futures. In Ann Lovell's case, she created the trust in order to protect her property from her scoundrel husband. But husbands sometimes agreed to such an arrangement, particularly after the 1819 panic, as insurance against their own losses in an increasingly treacherous market.[48] Similarly, fathers sought to protect their daughters and their own familial property by creating such an arrangement as part of the daughters' marriage settlements.[49]

Ann continued to add to her holdings. In 1824 her brother Andrew died, leaving her one-third of his estate. She bought the other two-thirds from her sisters Sophia Dulles and Rachel Richardson. Lovell attempted to seize the property as his own, but Ann shrewdly bought out his portion.[50] This maneuver clearly grated on him. "Since the settlement of the estate," he wrote to her in 1826, "I have the six thousand dollars instead of enjoying the whole which I was entitled to." Furiously, he continued: "[Y]ou have appeared to me as if I had no business there [on the plantation,] having property of my own to support me." Ann may have hoped that he would take his money and move on. He acknowledged as much: "[You said] that you could live without me having made over all your property to be at your disposal, by will or other ways." He concluded: "I have now determined to gratify you *by getting as far from you as possible,* that you may do better without me as you have often told me."[51] With that, he once again disappeared.

47. Indenture between James Lovell, Ann Lovell, and Edward Richardson, June 13, 1811, LCI.

48. Notes in Ann Lovell Papers.

49. Suzanne Lebsock, *The Free Women of Petersburg: Status and Culture in a Southern Town, 1784–1860,* 57–61; Marylynn Salmon, "Women and Property in South Carolina: The Evidence from Marriage Settlements, 1730–1830," 296.

50. Indenture between James Lovell, Ann Lovell, and Edward Richardson, November 10, 1825, LCI.

51. James Lovell to "Mrs. Lovell" [Ann Lovell], July 4, 1826, LCI.

Ann understood that the dark underside of married life might leave a woman of property destitute, and she took steps to protect herself from a turn of fortune. In her will she took care to ensure that the women of the Cheves and Richardson families would benefit from her wealth. To Langdon Cheves, she gave her plantations Home Place and Goshen. She left her plantation Cave Hall and a thousand acres of her plantation Good Hope to her grandniece Rachel Susan Bee, the orphaned granddaughter of her sister Rachel, should she find herself single at the time of Ann's death. She also left several slaves to Bee and to her other grandniece, Mary Elizabeth (Bet) McCord, Bee's half-sister. After dividing the majority of her property, she bequeathed the remainder to Joseph Dulles, Edward Richardson, and Mary Cheves, to be divided equally. Should Richardson die before Ann, his share would go to his wife. In all of her assignments, she carefully ensured that the line of succession proceeded from husband to wife, or to a single woman, so that no woman would find herself alone and without means of survival.[52]

Although Ann left nothing directly to her grandniece Louisa, the property that she left to Langdon Cheves enabled him to gift Louisa with a substantial plantation of her own near Abbeville, South Carolina. Cheves combined Home Place and Goshen into one property, which he renamed Lang Syne. He ran this plantation until his daughter Sophia's marriage to Charles Haskell in 1830. Haskell ran the plantation for Cheves until Louisa's marriage in 1840, at which time Cheves deeded the land and its slaves to her.

By the time she became a landholder, Louisa had already been a slaveholder for ten years, courtesy of her grandmother. Sophia Dulles had retained title to approximately a hundred slaves, inherited from her brother Andrew. In 1830 she divided these slaves among her granddaughters. She gave forty slaves to Sophia Cheves as a marriage gift. Louisa received approximately the same number.[53] At age twenty she now had a vested interest in the institution of slavery.

52. Will of Ann Lovell, December 12, 1832, LCI. Ann left nothing to her absent, but still living, husband, James Lovell. The probated version of the will no longer exists, and is presumed to have burned with the Orangeburg courthouse during the Civil War (Moss and Lide to Langdon Cheves [III], April 11, 1916, LCIII).

53. Sophia Dulles to Joseph [Heatly] Dulles, December 6, 1830, LCI; Langdon Cheves to Alexander Cheves, May 24, 1838, LCI.

Moreover, these slaves were the only property held by Louisa, a single woman. With the memory of her great-aunt's experience fresh in her mind and with the possibility of spinsterhood stretching before her, ownership of these slaves gave her real financial security and the chance for independence, a rare luxury for women in the nineteenth century.

"The existence of society is an inherent necessity to man's existence; what therefore is needful to the existence of society cannot be unjust," Louisa later argued. "Thus, then, slavery is sometimes and to certain extents proved just."[54] Her upbringing during the upheaval of industrialization, which led her to the conclusion that wage labor threatened social stability; her observation of the poor conditions of free blacks; and her firm commitment to a paternal hierarchy had paved the way for her acceptance of slavery as beneficent. Her ownership of slaves sealed her defense of the institution in her mind.

Louisa had learned that society depended upon order and property, to the exclusion of equality. Inequality, then, was right, particularly if she were the beneficiary of that inequality. Yet, as a woman she found herself in an inferior position to the men around her. Her intellectual ambition demanded that she challenge her submission, while her desire for order tied her to the same hierarchy that subverted that ambition. One of the central tasks of her life would be the reconciliation of these two impulses.

54. LSM, "Slavery and Political Economy," 442.

4

"Submissive Bow, and *Be Content*"

The Cheves family returned to South Carolina in 1830, and the two eldest daughters were tossed into a whirlwind of social activity in Charleston, Columbia, and the upstate summer retreat Pendleton. Sophia Cheves wrote that old family friends "seemed to receive us like the prodigal son" and treated the family to "six dances, two tea parties, two dinner parties, besides several that we were obliged to refuse as Mother was not able to bear any more."[1] Several older gentlemen flirted with the two sisters, offering marriage in jest as a means of keeping them in the South. Courtship was, in fact, the purpose of these outings for these eligible young ladies. Their father quickly purchased land along the Savannah River in Abbeville and in the western reaches of the state in an effort not only to establish himself as a planter, but also to assist his children in attracting spouses that would join his family with others of the South Carolina planter aristocracy. Perhaps one of his daughters' proposals, from someone named Rutledge or Middleton or Pinckney—three of the most prominent families in South Carolina—would be in earnest.[2]

By July, a wedding topped the Cheves social agenda. Sophia wrote to her friend Eleuthera DuPont that she "had promised so silly a thing as to be Mrs. Charles Thompson Haskell before New Year's Day." Although not a Rutledge or a Middleton or a Pinckney, Mr. Haskell proved an acceptable suitor. The Haskell family had long been connected with the Lovell family in St. Matthews Parish, where Sophia had met Charles while visiting her great-aunt Ann several

1. Sophia Cheves to Eleuthera DuPont, January 2, 1830, LCIII. "Mother," of course, was entering her second trimester of yet another pregnancy.
2. Charles Cheves would marry a Middleton, Isabella, in 1846; and Anna Cheves would marry a relation of the Pinckneys, Thomas Huger, in 1841.

years earlier. She found him "well looking enough for to think him as handsome as I choose." The couple developed a friendship, and "now we are the best in the world." Neither was intellectually inclined, nor particularly ambitious beyond the desire for family and for property to support that family well. By December the newlyweds had ensconced themselves in a St. Matthews Parish house "where the patriotic Mrs. Motte once lived."[3] Later, in 1840, they moved to a plantation in Abbeville where Charles grew rice and Sophia gave birth to ten children.

Louisa, being a year younger, should have followed in her sister's footsteps. She was never known for her beauty, described most frequently as "strong" or "masculine" or "opinionated," not necessarily the sort of attributes attractive to a potential fiancé. Nevertheless, she was the daughter of the famed Judge Cheves and a woman of property who had been presented to society. Some man should have found her to be eligible marriage material. If he did, then she certainly did not reciprocate his sentiments. She remained single until the scandalously old age of thirty years. Her decisions, first to remain single and then to marry, can be seen as attempts to reconcile her personal independence with her conception of social order. This conflict was one of the central struggles of her life, and its resolution would be the defining event of her life.

Louisa's prolonged "spinsterhood" was probably prompted by several factors. First, she identified so strongly with her father that she could not allow him to be supplanted by a husband in her affections. Second, as an unmarried adult, she enjoyed freedom from the responsibilities of being a wife and mother and could pursue her intellectual interests. Finally, she was apprehensive about many aspects of marriage, particularly childbearing.

For her entire life Louisa's primary loyalty lay not with any sister, mother, or friend, but with her father. Marriage would require a transfer of loyalties as her duties and very source of identity moved from her father's household to her husband's. The choice of a husband, then, would take place in some very complicated psychological

3. Sophia Cheves to Eleuthera DuPont, July 20, 1830; Sophia Haskell to Eleuthera DuPont, November 9, 1830, LCIII. The British occupied the home of Elizabeth Motte during the American Revolution. She earned her heroic status by helping the American army burn her own home in order to drive the British from the district.

territory. Langdon Cheves had accomplished a great deal on both the state and national levels. He had been a successful lawyer and statesman, and was considered a man of high principle. Success never seemed to elude him. The husband of Louisa Cheves would have to equal her father in order to earn, first, her attention, then her respect, and ultimately her love. At the same time, however, this husband could in no way threaten the high position that her father held in Louisa's esteem. The necessity to both surpass and yet not surpass Langdon Cheves placed all beaux at an extreme disadvantage.

Moreover, Louisa's relationship to the primary male figure in her life would shift from the clearly subordinate one of daughter to the quasi-partnership of helpmeet. She would have to find a man whom she admired as much as she admired her father, yet one with whom she could also assume a personal status of "rhetorical equality" in a "companionate marriage."[4] Yet, because the standard for admiration had been set so high, any man with whom she might feel a companionship would be perceived as lowering himself. He would descend from equality with Langdon Cheves to equivalence with Louisa Cheves, the inferior of the two. In her twenties, Louisa's pride and sense of self would not allow her to join her life with any man whom she considered beneath admiration. Every suitor inevitably fell short.

Though Louisa found no man of suitable marriage material, she did not seem to mourn this failure. In literature, the story of a woman's life often climaxes with a wedding. Everything else that follows falls under the category of "happily ever after."[5] To some extent, that traditional narrative in art follows the example of life. Most women of the nineteenth century implicitly understood that the central, in fact only, real choice of their life was who to marry. Some rare women, however, purposefully chose no one. Louisa, by design or default, fell into this category.

4. These terms refer to the doctrine of separate spheres, in which a husband and wife were supposedly in an equal partnership, although their responsibilities differed. Theoretically, women did not require equality outside of the home because that would mean intrusion into the male sphere. This is not to imply that Louisa and her husband would be equals, but that her relationship to a husband would more closely approach equality than her relationship with her father. See Cott, *Bonds of Womanhood*, 71–74; Jabour, *Marriage in the Early Republic*, 1–7; Suzanne Lebsock, *Free Women of Petersburg*, 16.

5. Heilbrun, Carolyn G., *Writing a Woman's Life*, 20–23.

For many women, remaining or becoming single did not necessarily translate into freedom. Independence meant earning a living, and careers for women were limited. Most work, such as domestic work, was hard; some, such as teaching, paid very little. Other work, such as acting, even bordered on the scandalous. Moreover, all work thrust women into the "male" sphere where they supposedly did not belong.

Some women of education and class found satisfaction in an unmarried state, regardless of this taint. Catharine Beecher spent her life training other women how to take care of children both in the home and in the classroom, although she herself never married. Louisa May Alcott declared at an early age that she would never marry and would earn her living by her pen. Sarah Grimke, a southern woman of Louisa Cheves's own class, chose to devote her life to a cause rather than to a husband and children. Her work in the abolition movement made her sensitive to the legal status of women, particularly in marriage, in both the northern and southern states, and she went on to fight for women's rights.[6] Even women who had been married often found widowhood to be a preferable state, and refused to remarry. Some made this choice to retain control over the property they had inherited from their husbands. Other widows found unexpected careers, such as Sarah Josepha Hale, who had been a neighbor of the Cheves family in Philadelphia. After her husband's death, she became the editor of the magazine *Godey's Ladies Book* and the author of several novels.[7]

Most of these women, in choosing to remain single, needed to earn a living either because of their family's economic circumstance or because they lived away from their family. Louisa Cheves, remaining under her father's ample roof, did not have to support herself or

6. Like Louisa, Grimke was the daughter of a slaveholding South Carolina judge and lived for a time in Philadelphia, but she held opposing views from Louisa on slavery and women's rights.

7. Kathryn Kish Sklar, *Catharine Beecher: A Study in American Domesticity*, 60, 180–82; Sarah Elbert, *A Hunger for Home: Louisa May Alcott and* Little Women, 95, 203; Gerda Lerner, *The Grimke Sisters from South Carolina: Pioneers for Women's Rights and Abolition*; Sherbrooke Rogers, *Sarah Josepha Hale: A New England Pioneer, 1788–1879*, 21–27. The married women in the abolition and women's movements, even those with supportive husbands, found it difficult to dedicate their lives to both a cause and a family. Such frustrations often strengthened their resolve to pursue equality for women.

contribute to the income of her family. As mentioned, she herself
owned property. In 1830, Sophia Dulles presented her granddaughter
with nearly forty slaves. Three years later, Langdon Cheves ensured
his daughter's future, either as a single or a married woman, by ear-
marking for her a cotton plantation of over 1,500 acres in Abbeville.
Louisa turned the management of the slaves over to her father and
of the land to her brother-in-law Charles Haskell, although she kept
abreast of the well-being of both. Profitable land with slaves ensured
that Louisa would not have to work for an income, either on the farm
or in any other capacity.[8]

Families did, however, expect single daughters and sisters to contribute to the functioning of the household.[9] Louisa was no exception. She became the tutor of her youngest siblings, Hayne, Charles,
and Anna. She would, in fact, come to see these children as something more than merely brothers and a sister. Hayne, in particular,
being so young a child, would become almost her own child over
time. A third brother, John, five years younger than Louisa, assisted
her briefly in educating the younger children after receiving the boot
from West Point.

Louisa also filled in as nurse for the household. From 1830 to 1836,
the Cheves family had need for her skills. Sophia Dulles had moved
in with the Cheves family in 1824 after suffering a stroke. She recovered most of her faculties, but found herself impaired by some
paralysis and by her advancing age. As for Mary Cheves, the family
had not been in South Carolina six months before she gave birth to
her fourteenth child. David Johnson appeared only fourteen months
after his next-eldest sibling, Robert Hayne. Mary, who had been in
some stage of pregnancy for most of the previous twenty-three years,
had not had time to recover from Hayne's birth before becoming
pregnant with David. David died within a few months, and Mary
never fully recovered from that pregnancy. Mercifully, she did not
become pregnant again. Louisa, meanwhile, nursed her mother, her

---

8. Sophia Dulles to Joseph Dulles, November 12, 1833, LCI; Sophia Haskell to Ann
Lovell, July 26, 1834, LCI; Huff, *Langdon Cheves*, 153–54, 188, 196, 203.

9. Catherine Clinton, *The Plantation Mistress: Woman's World in the Old South*, 38–39;
Anne Firor Scott, *The Southern Lady: From Pedestal to Politics, 1830–1930*, 35.

grandmother, the children, and the slaves of the household as the need arose.[10]

When other tasks around the household arose, Louisa stepped in to assist, whether she liked the job or not. In one instance, Mary ordered her daughter to sew clothes for the household staff. Louisa, who had carefully avoided such duties in the past, set herself to the needle and thread. By evening, according to her mother, "Louisa who had never before had any such business to attend to sat to work and cut and made a frock coat (they call Jackson Coats) and pantaloons in a day, sometimes 2 coats a day and sometimes more. . . . In fact," Mary Cheves continued, Louisa "made all the clothes for the men and children including shirts."[11]

Louisa's assistance was also called upon during the family's several moves during this period. Langdon Cheves seemed incapable of keeping his family in one home for longer than a year or two at a time. When the Cheves family first returned to South Carolina they stayed with Ann Lovell on her plantation in St. Matthews, outside of Columbia. Then they moved to Orange Grove, on the northern neck of the Charleston peninsula. Before completely settling into Orange Grove, Cheves bought a plantation on the South Carolina side of the Savannah River. He moved his family there for the winter, then upstate to Pendleton for the summer.

By 1834, he had bought a farm in Pendleton, where his family would reside year-round. The house on the farm was a subject of note for visitors. Cheves had taken two rows of cabins, enclosed the lawn between the rows to create a great hall, then built a study at one end of the hall and a dining room at the other. Each cabin became a private chamber. The construction of the home, which was not finished until after the Cheves family had installed themselves in the structure, created havoc in the household. During this time, Louisa was a welcome asset to her mother.[12]

---

10. Huff, *Langdon Cheves*, 143, 152–53, 205.

11. Sophia Haskell to Ann Lovell, c. 1831, Ann (Heatly) Reid Lovell Papers, Perkins Library, Rare Book and Manuscript Collection, Duke University; Mary Cheves to Ann Lovell, November 28, 1833, LCI.

12. Huff, *Langdon Cheves*, 150–54, 177–83.

Nevertheless, her role was ancillary. Her mother oversaw the day-to-day operations of the household, where the many little tasks of management took so much energy. Slaves performed the heavier work of household production, such as cooking, cleaning, child care, livestock slaughter, and dairy processing. Louisa's role as teacher was sporadic. The children now attended local schools in Charleston, Savannah, and Pendleton. Louisa filled in only in the absence of a local instructor, a common occurrence in Pendleton. In 1836, Langdon Cheves prepared to send Charles and Anna to school in Philadelphia.[13] Sickness, while frequent, was not constant, and the bulk of the nursing duties involved sitting by the convalescent's bedside and reading aloud.

Unless called upon in emergencies, Louisa could now spend much of her time in intellectual pursuits. She avidly read classical literature, science, and politics, as well as the Romantic poets and William Shakespeare. Shakespeare had been a constant companion in her childhood, through her father's love of his language. As an adult, Louisa pursued that affection, quoting Shakespeare copiously and mirroring his style in her own play, *Caius Gracchus*. That play also reflects two other influences. First, it demonstrates Louisa's keen knowledge of ancient history, particularly the works of Plutarch. Second, it follows the dramatic style of several Romantic poets. College of Charleston professor William Porcher Miles criticized *Caius Gracchus* as a "closet drama," to which Louisa responded: "[W]hat else can a Woman write? The world of action must to her be almost entirely a closed book."[14] In her play, however, Louisa was mimicking such poets as Byron and Keats, who wrote this sort of "closet drama," or plays that were never intended for staging.

During these years, Louisa seems to have had nursed an ambition to become something more than a wife and mother. In her book of poetry, published in 1848, she describes a yearning to rise above her station. This yearning she often personifies through common or even whimsical creatures that seek goals far beyond their reach. The

13. Scott, *Southern Lady*, 186–87; Sophia Haskell to Ann Lovell, July 26, 1834, LCI; Sophia Dulles to Joseph Dulles, October 1, 1836, LCI.

14. LSM to William Porcher Miles, June 12, 1848, William Porcher Miles Papers, Southern Historical Collection, Manuscripts Division, University of North Carolina–Chapel Hill.

subject of "The Fire-fly" wishes to join its own light with those of the stars as it "apes the sky's bright beam." Likewise, in "The Sunbeam Sprite," an elfin creature journeys across mountains and seas in an attempt to capture a sunbeam. Similarly, the narrator of "The Mirage" tries to catch "phantom shapes on sea or sand" and other dreamlike images in her hands.[15]

In other poems, the narrator feels a spiritual power pulling her beyond her own station. The narrator of "To a Fly" brushes away the pest, saying: "Know I was born for nobler things / An have not time to lose on thee." The fly represents the common household world in which such bugs are found, while the narrator hopes for greater things. Less whimsically, in "The Spirit of the Storm," the narrator identifies with the raging power of a thunderstorm, declaring her sympathy with the cries: "Would I could roam with thee!" and "Wild spirit of the storm! Like thee, I would be free." In "My Dream Child," the creative force rouses "wild" emotions in the narrator, and lets loose "thoughts' untamed creation."[16] In these poems, Louisa moves from youthful self-importance to full-blown passion for a powerful force that transcends her own being.

Louisa began writing poetry in the 1830s. By her own admission, *My Dreams* was written about 1836, but she did not pursue publication until after her marriage and the birth of her children.[17] As one critic pointed out, she was not moved by economic necessity to earn her living by her pen, and so did not publish. Moreover, to pursue a public life when she had not yet established herself in her proper role could lead to charges that she was not feminine or, more important, that she was challenging the social order. Still, the command of language and rhetoric in the essays she published between 1849 and 1856 suggest that Louisa had had much practice. She also worked to maintain fluency in French, possibly reading many books in that language, which led to her translation of the work of Bastiat. She acquired this practice, as well as the background of knowledge displayed in all of her work, during those years that were free of customary female responsibilities.

15. Lounsbury, ed., *Louisa S. McCord: Poems, Drama, Biography, Letters*, 95, 97–98, 135.
16. Ibid., 127, 130–31.
17. LSM to William Porcher Miles, June 12, 1848, William Porcher Miles Papers.

In marriage, Louisa's responsibilities would increase and the comfortable life of study that she had created for herself would come to an end. The duties in which she had only assisted would become full-time responsibilities. Time for reading, writing, and study would have decreased if not disappeared altogether, particularly after the birth of her children. Children, in fact, lay behind Louisa's third apprehension about marriage. Marriage, while not synonymous with motherhood, seemed inevitably to lead to childbearing. Motherhood, in and of itself, and in relation to one or two children, could be joyous and welcome. Indeed, many women saw motherhood as the fulfillment of their biological and social destiny. Louisa shared these ideas. "Be she true woman," she wrote in her dedication to *Caius Gracchus*, "with a woman's heart," a woman was "[i]in bondage to her child."[18] At the same time, she also witnessed a more sinister side of childbearing. She needed only to look about her in her home to see that motherhood was not limited to the idyll of Madonna and child.

In the 1830s, particularly in rural areas, women gave birth to many children, as Mary Cheves had. Persistent pregnancy was a burden that took its toll on women's health. The threat of death for both mother and child accompanied every confinement. Women frequently expressed fear at the imminent arrival of a child, and heaved a sigh of relief at every act of sexual intercourse that did not lead to pregnancy.[19]

Moreover, care of infants took much time. Even in families where servants or slaves took over child-rearing responsibilities, mothers usually cared for babies for approximately three years. By that time, however, another infant had usually replaced his elder sibling at his mother's breast. What with her continuing responsibilities as mistress of the house, a woman would have little or no time and energy to read or write. The toll that childbearing would take on her health and time, as well as the potential for grief and death, may very well have contributed to Louisa's decision not to marry. Unlike her sister Sophia, who gave birth to ten children, Louisa could avoid facing

18. LSM, *Caius Gracchus*, dedication, lines 8, 11.

19. Clinton, *Plantation Mistress*, 153–55; Drew Gilpin Faust, *Mothers of Invention: Women of the Slaveholding South in the American Civil War*, 123–29.

her fears because she had other interests to occupy her time and her passions.[20]

Remaining single, however, presented her with a conundrum. Her defense of slavery, and hence her claim to her only real property, emerged from a belief in a hierarchical social order. The security and persistence of that social order required her participation in the particular role of wife and mother. Her rejection of such a role, then, constituted a threat to the very social order in which she was so comfortably living. Widows, particularly those with children, could reject remarriage because they had already fulfilled their role. Louisa May Alcott and Sarah Grimke could embrace an unmarried state because they rejected, and even challenged, the social status quo. Catharine Beecher was an exception because she taught other women how to perform their role more effectively.[21]

Louisa, however, could not exempt herself from her prescribed role. She did not help other women become better wives and mothers, and she saw no reason to challenge the hierarchy and thereby threaten her own claim to property and future income. She used her freedom for her own satisfaction. But to opt out of marriage and motherhood in order to keep herself happy, without making any contribution to society beyond the occasional assistance at home, seemed to her a selfish indulgence. As the abolition movement gained momentum in more northern regions, and as southern defense of slavery grew, this indulgence might even seem dangerous to society. She realized she would have to sacrifice her own comforts, face her own apprehensions, and find a husband.

In 1836, Louisa's struggle toward an acceptance of marriage was delayed when Mary Cheves thrust the entire burden of housekeeping upon her second daughter. In March, Louisa wrote to her sister Sophia, "Mother has been very sick, or should I say *ill*." Constipation plagued Mary, and she got no relief from the doctor's medicines,

20. Fox-Genovese, *Plantation Household,* 80–82; Anne Firor Scott, "Women's Perspective on the Patriarchy in the 1850s," 77.

21. Fox-Genovese, *Plantation Household,* 80–82; Scott, "Women's Perspective," 77; Elbert, *Hunger for Home,* ix–xiii; Lerner, *Grimke Sisters,* 4–12; Sklar, *Catharine Beecher,* 180–82.

which "only produced violent pains." The doctor diagnosed "inflammation of the bowels," which could have been either intestinal cancer or a ruptured appendix. She seemed to recover for a few days, then suffered a relapse. Louisa consulted with her brother John, now a medical student, and a physician friend of his. Neither could find a cause for Mary's distress. Louisa reported: "[E]xcessive constipation unrelieved now for 16 days and the danger is of inflammation—Dr. de Leon thinks that there must be a crisis soon."[22] While Mary had no fever, her strength began to fail. Louisa, wracked with worry, stayed awake for nearly two weeks straight, looking after her mother.

Mary called for a pen and paper, onto which she spilled her emotions for her husband. She asked him particularly to attend more to religion "that you may become a family in Jesus." Perhaps in this final moment she found comfort in the hope that she might see her family in the afterlife, but worried that they would not find themselves in the same place as she if they did not become more devout. She signed her letter, "a last Farewell." On Tuesday, April 5, she remained alert all day, "quite conscious of her state, and talking to us all." Then, "it was all over sooner than I expected," Louisa wrote. "Poor Mother's troubles finished."[23] Less than an hour after last speaking with Louisa, Mary slipped away. The family buried her on Lang Syne, near Ann Lovell, the day after her death.

"Father seems to feel it very much," Louisa wrote, "so did Anna for the first day or two." Her father, in fact, never recovered from the loss, she would come to believe. The younger children, not quite understanding death, did not comprehend what had happened, according to Louisa. As for herself, she wrote: "I feel as I wander about the house and have to take her place in a thousand things as if I were doing wrong all the time."[24]

Louisa replaced her mother in the Cheves household. Assisting with the daily duties had given her some familiarity with the operation of a large household. The work of a plantation mistress fell into four categories. The first involved daily housekeeping and management, such as the preparation of menus and maintenance of house-

22. LSM to Sophia Haskell, March 20, 1836, and March 28, 1836, LCIII.
23. Mary Cheves to Langdon Cheves, April 4, 1836, LCI; LSM to Sophia Haskell, April 8, [1836,] LCIII.
24. LSM to Sophia Haskell, April 8, [1836], LCIII; LSM notes, LCI.

hold provisions. Slave supervision constituted the second major task, and was the one that received the bulk of mistresses' complaints. The third task was sewing, not only clothes for herself and for the immediate family, but also for the slaves. Finally, mistresses acted as caretakers for the entire household, a role that included education or training, and nursing.[25] Louisa had stepped into each of these roles when assisting her mother. After her mother's death, she took over all these tasks.

Louisa could have argued to herself that by filling her mother's position she was now fulfilling her prescribed role. As mistress of the household and caretaker of her younger siblings, she acted as "wife" to her father and "mother" to her brothers and sister. She became a helpmeet to the greatest man that she knew. As for the children, only three remained in the Cheves home, and the older two soon moved off to school. Louisa then had only little Hayne to care for, and a slave nanny did most of the daily work in that area. The sewing tasks she either delegated to slaves or eliminated by purchasing manufactured clothes. All that was left for her to do was to oversee the operation of the household and its slaves. While this was more work than she was used to before 1836, the increased responsibilities did not occupy all of her time, and she was very soon able to return much of her attention to reading and writing.[26]

Her conscience still must have pricked her, though, particularly in the political context of the 1830s. Soon after the Cheves family returned to South Carolina at the start of the decade, they found the state in the grip of the Nullification Crisis. Led by John C. Calhoun, a faction of elite low-country planters used the rhetoric of states' rights in an attempt to nullify the tariffs of 1828 and 1832 within the borders of South Carolina. The federal government, they argued, had passed these high tariffs to the detriment of South Carolina. Through the winter of 1832–1833, nullifiers gained seats in the state

25. Marli F. Weiner, *Mistresses and Slaves: Plantation Women in South Carolina, 1830–1880*, 30.

26. The amount of actual work that slave mistresses did has been the subject of a minor historiographical debate. Overall, the number of slaves that a woman had at her disposal usually determined the extent of her physical labor, and most of her work was largely supervisory. See Clinton, *Plantation Mistress;* Fox-Genovese, *Plantation Household;* Scott, *Southern Lady;* Weiner, "The Work Lives of Plantation Mistresses," chap. 2 in *Mistresses and Slaves.*

legislature. Militias in the low country prepared for what would almost certainly become an armed confrontation with federal troops
and volunteers. The state sat on the brink of civil war, both with the
U.S. government and with internal opposing factions. The crisis was
defused when South Carolina agreed to a lower, compromise tariff
under threat of invasion by one of the largest armies ever mustered
on the continent.

Tariffs had provided a trigger for nullification, but what many
southern slaveholders both within and outside of South Carolina
began to fear was abolition. Taxes on imports and the emancipation of slaves might seem to have little to do with each other. To
many southerners, however, the move toward a higher tariff seemed
to indicate that northern manufacturers were infiltrating Congress
and manipulating laws not only for their own benefit, but also to
the detriment of the slave-owning South. Northern industry in the
1830s was still in its childhood, and had not yet taken on the political
rhetoric of free labor. Yet some southern planters understood the
connection between manufacturing and wage labor. South Carolina
contained the largest faction of planters who perceived that this connection might eclipse their own agricultural interest, based as it was
upon slave labor.[27]

The Nullification Crisis also took place within the context of a
growing abolition movement. In 1831, William Lloyd Garrison began publication of *The Liberator,* in which he adamantly argued for
an end to the institution of slavery.[28] Abolition was not a new issue for the nation. Quakers had argued for the end of slavery since
the eighteenth century. The American Colonization Society gained
popularity in the early part of the nineteenth century with its plan to
purchase slaves for emancipation to Africa. All states north of Maryland and Delaware had abolished the institution, and the Northwest Ordinance had forbidden slavery north of the Ohio River. This
North-South division continued with the Missouri Compromise of
1820, which allowed Missouri to enter the Union as a slave state,

27. Many scholars of the Jacksonian era have discussed the Nullification Crisis and
its relationship to slavery; the work that most fully develops this theory is William W.
Freehling, *Prelude to Civil War: The Nullification Controversy in South Carolina, 1816–
1836.*
28. Henry Mayer, *All on Fire: William Lloyd Garrison and the Abolition of Slavery,* xiii–
xxiii.

with Maine as its counterpoint. A dividing line extended through the remaining territory of the Louisiana Purchase, permitting slavery only in a relatively small area. This trend toward limiting slavery alarmed many slaveholders, particularly as the economy of many southern states was ever more reliant upon cotton cultivation and its attendant dependency on more slaves and land.

The publication of *The Liberator* incensed planters. In their minds, the First Amendment to the Constitution did not entitle attacks upon their property; indeed, upon what they considered their very economic survival. Nor did they believe that the U.S. Post Office should allow abolitionists to use federal services to distribute inflammatory material. Hackles up, slave owners in South Carolina organized to block the delivery of all mass-mailed abolitionist literature. At one point, vigilantes in Charleston seized mail sacks delivered to the Custom House's Post Office.[29] Taken together, the tariff and the distribution of abolitionist literature caused many planters to believe that their institutions were under an attack that the federal government both supported and sponsored.

Slave owners feared the effects of abolitionist ideas not only upon the federal government, but also upon their slaves. Denmark Vesey's attempt to take over Charleston, although thwarted, had left its imprint upon South Carolina law and in the minds of South Carolinians. In 1831, southern slave owners daily read of the progress of Nat Turner's rebellion and trial. These events seemed to crystallize the nightmares of southern whites. News of the revolt on the Spanish slave ship *Amistad* reached American shores along with the ship of rebels itself in 1839. Planters were frightened both by the violence of the revolt and by the ensuing trial, which gave the rebels their freedom and questioned the borders of slavery.[30]

Tucked away in the upcountry village of Pendleton, the Cheves family was not immune to the effects of these events. Langdon Cheves, fresh from Philadelphia and still a bit of a nationalist, did not believe that nullification was the best response to the federal

29. Ibid., 196. See also Clement Eaton, *Freedom of Thought in the Old South*, for the role of Calhoun and the Nullification Crisis in the suppression of free thought through censorship in the South.

30. Thomas Wentworth Higginson, *Black Rebellion: Five Slave Revolts*, chap. 4; Iyunolu Folayan Osagie, *The Amistad Revolt: Memory, Slavery, and the Politics of Identity in the United States and Sierra Leone*.

tariffs. Wary of excessive federal power and newly established in the planter class himself, however, he did sympathize with other planters on the larger questions of the day. He particularly worried about the influx of abolitionist literature into South Carolina. In 1835, he and other low-country planters living in Pendleton organized to prevent the distribution of *The Liberator* and other like-minded material. He also urged the southern states to unify against this growing threat. As his land and slaveholdings grew, so did his suspicion of abolitionist influence in the federal government.[31]

As manufacturing, with its reliance on wage labor, grew, so did southern slave owners' fears of those interests gaining control of Congress. They became defensive of their economy and their source of labor. Moreover, as industrialization changed the very way of life in the North, drawing more people to cities and leading to the development of an urban middle class with its own concerns and interests, many southern planters began to associate agriculture and slavery with a particular society, regardless of that society's similarities with that of the majority of northern farmers or the hierarchy of social class in northern states. Defensiveness begat cultural conservatism, even for those planters, like Cheves, who were relatively new to the planter aristocracy.[32]

As the country seemed to split into one society that was entrenched in agricultural cash crops and one that was more urban and industrialized, women struggled to define their own roles. Most women, even those involved in radical movements such as abolition, saw their role mainly as that of caretaker. As early as the American Revolution, white women had begun to define themselves, as Louisa put it, as the "world's soothing mother."[33] Their rejection or acceptance of marriage and motherhood incorporated that rhetoric of Republican Motherhood and expanded it to argue either for an enlarged public

31. Huff, *Langdon Cheves*, 215, 217, 224.

32. Studies of the changing American economy and its political and sectional implications include Jesse T. Carpenter, *The South as a Conscious Minority, 1789–1861;* John McCardell, *The Idea of a Southern Nation: Southern Nationalists and Southern Nationalism, 1830–1860;* James Oakes, *The Ruling Race: A History of American Slaveholders;* and Sellers, *Market Revolution in Jacksonian America, 1815–1846.*

33. LSM, "Woman's Progress," in *Louisa S. McCord: Poems, Drama, Biography, Letters,* ed. Richard C. Lounsbury, 152, line 72.

role or for a further retrenchment into the private sphere and the "cult of domesticity."[34]

Louisa would argue for further retrenchment of women into the private sphere. In fact, she viewed such a retrenchment as a duty. Her struggle to accept this duty permeated *My Dreams* and *Caius Gracchus*, published after her marriage and the birth of her children. In these works, she defines duty, in and of itself, as a genderless concept. Both men and women should "Up and be doing! 'Tis our being's law." Idleness is "fancy," which, while fine as an occasional escape from the harshness of life, cannot lead to happiness.[35] Satisfaction can come only by recognizing that "Life yet has duties," she wrote, "and my comfort is / yet to fulfill them." This nongendered duty consists of "not shrinking from the trial, nor yet leaping / Beyond the marked outline of licensed right," whether that trial be the death of a parent, mundane daily chores, or the sacrifice of independence for the responsibilities of marriage and children. A man should concentrate upon "Curbing his passions to his duty's rule," and a woman should do the same.[36]

In curbing her own passions, a woman should "kneel / To nature's inborn majesty in man." Rather than striving to be the equal of men by taking on masculine duties, women should "stay within doors, . . . 'tis the place / Most meet and fitting woman." With "meek endurance, quiet fortitude,"[37] women should seek "to labour and to pray; to help, to heal, / to soothe, to bear; patient, with smiles, to suffer; / And with self-abnegation nobly lose / her private interest in the dearer weal / Of those she loves and lives for." A "true" woman's duty is in "teaching man," both husband and son, to fulfill his "destiny."

34. Studies on the role of women in defining their place in a changing American society include Cott, *Bonds of Womanhood*; Kerber, *Women of the Republic*; Mary P. Ryan, *Cradle of the Middle Class: The Family in Oneida County, New York, 1790–1865*.

35. LSM, *Caius Gracchus*, act 5, scene 4, lines 50–51; LSM, "Daughters of Hope," in *Louisa S. McCord: Poems, Drama, Biography, Letters*, ed. Richard C. Lounsbury, 108. In this whimsical poem, Louisa personifies Fancy and Happiness as the two children of Hope. As Man plays with Fancy, Happiness runs away. Man and Fancy join with Hope to search endlessly for Happiness.

36. LSM, *Caius Gracchus*, 5.1.220–21, 3.1.38–40; Steven M. Stowe, "Coming of Age: Duty and Satisfaction," chap. 3 in *Intimacy and Power in the Old South: Ritual in the Lives of the Planters*, esp. 131.

37. LSM, *Caius Gracchus*, 3.1.61–62, 1.3.1–2, 17.

In doing so, she "purifies, exalts and guides" them to their "duty."[38] A woman can only counsel her husband, but she can mold her sons to be better men than their fathers.

In 1852, Louisa would write that even a "high-minded, intellectual woman" should not "put aside God's and Nature's law, to *her* pleasure." Instead, she should be "an earnest woman, striving, as all earnest minds *can* strive, to do and to work," because "While man *writes,* she *does;* while he imagines the hero-soul, she is often performing its tasks."[39] By the time that Louisa had *written* these words, she was confident that she had herself *done* those tasks and that work. In 1839, however, that work still stood before her. Well past the usual age for marriage, Louisa found herself unable to accept marriage and motherhood, yet unable to either reject or transform those two institutions. After the death of her mother, she possibly believed that she had filled those roles in her mother's place. Perhaps even before her mother's death, she believed that her support in the house constituted a fulfillment of those roles.

In 1839, Louisa faced a crisis. With her younger siblings gone, Hayne soon heading for boarding school, and a household that now required relatively little supervision, it must have dawned on her that she was not, nor ever had been, truly a wife or mother. If she believed something similar to those words she would write thirteen years later, she must also have known that she herself was not an "earnest" woman, regardless of her "high-mindedness" and "intellect." More important, as a South Carolinian and the daughter of a public man, she lived in a political climate that had strong undercurrents of class-consciousness and desire for social order. Well aware of her position in that social order, and of her responsibilities in that position, Louisa realized that she must now, in her own words, "Submissive bow, and *be content,*" by finding a husband and starting her own family.[40] On May 20, 1840, she married David James McCord in a subdued ceremony at Lang Syne.

The McCord family had settled in the Orangeburg District from Ireland in the mid-eighteenth century. The earliest McCord, John,

38. LSM, "Woman's Progress," 152, lines 65–70; LSM, "Enfranchisement of Woman," 119.
39. LSM, "Enfranchisement of Woman," 108, 122.
40. LSM, "The Voice of the Star," in *Louisa S. McCord: Poems, Drama, Biography, Letters,* ed. Richard C. Lounsbury, 66, line 60.

was an Indian trader who became a planter and built a ferry across the Santee River. One of his plantations bordered that of William Heatly, the father of Ann Lovell and Sophia Dulles, and the two families had a long association, with McCords and Heatlys acting as godparents for one another's children. John McCord had six sons, all of whom inherited portions of his plantation and added to it during and after the American Revolution. The youngest of these sons, Russell, became the father of Russell Paul McCord and David James McCord, born in 1793 and 1797, respectively. By this generation, however, much of the McCord land had passed out of the family's hands, driving most of the younger men west. Russell Paul and his uncle Joseph moved to Alabama, while David James chose to stay in South Carolina and pursue a legal and political career.[41]

In many ways, McCord's public career resembled that of his future father-in-law. As a lawyer, he published *McCord's Reports,* a lengthy review of South Carolina court decisions. While Cheves cautiously moved toward a states' rights position, the younger McCord edited a pamphlet that supported nullification, and he became an avid defender of states' rights rhetoric. His fiery and outspoken nature made him a popular politician in an era that required showmanship and charisma from its statesmen. McCord served in the South Carolina legislature for eight years, during which time he also became president of the Columbia Branch of the Bank of South Carolina.[42] First a lawyer, then a politician, and finally a banker: the resemblance to her father could not have escaped Louisa.

In both his public and private life, McCord had many opportunities to cross paths with the Cheves family. He had met Cheves in the legal and banking circles of Columbia, and corresponded with him as early as the 1820s. His sister-in-law was the daughter of Cheves's factor, Ainsley Hall, while his mother-in-law, Ann McCord, was a frequent visitor to Ann Lovell's home.[43] Most important, his eldest daughter, Charlotte, married Langdon Cheves Jr. only six months before he himself married Louisa Cheves. By the end of 1839, Louisa

41. Susan Smythe Bennett, "The McCords of McCords' Ferry, South Carolina," 177–87.
42. Ibid., 188–90.
43. Ibid., 187; Ann Wagner to Effingham Wagner, June 15, 1818, Cheves-Wagner Family Papers, Southern Historical Collection, Manuscripts Division, University of North Carolina–Chapel Hill.

and David were well acquainted. Sometime after the death of his wife, Emmeline, in August 1839, they found they were attracted to each other and decided to marry.

The reasons that they chose one another were complex. Louisa's poetry suggests that romantic love was not necessarily part of the arrangement. At first glance, some of her poems seem to suggest that she felt a deep love for McCord. In "'Tis but Thee, Love, Only Thee," the narrator contemplates the sunbeams and the summer breeze, thinking of "thee, love, only thee." When she becomes frightened or sorrowful, in need of comfort, the balm is "thee, love, only thee."[44] Similarly, in "The Falling Star," a river and a star fall in love. In an effort to consummate their love, the star "fled / From its home of light and power" to join the river. "May the star not love its fate?" asks the narrator. "Perchance," she continues, the star "deems not dearly bought / That home, where it forgotten lies."[45] These poems contain a sentimentality that seems to indicate that the narrator is truly in love with the object of her affection.

But the love in the first poem is more dependent than mere romantic affection, particularly in light of a third poem, "The Comet." In "'Tis but Thee, Love, Only Thee," the narrator depends upon her beloved to soothe her sorrow. In "The Comet," she reveals a fear that might be driving her to her beloved for comfort. She pities the comet, the celestial "emblem of the soul." Whether it represents good or evil, as most civilizations in the past have perceived this phenomenon, she cannot envy it, "for thou'rt *alone*, / And *loneliness*, methinks—is *misery*."[46] The lover who provides the comfort discussed in the first poem could also ward off the loneliness feared by the narrator in this poem.

Louisa, at thirty, without a mother and without children around her in the house, and with her father constantly away looking after his plantations, may have felt lonely and longed for a companion. Most women turned to other women for such comfort, something

44. LSM, "'Tis but Thee, Love, Only Thee," in *Louisa S. McCord: Poems, Drama, Biography, Letters,* ed. Richard C. Lounsbury, 119–20.

45. LSM, "The Falling Star," in *Louisa S. McCord: Poems, Drama, Biography, Letters,* ed. Richard C. Lounsbury, 110–12, lines 27–28, 32, 39–40.

46. LSM, "The Comet," in *Louisa S. McCord: Poems, Drama, Biography, Letters,* ed. Richard C. Lounsbury, 112–13, lines 2, 53–54.

Louisa did not seem often to do. But even those women who had close female friends suffered at their prolonged absences.[47] Louisa, then, may have hoped that a husband might ease some of her loneliness.

Finding a companion, however, could be dangerous business, particularly if love were involved. In "Love, Wisdom and Folly," Love understands that Wisdom is his best partner, a "friend, or brother, / Some one, to whom to look for aid." Yet, when Love courts Wisdom, Wisdom realizes that Love "thought to rule." Wisdom then spurns Love, and Love runs off to live with Folly, "who had not Wisdom's fear / Of being by Love's power ruled."[48]

Similarly, in "Pretty Fanny," a wise grandmother warns her young granddaughter, "That man's a heartless, false deceiver," and says that "a husband or a lover / Is a thing to shun indeed." Fanny, in her innocence, listens intently to her grandmother, whom Louisa might have based upon her late aunt Ann Lovell. Then, "one day, when, o'er her bending, / Softly woo'd a lovesick youth," Fanny questions her grandmother's counsel. "'Perchance 'tis but to Grannie's seeming / That men act so sad a part,'" she thinks, and allows herself to fall in love with the young suitor. Before long, alas!, "Fanny soon was what she dreaded, / And a wedded life her lot." The narrator asks, "Would ye follow pretty Fanny? / Learn the end of her career?" Her experience causes Fanny to grow as cynical as her grandmother. She finds love, but that love clouds her judgment and leads to a life of disappointment.[49]

In "The Blood-Stained Rose," Louisa personifies Love rather typically as Cupid with a bow and arrow. Some fairies frolic among flowers until Love, described as "the tyrant," invades their bower. Having "aimed his sharp arrows at each heart," he hits his mark; one fairy is said to have "writhed with suffering, as he felt / The point pierce deep into his heart." Love counsels the fairies to accept their fate, saying, "To who submits, my wound is light, / But hard to him who would

47. Smith-Rosenberg, "The Female World of Love and Ritual," in *Disorderly Conduct*.
48. LSM, "Love, Wisdom, and Folly," in *Louisa S. McCord: Poems, Drama, Biography, Letters*, ed. Richard C. Lounsbury, 116–19, lines 5–6, 62, 111–12.
49. LSM, "Pretty Fanny," in *Louisa S. McCord: Poems, Drama, Biography, Letters*, ed. Richard C. Lounsbury, 132–34, lines 30, 35–36. 59–60, 87–88, 89–90, 93–96. For a similar interpretation of this poem, see Fox-Genovese, *Plantation Household*, 271–72.

resist." One lady fairy, however, escapes the arrows, declaring, "No power shall see me bow my head, / Or crouch beneath a tyrant's rod; / With servile voice I ne'er have prayed . . . / 'Tis not today I'll learn to stoop." Nevertheless, Love chooses a "barbed point" and "a bleeding wound / Deep in her inmost heart was made." The fairy bleeds, staining red the white rose upon which she stands. When maidens look upon a red rose, the poem concludes, they should remember to "bow to Love, before he dooms / You, like the fairy of the flower."[50] Louisa takes the symbol of love, a red rose, and gives it a sinister and cautionary twist. Love is inescapable, and also painful.

Taken together, these poems illustrate Louisa's ambivalence toward romantic love in marriage. Lonely and in need, she would rely on love to help her find a companion. David McCord is said to have been quite attractive, with dark hair and blue eyes. His daughter Lou, as enamored of him as her mother Louisa had been of her own father, would describe him as "handsome and irresistible." "I wish it were possible to convey to you," she wrote in her memoir, "the charm of his quiet, witty voice and keen bright eyes, noticing all of your little ways and doings." Louisa may have seen something similar.[51] Intellectually, both she and he agreed on many topics, and their conversations were likely quite engrossing for her, if not for both of them.

She also viewed love with caution and perhaps regret. Giving in to passion could lead to folly. In a time when women had little recourse to amend a bad choice in a husband, passion could even be disastrous. Like Louisa's imagined "Pretty Fanny," she too may have fallen under a man's charm and later realized that she had not chosen wisely. As her daughter Lou wrote, McCord could snub one "violently with a glance," and was given to emotional outbursts with other men that could lead to duels.[52] Some of Louisa's work provocatively suggests that violence may have simmered just below the surface of her relationship with her husband. "When have the strong forgotten to oppress the weak?" she wrote in an essay in which she examined woman's physical weakness in relation to man's physical strength. In

50. LSM, "The Blood-Stained Rose," in *Louisa S. McCord: Poems, Drama, Biography, Letters,* ed. Richard C. Lounsbury, 81–86, lines 73, 85–86, 93–94, 115–20, 144, 137–38, 163–66.

51. Smythe, "Recollections," 9; Fox-Genovese, *Plantation Household,* 274.

52. Smythe, "Recollections," 9.

"Woman's Progress," she made a case for women's acceptance of verbal abuse: "Man may rail, / Or mock, or pity her; with tyrant strength / May trample on her weakness, or may sneer / As though his being were of high mould; / But not for this is she degraded; rather / Ennobled, in the gently bearing it."[53]

A woman had a duty to marry, and she should love her husband if for no other reason than that love made duty more bearable. As in "The Falling Star," love would make her enjoy her fate. Still, love could lead to disappointment. Because Louisa realized that marriage was the only way to preserve her society, she may have attempted to convince herself that her love for McCord sprang more from her sense of duty than from romance or infatuation.

Romantic love and the desire for companionship played only a small and ill-defined part in bringing Louisa and David together; each partner had other motives for marriage. These centered on social status, property, and children. Both Louisa and David were well placed socially before their marriage, she as the daughter of Langdon Cheves and he as a banker, lawyer, and politician in his own right. By marrying, however, Louisa would gain social legitimacy as an adult.[54] In the eyes of nineteenth-century society, Louisa held a place of little value as a single woman. Though no longer a child, she had not yet moved from the child's position as a dependent of her father. Marriage, particularly to a man of her class, gave her the status of an adult. In addition, she harbored an ambition to publish things that she wrote, and marriage would shield her femininity from criticism.

For David, marriage to Louisa connected him to one of the most respected men in South Carolina, one who also had a prominent national career. Up to this point, McCord's career had been limited to the state arena. Connection to the Cheves name would most certainly give him greater prominence in the state and might propel him onto the national stage. Moreover, it would give him access to the wealth and property that he himself did not have.

Property was the second thing that brought David and Louisa together. David had not owned any significant property for most of his

53. LSM, "Enfranchisement of Woman," 108; LSM, "Woman's Progress," 154, lines 140–45.
54. Fox-Genovese, *Plantation Household*, 273; Lebsock, *Free Women of Petersburg*, 26.

life. Although his family had once owned plantations in the Orange-burg District, near Lang Syne, its fortunes had dissipated over the last few decades. By the time David and his brother, Russell Paul, came of age, they had no plantation to inherit. Russell Paul moved westward to Alabama, where he became a cotton planter. David re-mained in South Carolina to pursue a legal career. By the time of his first wife's death, he had eight children for whom he had to provide an inheritance. His wife, the daughter of a merchant, did not leave David or her children any property. Her death provided David with the opportunity to marry again, this time to someone with property.

For several years Langdon Cheves had earmarked Lang Syne as Louisa's plantation, and it was referred to as such among the family, although she did not hold its legal title. This plantation was to be her dowry. Under common practice, upon her marriage the title to Lang Syne would pass from Louisa's hands to her husband's. Louisa may not have particularly cared for such an arrangement, and her father seemed to like it even less. Perhaps he had expected her to choose a husband who had some experience with the operation of a plantation, or at least someone who did not have an existing brood of children to provide with an inheritance in addition to any that he might have with Louisa. Cheves probably envisioned the property passing from his family to the McCord family, which bore the stigma of having been incapable of managing property well enough to keep it.

Cheves drew up a contract whereby the plantation would become Louisa's upon her marriage and would remain entirely hers in the event of McCord's death.[55] No children from McCord's first mar-riage would have claim to Lang Syne, and the plantation would stay in the Lovell-Cheves line. In several southern states the prac-tice of setting aside a bride's property in her own name had become common. Fathers wished to prevent their hard-earned and inherited property from leaving their own line of descent, and from passing to unscrupulous sons-in-law. Husbands acquiesced because, after the Panic of 1819, the unstable marketplace could threaten even the most successful planter with bankruptcy. Keeping property in the name of the wife protected it from the husband's creditors, giving the family a sort of insurance policy against complete financial disaster. Generally,

---

55. Abstract to Title of Lang Syne and Abstract of Marriage Settlement, LCI.

in all but legal title, the husband acted as master and manager of his wife's estate.[56]

On the eve of the wedding, Cheves and Louisa presented David with the contract. As a banker, McCord saw the wisdom in signing away his claim to Louisa's property. The plantation might not actually be his, but he could use its profits and borrow against it in order to purchase his own land. He may have hoped to become a landowner in Alabama, as his brother had. In 1845, while scouting land opportunities in Texas for Langdon Cheves, he hoped to find parcels for himself.[57] Yet none of these possibilities played out.

McCord's failure to become a planter in his own right may have been because he controlled neither the title to Lang Syne nor its business. All of the papers for the plantation were burned or lost during the Civil War, but evidence suggests that Louisa herself ran the plantation. First, she seamlessly took over its operation after the death of McCord instead of handing the business over to a brother or to her father, as was customary. She also saw to the business of her father's plantation when his health began to decline and he entered her care, which suggests that she had already acquired the experience to do so. Second, her daughter Louisa referred to the business papers of the plantation as belonging to her mother. "In the middle of the room stood the old pigeon desk," the younger Louisa wrote, describing the study at Lang Syne; "it held my Mother's business papers."[58] Louisa held the purse strings, and she may have decided not to invest in land further west, nor allow McCord to invest.

Such a decision would have been a missed opportunity on her part, since many eastern planters bought western land for speculation or to replace exhausted land in places such as South Carolina. She repeatedly referred to herself as a bad businesswoman. "I am very ignorant of business," she wrote to her brother Langdon Cheves Jr., "and having nobody to help me, stumble along very blunderingly." In this case, she might have been correct about herself. Nevertheless, that statement was written in one of a series of letters in which she showed a

56. Salmon, "Women and Property in South Carolina," 296, 304; Lebsock, *Free Women of Petersburg*, 58–67.

57. McCord left a diary of this expedition, but it was apparently abandoned in the middle of the trip and reveals very little; LCIII. Neither McCord nor Cheves seem to have invested in Texas land.

58. Smythe, "Recollections," 10.

considerable knowledge of business affairs. She also downplayed her abilities as a writer.[59] Such self-deprecating remarks may have been her way of preserving her femininity when she ventured outside of the prescribed feminine world, of protecting herself from accusations of masculinity or charges of being unnatural. Her decision not to invest in land may have been wise if her intention was to keep control of the business. Another plantation might necessitate a move away from her home, or sending her husband to oversee it, something she seemed reluctant to do even for Lang Syne. But regardless of her accomplishments, she was a businesswoman, something quite unusual for a married woman to be in antebellum South Carolina.

McCord's sole role in the operation of the plantation seems to have been that of overseer. He rode around the plantation to ensure its smooth operation. When his son, Langdon Cheves McCord, became old enough, McCord carried him along to learn the business of planting in preparation for one day replacing both his father and mother as master and owner of Lang Syne. McCord seems to have done little else and to have remained uncomfortable with the fact that the property was never actually his. Even in his will, resentment seeps through his words. "I must state in the first place that I own in my own right no other property real or personal than Two Bonds due to me," he wrote. "The property of Lang Syne, real and personal, as well as that in Columbia is not mine, but my wife's." So adamant was he about this point that he also stated, "I wish it to be understood in case of my death and a balance should appear for or against me, it is in fact, not mine, but my wife's, Louisa S. McCord, and she is to receive the balance or pay the debt." He added, "I owe no debts whatsoever." He also expressed the belief that he had no obligation to his widow or their three children together because her property had supported them from the time of their marriage and would continue to do so after his death.[60]

McCord's resentment did not necessarily stem from merely disappointed expectations for his marriage. Naturally, he would have

59. LSM to Langdon Cheves Jr., March 23, 1858, LCI; LSM to William Porcher Miles, June 12, 1848, William Porcher Miles Papers.

60. Typescript of the Will of David James McCord, February 21, 1854, Dulles-Cheves-McCord-Lovell Papers.

liked to have owned Lang Syne. But the tension over Lang Syne that existed in his marriage could have stemmed from the inversion of gender roles and its implication about his manhood. Men in the South placed high social and economic status on landholding, and defined honor and liberty in relation to the property and people they controlled. McCord had shown himself to be a man concerned with such honor. Yet, in relation to property, his father-in-law and his wife subverted his position. Regardless of their benevolence and of his decision-making powers in regard to the day-to-day operation of Lang Syne, Louisa was the owner. Any major decision about the plantation, such as to sell or to mortgage or to gift the land, would require the consent of his wife.[61]

More important than McCord's discomfort, however, was the fact that by maintaining control of Lang Syne, Louisa was also living a contradiction. She deeply respected the social hierarchy, seeing it as both natural and necessary for maintaining order. She even sacrificed her own independence in order to fulfill her duty by marrying. But in that marriage, she was the superior spouse because she controlled the household wealth. There are two possible explanations for this situation. The first is that she lived this contradiction at her father's insistence. He had created the arrangement whereby the plantation remained in her name, and his frequent visits to her home may have required her to stay abreast of the production and operation of the property in order to keep him satisfied. Her father would have been the one person who could persuade her to go against any belief that she might have. Regardless of his own belief in the weakness of women, he may have insisted upon the arrangement out of mistrust of McCord. That theory has a flaw, however, in that he did later trust McCord to scout Texas land for him.

A second hypothesis is that Louisa herself wanted to control the business of Lang Syne. In light of the cynicism about love that creeps into "Woman's Progress" and "Enfranchisement of Woman," she would have wanted leverage in her marriage beyond the role of gentle advisor that she believed appropriate to a wife. If her husband were to become violent or to abandon her, as James Lovell had abandoned her aunt Ann, she would have protection for herself.

61. Bertram Wyatt-Brown, *Southern Honor: Ethics and Behavior in the Old South*.

The final thing that brought David and Louisa together was children. Louisa was an aging spinster by nineteenth-century standards. She may have offered enticing conversation and the prospect of property, but she was hardly young and nubile, waiting to be molded into a wife and mistress by a willing man. Most men looking for a wife would have been more inclined to court her younger sister, Anna. Yet McCord, a widower with eight children, was probably not looking for a fresh new bride to guide and to populate his house with heirs. Emmeline, the first Mrs. McCord, had died in August 1839, only ten months before David and Louisa's wedding, from complications of childbirth. She left David with eight children, five of them ranging in age from infancy to ten years old and requiring a mother. The seventeen-year-old Anna Cheves would not have been a suitable replacement for the thirty-six-year-old Emmeline. The thirty-year-old Louisa, a proven housekeeper who had contributed to the upbringing of her youngest siblings, would make a better caretaker. Moreover, McCord, with eight heirs and no plantation, may have worried that a younger wife would have produced another host of children requiring inheritances and dowries. Louisa would produce fewer, if any, heirs to disappoint.

The first indication that Louisa would not seamlessly replace the first Mrs. McCord occurred at her wedding. Charlotte McCord Cheves, who was the groom's eldest daughter as well as the sister-in-law of her new stepmother, did not attend, claiming illness. Married only six months to Langdon Cheves Jr., Charlotte may have been experiencing the early stages of a pregnancy that did not go to term. She may have been suffering from a spring cold or some other ailment. More likely, though, Charlotte avoided her father's almost too-hasty wedding out of deference to the memory of her departed mother. Later generations of the Cheves-McCord family and friends chose to gloss over the brief span between the death of Emmeline McCord and David's remarriage to Louisa. University of South Carolina professor and historian R. L. Meriwether refers to the span as "several years." Louisa's granddaughter, Susan Smythe Bennett, said that her grandfather "married for the second time, his first wife having been dead something over a year."[62] That two sources would downplay the

<hr>

62. Notes by R. L. Meriwether in Dulles-Cheves-McCord-Lovell Papers; Bennett, "McCords of McCords' Ferry," 190.

haste of McCord's remarriage suggests that the spring wedding was considered in questionable taste.

Charlotte's refusal to attend her father's wedding foreshadowed later strains between the couple and McCord's children with his first wife. Emmeline Wagner McCord had given birth to ten children. Two died before her own death, and two soon after. Twelve-year-old David passed away on November 13, 1839, only three months after his mother's death and six months before his father's remarriage. Another child, twenty-year-old Lorain, died in Alabama on September 11, 1840, four months after his father's remarriage.[63] Louisa may have been a comfort to her husband amid these losses, being herself no stranger to grief. Nevertheless, she did not act as stepmother to the remaining seven children.

The oldest child, Charlotte, had married Langdon Cheves Jr. on Christmas eve, 1839. Charlotte took in her younger sister, Mary Eliza, who was fifteen at the time of her father's remarriage. While McCord sent money to Mary Eliza and advised her on her education, she remained at the younger Cheves's plantation, Delta, just outside of Savannah, Georgia.[64] If Mary Eliza visited her father, she did not do so regularly or frequently.

McCord had five more children living, all under eleven years old. A third daughter, Emma, celebrated her tenth birthday just before her mother's death. Russell Paul was seven, Henry James five, Julia three, and the baby Turquand had arrived only a week before his mother died. All these children lived to at least age twenty, with the last known date of death being Julia's in 1920. When Emma died in 1851, she left McCord a granddaughter, Anna.

Louisa would have had quite a houseful of children on her hands with this brood. The baby and Julia would require her constant care, while the older three, who would certainly have a slave for a nanny, would still need Louisa for a tutor. Louisa had performed both tasks for her own younger siblings, but no evidence exists that she wished

63. Bennett, "McCords of McCords' Ferry," 188–89; McCord family Bible, South Caroliniana Library, University of South Carolina.

64. In 1999, this plantation passed out of the hands of the Cheves family and its descendants. The deed stipulated that the land never be sold to any "Yankees" or people by the name of Sherman. "Man Hopes to Prohibit Sale of His Land to 'Yankee Race' or Shermans," *Houston Chronicle*, February 7, 1998.

or was able to do so for these children. Her one comment on step-parenting, made in regard to her father's stepmother—that she "must naturally have cared little for a child so long a stranger to her"—suggests that she had no desire to take on the rearing of another woman's children. The three boys ended up in Alabama with Russell Paul McCord, their uncle, who oversaw their education. They may have moved there sometime between their mother's death and their father's remarriage. Emma may have joined them, or followed Mary Eliza to Delta. Julia was taken in by Ann Richardson, a relation of both Louisa's and the McCords who was known to accept the orphaned children of her extended family and distant relations.[65] None of the children lived with their father and his new wife. Nor did Louisa acknowledge that she was stepmother to them. She preferred that her husband's children refer to her as "aunt." She had Charlotte's children with Langdon Jr. use the same term because, as an acquaintance noted, she did not believe in the relationship of "half-sister."[66] As "aunt," she could gloss over or resolve any strain resulting from her position as the second Mrs. McCord, and conveniently explain her relation to those outside the family.

Instead of becoming mother to David's first set of children, within a year of her marriage Louisa began her own family. By the end of 1840, she discovered herself pregnant. On April 17, 1841, in the McCord apartment over the Bank of South Carolina, she became mother to a son, named Langdon Cheves McCord in honor of her adored father (and called Cheves by his family). Two years later, Louisa again entered her confinement in the summer village of Fort Motte, giving birth to Hannah Cheves McCord on September 18, 1843. The baby's first name came from her paternal grandmother and her second name from her maternal family. Hannah gained a sister two years later when Louisa gave birth to another daughter in Pendleton on August 10, 1845. Her parents named her Louisa Rebecca Hayne McCord, after her mother, the wife of family friend Robert Hayne,[67] and her uncle Robert Hayne Cheves.

65. Smythe, "Recollections," 103. Richardson had also taken in Rachel Susan Bee (who later married John Cheves) and her half-sister, Mary Elizabeth "Bet" McCord, who were grandnieces to Sophia Dulles and cousins to David James McCord.

66. "The Journals of Jane Caroline North, 1851–1852," in *An Evening When Alone: Four Journals of Single Women in the South, 1827–1867*, ed. Michael O'Brien, 174.

67. Robert Hayne had died in 1839. He had been a close friend of the family and one of Langdon Cheves's law students. His career included a term as South Carolina

Louisa Rebecca was the last child born to the McCords. Her mother was only thirty-four at the time of her birth. This fact is striking in comparison to the fertility of the other women in Louisa's family. Her mother, Mary, had given birth to fourteen children. Her sister, Sophia, would have ten children. Her husband's first wife gave birth to ten children. All three remained in some stage of pregnancy for the duration of their fertile years, but Louisa ceased childbearing at a relatively early age, considering her life span. She had not yet entered menopause, and she and David would remain married for another ten years. Louisa could easily have given birth to at least one more child.

There are several possible explanations for this limited number of children. Louisa may have conceived others, but miscarried. Her sister Anna had suffered an "abortive birth" and lost the ability to have any other children.[68] Because Louisa honored and celebrated the role of the mother in her writing, her own miscarriages or infertility, if they had existed, could have served her rhetorically or metaphorically. If nothing else, they might have afforded her an opportunity to sympathize with the inability of her friend, the diarist Mary Chesnut, to carry a pregnancy to term. In any case, she remained silent on the matter.

Perhaps either David or Louisa decided not to have any more than three children. He was already hard-pressed to bear the expense of providing for his existing children. Cheves, Hannah, and Lou could have been his concession to his wife's desire for children of her own. Conversely, Louisa may have decided that childbearing was too painful and exhausting to continue beyond her three children. She viewed motherhood as the duty and privilege of a woman. The reality was not quite as satisfying as the theory.

By the mid-nineteenth century many parents had begun to have fewer children. Urban centers were growing and children were a greater financial burden to city-dwellers, while an emphasis on motherhood placed the child at the center of the family's life. Mothers devoted more time to raising each child. This phenomenon has been associated with the rising northern middle class. The pattern certainly prevailed in that region, but others also felt the effects. In the

---

governor during the Nullification Crisis, a movement that he ardently supported, despite his mentor's opposition.

68. Langdon Cheves to Langdon Cheves Jr., March 19, 1843, LCI.

South some families, particularly those of the upper classes who lived in or had strong ties to cities, attempted to decrease the size of their families.[69] While Louisa and David lived in the world of the plantation, much of their social and intellectual life tied them to Columbia and Charleston, where they spent a good deal of each year.

In fact, while Louisa differed from her maternal grandmother, mother, and older sister by having only three children, her family size matched that of her younger siblings. Sophia Dulles and Mary Cheves began childbearing in an earlier generation that came of age in the late colonial and early federal eras in which women accepted frequent childbearing as a fact of life. Sophia Haskell began her family in the early 1830s, before the new pattern had completely emerged, much less influenced the South. Moreover, Sophia lived the greater portion of her life on her husband's plantation, seldom venturing to the city. Her life was focused on family and neighborhood, where rural patterns prevailed.

Louisa's younger siblings, on the other hand, produced an average of only three surviving children. Anna miscarried her first child, and was unable to conceive others. While her infertility was not a choice, her sisters-in-law did seem to choose smaller families. Langdon Jr. and his wife, Charlotte, had three children, Langdon, Mary, and Emma. John and his wife, Rachel Susan, had two children, Edward and Mary Elizabeth. Charles's wife, Isabella Middleton, gave birth to five children, Langdon, Henry, Harriott, Isabella, and a fifth child who died in infancy.[70] This pattern persisted into the next generation of Cheves descendants.

While nineteenth-century families had begun to place an emphasis upon the child, servants did the actual rearing of children in families

---

69. For discussions of nineteenth-century reproduction and sexuality, see Janet Farrell Brodie, *Contraception and Abortion in Nineteenth-Century America,* 3; James Lewis and Kenneth A. Lockridge, " 'Sally Has Been Sick': Pregnancy and Family Limitation among Virginia Gentry Women," 5–19; and James Reed, *The Birth Control Movement and American Society: From Private Vice to Public Virtue,* 4, 21–22.

70. These first cousins intermarried with one another and with their cousins by Sophia and Louisa. Charles's son Langdon married Sophia's daughter Sophia Haskell. Charles's other son, Henry, married Louisa's granddaughter Langdon Cheves McCord. Sophia's son Joseph married John's daughter, Mary Elizabeth. This pattern of cousin marriage was common throughout the upper classes and in the South, dating back to the colonial era.

that could afford nannies. By 1848, Louisa had weaned her youngest child. Presumably, by this time, she and David had found a reasonable method of contraception, even if that meant abstinence, and no other infant replaced little Lou at her breast. Louisa turned the primary care of her last child over to an enslaved nursemaid, Dinah, who already oversaw the upbringing of Cheves and Hannah.

Dinah, known as Maum Di, had been owned by the McCord family since her youth, first as a chambermaid and then as nursemaid. In her memoir, Lou presented Maum Di as the strongest maternal presence in her childhood. Maum Di scolded, protected, and comforted all three McCord children and earned their love and respect for their entire lives. Louisa, on the other hand, was more of a manager of her children's lives than a maternal figure. She treated her children much as she did her slaves. She acted as an authority figure, punishing the children with slaps or by placing them in closets, and she dictated their education, both religious and formal. She moved within the children's lives as a powerful figure who had to be respected or feared, but not one to whom they ran for comfort.[71]

Despite her removed position from her children's daily lives, her mothering also had some rather radical elements, particularly in the area of education. As mother, she was bound to see that her children learned their proper duties in society. Some of these were moral duties and entailed attendance at church. She herself had been baptized in the Scots Church in Charleston and had attended Presbyterian churches for much of her childhood. Yet she and her husband did not join any church throughout their marriage. In fact, they did not have their children baptized, nor did Louisa take the children to their father's funeral when he died in 1855. "Mamma and we little girls did not go to the church," Lou wrote, "but I recollect her taking us by the hands and walking very fast down to the bottom of the long garden path, where we could watch the procession going down the street and out of sight round the corner to Trinity Church."[72] Such an oversight in education is notable, particularly among the planter class and in an era in the throes of a Second Great Awakening. For the elite classes in nineteenth-century America, religion was more than an expression

71. Smythe, "Recollections," 19.
72. Ibid.

of spirituality. Religion could be used as a tool for social control. In industrialized areas, it became a means of creating a more productive and obedient worker, or of defending Protestant America from the influx of Irish Catholic immigrants. For slaveholders, religion worked in a similar fashion, as a means of convincing the slaves that God had ordained their bondage and of teaching obedience to their masters. To teach the working classes, both enslaved and free, the elite classes had to set a good example by attending church, regardless of their own level of morality or spirituality.[73] For someone like Louisa who believed in social order and the obligations of class, her failure to at least teach her children to attend church indicates the same sort of independence that manifested itself in her prolonged unmarried period and in her control of Lang Syne.

When it came to the formal education of her children, Louisa again was lax. Her daughter Lou, after describing the haphazard school attendance of her siblings and herself, wrote that she did not intend to give "the impression that my Mother had been at all negligent or indifferent in the matter of our education. She was neither, but she had her ideas, and one was that she saw no necessity especially for girls for so much school training." That statement seems shocking when applied to a woman who had to struggle so hard for her own education, hiding behind a parlor door as a child in order to learn more than was normally permitted to a girl. Lou went on to clarify her mother's opinions. Although Louisa hired various tutors and sent Hannah and Cheves to boarding school, ultimately "[s]he believed in letting an education be absorbed unconsciously as much as possible." Louisa brought her children up to be bilingual, speaking both French and English to them from their infancy. She read Shakespeare and Sir Walter Scott and "french books" to her children "everyday, as soon as we could understand," and the children would "listen absorbed." When Louisa's eyesight failed her, she took little Lou out of school and set her to reading aloud and writing for her. In such a way Louisa exposed her daughter to current events, such

73. Orville Vernon Burton, *In My Father's House Are Many Mansions: Family and Community in Edgefield, South Carolina*, 27–28; Erskine Clarke, *Our Southern Zion: A History of Calvinism in the South Carolina Low Country, 1690–1990*, 2; Paul E. Johnson, *A Shopkeeper's Millennium: Society and Revivals in Rochester, New York, 1815–1837*, 38–42, 121–28; Steven Mintz, *Moralists and Modernizers: America's Pre–Civil War Reformers*, 50–51.

books as "Kanes' Arctic Expedition, then just out," and the business of Lang Syne.[74]

Allowing a child to learn through experience was a relatively new method of education. Bronson Alcott, Henry David Thoreau, and Ralph Waldo Emerson, among others, all touted the idea, and ran many a failed school on the principle.[75] Their schools failed because this new theory ran contrary to the more accepted practice of rote memorization and harsh discipline. Louisa may have accepted harsh discipline as a necessity, but she rejected the more formal modes of learning, sharing with northern intellectuals the belief in the innate instinct of children to learn. If she was modern in the number of children that she bore, she was also transcendental in her education techniques. She perceived no contradiction in the iconoclastic religious and moral education that she offered her children and her otherwise conservative perception of social order. In fact, she may have perceived her iconoclasm as part of her elite privilege.

For the most part, her methods of child-rearing mirrored those of other elite mothers by turning the daily work of child care over to Maum Di. From spending so much time with the slaves, Lou might have known more about the actual operations of the plantation than her mother; she spoke of "hog-killing" and other such tasks with great knowledge and detail.[76] Having shed herself of the daily responsibilities of child-rearing, Louisa had the freedom to focus her attention on writing book reviews, essays, and translations. Now safely ensconced in the role of wife and mother, she could freely pursue publication without hazarding accusations against her femininity or seeming to threaten social order.

For the duration of her marriage she managed to negotiate between her desire for independence and her duty as wife, mother, and mistress. She had married because she could not defend slavery, her claim to property, as a means of social order if she herself defied that social order. In marriage she became both slaveholder and landholder, keeping control of that property from her husband. Although these responsibilities took time, they did not demand as much of her freedom as childbearing. Limiting the number of children she had gave

---

74. Smythe, "Recollections," 24, 10, 22.
75. Wesley T. Mott, ed., *Encyclopedia of Transcendentalism*, 53–57.
76. Smythe, "Recollections," 14–16.

her the liberty, later in her marriage, to return to the intellectual pursuits that she loved so dearly. She wrote and published from 1848 until 1856. With the death of her husband in 1855, however much sorrow that event may have caused her, she earned the status of widow and could openly manage her property, escape any possibility of further childbearing, and continue to write and publish. Moreover, she could do so while maintaining her social standing. She would even be respected.

Her career as a writer and her freedom in her household would be cut short, however. In 1856, a condition resembling dementia or Alzheimer's disease gripped her father. Once again she bowed to her duty as caretaker of those she loved and took Langdon Cheves into her home. Whereas duty had been the prime motivation for her marriage, love primarily drove her actions with her father. That love would also cause her greatest sorrow as she watched the true man of her life descend into helplessness and senility.

5

"Inferiority Is Not a Curse"

By 1848, Louisa had accomplished the major tasks of womanhood. She had married and borne three children. Having weaned the baby, Lou, and turned her over to the nursery maid, Louisa found the time to devote to her writing. Between 1848 and 1856, she published a volume of poems, a play, and several essays and book reviews, as well as a translation of Frédéric Bastiat's work on political economy, *Sophismes Economiques*. What fame she earned after her lifetime sprang from her work during these years. Moreover, the essays and play offer an eloquent statement of her belief system and demonstrate the extent to which she absorbed the intellectual styles of her time and place. They were a product of her experience and education and provided the framework from which she would act for the remainder of her life. The essays also offer the most dramatic illustration of the contradiction between her ideal of society and the way that society actually functioned. Therefore, the key to understanding Louisa McCord and her view of her world lies in the work that she generated during this decade.

Louisa firmly believed in a hierarchical world, one dictated by nature and by God, in which every person has a place according to his or her gender and race. In this world, superiors take care of their inferiors, who obey and respect their superiors. Louisa described this paternalism as placing those in the inferior position "under the sheltering arm of that master," while "putting a check upon individual selfishness" in that master.[1] As a woman, Louisa was in an inferior position, one subservient to men. Although she believed herself to be the intellectual equal of any man, she accepted her position. Her

---

1. LSM, "Diversity of the Races," 179; "Negro and White Slavery—Wherein Do They Differ?" 193.

reasons for doing so lay in her defense of slavery, which in turn lay at the heart of her belief system.

Louisa's defense of slavery consisted of three main arguments. First, that slave labor elevated white people, allowing them to pursue art, literature, science, and all other fields that led to the creation of "civilization." Second, slave labor acted as a form of social control. Embedded in both arguments, and backed by the scientific evidence of the nineteenth century, was the assumption that people of African descent were neither capable of creating their own civilization nor of functioning in an existing civilization without the guiding force of slavery. Therefore, her third argument was that slavery improved the condition of black people.

Like many educated people of her day, Louisa looked to ancient Greece and Rome as examples of great civilizations.[2] She was familiar with the history of Rome, and used it to illustrate the proper functioning of a republic in her play *Caius Gracchus: A Tragedy in Five Acts*. The society of ancient Rome had produced republicanism, Pax Romana, and the classical art and architecture that influenced Western civilization for nearly two millennia. This great civilization also had slaves. In fact, it was the very use of slaves that allowed Rome to achieve its historic greatness. With an enslaved laboring class, the privileged class was free to create Roman civilization. The same was true for the American South. "Our civilization of this world of the nineteenth century, *must fall* with negro emancipation," Louisa wrote.[3] She herself gained free time to pursue her own reading and writing through the labor of servants and slaves.

Historically, slavery was part and parcel of great civilizations. Without it, according to its supporters, society slipped into mere subsistence, its members focused solely upon survival and profit. Intellectuals throughout the South consistently pointed to northern capitalism as an example of greedy acquisition with little concern for high culture.[4]

Of course, most southern intellectuals also realized the deficiencies of their region in education and art. While many had attended

2. Lounsbury, "*Ludibria Rerum Mortalium*," 325–36.
3. LSM, "Negro and White Slavery," 198.
4. Drew Gilpin Faust, *A Sacred Circle: The Dilemma of the Intellectual in the Old South, 1840–1860*, 114–16.

college in the South, at either South Carolina College, the College of Charleston, William and Mary, or the University of Virginia, they were well aware that the wealthiest of planters usually sent their sons to northern universities such as Harvard and Yale.[5] Southern colleges could not compete with those schools in terms of reputation and exposure to an international intellectual society. Also, the major literary and artistic movements of the mid-nineteenth century all originated in such places as Philadelphia, New York, and Concord, Massachusetts.[6] Louisa was aware of these deficiencies. She was widely read, had several brothers who had attended northern institutions, and corresponded frequently with her Dulles relations in Philadelphia.

Unlike other southern intellectuals, however, she does not seem to have worried about this dearth of southern intellectual achievement. Her perception of the intellectual capabilities of the South was much more positive. Her home in Columbia, South Carolina, was on the edge of the college campus where her husband was a trustee and only a few blocks from the South Carolina State House. She counted among her acquaintances the southern intellectuals Francis Lieber, William Porcher Miles, William Gilmore Simms, James DeBow, and various members of the South Carolina College faculty and state legislature. While many of the southern intellectuals of her day came in contact with one another almost exclusively through letters, meeting only on rare occasions, Louisa lived in a world populated by the educated and influential people of her state. Thus, she assumed that white people were more suited to activities of the mind. "The white man, with his larger brain," she wrote, "and more highly developed faculties, is unfit for the position of the negro."[7]

Like her slave-owning contemporaries, Louisa believed that all societies were erected on the foundation of a laboring class. Physical labor was usually done by those of an inferior class. James Henry Hammond, a fellow South Carolinian, called them the "mud-sill" upon which civilization rested.[8] Many other political economists agreed

5. David Moltke-Hansen, "The Expansion of Intellectual Life: A Prospectus," 17.
6. Faust, *Sacred Circle*, ix, 7.
7. LSM, "Negro and White Slavery," 193.
8. Drew Gilpin Faust, *James Henry Hammond and the Old South: A Design for Mastery*, 346; George M. Frederickson, "Masters and Mudsills: The Role of Race in the Planter Ideology of South Carolina," 34, 48.

with this basic premise, although they disagreed upon the appropriate status for this class. Karl Marx argued that the working class should be elevated through governmental ownership of private industry. Republican ideologists in northern states believed that the working class was elevated by its status as free labor, through which its members could eventually earn the means to become landowners.[9] In the South, many agreed with Hammond that black people were a biologically inferior class suited only to manual labor. George Fitzhugh, although personally disliked by many who supported his ideas, went even further. He argued that not just blacks, but the entire working class, regardless of race, should be enslaved. "How fortunate for the South that she has this inferior race," he wrote, but "in the absence of Negro slavery there must be white slavery." Otherwise, he believed, "the white laboring class are remitted to slavery to capital, which is much more cruel and exacting than domestic slavery."[10]

Louisa agreed with Hammond that manual labor was best done by a race that was biologically suited for such work. Like Hammond, she echoed an earlier slave-owning intellectual, Thomas Jefferson, in claiming that blacks were incapable of any other type of work. "The observations of naturalists all go to confirm this position by his anatomical inferiority," she wrote, concluding that "the very virtues of the negro fit him for slavery, and his vices cry aloud for the checks of bondage," defining the virtues as physical strength and the vices as a wanton sensuality.[11]

Louisa also agreed with Fitzhugh that wage labor dehumanized the worker because it eliminated the paternalism supposedly inherent in slavery. An employer of a wage laborer had no need of "curtailing his luxuries to supply the wants of his subordinates." In fact, an employer would foist the "individual responsibility" for his workers onto a "charitable society, or an alms, which may serve, at most, to hold life together for a few weeks." Then "the rich man has done his duty, and passes on to his business or his pleasure," while

9. Eric Foner, *Free Soil, Free Labor, Free Men: The Ideology of the Republican Party Before the Civil War*, xi–xii.

10. George Fitzhugh, "Southern Thought," 276–77; Eugene D. Genovese, *The Political Economy of Slavery: Studies in the Economy and Society of the Slave South*, 8, 29.

11. LSM, "Negro-Mania," 231, 237.

"the poor victim of society, too, passes on, to toil, starve, and die—forgotten."[12]

To prevent this, Fitzhugh argued for the enslavement of all laborers in order to force employers to accept the type of responsibility for their subordinates' material condition that, he insisted, slave owners felt for their slaves. Louisa wholeheartedly agreed that the slave owner cared much more for his slaves than the employer did for his employees. "We love our negroes," she wrote. "They form to us a more extended bond for human sympathies."[13] Yet she did not believe that the absence of this responsibility in the wage labor system should lead to the enslavement of all laborers, regardless of race, as Fitzhugh suggested. Instead, she believed that the entire working class should be black slaves, eliminating the need for white laborers. In fact, she seems to argue for the expansion of black slavery not only into the western territories, but also into the North.[14] In such a way, all white people would then be free to pursue other, less physically strenuous professions.

Champions of "free labor" consistently attacked slave labor as degrading, inferior, and less productive than wage labor. An enslaved and degraded working class, they argued, was contrary to the ideal of voluntary wage labor as a means to becoming a landowner. This argument was designed to steer clear of incendiary abolitionist assaults on the condition of slaves, to deflect criticism of the condition of the white working class, and to gain support from both the northern working class and poor white southerners who did not own slaves. In fact, this argument was an attack specifically on southern aristocrats, casting them as a politically and economically backward class that opposed the ideals of democracy and capitalism, and even those of a progressing civilization.[15]

Louisa reacted to those charges by turning around the free-labor argument. Herein she diverged from Fitzhugh. The intellect of the

12. LSM, "Negro and White Slavery," 192.

13. Ibid., 193.

14. The Republican party played against just such an argument to gain support in northern states. See Marcus Cunliffe, *Chattel Slavery and Wage Slavery: The Anglo-American Context, 1830–1860*, 19.

15. Cunliffe, *Chattel Slavery and Wage Slavery*, 22–24; Foner, *Free Soil, Free Labor, Free Men*, 58–63.

white race, she believed, placed white people above the work of manual labor. Yet in nonslaveholding areas white people comprised the bulk of the working class. Moreover, she argued, the white working class of the industrialized North and even of England lived in conditions worse than those of slaves. "Our Northern cities, in their filthy crowded cellars and dirty lanes," she wrote, were rife with scenes of prostitution, starvation, disease, dilapidated and unhealthy housing, and child labor. In contrast, she insisted, the integrity of slave "family ties and social affections are respected and indulged in a greater degree than those of any laboring class in the world." Incidences "of crime, of deformity and insanity" in industrial working classes were much higher than among slaves, she argued, and rates of illiteracy equally high. She cited several studies of the working class in England, and her own experience in the North, to show that the wages of free labor did not enable a worker to support himself, much less his family.[16]

Ironically, as Louisa argued for the emancipation of the white working class from manual labor, she demonstrated little love for those of the working class with whom she came into contact. During the Civil War, while running a hospital, she criticized the enlisted patients and working-class nurses. She also expressed her disdain for an Irish washerwoman who left her service with the Union army.

Despite her personal dislike of the working class, her charges about the conditions of wage labor were astute and echoed those of other critics, in southern states and in England, of industrialization. The decades between 1830 and 1850 saw a rapid influx of immigrants from the American countryside and Ireland to northern U.S. cities, causing a national urban population growth of 92 percent. Crime, overcrowding, and poverty characterized the urban landscape. Low wages required every member of the family to earn an income, and the pursuit of jobs and better wages took younger generations away from home. Dwellings crammed with people led to the spread of disease, while dangerous working conditions resulted in maimed workers. The breakdown of old forms of social cohesion and control left the poor, the mentally and physically disabled, and the orphaned and elderly without a support network. These conditions became more and

16. LSM, "Negro and White Slavery," 195–97; "British Philanthropy," 286, 308.

more visible to the general public and a cause for concern among the socially aware. Urban reformers looked for solutions in the establishment of organizations and institutions designed to alleviate the misery associated with these problems, if not eliminate the problems altogether. Still, urban reformers refused to equate the condition of their laborers with those of the slaves. They responded to attacks from overseas with the retort that the problems faced by the working class came not from industrialization or capitalism, but from the refusal of the working class to improve their own conditions by refraining from drink, controlling their children and the number of their children, and eschewing crime.[17]

Louisa viewed this urge to reform with skepticism. "The fashion of our age is *cant,* a whining pretension to goodness," she wrote.[18] If the conditions of the working class were partly their own fault because they were free, then all the more reason to have an enslaved working class. Moreover, such institutional reforms accepted the breakdown of paternal relations and relieved the upper class from responsibility for their inferiors by placing all social responsibility into the hands of the government. Institutional solutions, according to Louisa, did not address the basic problem of wage labor, which was the absence of individual responsibility in class relationships. If class warfare were to be avoided, any institutional solutions would have to require the enforcement of such responsibility by the government.

Louisa saw the logic of bringing in government to support social reform. "The State," she wrote, "should succour the unfortunate, and palliate the effects of disastrous change, most willingly we agree." Yet, she added, "there is a point at which such efforts on the part of the State should stop—and this is, when governmental vigilance annihilates (by taking the place of) individual vigilance." She argued: "The only duty devolving upon the government is to watch over, and keep, each and all within the limits of their respective rights." Otherwise, individual rights would disappear because "in proportion as governmental power increases, the individual is necessarily effaced from the

---

17. Mintz, *Moralists and Modernizers,* 7; David J. Rothman, *The Discovery of the Asylum: Social Order and Disorder in the New Republic,* xxiv–xxvii; Cunliffe, *Chattel Slavery and Wage Slavery,* 16–18, 28–29.
18. LSM, "Right to Labor," 84.

direction of affairs."[19] Wage labor, then, was antithetical to, rather than a promoter of, individual freedom.

As long as the government did not become involved in alleviating the conditions of poor white workers, Louisa believed, a dangerous specter loomed. Without the checks of paternalism inherent in slavery, the working classes sank into the filth and misery of abject poverty. Since white men were, in Louisa's opinion, the intellectually superior race, they would not long tolerate these conditions. "The white man," she wrote, "made for liberty (i.e., for self-government, of which the instinct is implanted in his bosom), rebels at what 'the submissive, obsequious, imitative negro' finds, perhaps, his happiest existence." Since wage laborers would not rationally accept a position equal to a slave, and since their conditions were worse than those of a slave, they comprised a potentially dangerous class. "When men are fit for liberty," Louisa wrote, "they need *no prompting to make them claim it.*"[20]

The danger lay in the fact that the masses of free working people could easily be led to extremes given the conditions in which they lived and the radical ideas circulating in the North. Because white people are capable of rational thought, in her opinion, "those who are ahead in the race of knowledge" must teach "the masses to think rightly." In her play *Caius Gracchus,* she demonstrated, through the orations of her main character, the ways in which the public can be swayed by well-formulated arguments. Yet such a task is delicate. The enemy of Caius, Fluvius, perverts Caius's message and turns the populace of Rome into a bloodthirsty mob. Louisa worried that many in the northern states would fall under the similar influence of the more radical arguments made by "free-soilers, barn-burners, anti-renters, abolitionists," and socialists. "They see their rights," she wrote of the free working class, "and, knowing these withheld, fancy them greater than they are, and grasp beyond them."[21] She feared the result would be class warfare, social revolution, and anarchy.

Louisa believed that radical groups advanced their political position by exploiting the conditions of poverty and twisting the meaning

19. LSM, "Justice and Fraternity," 62–63; "Right to Labor," 87.
20. LSM, "Diversity of the Races," 173–74.
21. LSM, "Right to Labor," 80, 83; "Justice and Fraternity," 73; "Slavery and Political Economy," 450.

of freedom to incite social turmoil. "They forgot," she wrote, "that liberty was but enfranchisement." Socialists extended the meaning of freedom to not only the right to vote, but also the right to work and the right to own property. According to Louisa, political democracy and the system of capitalism entitled a person only to the opportunity to work and the possibility of owning property. To insist upon more, to require that the government guarantee more, would be robbery and tyranny. "Your fanciful equality," she wrote of the supposed socialists, "may, in truth, drag all down to one level of starvation and beggary."[22]

In Louisa's opinion wage labor degraded white workers by forcing them into manual labor for which they were not biologically suited and by leading them into living conditions worse than those of slaves, to whom white workers were supposedly superior. To improve the conditions of a free working class, either through institutional reform or socialism, the government would have to act in the role of benevolent master. This required the establishment of a large and intrusive system of government. The absence of such a system in a free-labor society, she believed, would lead to anarchy or even the end of civilization. Either alternative would destroy the freedom of individuals.

If a free-labor system is, as Louisa argued, a contradiction in terms because it degrades the white race and places at risk the very freedom that it celebrates, then the alternative, slave labor, must be the superior system because it elevates the white race and protects its freedom. Not only did slave labor allow white people the leisure to improve the arts and sciences that are the hallmarks of a great civilization, but, Louisa believed, the paternalism inherent in the system also ensured public morality and responsibility, something that seemed to her to be disappearing from the North.

Slavery also protected the white race from what Louisa believed to be a "savage" race living within the United States. Perhaps thinking back to the stories of Denmark Vesey in her youth, or to the more recent Nat Turner rebellion that caused some Virginians to contemplate emancipation, Louisa wrote: "The negro, *by his nature*, has crouched contented in the lowest barbarism." Thousands of years had

22. LSM, "Right to Labor," 85.

not produced any great African civilization, she believed, pointing to the lack of monumental ruins through sub-Saharan Africa and to the lack of any great African philosopher, artist, or philosopher.[23] The contemporary African king, she argued, citing the observations of white explorers, is "indifferent as to whether his subjects regale themselves with a cannibal feast of roasted Dominicans, or ride naked about his dominions, in palm hats and golden spurs."[24] She pointed to places outside of Africa where blacks had gained control of the government with what she saw as disastrous results. "Jamaica," she wrote, "shows what, under the best auspices, is the rapid tendency of this people, when set free from control." The corruption of the Haitian government similarly resulted from its control by former slaves and their descendants, she argued, and she feared the same fate would befall the American South.[25] "Necessarily," she wrote, "in those regions where the negro race outnumbers its masters," as in South Carolina, "a barbarism tenfold worse than Gothic or Vandal" would follow. Consequently, if returned to a state of freedom, she argued, people of African descent would only revert to savagery, "for negro emancipation is the emancipation of brute force."[26] Slavery was the only way to prevent such a disaster from happening.

If slavery elevated and protected the white race, Louisa argued, it also elevated the black race. Slavery exposed blacks to western European civilization, which they could imitate. "Only under the guidance of the white man has he, with a kind of monkey imitativeness, sometimes followed, to a very limited extent, the white civilization," she wrote. Slaves, however, would never fully adopt Western civilization

23. LSM, "Negro and White Slavery," 199; "Negro-mania," 229–32. In response to suggestions that the ancient Egyptians were African, Louisa cited arguments that the pharaohs were, in fact, white.

24. LSM, "Negro and White Slavery," 200. By "Dominicans," Louisa probably meant either missionaries or Dahomians. In other essays, she suggested that the Dahomian king would "roast" and eat his own people.

25. LSM, "British Philanthropy," 291. The British had voluntarily enacted abolition with compensation in their West Indies colonies, then criticized the decline of the territory shortly thereafter. See Cunliffe, *Chattel Slavery and Wage Slavery*, 15. Louisa's argument about Haiti reflects that of Englishman Thomas Carlyle, who roundly criticized emancipation in the West Indies, insisting that the freedmen there sat around getting drunk on rum and eating pumpkins all day. Louisa read his essay on the subject, "Occasional Discourse on the Nigger Question," quoting it in her own essay "Negro-Mania."

26. LSM, "Negro and White Slavery," 201.

because they copied most "often its follies, but never its higher points of development." Among those follies, she asserted, lay the mistaken belief that freedom meant leisure and wealth, without the effort to earn either. "They think of liberty as of a long holiday," she wrote of the slaves, "and would be surprised to find that hard work, scant pittance of food, sickness without help, rags for clothing, and shivering cold, without fire or house-room, are often the lot of the so-called freedmen." Slaves, she believed, were not capable of understanding the responsibilities that went along with freedom. Therefore, she wrote, emancipation "would consign the race to that gradual extinction which is already rapidly advancing upon that portion of it located in our Northern States."[27]

Laziness, however, was not the greatest threat to freedmen, according to Louisa. That lay in what she called "racial amalgamation," or the mixing of races on equal social terms, particularly through sexual intercourse. All races, she believed, lived in a state of mutual incompatibility if set on equal ground. She wrote: "The antagonism of races is working itself out in every instance where two races are put in collision, by the quicker or slower extinction of the inferior and feebler race." She pointed to "the case of our native American Indians," who had been removed from the eastern states, and "the negroes located in our free states." She also cited British colonization in Ireland, Asia, and Australia, places inhabited by people whom Anglos did not consider white. In each instance, the invaded people all fell before the advancing British.[28] This, she concluded, proved that "extermination seems to be the fate of the dark races, when invaded by or otherwise brought into juxtaposition with the white." The only alternative, according to her interpretation of history, was enslavement, which "has come to the rescue and protection of the weaker race."[29]

Slavery, Louisa argued, protected nonwhite races by placing them "under the sheltering arm of that master" and by giving them ben-

27. Ibid., 199; LSM, "Diversity of the Races," 183–84.
28. LSM, "Negro-mania," 239; "Diversity of the Races," 178. For centuries, the English described the Irish as "savage," and used much of the same imagery in describing the Irish as they did in describing Africans and Native Americans. They also used the same brutal tactics against them. The invasions of Ireland, Asia, and Australia, as well as the condition of the English working class, was an ever-present issue in both Britain and the United States. See Cunliffe, *Chattel Slavery and Wage Slavery*, 14–15.
29. LSM, "Diversity of the Races," 182; "Negro-mania," 239.

eficial work that suited their nature. "The negro," she insisted, "is satisfied and happy in the half-civilized condition which, with us, his imitativeness enables him to attain." In fact, she believed, slaves recognized and enjoyed their allegedly elevated condition. "Our negro," she wrote, "feels by instinct that his condition is suited to his powers; and would, but for mischievous interference, never seek, never wish to change it."[30]

Slavery, then, allowed a mass of people a life of contentment, free from the degradation of the poor white working class, safe from the threat of the supposedly superior white race, and in a position to benefit from Western civilization. Similarly, the institution also protected white people from the alleged savagery of the black race, while freeing whites to pursue the arts and sciences that characterized civilization and allowing them to daily demonstrate Christian benevolence through their care of their slaves. Louisa had, in fact, inverted the arguments of the abolitionists. Slavery was not the highest form of tyranny, in her opinion, but the highest form of charity. "If there is any community whose system of government works better for *all classes* than our own," she entreated, "we are willing to abandon the defense of ours." Meanwhile, she believed, slavery had developed to become a more perfect institution within American borders. "Shorn of the barbarities with which a slavery established by conquest and maintained by brute force is always accompanied," she wrote, "we have begun to mingle it with the graces and amenities of the highest Christian civilization."[31]

Louisa's faith in the benevolence of paternalism was belied by the violence that she herself recognized as inherent in the perpetuation of slavery. She willingly recognized the violence of slave rebellions, yet would not acknowledge the violent behavior of masters towards their slaves. This violence took many forms, of which the most common and visible were rape and beating.

---

30. LSM, "Diversity of the Races," 179, 170; "Negro-mania," 240.

31. LSM, "Uncle Tom's Cabin," 253, 279. A defense of slaves as property appeared in the court system, as in the Dred Scott case and in the formation of such legislation as the Fugitive Slave Law, but was not a large part of the intellectual defense of the institution. Louisa discussed slaves as property only in passing. As property, she argued, slaves were protected from absolute brutality because a master would not willingly damage or destroy his possessions. See Faust, *Sacred Circle*, 114, and LSM, "Uncle Tom's Cabin," 273.

Strangely absent from Louisa's analysis of slavery is the subject of miscegenation. Despite her dread of racial amalgamation, she failed to observe the existing amalgamation from masters' sexual abuse of their female slaves. The subject of miscegenation lay somewhere between a taboo and a source of rage for most southern women. Mary Chesnut accurately observed that "every lady tells you who is the father of all the mulatto children in everybody's household, but those in her own she seems to think drop from the clouds, or pretends to think so." Chesnut, in fact, proved a bit more honest than Louisa in addressing the abuses that masters inflicted upon their slaves, though she overstated the latent abolitionism of most mistresses. Yet she also fell victim to the fallacy of her own observation, attributing the paternity of the fair-skinned slaves on the Chesnut plantation solely to her father-in-law, at whom she directed much ire.[32]

While sexuality remained a delicate subject in general for antebellum audiences, antislavery activists directly addressed miscegenation. Frederick Douglass made public his belief that his former master was also his father.[33] Harriet Jacobs, veiling her identity behind the pseudonym "Linda Brent," described her own rapes in *Incidents in the Life of a Slave Girl*. Abolitionist fiction also contained characters of mixed-race heritage, such as Eliza in Harriet Beecher Stowe's *Uncle Tom's Cabin*. Such authors used the symbol of the tragic mulatto as evidence of the injustice of an institution that not only debauched black women but also permitted the enslavement of people who were partially white. Often, the mulatto character was used to elicit identification and sympathy from a white audience. Louisa, too, acknowledged the mulatto. She, however, used the figure to castigate white northern audiences for what she saw as their failure to face their own deeply rooted belief in the inferiority of blacks. She offered the fictional mulatto as proof that, even in the imagination of abolitionists, amalgamation would fail. However, she did not address how people of mixed racial parentage came into being.

It could not have been easy for Louisa to ignore the subject of beatings. Every fugitive, freedman, and observer testified to the brutality

32. Elisabeth Muhlenfeld, *Mary Boykin Chesnut: A Biography*, 109–10; Chesnut diary, 29.

33. Frederick Douglass, *Narrative of the Life of Frederick Douglass, an American Slave, Written by Himself*, 13.

inflicted by slaveowners or their minions. The ever-present specter of the whip, wielded by both master and mistress, haunted every slave narrative. Even proslavery advocates commented upon its use. James Henry Hammond, for instance, was known for beating his slaves excessively. Although bystanders might disapprove of the frequency of the beatings, none questioned the beatings themselves nor made efforts to curb their neighbor's use of the lash.

In some instances, slave owners went to extremes of violence. Douglass wrote of his experience under the "slave breaker" Edward Covey. Covey not only beat, but also mentally tormented and physically exhausted, slaves into submission. In cities, workhouses took the place of breakers, acting as prisons and places of torture for slaves who were not easily controlled by their masters. At the Charleston workhouse, slaves were beaten, branded, and forced to run on a treadmill. There, too, free black seamen and unsponsored free blacks found themselves. The treatment of blacks in this workhouse deeply influenced Angelina and Sarah Grimke and helped to push them toward the abolitionist cause.[34]

Because her plantation records were destroyed during the Civil War, ironically by the same slaves whose lives may have been illuminated by those records, no documentation exists as to Louisa's or her husband's methods as slave managers. Letters to her brother Langdon during the mid-1850s do survive, and they reveal how she behaved toward two slaves in her household at that time. These letters show that Louisa was not only familiar with the workhouse, but also used its services. In 1856, during her father's final illness, she became disgusted by the behavior of two of his slaves, June and Cilla, who may have been June's wife. Langdon Cheves Sr. had promised both their freedom, and they persisted in reminding him of that promise. Louisa classified this behavior as "tormenting" her father, but, given Cheves's failing memory, June and Cilla may have felt it necessary to ensure that his promise did not slip his mind. Louisa grew so angry with June that she sent him to the Charleston workhouse, then sold him.[35] She does not seem to have honored her father's wishes

34. Ibid., 46–57; Walter J. Fraser Jr., *Charleston! Charleston!* 203; Lerner, *Grimke Sisters,* 77–78.
35. LSM to Langdon Cheves Jr., December 18, [1856], LCI.

by emancipating Cilla or her infant child. Moreover, her sale of June separated them from him, despite her insistence that slavery encouraged the unity of slave families. Thus, even as Louisa argued that "the master gives protection, the slave looks for it," she herself proved the opposite.[36]

The slave society of the South was dependent upon a hierarchical social order that placed the white race over the black race. Most southern theorists of the time were male, and left the question of gender out of their arguments. The premise that women were inferior was not debated because the social status of women in the South was not under attack, as slavery was. In fact, northern and southern males could agree that women were inferior. Even as abolitionist ideas began to influence northern political ideology, ideas about the equality of women, first publicly proclaimed in 1848 at the Seneca Falls Convention, remained marginal until the twentieth century, well after issues connected with slavery had been supposedly settled.

For Louisa, however, the question could not be so easily dismissed. Experience told her that women were the intellectual equals of men. If intellect was the key to the superiority of the white race over the black, as in her worldview, she should have been on an equal social, political, and legal footing with men. Yet she was not. Therefore, unlike the men, who simply assumed that women were not their intellectual equals, she had to refine her defense of her hierarchical society to both explain and justify her inferior position. For this, she turned to the issue of physical strength.

"In more advanced stages of society," she wrote, "where mind asserts its supremacy, intellect makes the master; intellect is the true strength, and mere muscular power needs not only the guidance, but the protection of that mighty power which man's intellect teaches him to sway." This was, to her, clearly the difference between the black and white races. Between men and women, however, intellects being the same, the main difference was the superior physical strength of men. "The woman, classed as man, must also be inferior," she wrote, "if only (we waive for the moment the question of intellect) because she is inferior in corporeal strength. A female-man must necessarily be inferior to male-man, so long as the latter has the power

36. LSM, "Uncle Tom's Cabin," 272.

to knock her down." Since the world was a physically brutal place, particularly on a plantation where physical force lay behind the authority of the master, a woman was completely vulnerable without the protection of a white man. "Turned out upon the waste common of existence, with no distinctive mark but corporeal weakness," Louisa wrote, "she becomes the inevitable victim of brutal strength."[37]

If superior intelligence placed the white race above the black, then, among white people, physical strength placed men above women. This was not a contradiction in Louisa's mind. White women were superior to black men because white women were more intelligent. White men, however, were both more intelligent than black men and stronger than white women. White men, in other words, possessed what the other two groups lacked. Presumably, black women lay at the bottom of this hierarchy, allegedly possessing neither great strength nor intelligence.

Thus, the fundamental difference between the role of a slave and the role of a woman lay in the distinction between intellect and physical strength. If white male dominance was based upon possession of both of those traits, then, logically, slaves and women were equally deficient. Intelligence supposedly elevated white women above black men; but the very characteristic that designated black men inferior, physical strength, elevated white men above white women. What entitled white women to their superior status over black men, then, was that they, being intelligent creatures, had free will. Slaves did not. Women could, and should, choose to accept their position as inferior to white men in order to preserve society.

The difference between male and female physical strength did not escape the northern feminists.[38] Indeed, many women were motivated to support the women's movement because of their experiences with or fears of domestic violence. Just as other groups reacted to the social upheaval of industrialization, urbanization, and immigration,

37. LSM, "Slavery and Political Economy," 442; "Enfranchisement of Woman," 114, 118.

38. I define the word *feminist* broadly in this context, using it to describe people who believed that men and women should be considered fully equal, socially and politically. Since this was the main goal of the nineteenth-century woman's movement, I use it as a sort of shorthand in referring to that movement. The word, however, did not come into popular use in the United States until the 1920s; therefore, I use it ahistorically.

the women's movement turned to the government to create solutions. Louisa opposed the intervention of government into private affairs because, as she had argued in her essays on political economy and the white working class, a more active government would lead to the suppression of individual rights. Instead, as with slavery, a woman should accept her inferior position in southern society in return for the protection of the physically stronger white male. This arrangement, as with slavery, lay outside of the bounds of the government or the law. The law should merely sanction the institution, slavery or marriage, in which this bargain was struck.[39]

The concept of female inferiority, however, made Louisa uncomfortable. She echoed the proponents of the doctrine of separate spheres by insisting that woman were not, in fact, inferior: "Woman is neither man's equal nor inferior, but only his different."[40] Only when a woman stepped outside of this "different" position did she become inferior, because she could not physically defend herself. Moreover, all people became inferior when they left their allotted position. "Each is inferior," she wrote, "when attempting to fulfill a position destined to the other." Yet she uses the position of women as an example that "[i]nferiority is by no means necessarily a curse," or, more emphatically, "Inferiority is not a curse."[41] In this instance, she refers not to women stepping outside their roles, but to women remaining within their roles.

The contradiction in her philosophy seems to stem from the context in which she addressed the issue. Her arguments that women fulfill a role that is different from, but not subordinate to, that of men, appeared in essays that specifically addressed the women's movement. Her audience comprised women who wanted to strengthen their

39. Susan A. Eacker, "A 'Dangerous Intimate' of the South: Louisa McCord on Gender and Slavery." Eacker refers to the paternal exchange of protection for servitude as "a kind of protection racket" (27). The strongest critics of domestic violence in the antebellum era were probably Angelina and Sarah Grimke, who saw a connection between slave discipline and the intimidation of women. Antifeminists like Louisa McCord, however, tended to turn a blind eye to the problem. See Lerner, *Grimke Sisters;* and Linda Gordon, *Heroes of Their Own Lives: The Politics and History of Family Violence.*

40. LSM, "Enfranchisement of Woman," 124. For the doctrine of separate spheres, see Cott, "Domesticity," chap. 2 in *Bonds of Womanhood.*

41. LSM, "Woman and Her Needs," 152; "A Letter to the Duchess of Sutherland from a Lady of South Carolina," 354; "British Philanthropy," 291.

position legally, politically, and socially, and women who might be persuaded to support the movement. That audience undoubtedly would have been alienated by an argument that stated that women were inferior creatures. In fact, Louisa used the threat of inferiority to undermine feminist arguments. By following the women's movement and its agenda of equality, she maintained, women would become inferior. But by remaining within her proper role, which might seem inferior on the surface, woman was actually elevated to a status similar to that of man.

Louisa avoided the term *equal* just as much as she avoided the term *inferior* in these essays, however. A woman's position gave her strength and influence, but could not be equated with man's. "Woman," she wrote, "is designed, by nature, the conservative power of the world. . . . she checks oftener than she impels." She believed that "nature hath made [woman] to persuade and not to combat—to entreat but not to force." While man can resort to violence as a defense, woman must rely upon the powers of her mind and the force of her emotions. Women, then, find strength in intelligence and emotional persuasion.[42] Men find strength in intelligence and physical power. The difference was too great to compare.

When Louisa argued that inferiority is not a burden, she did so in the context of defending slavery. Because her defense depended upon the acceptance of a natural hierarchy of superiors and inferiors, she felt compelled to explain that inferiority was actually a blessing. Superior or inferior, she argued, "no man is born free." If freedom is defined as "the power of exercising free will" or "the right and ability to act independently of the dictates and control of others," the master is no more free than the slave.[43] Those in a superior position have a multitude of responsibilities that keep them as tied to their inferiors as their duties and the law keep inferiors tied to their masters or husbands. Thus, being an inferior is not a punishment, but just a condition. The position of a woman, with power to influence the actions of men but not to directly act in the world herself, illustrates the benefits of an inferior position and should persuade those who question slaves' treatment as inhumane that inferiority is not only natural, but also important in the grand scheme of the world.

42. LSM, "Woman and Her Needs," 153, 140; "Enfranchisement of Woman," 122.
43. LSM, "Diversity of the Races," 171.

If, however, in that scheme woman is the intellectual equal of man, her physical weakness should not bar her from positions that do not require bodily force in which to excel, such as that of professor, scientist, or doctor. In fact, if a woman's strength lay in her powers of persuasion and in her conservative restraint, she should be allowed into the legal profession, and even into politics. Louisa herself stepped outside of her prescribed role by publishing her essays in journals owned, edited, and predominantly read by men.

The women's movement was sensitive to these issues as well. Only a few women challenged the notion of women's physical weakness. Many in the North, both connected to the movement and not, sought to address the issue of women's physical frailty through dress and health reform.[44] Unlike Louisa, however, they did not believe that physical weakness should consign them to an inferior position. They drew upon the philosophy of the Enlightenment in which all humans have equal worth, regardless of material circumstances. Most accepted the notion that women are different from men and held to the belief in separate spheres in which men dominate the public sphere while women dominate the domestic sphere.

Yet women used the image of separate spheres to expand their domestic sphere. By the early 1800s women were asking that education for women be improved in order to make better mothers for the nation. Catharine Beecher seized upon this idea, taking it further by arguing that teaching was a natural extension of the motherly role.[45] The expansion of the domestic sphere became a bedrock of the women's movement, rationalizing everything from suffrage to birth control over the following century.

Louisa agreed with the premise of these arguments. Women did belong in the domestic sphere, but their power and authority lay in

44. A notable exception to the acceptance of women's weakness was the abolitionist Sojourner Truth. She pointed to her own ability to do hard physical labor like a man, stating that physical strength had neither robbed her of her femininity nor elevated her status. Margaret Washington, ed., *Narrative of Sojourner Truth*, 117–18. Studies of female health reform generally focus on the late nineteenth century, but usually include some discussion of antebellum concerns. See Barbara Ehrenreich and Deirdre English, "Witches, Healers, and Doctors," chap. 2 in *For Her Own Good: 150 Years of the Experts' Advice to Women;* Hillel Schwartz, "The Thin Body and the Jacksonians," chap. 2 in *Never Satisfied: A Cultural History of Diets, Fantasies, and Fat.*

45. Kerber, "The Republican Mother: Female Political Imagination in the Early Republic," chap. 9 in *Women of the Republic;* Sklar, *Catharine Beecher,* 180–82.

remaining in the sphere as it existed, rather than in expanding its boundaries. A woman should "teach her woman-intellect to curb her man-intellect, and will make herself the stronger woman thereby." If women were the victims of injustice, the injustice should be remedied "by working with, not against—by seconding, not opposing—Nature's laws." The desire to move outside or to expand women's place was ambition, a masculine trait, she argued: "Woman was made for *duty*, not for *fame*." When a woman seeks fame, "she throws herself from her position, and thus, of necessity, degrades herself."[46]

Instead, woman should operate behind the scenes of history. "She may counsel, she may teach, she may uphold the weary arm of manhood—of the husband, the brother, the son—and rouse him to the struggle for which nature never designed her," Louisa wrote. "[S]ide by side she may stand with man, to guide, to strengthen, to check, or to soothe." Moreover, "no true woman feels that the noble weapons of life are denied her, because she cannot tinker at constitutions and try her hand at law-making," she wrote. "[H]ers are the noble weapons of philosophy and Christianity."[47]

In her play *Caius Gracchus*, Louisa created the character of Cornelia as the model of feminine behavior. Cornelia was the mother of Tiberius and Caius Gracchus, two Roman orators who became tribunes and then were assassinated by their enemies. Cornelia was legendary as a Roman matron. In a popular story, a woman brags about her jewels to Cornelia, who produces her sons and proclaims them her own best jewels. Louisa elaborated upon this legend. In the play, Cornelia becomes the driving force behind her sons' rise to power through her wise counsel.[48] "Be cool! Be cool!" she recommends, "and heed that you do not, / In blaming one extreme, to the other rush." When not advising moderation, she urges her sons to duty. To Caius she says: "Up! Up! And work! / How should we dare to make a whim our guide, / When obligations crowd us with their claims?" She even shames them to action: "My son, I know, can never thus be brought / By fear to shirk his manhood."[49] Yet

---

46. LSM, "Enfranchisement of Woman," 121, 108–9; "Woman and Her Needs," 132–33.

47. LSM, "Woman and Her Needs," 153, 149.

48. Lounsbury, "*Ludibria Rerum Mortalium*," 331.

49. LSM, *Caius Gracchus*, 1.3.97–98; 5.4.54–56, 82–83.

she never moves outside of her own sphere, remaining within her house for all but a single scene. Her character does not advance the plot of the play. She and her daughter-in-law serve as a Greek chorus, but more important, she demonstrates the proper behavior for a woman. By doing so, she asserts authority as a woman within the limits placed on her gender. While she has no real power, she persuades and influences.

The women of the women's movement, according to Louisa, had overstepped their boundaries in seeking to be the equals of men. Like Lady Macbeth, they had become unnatural, "unsexed things." Worse, they had set the genders against each other. While, as Louisa argued, "man is corporeally stronger than woman" and, "in the unjust use of his strength, has frequently, habitually (we will allow her the full use of her argument), even invariably, oppressed and misused woman," the feminist sought to "correct the abuse" by "pitting woman against man, in a direct state of antagonism." Being physically weaker, woman faced annihilation in the male sphere. If, however, she survived, as queens throughout history had, she would constitute an entirely different threat to society. "A single queen Elizabeth might be tolerated," Louisa wrote, "and, if suited to the task of the nation over which she ruled, even admired; but a race of such monster-women could only exist as a race of Amazons. *Men* must disappear from a world where *men-women* should gain the ascendancy."[50] And without the protection of white men, she believed, white women would succumb to the savage barbarity of black men.

If woman's authority was in the home and her voice meant to be publicly silent, Louisa had to explain why she was addressing political issues in the public sphere. By taking on a public voice, she too had entered the realm of "unsexed things" and threatened the hierarchy upon which social order was based. She dealt with this problem in two ways: she either avoided revealing her identity as female, or she unmasked herself as a woman who, of necessity, must defend her gender from attacks by other women.

In writing about political economy or slavery, Louisa avoided revealing her gender. Many female authors of the nineteenth century

50. LSM, "Enfranchisement of Woman," 110, 118; "Woman and Her Needs," 144.

hid their gender behind a false name. The Brontë sisters called themselves Currer, Ellis, and Acton Bell, rather than Charlotte, Emily, and Anne Brontë. The names George Eliot and George Sand concealed the identity of Mary Ann Evans and Amandine-Aurore-Lucile Dupin, respectively. Although Louisa did not use a pseudonym, she published her work under her initials "LSM" only. Her publisher and close friends knew her identity but her larger audience did not; thus her gender was hidden behind the assumption of masculinity.

In one instance, Louisa took the male identity a step further. She most explicitly used a male voice in "The Right to Labor." Explaining political economy, she speaks of laboring, profiting, and disposing of profits, and writes: "The last I do for my wife or children, when passing a life of toil in their service." A false identity gave women the courage to break convention and publish their work, allowing their writing to reach an audience. More important, by disguising their gender, female writers ensured that readers would focus on their ideas rather than on the sex of the writer.[51]

When writing about women, addressing women, or writing poetry, however, Louisa allowed evidence of her femininity to emerge. In her poetry, her imagery of submission to duty is specifically female in the context of her worldview. In "The Blood-Stained Rose" and "The Falling Star," the wounded fairy who attempts to avoid love and the fallen star who leaves her lofty home in the sky are both specifically female. Throughout the poems, Louisa personifies hope as a female.[52] Hope is seldom an actor in the poems, but she provides comfort and solace to the adventuring male, and this, Louisa indicates, is the preferable and more heroic role. Thus, while Louisa chastises and punishes those female characters who seek to avoid their duty, she idolizes those who fulfill it. By adhering to duty and submission as a central rather than a secondary theme, Louisa takes on a feminine voice.

In the poems she only suggests female authorship. In some essays, however, she overtly uses a female voice and identifies herself

51. LSM, "Right to Labor," 92; Gilbert and Gubar, "Infection in the Sentence: The Woman Writer and the Anxiety of Authorship," chap. 2 in *Madwoman in the Attic.*
52. See, for example, "The Home of Hope" and "The Voice of the Star," in *Louisa S. McCord: Poems, Drama, Biography, Letters,* ed. Richard C. Lounsbury, 61, 64.

as a woman. "We have been obliged to confess ourself woman," she wrote,

> because only as woman can we take the defensive in this question . . . Only as woman, therefore, can we attempt the defense of woman against a move calculated in every step of its progress to lower her from the position which nature has accorded to her. Only as woman can we efficiently enter our protest against the folly and madness of ideas of which, we do their woman-advocates the justice to believe, that there is not one in a thousand degraded enough to maintain them, could she logically deduce the inference from her own premises.[53]

When her definition of womanhood came under attack, she assumed the voice of a woman in order to lend credence to her argument. She was not a man telling women to remain in their silent and powerless place, a scenario with which the feminists were familiar. She was a woman telling women to embrace their position and arguing for the benefits of submission. This the feminists would not expect, but a larger audience might accept. Louisa phrased her arguments in the ideology of Republican Motherhood, separate spheres, and feminine physical frailty juxtaposed with moral fortitude, which the public already accepted.

Moreover, she framed her defense with her favorite metaphor, that of sacrifice. She would sacrifice her own femininity in order to defend that of women too proper to defend themselves. She wrote that at first the women's movement was so absurd to her that "to attack it seriously were scarcely less ridiculous than to defend it." When legitimate publications such as the *Westminster Quarterly* began to publish the proceedings of women's rights conventions, she wrote, she realized that "the poison is spreading" because "madness becomes contagious."[54] If radical ideas were going to be taken seriously by other intellectuals, then she, as an intellectual and as a woman, must raise her voice in dissent, although such an act might seem to contradict her arguments.

---

53. LSM, "Woman and Her Needs," 145.
54. LSM, "Enfranchisement of Woman," 111.

White women held a position in society defined by their physical frailty and their intellectual strength. This position was a necessary one in a society based upon slavery. Intelligence permitted the creation of the hallmarks of civilization in the arts, sciences, and government, while physical force was necessary to deal with emergencies such as a slave rebellion or military attack. In those instances, a woman's intellect would not protect her from brutality, and she therefore required the protection of white men. As abolitionist activity grew—agitating the slaves, in Louisa's opinion—physical force became more necessary. Should the southern states have to take measures to defend themselves from what they perceived as northern aggression, women would be unable to take up arms in that defense. Instead, they should use their position behind the scenes to influence the men making the major decisions. They should counsel moderation and prevent men from acting rashly. They should mediate between slaves, and between slaves and masters, to prevent confrontation; but they should never undertake action themselves because they did not have the physical strength to back up or enforce their decisions when rational discourse broke down.

Women's inferiority, then, was a product of the slave system. Some women concluded that the absence of a slave system would logically lead to women's equality. Even in the South, so eminent a person as Mary Chesnut lamented the ownership of slaves, and many women considered themselves the "slaves of slaves," either because slave management dominated their daily work or because their own inferior position was linked so strongly to maintaining the institution of slavery.[55] For Louisa, however, the end of slavery meant the end of civilization and the beginning of anarchy. No sacrifice was too great to preserve society because "society is an inherent necessity to man's existence; what therefore is needful to the existence of society cannot be unjust."[56] Slavery, the submission of women, and any other relationship of inferior and superior, although contradictory to the notion of equality and justice, were necessary to preserve social order and peace. Indeed, Louisa argued, people were happiest in those

55. Clinton, *Plantation Mistress*, 185–86; Fox-Genovese, *Plantation Household*, 359–62; Scott, *Southern Lady*, 46–47; Weiner, *Mistresses and Slaves*, 93–103.
56. LSM, "Slavery and Political Economy," 442.

es. If unhappy, their misery was not a product of inferiority or thwarted ambitions, but a natural part of life.

Given the facts of her own life, she seemed a likely supporter of women's rights. She had watched her mother's health decline while bearing child after child. She had watched each of her brothers go off to college to pursue a higher education that was barred to her, even as she proved herself their intellectual equal in their studies at home, and she had subordinated her own independence in order to marry and bear children. Therefore, she knew the sacrifices a woman of intelligence had to make in order to maintain the facade of inferiority. At the same time, she knew that it was, in fact, a facade because she herself controlled her plantation in both title and as a business after her marriage. Yet Louisa became a strong opponent of the women's movement, and addressed her essays on women's issues to the proponents of that movement.

Her opposition to the movement lay in the need to preserve a slave society. Slavery was necessary to civilization, she believed, because it elevated both the white and black races and controlled both the black race and the working class. White women, unable to enforce this order upon all concerned due to their own physical weakness, were consigned to a position near but not at the top of this hierarchy. Gifted with intelligence but not physical strength, women could choose to accept this position or reject it, as those involved in the women's movement had. If Louisa chose to accept this position, she also chose to preserve slavery. If she rejected it, she placed slavery at risk and, by extension, all of civilization as well.

Louisa's worldview reflected not only her personal experiences as a woman, a slave owner, a person who had lived in both northern and southern states, and an intellectual, but also the major issues facing the nation in the mid–nineteenth century. The breakdown of paternal relationships in the North influenced her defense of slavery as a means of social control. Yet, as paternal relationships disintegrated, the rhetoric of democracy led to attacks upon human bondage as a backward and archaic institution, which, in turn, led some women to question gender roles. Louisa, with other intellectuals of the South, reacted to those attacks by articulating a defense of slavery that cast it in an historical and humane light. However, she also had to argue for woman's inferiority, something with which she was not comfortable, having experienced the inequities of her position. Again, she turned to the paternalist model as the appropriate form for preserving social order while also protecting those in inferior positions. Yet, if her acceptance of paternalism laid to rest her personal conflict between ambition and duty, it opened an unacknowledged conflict between the benevolence of paternalism and the violence required to preserve paternalism.

Slavery provided the foundation for Louisa's social vision, as it did for most other white southerners, but it also lay at the root of sectional differences. In the years to come, Louisa's ideals would come up against a national crisis into which she and her family would be drawn. The Civil War would test her fortitude in defending those ideals, requiring ever greater personal sacrifice.

6

"The Most Disastrous
One to Me in Every Way"

Louisa had written extensively about a woman's duty to sacrifice her own ambitions, and even desires, for the good of her family and society. Life, however, brought sadness so frequent and painful that she could not rationalize it politically. Her husband, David McCord, died suddenly in May 1855. The blow of his death had not yet faded when three more disasters struck Louisa's family. The years 1855 through 1858 also brought the death of two of her brothers and her father. Moreover, the death of Langdon Cheves followed a year and a half of constant care and attention that required his residence in her home. After his death, a lawsuit contesting Cheves's will tore apart the remaining siblings in a bitter rivalry. Louisa's belief in women's domestic fortitude endured its greatest test, and her elite position that she had so vigorously defended could not save her from the indignities and sorrows of a shattered family.

On August 12, 1855, Louisa received the news that her brother Charles Manly had passed away. Charles had succumbed to "country fever," one of the many epidemics that hit the plantations like clockwork every summer. He and his infant son died within hours of each other. The loss of this "intellectual, handsome, and fascinating" brother hit his family hard. "It was so sudden and unexpected," wrote Sophia Haskell. "He was snatched from all, after a few days sickness when no one, not even the physician, was anticipating danger."[1] Langdon Cheves was so distraught at losing yet another son that he suffered a stroke, and never fully recovered from the impact.

For Louisa, her husband's and brother's deaths were only the beginning of a year that she would call "the most disastrous one to me

---

1. Sophia Haskell to Eleuthera DuPont, November 11, 1856, LCIII.

in every way." As the Cheves family grieved for Charles, they received terrible news from Europe. "Our poor Hayne," wrote Sophia,
"almost on the same day received his death blow in Florence." The
youngest Cheves son, while traveling overseas, had suffered an attack
of tuberculosis that brought on "a dreadful hemorrhage of the lungs
which threatened him with immediate death."[2]

Hayne was a dear son, uncle, and brother in the Cheves family.
Louisa and Sophia had coddled him in his youth, giving him a strong
sense of self-confidence. His niece, Lou McCord, remembered him
fondly as a long-legged young man who "insisted upon wearing a
rattlesnake skin for a cravat and was altogether a great affliction and
delight to us." She recalled him as her and her siblings' favorite uncle,
who would place them on top of the piano and who would playfully
chase them with an apple peeler as they screamed with excitement.
She adored hearing stories of his youth, of which her mother had
plenty.[3]

Louisa considered Hayne to be her son. Their mother had been
so weak after his birth and had died while he was so young that
Louisa had come to replace her. "He belonged to me so young and
so long," she wrote, "I cannot but feel that it is my child." She anx-
iously awaited news from Europe about his condition, begging her
brothers and sisters to send any scrap that they might hear. "Let it be
the worst," she wrote, "it cannot kill my hope for I have no hope to
kill. But I want to know about my poor boy."[4]

Throughout 1856 Hayne did write, but he carefully protected his
sisters and brothers from any ill news. "He wrote quite cheerfully
himself," wrote Sophia, "so that we began to think he would come
back to us." Referring to the receipt of a long-awaited letter, Louisa
noted: "Poor Hayne's gives no information. It is patient, uncomplain-
ing, and trying to give hopes to comfort us." Yet she could tell this was
hope that "plainly he does not himself feel." Any news that seemed
positive became something she mistrusted. "Perhaps I ought to be
satisfied that this is good news," she wrote, "but some how or other
I do not feel it so."[5]

2. LSM to Langdon Cheves Jr., January 7, 1857, LCI; Sophia Haskell to Eleuthera
DuPont, November 11, 1856, LCIII.

3. Smythe, "Recollections," 2, 98.

4. LSM to Langdon Cheves Jr., January 25, 1856, LCI.

5. Sophia Haskell to Eleuthera DuPont, November 11, 1856, LCIII; LSM to Langdon
Cheves Jr., April 21, 1856, and February 29, 1856, LCI.

Her suspicions were well-founded. Most of the news about the true nature of Hayne's condition came from his friend, Joseph Manigault Heyward, who tenderly cared for Hayne throughout 1856. Heyward proved "most kind but [gave] no hope" with his reports. Louisa also consulted with Dr. John W. Powell, her personal friend and physician. Powell reviewed the letters from Heyward and Hayne, then offered his professional advice. After Hayne's initial attack, Louisa reported Powell's assessment to her brother Langdon Jr. "He says that an *active* hemorrhage for *ten days* would be impossible; that anyone would die under it," she wrote. Additional news from Europe failed to reach her when the steamship *Pacific* sank with more of Heyward's reports. Louisa finally permitted herself a single hope, "that my poor boy would at least get home to us to die."[6]

Louisa would have rushed to Florence herself to retrieve and nurse her brother, but she faced a yet greater trial that prevented her from leaving South Carolina. In the final years of his life, Langdon Cheves declined rapidly. His memory slipped away and he became addled and confused. He gradually became unable to care for himself and lost the ability to walk. Louisa, who probably considered herself his most devoted child, dedicated more and more time to taking care of her father. As the months passed, the roles of parent and child reversed, to the frustration and grief of both.

During his peak years as a planter, Cheves had seldom remained in one place for many months. He traveled down to Langdon Jr.'s plantation, Delta, north of Savannah, where he and his son mulled over problems of rice and climate. Then he would move upriver to Abbeville to do the same with his son-in-law Charles Haskell. Occasionally he stopped by Pendleton to check on whatever children remained there. At some point he might also stop by the Huger household in Charleston or their plantation in Ogeechee, Georgia, to make sure that his son-in-law Thomas was not abusing Anna's finances. Then he would ride out to St. Matthews Parish to oversee his own plantation, Sand Hills, and look in on Louisa and Lang Syne.

While Cheves remained active overseeing the operation of these plantations, he continued to search for new ventures throughout the 1840s. In 1845, Texas land beckoned. He attempted to take advantage

6. LSM to Langdon Cheves Jr., January 25, 1856, and April 12, 1856, LCI.

of the abundant land in the fledgling republic by sending David
McCord to investigate opportunities for planting and speculation.[7]
In 1846 he started up a plantation for his son Hayne, who was still
just a boy but who would soon require a livelihood for himself.[8]

Although ostensibly retired from public life since 1829, Cheves occasionally returned to politics in the following decades. He styled
himself after the statesmen of the early republic, who believed politics to be a responsibility that called them from their daily routine.
Over the years Cheves found reason to turn his attention from his
plantations to issues affecting the South. This former head of the National Bank grew increasingly suspicious of federal power. Although
he opposed nullification in the 1830s, he worried that abolitionist literature, one of the underlying issues of that crisis, would infiltrate
the South. He and his neighbors organized a committee to investigate the matter in Pendleton.[9] In the 1840s, he followed the progress
of the Republic of Texas and its possible admission as a slave state.
Although aged seventy-four and having lost some of his former vigor,
he attended the Nashville Convention in 1850, a meeting of delegates
from southern states who were alarmed at many of the provisions of
the Compromise of 1850 and at their perception of a growing northern conspiracy against the sovereignty of southern state governments.
There he urged southern secession in a rousing speech that many
critics believed saved the dignity of the meeting. He also argued vigorously for an alliance of southern states. Of his appearance at this
convention, however, he admitted: "[It] shall be the last public Act
of my life. I cannot write any more public letters."[10]

In fact, by 1855, Cheves could hardly write at all. In barely legible
script, he corresponded with Sophia, scrawling: "[W]riting letters
is a very disagreeable labor." Throughout that year he also became
increasingly disoriented in time and place. That he no longer could

7. Sophia supposedly inherited Texas property from her father, but none of the children could find titles or records for Texas land. Descendants of McCord currently live
in Houston, but their migration resulted from more recent circumstances, with no connection to Cheves's alleged property.
8. Huff, *Langdon Cheves*, 240–44.
9. Ibid., 224–25.
10. Langdon Cheves to Sophia Haskell, October 7, 1850, LCI; Huff, *Langdon Cheves*,
229; Thelma Jennings, *The Nashville Convention: Southern Movement for Unity, 1848–
1851*, 59, 109, 195–96, 198, 204.

care for himself was obvious to all. Of all the Cheves children, Louisa lived closest to her father. As a woman, she was expected to care for the babies and the aged in her family. She already felt responsible for Cheves, finding herself, she said, "unwilling to leave my Father" to attend to her plantation and insisting that he visit her frequently for extended periods of time.[11] She even carefully kept the news of Hayne's illness from him, lest grief for another son bring on a fatal heart attack or stroke.

She loved her father deeply, and to see him wander about his house or into others wearing threadbare clothing, soiling himself, and forgetting to feed himself tormented her possibly more than any other event of her life. "I have always felt," she wrote many years later, "that the height of sorrow/agony is that which makes the strong man weak."[12] She intimately and painfully witnessed this transformation in the person whom she most admired.

On January 14, 1856, Louisa went to Sand Hills to permanently remove her father to her own home in Columbia. Cheves was resistant. "He has never assented to the idea of change," she admitted, suggesting that she had unsuccessfully sought this move for some time. Now he refused to acknowledge the finality of the move and, she wrote, "seem[ed] constantly to think himself on a journey and in a boarding house." She continued: "[He] refers now to the Sandhills as his home, and frequently asks when we will get back. He seems anxious indeed to get back . . ."[13] To avoid agitating him any more than necessary, she found herself tactfully putting off his inquiries.

As Louisa observed, Cheves would not accept—perhaps could not accept—his dependent status. Daily he attempted to escape his daughter's house. Daily, she found new reasons why he could not go. Everyday, of course, the doctor would visit. Cheves grew impatient with this constant medical attention. He tried to storm from the house, and repeatedly broadcast his intention to leave. Louisa then contrived other obstacles. When her father called for his horse and carriage before the doctor arrived, she "concocted [a] falsehood about the horses and the roads to stop him . . ." He accepted her excuse on

11. Langdon Cheves to Sophia Haskell, July 3, 1855, LCI; LSM to Mary Cheves Dulles, [after August 1855], Dulles-Cheves-McCord-Lovell Papers.

12. Notes of LSM, LCI.

13. LSM to Langdon Cheves Jr., January 16, 1856, LCI.

that morning and, Louisa wrote, "[i]n this way he is put off from day to day, but is getting out of patience at being trifled with." Lying to her father gave her pangs of guilt, and contriving to hold him against his will, she said, "makes me feel like a jailer."[14]

Eventually Louisa seized upon a plan. She proposed to Langdon Jr. that their father might consent to his new residence if he were persuaded that he possessed the house. "Would it not be possible to make him go through the form of a purchase?" she asked her brother. "So long as he has the impression of owning that place [Sand Hills], so long as he thinks this [Louisa's house in Columbia] is not, and that is, his home, these attacks will constantly bring on the same results." She knew that her father's sense of self and dignity hinged upon property. "He must own property," she wrote, "he must be told 'this is yours,' wherever he stays." A mere lie would not do, however. "Some form, some apparent transfer must be gone through," she wrote, "before he will submit to be so told."[15]

This ruse, however, required the appearance of Langdon Jr. Louisa's father had already asked to see her brother: "[He] tells me I must write to you *every day* until I get an answer." She wrote: "I have, I believe, persuaded him to give up the idea of going until he sees *you*." She delayed her father's attempted departure by promising that Langdon Jr. would arrive any day and by feigning the receipt of his letters, "as I could not get on without a lie." She could not deceive her father with the ownership ploy. The elder Cheves would discuss business only with his son. "I do assume a great deal [of responsibility] in other points," Louisa wrote to her brother, "but the moment business of any kind is spoken of, Father immediately speaks of you and says it will be arranged when he sees you."[16]

While Louisa wrote to her brother "every few days" through the early months of 1856, she seldom heard from him. She pleaded with him for a letter, and especially for a visit. "My position is here so intensely distressing that you must excuse me if I press upon you more urgently than you think right," she wrote to him. "I know you have troubles, I know you have cares; perhaps even, you are not well

14. LSM to Langdon Cheves Jr., February 1, 1856, and January 16, 1856, LCI.
15. LSM to Langdon Cheves Jr., January 25, 1856, LCI.
16. LSM to Langdon Cheves Jr., March 7, [1856], February 1, 1856, and January 25, 1856, LCI.

yourself, perhaps I am goading you beyond endurance; but God help me what can I do?" She even allowed her father to attempt some feeble, scrawled lines to his son at the top of one of her letters to persuade her brother.[17]

Her other siblings offered little support. The sisters, Anna and Sophia, presumably wrote occasional letters. Anna and her husband, after some prodding on Louisa's part, sent a decent carriage for Cheves's use because "[t]he one in which Father rides is really dangerous."[18] John had his own hands full planning a trip to Florence to care for their brother Hayne. Langdon Jr. seemed her only lifeline, the only person in her family on whom she could depend to help with her father.

Langdon Jr.'s silence did not necessarily result from lack of concern. Only the coldest of hearts could ignore the feeble jumble of lines that topped Louisa's letter of March 5, 1856. Moreover, of the Cheves sons, he had been the closest to their father. However, he had his own troubles. He suffered from the flu. Then, an epidemic of measles hit his plantation, requiring a self-imposed quarantine of all inhabitants lest the disease spread throughout the countryside. To make matters worse, the epidemic hit at planting time, increasing Langdon Jr.'s worries.[19]

On hearing this news Louisa found herself torn between the need for her brother to come help her with her father and her fear that a journey from Savannah to Columbia would cause her brother an illness that would send him, too, to his grave. The loss of a third brother, after her husband and in the face of her father's condition, would be more than she could bear. So, even as she pleaded with him to visit, she also admonished him: "Take care of *yourself* my dear Brother, in the midst of all this trouble and sorrow" and "*Do not come* until you do so with perfect safety. You are almost all that we have left. You must take great care of yourself." Yet, even when the measles had passed and the planting season was completed, Langdon Jr. still did not arrive, nor did he increase the frequency of his missives to Louisa or their father's satisfaction. Charlotte, his wife, however,

17. LSM to Langdon Cheves Jr., January 23, [1856], and March 5, [1856], LCI.
18. LSM to Langdon Cheves Jr., March 12, 1856, LCI.
19. John Cheves to Langdon Cheves Jr., May 5, 1856, LCI.

began writing with more frequency, and Louisa wrote: "[H]er letters have helped me very much."[20]

Louisa became a ready cause or cure for her father's every anxiety. Desiring to see Langdon Jr., he blamed Louisa for his son's absence. "He is very anxious to hear from you," she wrote, "and evidently much irritated with *me* because he does not do so. He seems to think it is *my fault*." Cheves also became worried about his financial state. "His besetting idea is now that *he is ruined*," she wrote, and "He insists that he is in debt . . . to somebody he does not know who; that the debt will accumulate and ruin him and all his family." He became verbally abusive on the subject, "alternately moody and violent." No wonder she felt relief on those occasions when he would cast Langdon Jr. as the villain. "He frets much less when he has not me to be displeased with," she wrote.[21]

Louisa could not convince him of his financial security. If she tried to explain that he was not bankrupt, she wrote, "he says I do not know what I am talking of and that he is tired of being dictated to and does not want to be advised." Yet if she agreed with him, he insisted that she enumerate all of his lost property. He would then blame Louisa and Langdon Jr. for his imagined destitution. "Father is very unhappy today," she wrote, "thinks he is ruined, that I am cheating him, you are cheating him and every thing is wrong." On another day, she wrote: "The Doctor has combined he supposes with me to deceive him." When she could not account for the property that he believed he had lost, she said, he "accuses me of having managed things for my own benefit and made him a beggar."[22]

Nor could she escape him. "I try to stay away from him as you advise," she wrote, "but he sends for me constantly and constantly the same scene follows." On top of his accusations and his constant summons, he insisted that she write letters upon letters for him. "He thinks he has a hundred important communications to make," she wrote, and he expected her to take his dictation. "If I were to send you all poor dear Father's messages I would do nothing but write,"

20. LSM to Langdon Cheves Jr., January 20, [1856], February 1, 1856, and May 17, 1856, LCI.

21. LSM to Langdon Cheves Jr., March 5, [1856], March 1, 1856, and March 7, [1856], LCI.

22. LSM to Langdon Cheves Jr., March 1, 1856, and February 29, 1856, LCI.

she continued, "for he sends them hourly." She attempted to accommodate his other wishes, as well. "I have given up my whole lower story to him except one small room," she wrote, "have shut the door on every acquaintance and done everything I can imagine to satisfy him; but it will not do."[23]

Pain tinged all of Louisa's complaints and worries. She struggled alone to help her father, yet he often did not recognize her. In fact, she said, he developed "a habit of imagining that there are two of sundry persons habitually about him, and particularly myself." She had split into two people in her father's mind. One he despised for imprisoning him in her home; the other he loved and pitied. "I have a double," she wrote, "whom as I cannot give a name for, he constantly calls the 'nameless one' and 'the lonely one.'" He began to believe that the undesirable Louisa had displaced the sympathetic Louisa: "He is constantly annoyed with the fear that I am doing her some injustice and says he is sure I must have some dispute with her; otherwise he would see us together or at least I could tell him where she is."[24] On another occasion, he questioned her, "Are you not my daughter?" She kissed him in reply, grateful for the recognition. "I thought you were my daughter," he answered.[25] Whether this was a dismissal or an acknowledgment, Louisa never knew.

The doctors who treated Cheves's immediate symptoms did not offer a prognosis for his condition. His age seems to be the reason that they simply accepted his illness. That, along with his lapses in memory and his disorientation, suggests that he may have suffered from Alzheimer's disease, which was unidentified in the nineteenth century.

Caring for her father in his agitated and failing condition took the bulk of Louisa's days, so much so that she feared neglecting her children and worried about their reaction to their confused and often raging grandfather. Living in an environment "with nothing to soothe and every thing to excite them," she wrote, "must affect their young minds dangerously and is enough to turn them all into maniacs." She insisted, "I *must* have a hiding place for them, if this state of affairs

23. LSM to Langdon Cheves Jr., March 1, 1856, May 5, [1856], and January 28, 1856, LCI.

24. LSM to Langdon Cheves Jr., April 13, 1856, LCI.

25. Notes of LSM, LCI.

is to continue long." She found herself longing for the solace of little Cheves, Lou, and Han, "but to go on and on and on with not a corner of the house sometimes where I can sit with them quietly as a mother with her children" became almost unendurable.[26]

Louisa finally hit upon a solution to both her desire for privacy and her father's need to be master of his own home. She would build a small cottage, she wrote, "where my children could be sent (calling it their homes) or where I could myself go . . . where in fact we could stay in case of necessity." She would have slave quarters constructed in the same area to accommodate the increased size of the household and her father's need for space. Additionally, one of her father's slaves, Cilla, required a separate place for her confinement and for the protection of her new infant. The new slave quarters would be small, and the little house would have only four rooms without even a kitchen, but it would suffice for the immediate need to escape.[27]

Louisa first attempted to purchase the lot neighboring hers, but found it "unsaleable." She then sectioned off a portion of her own crowded lot, and "had a workman to run a fence across the lower portion of it." The fence would block the construction from Cheves, lest he suspect he was being moved yet again. When he discovered the activity on the far side, however, he deduced that his daughter had told the truth when she said that the larger house was his own. She wrote: "[He] begins to believe that I have really renounced claims upon this establishment." Just as she suspected, Cheves found the prospect pleasing, and often mentioned Louisa's leaving. "He watches its progress," she wrote, "and seems now thoroughly satisfied, not only that *this* is *his*, but that it is my intention some day to leave it."[28]

Still, he did want his daughter nearby. "He wants me," she wrote, "but cannot bear that he should be *obliged* to keep me; and thus the sight of a house in which he thinks I can live, keeps things right."[29]

26. LSM to Langdon Cheves Jr., March 1, 1856, LCI. Louisa may have exaggerated the effect of her father upon her children. Lou McCord remembered that her grandfather had become weak in his final years, but among her chief memories was that he had loved children and kept a room for them at his Sand Hills house: "[I]t was there that I was introduced to the joys of coffee" (Smythe, "Recollections," 14).

27. LSM to Langdon Cheves Jr., March 1, 1856, and February 29, 1856, LCI.

28. LSM to Langdon Cheves Jr., March 7, [1856], and April 13, 1856, LCI.

29. LSM to Langdon Cheves Jr., April 13, 1856, LCI.

She embodied his loss of independence, but he also could order her to do his bidding. Moreover, she offered tangible evidence that someone in his family cared for him. Therefore, he did not want her to leave entirely. Her move next door would keep her in sight, but also seemingly establish his own independence from her.

As events turned out, Louisa does not seem to have ever moved into the little house herself. With only "two rooms and two little closet rooms and a piazza to look as if it was a sizeable house," the building could not offer Louisa and her children the comfort to which they were accustomed. "I will never live in it," she declared, "but it will do to go to if needed, and to hide my children when he is as he has lately been." Instead, Cheves seems to have been moved into the smaller house; Louisa referred to "*four* large fires constantly kept up in his house."[30] Two decades later, she wrote: "I caused to be built in my garden a house of four rooms where he stayed."[31] If Cheves objected to his moving to the smaller house, he soon recovered and accepted the dwelling as his own. As Louisa suspected, the belief that he owned property was of the most importance to her father.

Langdon Cheves, of course, was not destitute as he believed. In fact he had property about him constantly in the form of his slaves June and Priscilla. As a show of authority and benevolence, he had promised freedom to them and their children upon his death. June and Cilla seem to have been married. June had two other children by an earlier marriage, one of whom, Marianne, was born around 1840 and became Louisa's personal maid. Lou later remembered June as being "wonderfully clever, but a hard drinker and very bad-tempered" and quite neglectful of his children.[32] Cilla seems to have given birth to a child during 1856, although Louisa made no mention of the infant other than writing of her concern over Cilla's requirements during her confinement.

That Cheves made his wishes known to Cilla and June was a source of further friction between him and Louisa. Naturally, the two slaves became excited about their impending freedom and very concerned that Cheves's daughter would not fulfill his wishes. "This is a constant, daily, sometimes hourly, subject of discussion with them," she

30. LSM to Langdon Cheves Jr., March 7, [1856], and December 20, 1856, LCI.
31. Notes of LSM, LCI.
32. Smythe, "Recollections," 8.

wrote, "and I am called in to promise etc., which I have been obliged to do over and over 50 times, in the most solemn manner, to the servants themselves as well as to Father." To Louisa's horror, her father intended to call in James D. Treadwell, a member of the state legislature and a notorious alcoholic, to oversee the transaction. Louisa agreed to free both slaves, but not from a desire to honor her father's wishes or from any sense of paternalism. "They will be perfectly worthless after all that has passed," she wrote, "and I would ask nothing better for my own comfort than to let them go if they choose it."[33]

Both slaves, attending to the old man every day, knew the state of his memory and endeavored to ensure that he did not forget this one important promise. This upset Louisa, because she continually found herself responding to the older man's summons on the subject, and she constantly referred to his agitated state in her letters to her brother. She wrote: "I am convinced now that they have been tormenting Father about it (at least the woman has) for a very long time."[34]

The fact that Louisa described Cilla in this way raises interesting if unanswerable questions. An enslaved woman, particularly one expecting a child, would have great concern for her own liberty. She could deliver a free child if she herself were free, and never have to fear that she and her child would be forcibly separated or that a daughter would face almost certain rape. That Cilla could not guarantee the delivery of her child until after her own emancipation would explain her concern with securing a promise not only for herself but also for her child. Moreover, her agitation of her master suggests that she understood his paternalist belief system enough to attempt to manipulate it to her favor. Perhaps there was even some concrete reason for her influence over her master. He may not have sired her child, but perhaps he fathered others, although no mention of this possibility ever seems to have arisen around Cheves, even in the decades after his wife's death. In any case, Cilla seized upon an opportunity to improve her life, and would not let her master or her future mistress forget the promise that she had procured.

---

33. LSM to Langdon Cheves Jr., April 13, 1856, LCI.
34. LSM to Langdon Cheves Jr., April 21, 1856, LCI.

Louisa's use of the word *tormenting* also raises questions. It may have been hyperbole, or written in her frustration at June and Cilla's persistence in setting a dangerous precedent with her father. After all, if two slaves managed to gain freedom from her father, others might follow suit. Moreover, if two slaves managed to get their way with the master and mistress, others might become recalcitrant and all discipline in the household evaporate. Louisa described her slave Ben as "still much the worse of the treatment received from him [June] and indeed will I presume always be the worse for it."[35] Ben, too, seemed to want a life of his own. Louisa may also have objected to the effects of June and Cilla's persistence upon her father, whom she preferred to remain calm and relieved of all business concerns.

Still, perhaps June and Cilla did, in fact, "torment" the old man. Many masters and mistresses, and even their descendants, needed to believe that their slaves were happy, content, and loving toward their masters. Slaves may have put on such faces for their own survival, but many slipped in retaliation for harsh treatment. Such retaliation might seem like an accident, such as dropping a baby or breaking a plate or spilling a bowl of soup in an inopportune place at an inopportune moment. From the point of view of June and Cilla, Langdon Cheves may have been an unpleasant man. Even before his decline, he may have berated them, beaten them, or made demands upon them that made their lives miserable. If nothing else, he represented, for them, the entire institution that attempted to rob them of their very humanity. If they irritated him in any way, they saw themselves as completely justified. His discomfort was a small thing in comparison to their enslaved condition.[36]

Louisa, angry with Cilla for her persistence on the emancipation question, focused her anger on June with excessive cruelty. By the end of 1856, she had decided to rid herself of June altogether, regardless of her father's wishes. "I send him down by this evening's cars to Charleston," she wrote, "to be placed in the Work House in care of Messrs. Capers and Heyward."[37]

Louisa instructed Capers and Heyward, slave auctioneers, to sell June out of South Carolina. She also contemplated sending Cilla and

35. LSM to Langdon Cheves Jr., January 7, 1857, LCI.
36. James Oakes, *Slavery and Freedom: An Interpretation of the Old South*, 138.
37. LSM to Langdon Cheves Jr., December 18, [1856], LCI.

her child along but reconsidered, saying that she believed June "cares nothing about" his wife. She felt some pangs of guilt for sending June away, writing: "It pains me to think of on *his* account." Yet, she wrote, "I cannot regret my dismissal of June," adding: "I had no alternative. He had become really dangerous for me and mine."[38] Again, the danger did not stem from any real physical threat, but from the fear that June might instigate further agitation for freedom or undermine her authority over her other slaves. Facing a future with neither a husband nor father to wield the threat of physical punishment, Louisa knew that the preservation of her authority over the slaves in her household was paramount to maintaining discipline and order.[39]

She refused to replace June with another slave to care for Cheves. Instead, she hired a Scotsman named Boyd. Boyd, paid a wage by Louisa, made no demands for freedom. In addition to the usual nursing that Cheves required, Boyd read to Cheves in the brogue so familiar to the older man from his childhood. Louisa insisted that her father was "doing better than he did with June."[40] Boyd's accent may have soothed Cheves. More important, Boyd held a position less charged with the abuses of power. If June and Cilla had, in fact, vented their frustration on their master, Cheves would have found Boyd's care to be much more calming.

Cheves lived with Louisa for a year and a half. His mind wandered through time and space. He often believed himself to be in Savannah or Charleston or on some plantation. He either could not remember his daughter or believed that she had a double. He raged at his inability to command either his own memory or the household in which he found himself. He entered Louisa's care afflicted with a condition that she described only as "a most painful feature of his case . . . making it doubly imperative that he should reside constantly and permanently with one of his children." This, and a subsequent mention, seems to refer to incontinence, which would only make his already addled state seem all the more pitiful. Then he lost his ability to walk, so Louisa ordered "a large chair made for him with wheels,

38. Ibid., LSM to Langdon Cheves Jr., January 7, 1857, LCI.
39. Many women, particularly during the Civil War, faced similar difficulties in exerting command over their slaves. See Faust, *Mothers of Invention*, 54–56, 66–70; Fox-Genovese, *Plantation Household*, 205–7.
40. LSM to Langdon Cheves Jr., January 7, 1857, LCI.

which pleased him only for a few days." After having her father in her care for a year, she wrote that he "needs constantly more and more attention and appliances for comfort." Yet his body remained relatively healthy. "He is with his full weight and size," Louisa wrote, but "helpless almost as an infant."[41] He had the energy to fight with his strong-willed daughter for almost eighteen months.

From the moment that her father entered her house, he became her consuming duty. As much as she loved and admired him and as much as she committed herself to caring for him, she had other passions and duties that became neglected in the wake of his arrival. As she wrote, her children could not receive her attention. She periodically rode to Lang Syne to oversee business on the plantation, but fretted about the disasters that might befall her home in the meantime.

Toward the end of the summer of 1856, Langdon Jr. finally arrived in Columbia to watch over his father.[42] His long-awaited arrival allowed Louisa to seek refuge and medical advice for herself in Philadelphia. Desperate for escape, she also spent a month in Narragansett, Rhode Island, with her cousins the Dulleses. There she tried to resume her writing, which had fallen by the wayside since her father had moved into her home.[43] Escape from her emotions was not so easily achieved, however. On a quiet evening in Rhode Island, with the waves lapping the shore outside the window, Joseph Heatly Dulles began reading from Charles Dickens's recent novel, *David Copperfield*. The trials of the characters in the book stirred Louisa's already strained emotions. Her daughter Lou recalled "being so surprised at seeing . . . Mother who was very sad and very nervous, break down and cry at some of the scenes."[44]

Returning to Columbia, Louisa found her father more complicit in his change of residence. His frustration at his condition remained, though, and she bore the brunt of it alone. As she had written earlier: "The most painful part of it all is, that he is almost always dissatisfied

41. LSM to Langdon Cheves Jr., January 28, 1856, May 17, 1856, and February 5, 1857, LCI.

42. William deSaussure to Langdon Cheves Jr., August 10, 1856, and Cheves to deSaussure, December 22, 1856, LCI.

43. LSM to James Henley Thornwell, July 1856, LCI.

44. Smythe, "Recollections," 21.

and unhappy." A man so accustomed to independence, authority, and clarity of mind grieved the loss of it all. Louisa accurately understood his feelings when she wrote: "I sometimes think that he has a jealousy of the part I act in retaining him here."[45] In his grieving, he lashed out at the person who most represented his state of dependency, the person who now acted as his nursemaid: his daughter.

Moreover, her finances were dwindling. One of her complaints to her brother was that the cost of caring for their father exceeded the income of both of their plantations. She first estimated that her father would require "$2000 at present, with $500 quarterly from 1st April." His need for a wheelchair and other appliances, a separate house, and the added servants' quarters, as well as Boyd's pay, added considerably to her expenses. "I cannot command more than $100 without borrowing," she wrote, and "I am really getting embarassed for want of funds." After her father had lived with her a year, she tallied up her expenses and found herself in debt "*minus* some 700 dollars." Her situation would only become worse: "Each day some new expense occurs." Now, she realized, "$2000 a year is entirely insuficient for Father's expenses."[46]

She complained that she had no sense for money, and she does seem to have spent extravagantly rather than economize. Yet she also seems to have kept careful records of expenses and pleaded with her brother to have her credit extended at the bank of Fraser and Company to cover mounting costs. Frustrated at her brother's leisurely pace, she finally wrote to the bank herself. She understood that she had stepped outside the bounds of proper procedure, particularly for a woman. "I do not blame you at all for not writing about my little wants," she wrote to her brother, "only I can't do without money and I hope you will not be displeased with what I have done." She apologized to the bank for taking "liberty." Still, she added, "For the future I must beg you to have an understanding with him [Langdon Jr.] that I may draw upon you to a larger amount than hitherto."[47] Deferentially, she had taken matters into her own hands.

45. LSM to Langdon Cheves Jr., January, 28, 1856, LCI.
46. LSM to Langdon Cheves Jr., March 12, [1856], March 19, 1856, February 5, 1857, and January 29, 1857, LCI.
47. LSM to Langdon Cheves Jr., February 5, 1857, LCI; LSM to Messrs. John Fraser and Co., February 5, 1857, LCI.

The years 1856 and 1857 were horrible ones for Louisa. Surviving those years was worse for knowing how the ordeal must end. The end, moreover, came with a double blow. In November 1856 she learned of the death of her baby brother, Hayne. Tuberculosis finally took him on August 14, 1856. Sophia's son Langdon Haskell had rushed to Italy and was with him in his final hours. John Cheves and his wife Rachel arrived too late.[48] The emaciated body was shipped back to South Carolina, where Thomas Huger, Anna's husband, received it and consulted with Louisa on the funeral arrangements.[49] The family lay the youngest child to rest in the family plot at Magnolia cemetery as the year turned.

Louisa had carefully concealed Hayne's illness from her father. Now she kept his death a secret. She did not want to upset her father, who was already so disturbed by his own decline and who had taken the death of Charles so badly. He would die not knowing that his son had preceded him to the grave, a fact that would have unfortunate repercussions.

Langdon Cheves clung to life until June 26, 1857. How horrid it must have been for Louisa to have her final memories of her father in his debilitated state. How relieved she must have felt that he had moved on from this life. How guilty she must have felt for her relief. As her final gift to him, she would attempt to preserve his memory, depicting him as the strong and able man that she admired in an attempt to erase the weak invalid that he had become. She and Langdon Jr. commissioned a statue of their father to be placed in the speaker's room of the South Carolina State House.[50] They also set about fulfilling his wish for "the erection of three tomb-stones or monuments of some kind, over his Mother's grave in Abbeville and our Mother's and Aunt Lovell's on this place [Lang Syne]." Finally, Louisa undertook the commission of a bust of her father from Hiram Powers, whose powerful and elegant sculptures gained acclaim during the mid-nineteenth century.[51]

48. Sophia Haskell to Eleuthera DuPont, November 11, 1856, LCIII.

49. Thomas Pinckney Huger to Langdon Cheves Jr., November 29, 1856, LCI.

50. William deSaussure to Langdon Cheves Jr., August 10, 1856, and Cheves Jr. to deSaussure, December 22, 1856, LCI.

51. LSM to Langdon Cheves Jr., December 26, 1857, and February 5, 1858, LCI; LSM to Hiram Powers, July 9, 1858, Hiram Powers and Powers Family Papers, Smithsonian Institution, Washington, D.C.

After a death, the family must dispose of the property of the departed. Louisa was left to care for the personal items. Cheves's slaves fell under her responsibility, and she saw to their relocation among her siblings' plantations.[52] She gathered together her father's papers and sent them to Langdon Jr., executor of his will. She gratefully allowed Langdon Jr. to handle their father's estate without interference or advice from herself, if for no other reason than the cost of lawyers. "If I only look at the tip end of the nose of one," she wrote, "he makes me pay fifty Dollars." She already had enough bills from the debts that she had incurred for her father's care. To pay these, she sold Sand Hills, her father's plantation that she inherited. The price that she received was so low that she lamented that she had "thrown away" the plantation, and she found that she must sell her inherited stock in railroads to make up the difference.[53]

This would be the end of a chapter in Louisa's life. She had lost her husband, two of her brothers, and her father in the space of three years. Under the strain, her eyesight had begun to fail her, and she planned a trip to Europe to seek medical consultation and to find respite from her seemingly endless grief. Charles Haskell, however, prolonged the year's sadness. He challenged Cheves's will, and was joined by John Cheves.

The lawsuit stemmed from Hayne's inheritance. Since Cheves had not learned of his son's death, he had not amended his will. Moreover, he would not have been considered competent enough to do so had Louisa apprised him of this news. Langdon Jr. automatically considered Hayne's portion of the estate as intestate.[54] Intestate property would be divided equally among all surviving children.

One item of Langdon Cheves's will, however, stated: "As to the rest, residue and remainder of my estate, real and personal or in action, I give devise and bequeath the same unto my daughters and their issue."[55] Haskell and John insisted that Hayne's inheritance fell under residual property, which should be divided according to

52. LSM to Langdon Cheves Jr., December 26, 1857, LCI.
53. LSM to Langdon Cheves Jr., March 23, 1858, and April 3, 1858, LCI.
54. Statement of Langdon Cheves Jr., *The State of South-Carolina, Charleston District, in equity*, 3, LCI.
55. Will of Langdon Cheves [Sr.], LCI.

that item. Haskell, of course, would benefit from that interpretation through his marriage to Sophia. John did not explain his motives.

John's position shocked Louisa: "The property given by Father to his daughters . . . was so *very much less* than that given to his Sons that I could never have anticipated opposition from any of them."[56] That may have been the very reason that John supported Haskell. He may have inherited his father's concern for the "helplessness of females"[57] and believed that his sisters had been unfairly treated by Langdon Jr.'s division of property.

John may have been concerned with not only the property itself, but the fact that he was not named executor of the will. Of his adult sons, Cheves had named Charles and Langdon Jr. as executors. With Charles gone, Langdon Jr. alone carried out what he supposed to be his father's wishes. Moreover, Cheves had charged his executors with the management of South Field, on the Ogeechee River in Georgia, the plantation that became the focus of the dispute. John may have challenged Langdon Jr.'s interpretation as a means of questioning his sole authority in the dispensation of property and his seeming advantage in the control of property left in the will.[58]

Louisa, for her part, agreed with Langdon Jr. although she stood to gain less property from such a decision. Her opinion was shaped by what she believed were her father's wishes and by "justice to her brothers." She wrote: "The last time I read over Father's will to him, he remarked of that clause [regarding the residual property] to the effect that it could cover nothing but his clothing and trifling personal effects."[59] She thought Cheves believed that he had sufficiently provided for his daughters in life and was leaving them sufficient funds in trust up to 1860. She believed that had he known of Hayne's death, he would never have divided Hayne's inheritance among only his daughters since "he conceived that he had done ample justice by his daughters." Once he had provided for his daughters, Louisa believed, Cheves had attempted to provide for each surviving child equally, although "he did not mean an arithmetical equality." In fact,

56. LSM to Langdon Cheves Jr., March 23, 1858, LCI.

57. Langdon Cheves [Sr.] to Alexander Cheves, May 24, 1838, LCI.

58. Will of Langdon Cheves [Sr.], LCI.

59. LSM deposition before the Equity Court of Appeals, Charleston District, printed copy, LCI; LSM to Langdon Cheves Jr., February 5, 1858, LCI.

she stated, "the plantation which he gave to his son John was far less valuable than those which he afterwards gave to his sons Langdon and Charles."[60] John, therefore, should be satisfied with the intestate decision.

John's role in the lawsuit hurt Louisa deeply. She fired off an angry letter to him, but quickly regretted her action and asked that it be burned without being read.[61] Ultimately, she could not bring herself to accuse one of her remaining two brothers of any misdeed. Instead, she placed the whole of the controversy upon her brother-in-law's shoulders, although she carefully did not implicate her sister in Haskell's behavior. Instead, she grated at the refusal of Haskell's lawyers to allow her to testify. "They object," she wrote, "to my speaking out the truth." A woman of opinions, she could not bear to be silenced, and thought it a great injustice. She warned Langdon Jr. not to trust Haskell. "I have had business connections with him off and on, for Seven and Twenty years," she wrote, "and I think I know him." She suggested that he was not the best nor most honest businessman, quoting Shylock from *The Merchant of Venice* to reinforce her point.[62] No records exist to prove or disprove Louisa's accusations, however, which may have sprung from her anger at the lawsuit.

After giving her statement to the equity court hearing the case, Louisa resigned herself to the court's decision. "I have done . . . all that can be done," she wrote. "I can only hope that it will be decided as it should be." She wished to relieve herself "from the embarrassment of apparently conniving at, and profiting by what I consider an unjust and disgraceful procedure (whether or not the law sanctions it)." Yet she did not entirely leave the situation behind her, asking "to be informed if any thing I can do will be useful in bringing about the proper result."[63]

Haskell and John Cheves were probably correct in their interpretation of Langdon Cheves's will.[64] Cheves had not provided Hayne with a plantation, but with an income of $3,500 annually until 1860.

60. LSM deposition, LCI.
61. LSM to Langdon Cheves Jr., April 23, 1858, LCI.
62. LSM to Langdon Cheves Jr., May 26, 1858, and April 23, 1858, LCI.
63. LSM to Langdon Cheves Jr., May 26, 1858, LCI.
64. Statement of Charles T. and Sophia L. Haskell, *State of South Carolina, Charleston District, in equity,* 4–10, LCI.

This sum would come from the profits of Cheves's plantation South Field. Cheves ultimately intended South Field for Hayne's use, but at the time he created his will, he had it remain in the hands of Langdon and Charles, with the remainder of its profits divided among Sophia, Louisa, and Anna. Thus, as Haskell and John guessed, with Hayne gone the profits from the plantation should have continued to be divided among the daughters as specifically stipulated in that item and as suggested by the final item regarding residual property.[65]

In June 1858, the Court of South Carolina ruled in favor of Haskell and John. While the court considered residual property to be specific in nature, it did not find that Cheves had in any way restricted the residual gift to his daughters. In fact, it found, his bequest had been quite generously unlimited. Thus, the court had legal room in which to consider the Ogeechee plantation as residual property. Moreover, the court determined that Cheves had not intended to die with any part of his estate intestate. Not knowing of Hayne's death, that is exactly what Cheves believed he had accomplished at his death. Therefore, to rule that the Ogeechee plantation was intestate would go against his wishes and intentions. The court fell back on the item regarding residual property and granted the proceeds of South Field to Louisa, Sophia, and Anna.[66]

Langdon Jr. appealed the decision. He did not believe that Cheves's bequest of a portion of the South Field profits to his daughters for a period of time implied his intention to bequeath the entirety of the plantation in perpetuity in the event of Hayne's death. In other words, Langdon Jr. believed that, had Cheves known that Hayne had died, he would have divided South Field among all of his children, as he had done with his Charleston Neck plantation.[67] The court, however, dismissed his appeal in 1859.[68]

Meanwhile, Louisa had taken her son and daughter Lou abroad to consult European physicians about Louisa's deteriorating vision.

65. Will of Langdon Cheves [Sr.], LCI.
66. Decision of the South Carolina Equity Court of Appeals, *Langdon Cheves, executor vs. Charles T. Haskell, and others*, Charleston, June Term, 1858, LCI.
67. Ibid.; will of Langdon Cheves [Sr.], LCI.
68. Decision of the South Carolina Equity Court of Appeals, *Langdon Cheves, executor vs. Charles T. Haskell, and others*, Charleston, January and February sitting, 1859, LCI.

Upon her return in 1860, she wanted as little as possible to do with the settlement. She authorized Langdon Jr. to act in her behalf in disposing of the Ogeechee inheritance. She considered herself, with her "permanently established defective vision," as "unfit" to be a planter. As with many southern slaveholding women, the management of slaves continued to frustrate her, and she refused to "consent to receive any more, for I am almost out of my senses with those that I have."[69] The slaves went to Langdon Jr.'s plantation and he sold the land for her profit. The entire business was now complete.

Duty, for Louisa, had always been a discipline. Subsuming her independence to marriage and motherhood had rewarded her with status and the satisfaction of having fulfilled her role as a woman. The loss of her husband offered the potential of independence once again, but she could not enjoy that possibility. In the aftermath of his death, she quickly lost one brother, awaited the death of a second brother, and helplessly watched her father deteriorate daily.

Caring for her father was the last act of love that she could show to the man who had so shaped her life and her mind. Yet, neither satisfaction nor reward came from the act. Duty translated into despair as she watched her father lose everything that had made him seem great to her. Their daily quarrels only deepened her pain by casting her in the role of villain. After his death, she attempted to avoid the disputes surrounding his will, but could not, and she watched her family fall into a feud at a time when they most needed to comfort one another. When she left for Europe to consult with ophthalmologists about her failing eyesight, she must have hoped that she would also find relief from the grief that plagued her at home.

Europe indeed offered a respite from that grief. Although depression clouded her early weeks in England, she settled comfortably into Paris society and journeyed farther south to Italy. But her happiness was temporary. She returned to the United States only to have her whole world once again tumble dizzily into ruin. Her physical strength and that of her ideals would face their greatest and bloodiest test, and she would bemoan her survival.

69. LSM to Langdon Cheves Jr., January 18, 1860, LCI.

7

"Mother of the Gracchi"

"There goes then this glorious Union," Louisa told her children in the fall of 1859. John Brown was on trial for his raid against the military arsenal at Harpers Ferry, Virginia, which was intended to start a slave insurrection that would spread from the Shenandoah Valley throughout the South. His story filled American newspapers in the North, South, and West that fall. Convicted of treason, he was executed on December 2, 1859. Throughout the North, sympathizers with the abolitionist cause declared him a martyr. In the southern states, however, slaveholders feared a contagion of similar plots among northern abolitionists. The number of local militias grew, and all trained with the expectation of imminent war. "Yes, you will see," said Louisa, "this is not the end of it, we will be forced to assert ourselves."[1]

Little did Louisa know that almost exactly a year later her words would come true with the secession of South Carolina from the Union. The rest of the lower southern states would follow, then part of the upper South. The ensuing war between this unrecognized confederacy of southern states and the United States of America lasted from April 1861 until April 1865. During those years, every family, both black and white, was affected by the war. The war provided Louisa with her greatest opportunity to perform "the hero-task," by infusing her feminine role as mother and caretaker with patriotic fervor. With the end of the war and the emancipation of the slaves, every idea upon which Louisa had based her life and her sacrifices no longer held meaning. Mary Chesnut observed of Louisa and other

---

1. James M. McPherson, *Battle Cry of Freedom: The Civil War Era*, 202–13; C. Vann Woodward, *The Burden of Southern History*, 53–68; Smythe, "Recollections," 37.

women of the South: "The thought that their lives had been given up in vain was very bitter to them."[2]

When Louisa learned of John Brown's raid, she had just returned to the United States from a yearlong stay in Europe. After the tragedies that bedeviled her from the death of her husband in 1855 through the death of her father in 1857, Europe seemed a respite from grief. Louisa went reluctantly, though, and only on her doctor's orders to see a French physician about her failing eyesight. She might have refused this advice, but her son, Cheves McCord, exhibited a similar disability. She could ignore her own health, but not that of her son. Thus, in July 1858, she had set sail for England. Her son and her youngest daughter, Lou, a self-professed "great Mammy's baby," accompanied her. The middle child, Hannah, chose to stay at home in a boarding school in order to be with her "friend and crony, Lottie" (Charlotte Reynolds), from whom she became inseparable.[3]

The French oculist's remedy for the eyesight problems of Louisa and Cheves was simple. Louisa suffered from an extreme sensitivity to light. By 1858, she could neither read nor write for long periods of time and confined herself behind a screen during daylight hours. Lou stayed home from school to act as her reader and secretary. To combat the problem, the doctor prescribed a set of dark-colored glasses, which Louisa wore constantly thereafter.

Louisa and her two children then toured Europe. They visited Scotland, where Louisa stumbled upon a druggist and a bank manager both named Cheves. The bank manager turned out to be "the son of a favorite cousin" of Alexander Cheves, Langdon Cheves's father, after whom he was named.[4] It was in Scotland that Lou first saw an edition of *Uncle Tom's Cabin*, the abolitionist novel that her mother had railed against five years earlier. Imbued with her mother's spirit, she referred to the book as "that mass of falsehood." She wrote: "Horror doesn't describe my feelings when I read it."[5] Surprisingly, however, neither Lou nor her mother mentioned meeting or hearing of British abolitionists.

2. LSM, "Enfranchisement of Woman," 122; Chesnut diary, 702.
3. Smythe, "Recollections," 22–23.
4. LSM to Langdon Cheves Jr., April 6 [1876], LCI.
5. Smythe, "Recollections," 23.

Otherwise, their trip went "much like those of other tourists" of their class. In addition to Scotland and the Orkney Islands, they toured London, Holland, Germany, Switzerland, and France. They stayed for some time in Paris while Louisa and Cheves underwent treatment for their eyesight. Then they traveled through Italy, where Louisa "was quite rich in letters of introduction to prominent people in Rome." Their journey south, however, was interrupted by battles in the Italian Alps during the unification of Italy. Surprisingly nonplussed by the dispute, Louisa and her entourage pressed through once the passes reopened and arrived in Rome for Holy Week. There they were granted an audience with the pope, met several cardinals, and "encountered" the Prince of Wales as they climbed the stairs to the Dome of St. Peter's Basilica.[6]

While in Italy, Louisa commissioned a bust of Langdon Cheves from the famed sculptor Hiram Powers. She hoped to commemorate her beloved father in marble, using his death mask. Unfortunately, the mask did not arrive before she did. Not wishing to waste the sculptor's time, and grateful for the opportunity to sit with him, she had her own bust made. Lou reported that the McCords "were not specially pleased with the likeness at the time as we thought it too hard and old"; however, "she grew more like it with years." In her old age, Lou became "inexpressibly thankful for it is the only likeness at all good that we have of her."[7] The sculpture of Langdon Cheves would have to wait nearly twenty more years for completion.

The McCords returned to the United States in autumn 1859. At their first stop, New York, they learned of the Harpers Ferry raid, which sent a shiver of excitement and dread through the family. After the first shock, however, they momentarily dismissed their sense of foreboding and returned to South Carolina. The Dulles cousins from Philadelphia joined them at Lang Syne for Christmas, which, unbeknownst to them at the time, would be the McCords' last at the plantation. The family enjoyed themselves greatly through the winter, attempting to shut out "the mutterings of the coming storm" and "the natural regrets for what the thoughtful so plainly saw in the

6. Ibid., 23–36.
7. Ibid., 30.

future—the absolute necessity for division among the States."[8] The following year, 1860, would decisively change everyone's life.

In the presidential election of 1860, a new party supporting the advance of free labor and industry ran a candidate who intended to limit the expansion of slavery. Although the Republican, Abraham Lincoln, firmly reiterated that the president of the United States did not have the power to free slaves, slave owners feared for their property and translated their fear into the rhetoric of states' rights. Drawing upon the tradition of the Virginia and Kentucky resolutions written by Thomas Jefferson and James Madison in 1798 and 1799 and upon the theory of nullification postulated by John C. Calhoun in 1828, wealthy slave owners argued that a Republican president would violate their rights to property, thereby requiring the state governments to protect their slave-owning citizens by withdrawing from the Union. Seven states in the deep South, led by South Carolina, vowed to secede should Lincoln win. The Democratic party split when southern slaveholding Democrats refused to endorse the nominee from Illinois, Stephen A. Douglas, and no ballots in the southern states carried Lincoln's name. Nevertheless, Lincoln won. In the winter of 1860–1861, the deep South made good on its promise.

The South Carolina Convention on secession met in Columbia in December 1860. Throughout that month, Louisa and her family passed drilling minutemen and uniformed militia as they went to join the throng gathered outside of the Baptist church, where the convention met. Every seat inside the church was taken. On December 17, 1860, the convention unanimously voted to leave the Union. The Ordinance of Secession was signed on December 20. Bells rang. Cannons exploded. People shouted. Louisa ordered that her horses be hitched to her new, white silk–upholstered carriage. She, her daughters, and their friend Lottie draped banners over the sides and paraded past the celebrations on Columbia's Main Street. Bonfires sprang up on every corner, and at every bonfire someone made a rousing impromptu speech. "Everything seemed possessed with the same idea," Lou wrote, "move—rush somewhere—do something to work off almost unendurable strain."[9]

8. Ibid., 38–39.
9. John Hammond Moore, *Columbia and Richland County: A South Carolina Community, 1740–1990*, 183; Smythe, "Recollections," 41.

Ten years earlier, when another convention of South Carolinians had met to discuss the possibility of secession, Louisa had shrunk in horror at the debates. Pen in hand, she blasted the meeting as unrepresentative of the majority opinion in South Carolina. Moreover, while the idea of secession in order to protect slavery appealed to her, she did not believe that the time was ripe for such an action. If the minority were to have its way in 1851, she knew that South Carolina would stand alone, as it had during the Nullification Crisis of 1832.[10] In 1860 and 1861 the tide changed. The town bell rang out the news as Georgia, Alabama, Mississippi, Louisiana, Texas, and Florida all followed South Carolina out of the Union. The states joined together in a confederation and elected Mississippian Jefferson Davis as their president. Louisa rejoiced at each toll.

Leaving the Union required the expulsion of federal officials and troops, now considered foreign by South Carolina, from the state. Some surrendered quietly, having received no orders from President James Buchanan as to how to react.[11] Major Robert Anderson, the commander of the garrison at Fort Moultrie on Sullivan's Island, just outside of Charleston, refused to surrender. He moved his men to the unfinished Fort Sumter, located on a tiny island in Charleston Harbor. South Carolina militia and cadets from the Citadel immediately took up posts at Moultrie and Fort Wagner, besieging the Union troops at Sumter. Supplies ran low. Buchanan agreed to reinforce Anderson, but the South Carolinians at Fort Moultrie fired on the ship he sent and forced it to retreat. Anderson and the rest of the United States, both northern and southern, waited and wondered what the next president would do when he took office.[12]

Expecting open resistance from the federal government, southern men flocked to military organizations. Louisa's extended family was no exception. Her son Cheves and a new family friend, Augustine T. Smythe, were among the students at South Carolina College who resigned from their classes en masse to join the fray. Her brothers Langdon Jr. and John also enlisted. Langdon Jr. became famed for

10. LSM, "Separate Secession," 211–12.

11. Ironically, Buchanan was a neighbor and frequent visitor to the Cheves household when they lived in Lancaster, Pennsylvania, in the 1820s.

12. Walter J. Fraser Jr., *Charleston! Charleston!* 244–50; McPherson, *Battle Cry of Freedom*, 264–67.

his design of the battery at Fort Wagner. John earned notoriety for his invention of an "infernal machine" that could detonate waterborne torpedoes from shore. From Abbeville, the eight sons of Louisa's sister Sophia also joined the army. Martial fervor ran high as all of these men converged on Charleston.

On March 4, 1861, Lincoln took office. He vowed that he would not allow Sumter to surrender, and followed Buchanan's example by sending relief. The Confederacy faced the choice of allowing the Union fort to be resupplied and continue the siege indefinitely or to fire upon the fort and take it. War seemed imminent. Indeed, the frenzied crowds in Charleston seemed to welcome the prospect. Confederate President Davis ordered that renewed supplies must not reach the fort. Twice, Anderson was offered the opportunity to surrender. Twice, he refused. With the last offer of surrender came a warning. A refusal would result in an attack within an hour.[13]

In Charleston on the morning of April 12, 1861, Mary Chesnut lay awake in her bed at the Mills House. "I count four—St. Michael chimes," she wrote in her diary. "At half-past four, the heavy booming of a cannon." Everyone in the city who was able ran to the rooftops to watch the bombardment. For thirty-three hours, Anderson and the Union forces held out. Then, on April 13, with the building half destroyed and on fire, Anderson surrendered. "Fort Sumter did not fire a shot," Chesnut reported. "Nobody hurt after all."[14] The war had begun.

In Columbia, Louisa threw herself into the "Cause." Like many other women, she vowed to take part in the war without compromising her femininity.[15] Throughout the war, she was the model of impeccable Confederate patriotism. While other women openly chastised their husbands and criticized the government and the military for inaction, cowardice, or weakness, Louisa remained constant. True to her ideal, she would not publicly undermine the image of male authority. Mary Chesnut witnessed "the scornful turn of her lip" when

13. Walter J. Fraser Jr., *Charleston! Charleston!*, 249–50; McPherson, *Battle Cry of Freedom*, 273.

14. Chesnut diary, 46, 49; Walter J. Fraser Jr., *Charleston! Charleston!*, 250–51; McPherson, *Battle Cry of Freedom*, 274–75. Chesnut was mistaken. Anderson did return fire of a thousand rounds, less than half of what the Confederates fired upon Sumter.

15. Faust, *Mothers of Invention*, 10, 29.

"a low-country gentleman who is dissatisfied" said, "This [Confederate] government protects neither person nor property." When men would "shake their heads and tell us what Jeff Davis ought to do," Chesnut wrote, "[i]t is pleasant to hear Mrs. McCord on the subject." Louisa railed at "the monstrous conceit, the fatuous ignorance of these critics!" With fiery passion she defended the Confederate soldiers. "Since the world began, there were never better," she exclaimed. She sang the praises of Stonewall Jackson: "He fights to win—God bless him—and he wins!" She even ended her subscription to the *Charleston Mercury,* one of the more adamantly secessionist newspapers, "when it published a map of the coast defenses."[16] She would not tolerate any slight upon the Confederate soldiery.

Louisa had more to offer the Confederacy than her verbal defenses. Like many other women, she formed a Soldiers' Aid Society. Such organizations flourished during the war as women used their domestic skills to contribute to the war effort. They sewed uniforms, rolled bandages, knitted socks, and held bazaars to raise money. Some were successful enough to provide the navy with articles as large as gunboats. Louisa's was one such association. She suggested that their gunboat be called the "she-devil" because "it is the devil's own work it is built to do."[17] Women performed a good portion of the manufacturing labor that helped the Confederacy field and feed its army.[18]

No material sacrifice was too great for Louisa. Her first gift to the Confederacy was her son. She swelled with pride when he enlisted. Later, when he formed his own company, the South Carolina Zouaves, she personally outfitted the entire group.[19] She repeatedly put her property at the disposal of the Confederacy. When the army required horses, she "sent in her five bays" and satisfied herself with using mules for transportation. While other women ventured into plantation management for the first time in the absence of their husbands, Louisa, an old hand at running her land, devoted some of its acreage to growing provisions rather than cotton. She managed

16. Chesnut diary, 304, 305, 361, 370.

17. Ibid., 329.

18. Faust, *Mothers of Invention,* 23–26, 93; Scott, *Southern Lady,* 81.

19. Chesnut diary, 304; Smythe, "Recollections," 43; "Flag of the South Carolina Zouaves," clipping in Dulles-Cheves-McCord-Lovell Papers.

to keep herself and the hospital at South Carolina College provided with food from Lang Syne until 1865.[20]

She took a special interest in the hospital because she was its matron. As the war progressed and the number of wounded mounted, women turned their energies to nursing. With Englishwoman Florence Nightingale as their model, they transformed their usually private task of caring for the ill and infirm into a patriotic task in the local military hospitals. The lack of organization in many of the hospitals caused some of these volunteers to seize control. For privileged women accustomed to maintaining a large household, the task of running a hospital differed little from that of running a plantation. They oversaw the preparation and distribution of food, clothing, and medicine to patients; ensured that the nurses completed their tasks; enforced the morality of their charges; and mediated disputes among the nurses and patients. Their husbands were replaced by military and political officials, from whom they cajoled extra supplies, space, or medication.[21]

Louisa was one of those who took control. When South Carolina College turned its campus into a military hospital, Louisa, with her indomitable strength, experience, and sense of obligation, zealously threw herself into her duties. Lou recalled: "[S]ock in hand and basket on her arm she would go over every morning to make her rounds among the poor sufferers to whom she was to the extent of her power, a help and a comfort." As caretaker, comforter, even surrogate mother to the wounded men who passed through her hospital, her feminine duties that had for so long been confined to her own household now assumed national importance.[22] The defenders of the Confederacy had been wounded in battle, and she would nurse them back to health to return to the field to continue the fight. The properly feminine role that she had spent so much ink in glorifying ideologically now took on a patriotic glow and would be elevated in the eyes of men.

Noble purpose aside, the operation of a hospital entailed many difficulties involving supplies and personnel. Neither the patients nor

---

20. Chesnut diary, 304 n; Faust, *Mothers of Invention,* 32; Scott, *Southern Lady,* 82; Smythe, "Recollections," 49.

21. Faust, *Mothers of Invention,* 92–94.

22. Smythe, "Recollections," 49; Faust, *Mothers of Invention,* 92; Scott, *Southern Lady,* 83.

the nurses always lived up to the ideals that Louisa set. Finding volunteers was often difficult. Most women were struggling to survive in the absence of their husbands during the war. Some were grappling for the first time with plantation management, while others found odd jobs with which to earn extra money. Thus, most volunteers tended to be either unmarried or widowed and without small children. Even then, not all of these women had the stomach to face a Civil War hospital. Amputated limbs, maggots, blood, disease, and the moaning and terror of the patients often cut short their well-intentioned nursing careers. Those who could manage the conditions of the hospital often could not overcome the socialized indelicacy of handling men's bodies on a regular basis, nor face the charges of being somehow masculine.[23]

Louisa was sensitive to such attitudes. While she, the experienced widow, worked diligently in the hospital, her teenage daughters stayed at home. There they oversaw food production, ran errands for their mother, and heard and retold stories of their mother's valor in helping men through hideous operations. They never, however, set foot in the hospital wards because "she did not believe in young girls at the hospital."[24] A grown woman sacrificing her own delicacy, sense of propriety, and even femininity for a greater cause was one thing, but corrupting young girls when they could be spared was quite another.

Louisa wanted women who would perform their work in the hospital in the way that she dictated. They had to be women who understood that they were sacrificing their delicacy and who took their work seriously. The women who followed soldiers and who were hardened to the effects of the battlefield, however, were often desperately poor. Louisa constantly complained that these women made bad nurses because they "eat and drink the things provided for the sick and wounded." Among the upper-class women, she had to guard against husband seekers who attended patients "angel sleeved, displaying all of their white arms, and in their muslin, showing all of their beautiful white shoulders and throats." One such lovely vision

23. Faust, *Mothers of Invention*, 102–13. The Union faced similar problems with nurses; see Kristie Ross, "Arranging a Doll's House: Refined Women as Union Nurses," 108–9.
24. Smythe, "Recollections," 49.

tempted a soldier to appeal to the nurse for a kiss. Louisa became infuriated, not so much at the request as at the nurse for repeating the tale because "[i]t brought her hospital in disrepute."[25] Such blatant sexuality was unacceptable for the ladies staffing the hospital, who should be doing their duty to defend the Confederacy.

Louisa was also sensitive to the mingling of classes among the hospital's patients. While idealistically she would nurse any soldier in the Confederate cause, she expected them to display what she considered noble behavior. "The better born—that is, those born in the purple, the gentry," she told Mary Chesnut, "[t]hey are better patients. They endure in silence. They are hardier, stronger, tougher—less liable to break down than the sons of the soil." Moreover, she would not tolerate any discontent. In one instance, a Frenchman in her hospital vented his anger at Confederate conscription and suggested that he would "as soon fight for the North as the South." Louisa wrote to Chesnut about this case as a means of notifying her husband, James Chesnut, Confederate secretary of war, of this possible threat to the Confederacy.[26] To be worthy of care, the patients had to be loyal to the "Cause." She understood the war as a fight for southern independence in order to preserve a society in which such "better patients" could thrive.

The worst problem that she endured at the hospital, however, was supply shortages. With little manufacturing in the southern states, the Confederacy relied upon foreign imports to sustain its war effort. The Union blockade prevented much of the materiel of war from reaching the Confederate military. Necessities such as medicine and bandages were in short supply. Louisa constantly appealed to James Chesnut for help.[27] She was frustrated with the blockade runners, probably because they wasted valuable cargo space with luxuries such as silk and lace for speculation rather than bringing in the items she needed in her hospital.

The war raged north and west of South Carolina. Port Royal, on the coast, and the Sea Islands fell under Union control early in the war, but most of South Carolina remained distant from the fighting.

25. Chesnut diary, 386, 414.
26. Ibid., 377, 675.
27. Ibid., 392.

In Columbia, constant reminders of the war existed, particularly in the presence of the hospital and in high inflation. Still, in some respects, keeping a facade of normality was possible from the initial excitement of secession in 1861 until the Union invasion in late 1864 and early 1865. In fact, war seemed an aphrodisiac as young people seized the opportunity to become engaged.

Cheves McCord and Charlotte Reynolds were one couple who fell under the spell. Charlotte, called "Lottie," was the daughter of Dr. John Reynolds, a professor at South Carolina College. She and the McCord girls had become as close as sisters. In an effort to make that emotional attachment real, Lottie and Cheves had been engaged "after a boy-girl fashion" since about 1858, when he was only seventeen years old and she fourteen. A year later they had not yet published banns but "understood each other," Lou wrote. "The thought of no other woman ever entered his head." When the war began, the two formalized their intentions. On October 14, 1861, while Cheves was on a four-day furlough, the couple married.[28] A year later, Louisa learned that she would become a grandmother.

Meanwhile, Lou had her own romance growing. In the fall of 1860, she looked out of a window at home and saw "a rather short, stoutish" freshman from South Carolina College crossing the street. A few weeks later, a friend of the McCord family introduced the young man as Augustine T. Smythe, the son of Charleston Presbyterian minister and proslavery advocate Thomas Smyth. By the time he left to join the army, Lou wrote, he "asked leave to correspond with my mother." Louisa agreed, "as by this time we were very intimate with him and she was very fond of him."[29] The object of his affection, however, was clearly Mrs. McCord's teenage daughter.

Gus's intentions became so obvious that Lottie insisted to Lou, "[S]ome of these days he is just going to bust out with 'Miss Lou, will you marry me' and you will get up and go." Lou claimed she was "struck dumb with astonishment, never having yet looked on myself in a marrying light." Even Lou's cousin Sophia Louisa Haskell "saw

---

28. Smythe, "Recollections," 23, 38, 44.

29. Ibid., 42, 46. The last names of father and son were spelled differently. Augustine wished to distinguish himself from his father and also to clarify the pronunciation of his name.

fit to make 'saucy' remarks."[30] Within a few days, Lottie's prophecy came true. Louisa received a letter from Gus asking for her daughter's hand in marriage. After a two-week delay to calm her nerves, Lou finally accepted, "and the wonder was accomplished—I was engaged." This took place in 1863, but the war forced a prolonged, two-year engagement during which Lou saw Gus "for as many days as would amount to two weeks."[31]

Hannah had no difficulties in finding beaux. At the start of the war, she was already a "young lady," riding about town with her female companions and attending parties in both Charleston and Columbia. Even during the Charleston fire of 1861, she attracted a young man, much to the envy of her little sister.[32] While in Abbeville visiting her Aunt Sophia and Haskell cousins, she became close friends with Jennie Haskell, a niece of Sophia's husband. The two developed strong affections for each other, which Louisa referred to as "the romance of the affectionate friendship"; and the two young women exchanged at least one letter of deep longing when separated.[33] When Jennie became engaged, the news took Hannah by surprise, and "she expressed her utter disbelief of any such possible result."[34] As with most participants in such intense friendships, she soon grew to accept her friend's choice, knowing its seeming inevitability.[35] Until her own marriage to John Taylor Rhett in 1869, she was the constant companion of either her mother, her sister, or her sister-in-law.

Although marriages, engagements, and new babies opened bright spots, maintaining the facade of a normal life became ever more difficult as the war took a heavy toll on provisions and the population. Supplies became short, and prices on those available were inflated

30. Ibid., 56; Louisa Rebecca McCord to Sophia Louisa Haskell, February 6, 1863, LCIII.

31. Smythe, "Recollections," 56; Augustine T. Smythe to "Aunts," February 7, 1863, Smythe-Stoney-Adger Papers, SCHS; Sue Ann Smyth to Augustine T. Smythe, February 10, 1863, Smythe-Stoney-Adger Papers.

32. Smythe, "Recollections," 47.

33. LSM to Louisa Rebecca McCord, August 22 [1864?], Dulles-Cheves-McCord-Lovell Papers; Jennie Haskell to Hannah McCord, n.d., LCIII. The latter letter was folded to fit into a tiny envelope, about one inch by 3/4 inch, which was enclosed in another letter addressed to Sophia Lovell Haskell.

34. LSM to Louisa Rebecca McCord, August 22 [1864?], Dulles-Cheves-McCord-Lovell Papers.

35. Smith-Rosenberg, *Disorderly Conduct*, 59, 68–70.

beyond reach. Confederate money lost value from the moment that it left the printer, as did state money. By 1865, Louisa was able to exchange $16,000 in Confederate bills for only $300 worth of gold. Such inflation placed outlandish prices on everything from necessities to luxuries.[36] Very little material could be found to make new clothes. Women cut and re-cut dresses to adapt to each season and occasion, finally resorting to homespun material when their existing clothes wore down to rags. The gas supply dwindled, then disappeared, and those who could afford tallow turned to candles for lighting their homes at night. All imported goods had to come through the Union blockade. Louisa refused to purchase such items when she could, believing that all smuggled items should go to the soldiers.

As for food, Emma LeConte, daughter of a science professor at South Carolina College, noted the high prices of refreshments at an 1865 bazaar: "A small slice of cake is two dollars—a spoonful of Charlotte Russe five dollars . . . a small-sized cake at the Tennessee table sold for seventy-five dollars." Of daily provisions, she wrote: "Corn itself is forty dollars a bushel." Meat rose from 15 cents to $3 a pound through the course of the war. Both were scarce. "Dinner consists of a very small piece of meat, generally beef," wrote LeConte, "a few potatoes and a dish of hominy and a pone of corn bread." This and bread for breakfast comprised the meals for a whole day, but, she realized, "we have no reason to complain, so many families are worse off."[37] Those families had no meat at all, and less flour for bread. Louisa struggled to keep the soldiers at the hospital fed well enough to recover. She boiled scraps of meat with cornmeal to make a mush and stretched milk with water in order to feed all of the men.[38]

Worse than material deprivation, however, was the human cost of war. An estimated 260,000 southern soldiers lost their lives during the four years of war, with as many more wounded or maimed.[39] "The paper began to be filled with long lists of killed, wounded, and missing," remembered Lou. In rural areas, arriving trains would signal if they brought news of the war. "A short whistle meant that nothing

36. Chesnut diary, 705; McPherson, *Battle Cry of Freedom*, 430–42.
37. Earl Schenck Miers, ed., *When the World Ended: The Diary of Emma LeConte* (hereinafter "LeConte diary"), 12–13, 17; Walter J. Fraser Jr., *Charleston! Charleston!* 265.
38. Smythe, "Recollections," 49.
39. McPherson, *Battle Cry of Freedom*, 854.

would happen," wrote Lou. Everyone could breath a sigh of relief. "But when instead of stopping short," she wrote, "the whistle seemed to swell louder and louder, hoarser and hoarser and would blow on and on and on . . . we all knew what it meant—battle—perhaps victory, but surely death to some we knew and loved!"[40] Few families were excepted from these losses, certainly not the extended Cheves, Haskell, and McCord families.

By 1862, when "[t]he big battles in Virginia were begun," the mounting losses of the war struck closer and closer to home. Louisa learned that her nephew John Haskell lost an arm that had been "shattered" in battle. "What a shadow he was," Lou remembered, "and how that empty sleeve used to hurt us!"[41] His brother, Alexander, was also struck, but survived. Alex's wife, Rebecca Singleton Haskell, delirious from infections contracted in childbirth, believed that her husband had died. She passed away not knowing the truth, clutching his letters to her chest.[42] Another nephew, Edward Cheves, nineteen-year-old son of Louisa's brother John, died in the Seven Days' battle. While his sister cried out in grief, his mother "sat dead still, white as a sheet, never uttering a word or shedding a tear," reported Mary Chesnut. "Are our women losing the capacity to weep?"[43]

Then, in August 1862, the papers filled with stories of the battle of Second Manassas. On the list of the wounded, Louisa found the name "Captain Cheves McCord." A ball had lodged in his head, and he had been hit in the leg and foot as well. Nearly frantic, Louisa rushed to Richmond, Virginia. When she got off the train, she immediately sought out William Porcher Miles, her old friend who had helped her essays to publication ten years earlier. Now he was a member of the Confederate Congress and head of the Military Affairs Committee.[44] She begged him for a pass to the battlefield hospital at Warrenton. Miles refused. The Confederate government was issuing no passes, and the trains were reserved for military use

40. Smythe, "Recollections," 51.

41. Ibid., 51, 52.

42. Chesnut diary, 397; Mary Elizabeth Cheves to Sophia Louisa Haskell, July 11, 1862, LCIII.

43. Chesnut diary, 406.

44. Eric Walther, *The Fire-Eaters*, 291.

only. "I let him talk," Louisa later said, "for he does it beautifully." Yet she was undaunted. "That very night I chartered a special train. We ran down to Manassas and I brought Cheves back in triumph," she said. Her tale inspired Mary Chesnut to call her "Mother of the Gracchi."[45] This, perhaps, was the highest compliment that Louisa could receive.

Louisa brought Cheves home to his sisters, who doted over "*our hero*." She made her house into a veritable hospital ward in which to keep her son. She brought in one of the doctors from the hospital at the college, who extracted the musket ball still lodged in Cheves's head. When the doctor left, the three women stepped in to give Cheves as much nursing as he required, and then some. "We had a wheeled chair," Lou remembered, possibly referring to the one that her mother had ordered during Langdon Cheves's last days at their house. "Round and round the garden and round the campus he would go," she wrote, "with one of his willing, worshipping slaves pushing him while the rest followed."[46]

Despite the adoring care that he received from his mother and sisters, Cheves became anxious to return to his company. Too much his mother's son to shirk his duty, and perhaps feeling a bit guilty that he enjoyed such attention and care while his comrades slept in mud, ate raw corn stolen from nearby fields, and sucked the grease from their haversacks for sustenance, he insisted upon leaving his mother's house as soon as the doctor declared him ready. When the time came, Louisa uncharacteristically slipped in her own sense of duty and resembled more the weaker Licinia from *Caius Gracchus* than the stoic Cornelia. She begged her son to request at least an additional ten-day furlough. He refused, and left for Virginia right away.[47]

One day in January 1863, Louisa was going about her duties at the hospital. Lottie Cheves was visiting her mother. Lou was at a piano lesson and Hannah was out with a friend. A messenger from the telegraph office came to the hospital and wandered around, looking for Louisa. Not finding her, he hurried over to Mrs. Reynolds's house and delivered the message to Lottie, who immediately ran with it to

45. Chesnut diary, 428.
46. Smythe, "Recollections," 52.
47. Ibid., 53.

the McCord house. When Louisa returned from the hospital that evening, she was the last of the family to hear that "Cheves was dying." His head wound had ruptured, causing a stroke, and he fell without warning. His "body servant" Tom carried him to Richmond on a wagon. Before Louisa could secure transport to Virginia, a second dispatch arrived with the news that "Cheves was dead!"[48]

Louisa's nephews William and Alex Haskell retrieved her son's body from Virginia. Lou saw her brother prepared for burial, "as spotless and as beautiful as marble. They did not dare let Lottie see him." Lottie was very near delivering Cheves's child and verged on hysterics daily. Cheves's funeral was held at Trinity Church, where his father had been buried. When the service ended, Louisa fell to her knees at the edge of the grave and dropped in one of her gloves. As the coffin was covered with dirt, a military salute was fired. Then, Lou remembered, "we went back home to face what of life was left to us."[49]

Louisa had lost not just a son, but also her connection to the public world of men from which she was barred by her gender. "The light of my life is gone," Louisa wrote to her friend Mary Chesnut, "my hope fled, and my pride laid low."[50] Her greatest gift to the world, she believed, had been this son. Now he was gone.

The grief of the McCord family was compounded throughout 1863. William Haskell, the nephew and cousin who proved comfort to the McCord women after the death of Cheves, fell at the battle of Gettysburg that summer. His older brother Charles died at Battery Wagner, shot through the head in an assault by black Union troops.[51] On

48. Sophia Lovell Haskell to Sophia Louisa Haskell, January 26 [1863], LCIII; Smythe, "Recollections," 53. Two stories exist as to how Cheves died. The official version is that he fell while on the parade ground. Years later, Lottie was told that he had actually fallen after a small skirmish with the Union army. "It makes little difference," wrote Lou. "In the midst of his duties he fell to the ground unconscious."

49. Smythe, "Recollections," 54; Sophia Lovell Haskell to Sophia Louisa Haskell, n.d., LCIII.

50. Chesnut diary, 788; Sophia Lovell Haskell to Sophia Louisa Haskell, February 8, 1863, LCIII.

51. Rev. William, chaplain, Scales's Brigade, to Charles T. Haskell, July 6, 1863, LCIII; W. E. Haskell to Charles and Sophia Haskell, July 11, 1863, LCIII; LSM to Sophia Lovell Haskell, July 16, 1863, LCI; Joseph Haskell to Sophia Louisa Haskell, July 20, 1863, LCIII; Hannah McCord to Sophia Louisa Haskell, July 1863, LCIII; Louisa Rebecca McCord to Sophia Louisa Haskell, n.d., LCIII.

the same day, Louisa's brother Langdon Cheves Jr. also fell. Of her seven brothers that had survived to adulthood, only John, her least favorite, was left.

The only bright spot in the months after Cheves's death was the birth of his child. All hoped for and expected a son, who would have borne his father's name; but on February 3, 1863, Lottie gave birth to a girl. At a loss for an appropriate girl's name, Lottie and her mother-in-law finally decided that, regardless of the child's gender, she should be known as Langdon Cheves McCord. Little "Chev" became the delight of the family. "She could always make us happy," remembered Lou, "even with her poor little cholics." Her McCord and Reynolds relatives bestowed on her any little treat they could. "Sheets, and pillow cases, and old muslin curtains were cut up," recalled Lou, "old knitted woolen shawls were ripped up for wool from which to knit her sacks and socks." Dolls, toys from the attic, anything possible was fixed up for the child. "Even soldier's work was laid aside when the baby wanted us," Lou wrote.[52] This was quite unprecedented in Louisa McCord's house, but this was her grandbaby, and the only real remnant that she had of her son.

The following year brought the danger of war closer and closer to the McCord family in Columbia. Except for the earliest months of the war, when the Union army invaded the Sea Islands of Georgia and lower South Carolina, most of the fighting had been concentrated in Virginia and in the West along the Mississippi River. After the fall of Vicksburg in July 1863, the fighting moved steadily east, through Tennessee and down into Georgia. The new commander of the Union army, Ulysses S. Grant, conducted a bloody and terrifying war of attrition. His general in the West was William Tecumseh Sherman, who consistently defeated the Confederates throughout the spring and summer of 1864. In September, he marched jubilantly into Atlanta.[53]

Now Sherman embarked on a total war. Leaving a burning Atlanta, he planned to march through Georgia to Savannah, then turn northward toward Virginia. He would destroy as much of the land,

52. Smythe, "Recollections," 55.
53. Joseph T. Glatthaar, *The March to the Sea and Beyond: Sherman's Troops in the Savannah and Carolinas Campaigns*, 3–5; McPherson, *Battle Cry of Freedom*, 751–56, 774.

railroad, and industry of the South as possible. Not only would he smash the ability of the South to make war, but he would also crush southerners' desire to fight. He declared that he intended to "make them so sick of war that generations would pass away before they would again appeal to it."[54] Wherever he went, a swell of fear preceded him, and a wake of destruction followed.

On Christmas, Sherman moved into Savannah. Refugees fled the city for Charleston.[55] Gus Smythe, stationed there, found several of his future relations among the refugees. Louisa's sister Anna Huger; John Cheves's wife and daughter, Rachel and Mary Elizabeth; and Langdon Cheves Jr.'s widow and daughters, Charlotte, Mary Elizabeth, and Emma, were given shelter by the Smyth family.[56] After a brief rest, Charlotte and Rachel relocated to Louisa's home in Columbia, where they believed they would be safe. Gus would soon join the fighting in North Carolina.

Most expected Sherman's next stop to be Charleston. Yet Charleston, battered by cannon volleys and consumed by fire, did not entice Sherman. While he let South Carolinians believe that he had the city as his object, the northern and western portion of the state interested him more. He sent one column of his army through the upcountry to Charlotte, North Carolina. The other, headed by General Oliver O. Howard, drove through the center of the state. Relatively untouched by the ravages of war, lying on the Congaree River and a stop on the path of two main rail arteries, Columbia was ripe for devastation.[57]

James Chesnut wrote to Louisa and to his wife, Mary, warning them "to make ready—for the end had come." On Louisa's advice Mary destroyed the letter, believing that it could create demoralization and panic.[58] That letter would have done little harm given

54. Glatthaar, *March to the Sea*, 4–7; McPherson, *Battle Cry of Freedom*, 807–9.

55. Glatthaar, *March to the Sea*, 10; McPherson, *Battle Cry of Freedom*, 811.

56. Augustine T. Smythe to Louisa Rebecca McCord, January 12, 1865, Smythe-Stoney-Adger Papers. Gus was attached to the Signal Corps and was placed on reconnaissance in the St. Michael's Church steeple, which had been camouflaged black.

57. Walter J. Fraser Jr., *Charleston! Charleston!* 268; Glatthaar, *March to the Sea*, 11–12; McPherson, *Battle Cry of Freedom*, 828–30; Moore, *Columbia and Richland County*, 192–93.

58. Chesnut diary, 704.

the daily rumors that flooded Columbia about the intentions of the dreaded Union general.[59] Most centered on his vows to make South Carolina, the heart of the secession movement, suffer horribly for the pain of the previous three years. "All through Georgia, it is said," wrote Emma LeConte, "he promised his men full license in South Carolina." Grace Brown Elmore, a single woman living with her mother and sisters in Columbia, wrote that "Sherman told a lady who asked him where to flee . . . to avoid Carolina." According to the rumor, Sherman said: "Hitherto I have endeavored to restrain my men, but when I pass to Carolina my orders shall be every man for himself." All feared for their homes and their lives. Elmore actually contemplated "the righteousness of suicide" in the event of the "worst of all horrors."[60]

The citizens of Columbia, now reduced to a few older men, the wounded, and women and children, stood resolute. They vowed to fight, and castigated Georgia for falling too quickly. Some refused to believe that Sherman would actually take the city. Subsequently, preparations to defend Columbia did not begin until too late. Even then, the mayor, Thomas L. Goodwyn, insisted that the city could be held.[61]

In January 1865, bolstered by overly optimistic forecasts, the ladies of Columbia held a bazaar in the statehouse. This was one of the most talked-about and anticipated events of that winter, rivaling Sherman's march. Mary Chesnut juxtaposed the two events in her diary: "Bazaar opens today. Sherman marches always—all RR's smashed." Emma LeConte described the magnificent decorations, made of such coveted items as lace and damask, and wrote: "To go in there one would scarce believe it was war times." With destruction looming, the frenzied preparations for the bazaar had held off panic and hysteria. Grace Elmore most accurately described the emotional meaning of the bazaar. "The gay and the tragic so closely intertwined," she wrote, "the utter abandonment of ones self to the pleasure of the

59. Marion Brunson Lucas, *Sherman and the Burning of Columbia*, 34–35.
60. LeConte diary, 59; Marli F. Weiner, ed., *A Heritage of Woe: The Civil War Diary of Grace Brown Elmore, 1861–1868* (hereinafter "Elmore diary"), 83, 81.
61. LeConte diary, 11; Lucas, *Sherman and the Burning of Columbia*, 34–40; Moore, *Columbia and Richland County*, 200.

present, when any brightness lightens our darkness by shutting out for the time the horrors that surround us."[62]

Even as they tried to cover their fear with bravado, they packed their belongings and searched for places to which they could flee. Louisa considered sending Lou and Hannah to North Carolina with Mary Chesnut, but changed her mind. Most families, whether they fled or stayed behind, attempted to stay together. Chesnut worried frantically about her husband. Emma LeConte refused to leave her mother and waited desperately for the return of her father, and Lou wrung her hands as she awaited news of Gus.[63] Those who remained in the city prepared for the worst.

Louisa wasted no time. She and her daughters attended only one day of the weeklong bazaar. Meanwhile, she had her slaves bury cornmeal and bacon beneath the bricks of her carriage house, telling them to leave no trace of their efforts. She also ordered them to bury the silver but they refused, having heard rumors that Sherman tortured slaves in order to discover the whereabouts of family treasures. Instead, she had them dig several holes in the garden, and she and her daughters chose a few in which to hide the valuables. Hannah and Lou "carefully sewed our little treasures up in two carpet foot stools." Louisa had workmen tear out the outdoor stairs to the second-floor piazza at the back of the house and then enclose the piazza, which she turned into a storeroom. This became known as the "McCord fortification." The fortification's inhabitants included Louisa; Lou; Hannah; Lottie and her toddler, Chev; Rachel Cheves and her daughter, Mary Elizabeth "Minna" Cheves; and at least five slaves, Tom, Marianne, Maum Lucy, Maum Di, and Maum Rache.[64] Despite Louisa's efforts, they felt extremely vulnerable.

By February 15, evacuation of the city had begun in earnest. The railroad depots were clogged with frightened citizens who argued with officers and guards to be allowed on the trains in place of medicine, supplies, cotton, and the wounded. "The streets in town are

62. Moore, *Columbia and Richland County*, 198–99; Chesnut diary, 705; LeConte diary, 12; Elmore diary, 93.

63. Chesnut diary, 715, 703; LeConte diary, 27, 29; Smythe, "Recollections," 60; Louisa Rebecca McCord to Augustine T. Smythe, March 31, 1865, Smythe-Stoney-Adger Papers.

64. Chesnut diary, 715; Smythe, "Recollections," 58–62, 63, 66; Louisa Rebecca McCord to Sue Ann Smyth, March 21, 1865, Smythe-Stoney-Adger Papers.

lined with panic-stricken crowds, trying to escape," wrote Emma LeConte. "Everything that could drag itself away went off," Lou reported, "some on crutches, some being almost carried by their friends." The hospital at the college emptied out, and the patients trooped by the McCord house. "As they passed," Lou wrote, "many of them would stop to say a word of comfort farewell to us who this time needed comfort if ever people did."[65]

Meanwhile, outside the city, at the bridge over the Congaree River, Howard's men locked in battle with General Wade Hampton's forces. The citizens of Columbia could hear the struggle in their homes. "For the first time I hear the roaring of a battle," wrote Grace Elmore, "the firing of the musketry." "Oh, it is heart sickening to listen to it!" wrote Emma LeConte. The gunfire was "frightfully near and sounding above the din of a tumultuous town," with shots exploding so close that LeConte "could not help shuddering at each one." The sound of the muskets particularly distressed Lou McCord because they "were so suggestive of men killing each other!"[66]

By the next morning, the city itself came under fire. Louisa's house, three blocks from the statehouse, lay within range of Union forces. The coterie of women fled from their observation point on the piazza to the first floor and locked themselves in. They expected the house to crash down around them at any minute. At one point, they believed that a shell had struck the house. Maum Rache ventured upstairs to assess the damage and returned with the rumor that General Sherman had entered the city.[67] This was not yet true. Still, everyone knew the arrival of the Union army was imminent.

On the morning of February 17, Hampton retreated, removing all Confederate forces from Columbia. "Shall I ever forget the utter desolation I felt when the last horseman disappeared," wrote Grace Elmore. In their wake, the soldiers burned the railroad depot. The city shuddered as the building exploded. Looting began on Main Street. Spreading throughout the city, vandals destroyed, stole, and burned anything that they could. No business was safe. The only

---

65. Moore, *Columbia and Richland County*, 201; LeConte diary, 30; Smythe, "Recollections," 61.

66. Lucas, *Sherman and the Burning of Columbia*, 39–49; Elmore diary, 99; LeConte diary, 33; Smythe, "Recollections," 60.

67. Smythe, "Recollections," 61.

alternative to this disorder was the approaching Union army. Before noon, Mayor Goodwyn surrendered the city. Lou remembered that "a horror of desolation seemed to fall upon us as we saw ourselves being left to face this long expected trial."[68]

Sensing disaster, Louisa ordered the women in her house upstairs. They stood at the window, trying to gauge the movement of the Union forces. A loud tumult moved nearer and nearer. Suddenly the back gate burst open. "In rushed, pell mell, crowding, pushing, almost falling over each other, such a crowd of men," remembered Lou. "They seemed scarcely human." Breaking into the storehouses, servants' quarters, and barn, they took or ruined everything they could find. They stabbed the ground with their bayonets, looking for buried stores. "They robbed even the negroes," mourned Lou, and "completed the ruin of all we had outside."[69] The Union army had arrived.

Satisfied that they had completely ransacked the yard, they turned their attention to the house. Led by "one horrible looking man in a coon skin cap with the tail hanging down behind," a group of the soldiers made for the front door. Louisa and Rachel, in an effort to stem their frenzy, greeted them. The soldiers streamed into the house. With "terrible system and skill," they "smashed, tore and pocketed everything they could get at." Louisa and Rachel stayed out of the looters' way, "only following them about trying to keep some sort of check on them." More important, Louisa hoped to keep the men from going upstairs. "The warnings and stories we had heard led us to expect no mercy from them," Lou remembered. The lives and honor of the women hung in the balance.[70]

Louisa's efforts were to no avail. The men turned toward the staircase. Louisa and Rachel stood on the bottom step. Louisa raised her arm to bar the soldiers' advance. Their leader struck her arm away. He grabbed Louisa and pinned her to the wall by her neck. Then he snatched her watch, which had belonged to her father, then to her son, and finally to her nephew. Other soldiers gathered around, brandishing knives in her face. Rachel ran upstairs, screaming that

68. Elmore diary, 101; Lucas, *Sherman and the Burning of Columbia*, 68–71; Moore, *Columbia and Richland County*, 201; Smythe, "Recollections," 61.

69. Smythe, "Recollections," 62.

70. Ibid.; Louisa Rebecca McCord to Sue Ann Smyth, March 21, 1865, Smythe-Stoney-Adger Papers.

the soldiers were murdering Louisa. All of the women must escape, she insisted. They must jump from the upstairs veranda to the magnolia tree in the side yard, then climb down and run for help. The women very nearly pursued her plan.[71]

At that moment the doorbell rang. The soldiers paused. Their momentary surprise allowed Louisa to regain her wits. The bell rang again. "There are some of your officers," she said. "You had better not let them find you here." "In one minute they were gone!" Lou remembered. "Just like a flight of vultures." Then, in walked General O. O. Howard. "His coming was a relief unspeakable at the time," recalled Lou. The Confederate women actually "danced a jig around the room with excitement" at the arrival of the Union general, second in command to the dreaded Sherman. They stopped short, however, of accepting his invitation to dinner.[72]

As the day progressed, Sherman attempted to establish some sense of order. "Guards have been placed to protect houses," wrote Emma LeConte, "and Sherman has promised not to disturb private property." Over at the Elmore home, Grace's mother "went as early as possible to the provost martial and applied for a guard, she came back attended by one, and we were not troubled afterwards in the house." The McCord household was afforded extra protection, since it was now the headquarters of General Howard. Although the ladies regularly vented their spite at their unwelcome guest, Howard treated them courteously, and Lou later somewhat regretted their behavior toward him.[73]

The efforts of Sherman and his officers, however, were to no avail. The enlisted men, embittered by four years of bloody war, vented their anger. Whiskey made their aggression peak. Emma LeConte stood on the back porch of her father's house and saw "the wretches walking—generally staggering—back and forth from the camp to the

71. Smythe, "Recollections," 62; Louisa Rebecca McCord to Sue Ann Smyth, March 21, 1865, Smythe-Stoney-Adger Papers; LSM, "The Burning of Columbia," in *Louisa S. McCord; Poems, Drama, Biography, Letters,* ed. Richard C. Lounsbury, 242–45. Mary Chesnut incorrectly identified the raccoon-hatted soldier as Major General John A. Logan (Chesnut diary, 750). Louisa testified that the man was in a sergeant's uniform.

72. Smythe, "Recollections," 62; Louisa Rebecca McCord to Sue Ann Smyth, March 21, 1865, Smythe-Stoney-Adger Papers.

73. LeConte diary, 42; Elmore diary, 102; Smythe, "Recollections," 62; Louisa Rebecca McCord to Sue Ann Smyth, March 21, 1865, Smythe-Stoney-Adger Papers.

town—shouting hurrahing—cursing South Carolina—swearing—
blaspheming—singing ribald songs, and using such obscene language that we were forced to go indoors." The men caroused through
the streets of Columbia, and what earlier looters had not destroyed
or taken now became their pillage. They started small fires in the
yards of several homes and on street corners and burned some of the
outlying homes as citizens watched helplessly. "If I were but a man,"
declared Grace Elmore, "how firm my arm would be to strike." Ironically, since the citizens of Columbia had expected much worse, they
merely stewed in anger as they watched the raucous behavior play
out before them.[74]

The worst of the "devilish orgy" was yet to come. That evening,
the women stood on the upstairs porch and watched fires burning in
the distance. "We could locate these fires and knew them to be at the
homes of our friends," remembered Lou. Before long, the conflagration seemed much nearer. "The whole heavens were red with fire,"
wrote Grace Elmore, "all Columbia seemed to be burning." Lou had
the same impression. "Fire in every direction sweeping the whole
earth as it seemed, and the wind blowing it right towards us at the
most furious speed," she wrote. Emma LeConte described the sight
as a "great sea of flame" in which "night turned into noonday" and
"a quivering molten ocean seemed to fill the air and sky." She continued: "Columns of black, rolling smoke glittering with sparks and
flying embers" rose above the city into a "copper colored sky," rain-
ing "showers of burning flakes."[75] To the Confederate population,
Sherman truly had brought hell.

This fire had not been Sherman's intention. Although many of
his enlisted men had expressed a desire to see the capital of South
Carolina torched and shed no tears as the fire spread, the fire that
consumed the city developed out of several smaller fires that grew
out of control as the winter wind gusted through the streets. Bales of
cotton abandoned by the Confederate soldiers who had retreated that
morning provided fuel for the flames. Sparks from gunfire, from the
explosion of the depot that morning, and from the torches carried by

74. LeConte diary, 44; Elmore diary, 102; Lucas, *Sherman and the Burning of Columbia*,
88–90; Moore, *Columbia and Richland County*, 202–3.
75. Smythe, "Recollections," 63, 66; Elmore diary, 102; LeConte diary, 45–46.

looters became embedded in the soft, flammable material. The cotton could burst into flame within seconds or smolder for hours. The wind that evening made conditions worse; both Union soldiers and Confederate citizens scrambled to contain the damage, but to little effect. The final conflagration gutted Main Street. Nothing was left of the business district. Buildings for a block to the east and up to four blocks to the west became ruins. Even the statehouse was lost.[76]

The intersection of Pendleton and Bull streets, where Louisa's house lay, was spared. That her house survived she attributed only to General Howard's intercession. "The house was twice set on fire," Lou remembered, "and would of course have been burned had it not been for Gen. Howard's regard for his own reputation. . . . But it was most evident the determination of the soldiers to burn it." Unable to contain herself, Louisa upbraided Howard for the fire and for the invasion. When he commented in amazement on the blazing flurries of cotton that flew about, she put out a burning boll in the back entry and retorted: "Yes, General, very remarkable, through closed doors." Attempting to smooth Louisa's ruffled feathers, Howard apologized for the previous days' shelling, and tried to explain the losses that he and his men had suffered during the war. "Mamma listened quietly," wrote Lou, "and expressed her sorrow at any one's suffering, but said incidentally as it were, that it was a new idea to make women and children atone for the wounds and death of soldiers." She was wrong, but Howard kept his counsel.[77]

Louisa, like other southerners, wholly blamed the Union army for the fire. "The men openly acknowledged that they received orders to burn and plunder before they crossed the river," Emma LeConte wrote. Grace Elmore recorded: "Sherman had the brass to say before my Mother, the negroes burned the town . . . Liar that he is, none know better than he that his own men did it, and with his sanction if not by his order." Others charged Sherman with barbarism and murder. Sherman and Howard, however, flatly denied any culpability. Historians disagreed as to the cause of the fire for over a century afterward, citing both Union and Confederate accounts. Clearly Sherman

76. Lucas, *Sherman and the Burning of Columbia*, 83–118; Glatthaar, *March to the Sea*, 143–44; Moore, *Columbia and Richland County*, 202.

77. Smythe, "Recollections," 63, 64; LSM, "Burning of Columbia," 242–45.

did not officially order the blaze, although some of his enlisted men may have encouraged it. He was too astute a general to torch a city that he and his men occupied. Nor would he have bothered to fight a fire to save a city that he intended to destroy. Moreover, fire was a common hazard throughout the nineteenth century, particularly during wartime. For the people of Columbia, however, the possibility that blind chance or the carelessness of Confederate soldiers had caused the devastation of their city was beyond consideration.[78]

By dawn of February 18, the fire had been contained. The Union army then set about the business of securing and abandoning the city. The ladies in the McCord house perched themselves on the upstairs piazza and watched "the coming and going, grouping and talking of officers of every rank from General Sherman on down. The whole space in front of the house was filled with them." Well-fed and uniformed, they cut such an appealing figure to the war-wearied women that "it was hard to look at them and not sin." That is, except for General Sherman. The women caught a glimpse of him that day, and Lou described him as "a dreadful looking creature . . . red headed, stubby bearded and fierce eyed." Hannah shook her fist at him from her bedroom window and cursed him in a "truly feminine though not very Christian" manner. Fortunately, he did not see his young nemesis, and the women "had to grovel on the floor not to be caught laughing at our persecutor."[79]

Meanwhile, a steady stream of women wove their way through the intimidating crowd in the yard. They came to entreat Louisa to intervene on their behalf with Howard. Most requested extra protection and assurances that their homes would not be burned that evening, as some of the soldiers had taunted them. Others asked for food or shelter, having lost everything in the tragedy of the previous night. Louisa could not possibly help them all, so, after gaining an audience with the dreaded Sherman himself, she pled the cases of only those she liked. Louisa's generosity seemed to slip away from her, no matter

78. LeConte diary, 50; Elmore diary, 103; Glatthaar, *March to the Sea*, 144–46; Moore, *Columbia and Richland County*, 202–4. Glatthaar suggests that the Union soldiers encouraged the fire; Moore disagrees. In *Sherman and the Burning of Columbia*, Lucas argues that responsibility for the fire lay primarily at the feet of the retreating Confederates, who, in their haste, created the conditions for the disaster (163–67).

79. Smythe, "Recollections," 64, 65.

how often she reminded herself of her duty to those in need. Her emotions had worn thin and her temper had become short, driving her sister-in-law Rachel to a boardinghouse and then to Abbeville. The paternalism that she so cherished had not only broken down throughout the countryside, it had also withered in herself.[80]

After destroying the railroads around Columbia on February 18 and 19, the Union army departed on February 20. Concerned that anarchy would erupt once the troops left town, Sherman posted a guard and left a herd of cattle on the college common for provisions. Then the officers appropriated as many horses, mules, and carriages as possible, and left town. With them went several residents who had originally hailed from the northern states, a handful of freedmen, and an Irish seamstress employed by Louisa.

In the aftermath, the residents of Columbia began to assess the extent of the damage. Once again looters combed the city, and the few Union soldiers left behind as guards either could not or would not contain them. Eventually wagons from Georgia brought provisions, but nearly every family had to scavenge for food. Louisa managed to find some provisions, but "the flour was musty and the meat tainted." When not searching for the next meal, most people frantically wrote letters to inform loved ones of their survival and to relay news of the damage. Louisa wrote a letter to Mary Chesnut, venting her "futile rage at the senseless destruction," but destroyed it and sent another more "like herself—cool and businesslike."[81]

Then the worst news came, "the fearful, astounding, crushing blow of Lee's surrender." Even as Sherman marched through the town, many still dared to hope that the southern armies would rally and drive the Union out of the Confederacy. Rumors of a French alliance fueled this unfounded optimism, even as news of defeat rolled in from Richmond and Petersburg. The final surrender of the Confederacy hit all of its supporters hard. "Our people were bowed," wrote Grace Elmore, "they were bent to the earth by the blow, the fall of our bulwark." When Louisa received the news, she "sat in her old place by the window, but she no longer knitted and she had not soldiers to nurse." The last bit of purpose in her life had evaporated, and "she

80. Ibid., 65.
81. Ibid., 79; Chesnut diary, 777.

became then an old woman."[82] Even the news of Lincoln's assassination brought her no joy, as it did to many other white southerners.

For many southern women, sacrifice was the metaphor for the Civil War. This was certainly true for Louisa. The concept of sacrifice had been central to her life up to this point. She would give up any hope or ambition she might have for a public life in order to preserve the patriarchy. Her subordination within the patriarchal order was required in order to perpetuate the institution of slavery, upon which rested her vision of civilization. Secession and Civil War were also necessary to preserve that society; therefore she had supported both with her whole heart.[83]

War, however, also required sacrifice. Painful as her work in the hospital may have been, it allowed her to step outside of the confines of her particular domestic sphere and serve a higher cause. Real sacrifice, such as the loss of her son, was more painful. Moreover, sacrifice implied that she would receive something in return, but with the loss of the war those hopes were dashed. In the end she believed that her sacrifices were for nothing. As Reconstruction progressed, and the extent of the damage that the Civil War had wrought upon her life and her vision of civilization became more apparent, she sank deeper and deeper into a depression from which only her greatest hero, her departed father, could save her. Reconstruction, then, became not only the metaphor for the southern states in the Union, but also for her own life.

82. Elmore diary, 116; Smythe, "Recollections," 71.
83. Drew Gilpin Faust, "Altars of Sacrifice: Confederate Women and the Narratives of War," 171–99.

8

"At Rest"

In 1865, the business of Reconstruction began in earnest. Throughout the summer, Reconstruction under President Andrew Johnson suggested that the process would be short and painless for the former Confederates. When Congress reconvened in the late fall, however, it overruled the actions of the president and began a more radical program designed to grant suffrage to the freedmen, install the Republican party in the South, and increase the industrial capacity of the southern states. Lawmakers hoped to reduce the differences between the North and South, and some of the more radical congressmen wanted to make the South a model for nineteenth-century racial civil rights.[1]

The policies of Reconstruction touched Louisa in two ways. The end of slavery and the requirement of swearing an oath of loyalty to the Union in order to conduct property transactions underscored the defeat not only of the Confederacy to which she had been so dedicated, but also of her very understanding of society. All that she had sacrificed in the war became glaringly obvious to her as she wandered, virtually homeless, in the ensuing years, even exiling herself to Canada for a time. In the end she finally found purpose in commemorating the man most important in her life: her father, Langdon Cheves.

Regardless of how both the Union and the Confederacy argued, the institution of slavery lay at the heart of the Civil War. Slavery was the foundation on which Southern civilization and its doctrine of states' rights sat, and its abolishment became a tactical war aim for preserving the Union. In 1863 Lincoln signed the Emancipation Proclamation, freeing slaves in all of the rebelling regions. Two years

---

1. Eric Foner, *A Short History of Reconstruction, 1863–1877*, 1–15.

later, Congress signed into law the Thirteenth Amendment, which ended the institution of slavery in the United States. Considering themselves a separate nation, the Confederate states ignored these decrees. Moreover, southerners did their best to keep the news, or even rumors, of emancipation from their slaves.

As the Union army closed in on the Confederacy, however, many slave owners watched their slaves closely and wondered whether their behavior masked a desire to flee, or to do worse, the instant the army arrived. Louisa, prevented by her hospital duties from riding out to Lang Syne, had her overseer deliver a weekly report because "it was essential to get the report of the negroes themselves so that she might know of any possible abuses or troubles."[2] While such rumors as the Union army torturing slaves to learn the whereabouts of family treasures may have inconvenienced her in causing her to hide her silver, she probably did little to discourage such tales because they kept her slaves dependent on her care.

When Sherman's army passed through Columbia and the surrounding countryside, most of the McCord slaves remained in the household or on the plantation. At first this was interpreted as loyalty. "They had remained perfectly faithful," recalled Lou, "and even now when we think what they *might* have done with all the pressure brought to bear on them by our enemies." In fact, the only member of the household who deserted with Sherman was an Irish seamstress who had been hired earlier in the war. She left riding in Louisa's carriage, which the Union army had confiscated.[3]

Soon, however, the truth became apparent. "They one by one began to disappear from the yards of their former owners," wrote Lou of the freed slaves. "Where they went, why or when they went, no one knew. Simply when called they did not appear, and in many instances never appeared again to *our* eyes at least." Many jubilantly embraced their freedom. For them, the human right to freedom transcended any southern arguments for the benefits of paternalism. Freedom meant release from white control, it meant autonomy, and it meant the choice to pursue their own lives.[4] The freedmen that disappeared were exercising this right.

2. Smythe, "Recollections," 49.
3. Ibid., 72, 67.
4. Ibid., 73; Foner, *Short History of Reconstruction*, 35–36.

Many, however, stayed with their former masters or on their land. The whites interpreted these actions as signs of loyalty, but most freedmen had few other options for survival. On Louisa's plantation, as on others throughout the South, blacks took a much different attitude toward the land than they had before emancipation.[5] On first learning of their freedom the slaves on Lang Syne appropriated various items of furniture from the house; it was at this time that the business papers of the plantation were also lost. They probably believed that the McCord family, absent for five years, would not return. They may also have seen this as their entitlement for the generations of service that their families had been forced to give to the plantation.

Similarly, when the freedmen returned to the usual business of the plantation, they intended to take the proceeds of the planting for themselves as payment for their labor. In the case of Lang Syne, the only crop being planted was potatoes. Augustine Smythe, now married to Louisa's daughter, had taken over the management of the plantation and would soon be its new owner. Just after the war ended he rode out to check on the harvest and to make arrangements for himself and his bride to move to Lang Syne. When the women of the plantation heard that he intended to bring the potato crop back to Columbia they planned "an attack on the potato hills." They "took the stand that they [the potatoes] belonged to them [the freedmen]," wrote Lou. "[T]hey had worked for them and 'Mr. Smythe didn't hab nuttin to do wid 'em anyhow.'"[6] Louisa, their former mistress, no longer had any claim to their work, as far as the freedmen and women were concerned. As a result, Gus and Lou moved to the plantation shortly thereafter to keep control of the freedmen still working there.

Emancipation brought mixed feelings for Louisa and her daughter. On the one hand, they expressed some relief when one of their former slaves disappeared. It was one less mouth that they had to feed. On the other hand, they came to realize how dependent upon slave labor they had been. Living without servants became a great inconvenience for them. Moreover, the former mistresses did not understand why "[t]he negroes were in a curious turbulent condition." "They were

5. Ibid., 45–46.
6. Smythe, "Recollections," 81.

just like children," Lou insisted, "one minute asking and accepting favors, the next raising a great fuss about some nonsense."[7] What Lou did not realize was that the ability to question the judgment of their former mistress or master on any subject was of great symbolic importance to the former slaves. This was the essence of freedom. Lou could not comprehend, after a lifetime of believing herself entitled to the proceeds of the work of her mother's slaves, that those former slaves might now revoke that privilege.

As for Louisa, she sank into a deep depression at the end of the war. She wished to shed herself of responsibilities. When Gus Smythe returned to Columbia, she insisted that he and Lou get married immediately, "as a protector was sorely needed in those days." On June 27, 1865, the two married in a shabby, makeshift ceremony in Louisa's house. That same day, Louisa turned the title to Lang Syne over to Gus. Within a year, however, Gus realized that the plantation was not doing well. "There was no money in it," wrote Lou, "at least plenty went in it and none came out." The business became steadily worse. In December 1870, Gus sold the plantation to Daniel Zimmerman, retaining rights to the family cemetery, access to the cemetery, and a small log cabin that was turned over to Maum Di and her family.[8]

Meanwhile, Louisa longed to leave South Carolina. This was an idea expressed by many southerners during this period of defeat. Many exiled themselves to South America. Hawaii enticed Louisa the most, but she could not afford to travel. She therefore determined to sell all of her possessions. The sale of furniture and other incidentals proved no problem, but she could not sell her house in Columbia without taking an oath of loyalty to the Union. She had sacrificed her son and the previous five years of her life to the southern "Cause." The loss of that "Cause" had been painful and made all of her sacrifices seem worthless. In taking the oath, she would be recanting her dedication to the Confederacy.

---

7. Ibid., 81.

8. Ibid., 74, 84, 7; Abstract to Title of Lang Syne, LCI. The title to Lang Syne passed through several hands in the next decade until it was purchased by William G. Peterkin. Peterkin's wife, Julia, began writing novels about the black tenants on the plantation. One of these novels, *Scarlet Sister Mary*, won her the Pulitzer Prize for literature in 1929. See clippings in Dulles-Cheves-McCord-Lovell Papers.

Her friend Dr. Reynolds, the father of her daughter-in-law, persuaded her to take the oath. Perhaps, he argued, she would not be recanting. Most southerners understood that people who took the oath did so only to reclaim property that was rightfully theirs. Augustine Smythe had done so. Louisa's neighbors would understand why she took the oath and would not view it as a betrayal. Reynolds in fact offered to accompany her and take the oath himself. Louisa put on the black mourning dress that she had worn for the past several years. Her daughter recalled: "One of the saddest sights I ever saw was that couple walking arm in arm to the Provost Marshall's office . . . It was like a pitiful, pitiful funeral."[9] In Louisa's case, her daughter's metaphor was appropriate.

From 1865 to 1869, Louisa and Hannah wandered from Columbia to Abbeville to Charleston, staying with relatives and in boardinghouses. When Hannah married John Taylor Rhett in March 1869, Louisa settled in Charleston for two years. Like many women she became involved in the commemoration of the "Lost Cause," and became president of the South Carolina Monument Association.[10] This work, however, did not give her the sense of purpose that she sought. She could not salvage any meaning out of the preservation of the memory of the Confederate dead. The association could cover South Carolina with monuments, but every day martial law reminded her of the Confederacy's defeat. Union soldiers on every corner, freedmen who no longer deferred to white people on the street, racial mingling in places that had once been "white only" all served to remind her of the social order that had been lost. Moreover, with the loss of that social order, the sacrifice of her independence throughout her life was rendered meaningless. The guerrilla warfare between the Union army and the newly organized Ku Klux Klan, which she supported, only intensified her sense of defeat. "South Carolina is fast becoming to me, but as one great grave of the great past," she wrote in her resignation from the Monument Association.[11]

9. Smythe, "Recollections," 79.
10. Gaines M. Foster, *Ghosts of the Confederacy: Defeat, the Lost Cause, and the Emergence of the New South, 1865 to 1913* (New York: Oxford University Press, 1987), 38–45.
11. Foner, *Short History of Reconstruction*, 184–91; LSM to Augustine T. Smythe, November 24, 1871, Smythe-Stoney-Adger Papers; LSM to the Board of Managers of the South Carolina Monument Association, Dulles-Cheves-McCord-Lovell Papers.

Louisa left South Carolina in 1871 and traveled north to Canada, touring resorts around Lake Ontario and visiting distant relatives of her late husband. The death of Hannah after the birth of her second child in 1872 only served as a reminder of why Louisa had left home. She would not return to South Carolina until 1876. What drew her home was the end of Reconstruction and a project that held no grief, both of which allowed her to return to an era before sectional tension.

At the beginning of 1876, South Carolina was one of the few states still under Reconstruction. The white citizens of the state had proved highly resistant to the laws passed during the preceding decade. Klan activity was high, and membership in "rifle clubs" soared. Former Confederates, unable to vote—their punishment for treason during the Civil War—violently directed their ire at the Union army, freedmen, and Republicans. During the elections of 1876, riots repeatedly broke out at Republican gatherings, and the Democratic candidate for governor, General Wade Hampton, directed much of the violence. Through a campaign of voter fraud and intimidation, he won the election, and the government of South Carolina returned to the hands of the former slave owners.[12]

On the national level, the presidential race had become the center of controversy. White southerners, overwhelmingly Democratic, hoped that their candidate, Samuel Tilden, would end Reconstruction entirely if he won. The outcome of the contest between Tilden and Republican Rutherford Hayes was so close, and voter fraud within both parties so widespread, that the Democrats seized the opportunity to challenge the results in South Carolina, Florida, and Louisiana, three states where Reconstruction was still under way. The leadership of both parties debated through the winter of 1876. In early 1877, they reached an agreement whereby the Democrats would cease to contest the election and allow Hayes to become president in exchange for the end of military rule in the unreconstructed states.[13] In South Carolina, freedmen watched as the Republican party abandoned them to white supremacist rule. Louisa, however, probably shared her daughter's jubilation that "order" would be re-

---

12. Foner, *Short History of Reconstruction*, 240–41.
13. Ibid., 241–47; C. Vann Woodward, *Reunion and Reaction: The Compromise of 1877 and the End of Reconstruction*, 5–8.

stored to their state. She believed that she could return without being constantly reminded of all that she had lost.

Meanwhile, Langdon Cheves III, the son of Langdon Cheves Jr., had become interested in the life of his grandfather. He turned to his Aunt Louisa to provide him with tales of her father in his prime. She found such joy in writing these memories that her nephew suggested she compose a memoir. At first she declined, writing, "[M]y Father always kept off questions which appeared to aim at giving material for a written life" and "[A] few scattered anecdotes, and those perhaps already given to you by others, would be all I could do."[14] Yet she began to make notes on odd scraps of paper, recording any bit of information that she could find or remember about her father. In doing so, she found, she could revive the memory of a man whom she considered the greatest influence upon her life and, at the same time, return to a time before sectional conflict became so intense that it led to the war and to the losses of the war. Her work with the Monument Association had been to preserve the memory of the "Lost Cause," which was depressing work. Writing of her father returned her to a time before that "Cause" had come into being.

Two years later, she continued her work in commemorating her father. The bust that she had commissioned of Langdon Cheves after his death had never been completed. The materials, photographs, and death mask had not arrived at Hiram Powers's studio as scheduled in 1858. When the war came, it pushed the project out of her mind for fifteen years. In 1878, she wrote to Powers to ask him to resume work on the bust. Although Powers had died in 1874, his son, Preston Powers, completed the sculpture in 1879.[15]

By that time, Louisa had moved in with Lou and Gus and their four children. Gus had become a successful lawyer, and the Smythe family now lived on fashionable Legare Street in Charleston. There, Louisa found solace in a new role as matriarch. She gave constant advice on all matters to her son-in-law and helped her daughter in managing her household. The grandchildren gave her particular joy. She suggested that one child be christened Hannah, and "Loula was

14. LSM to Langdon Cheves III, April 6 [1876], LCI.
15. Correspondence between LSM and Preston Powers, Hiram Powers Papers, Smithsonian Institution, Washington, D.C.

like her own child," Lou wrote. Louisa bought the house next door to the Smythe home and contracted for improvements upon it, clearly hoping to live many more happy years near her family. By autumn 1879, her daughter wrote, "she had been her old self."[16]

Throughout November 1879, a pain in Louisa's stomach grew worse. On November 18, she suffered a severe attack of what she called "Gout in the Stomach." "She was sick five days in all," wrote Lou, "suffering intensely all the time—but the last three days were terrible." A doctor was called in and he said he did not expect her to survive. Lou turned to her mother and asked if she was willing to die. "Willing, my child?," Louisa replied. "Glad—glad to rest." The family gathered around her bedside and awaited the end. One of the last things Louisa did was to call her baby granddaughter, Susie, to her room to play. On November 23, 1879, Louisa McCord died.[17]

Louisa's life had spanned one of the most important eras in American history. Born just before the War of 1812, she lived through the Age of Jackson, the sectional crisis, the expansion and abolition of slavery, the Civil War, and Reconstruction. She also lived during a time when women expanded and developed their traditional roles from caretakers of the house and family into a broader, more public sphere. While many Americans, including women, believed the United States to be a nation capable of fulfilling all sorts of possibilities for individualism and democracy, Louisa saw her own life as one of sacrifice. She belonged to a conservative strain of thought that believed inequality to be a natural state that society should encourage through paternalist relationships.

As a child she observed the interactions of class in both a slave society and a free society. She shared the concerns of other American elites over the seemingly unruly nature of the working class. In doing so, she demonstrated more of a class identification than a sectional identification, and would continue to do so throughout her life on subjects of political economy. Where she differed from the northern elite, however, was over the issue of labor. She, along with other southern intellectuals, came to the conclusion that enslavement

16. Smythe, "Recollections," 90–91; LSM mortgage, Dulles-Cheves-McCord-Lovell Papers; Louisa Smythe to Sophia Lovell Haskell, December 4 [1879], LCIII.

17. Louisa Smythe to Sophia Lovell Haskell, December 4 [1879], LCIII; Smythe, "Recollections," 90–91.

was the best and most humane method by which the working class could be contained, and she believed that the working class should be exclusively African American. Slavery, however, was an institution that required a hierarchy of both race and gender. In this system, she believed, she had to accept an inferior position.

Louisa, however, became quite father-identified. Although she loved her mother, she did not particularly admire Mary Cheves's life of endless childbearing, with no power of self-determination. Her father had the power and influence both in the home and out in the world of politics. This Louisa envied. At the same time, she demonstrated a propensity for intellectual work in philosophy, economics, and mathematics that was supposed to be closed to her as a woman.

She could have rebelled, as had two other women of the South Carolina elite, Angelina and Sarah Grimke, but she did not. Nor did she find empowerment in a protofeminist "female world of love and ritual."[18] In fact, she disdained most activities of young women as frivolous. She preferred stoicism, which caused others to call her "masculine," but which she framed as subordination to "duty." Yet, in giving that impression and in remaining single until the age of thirty, Louisa seemed to be rebelling against her prescribed role as wife and mother. In this way, she was repudiating the world of her father, the slaves that she owned, and the ordered society in which she lived. She actually had no quarrel with that society as a whole, only with her position within it. In fact, she believed that the prevailing hierarchy was the only means to avoid the anarchy of socialism and racial "amalgamation." Thus, she sacrificed her own independence for the maintenance of a social order based upon slavery. She married and bore children.

Much of her marriage, however, was a facade. On the surface, Louisa seemed to be a dutiful wife and mother, submissive to her husband. But she bore only three children and maintained control of both the property and the business management of Lang Syne. She had made the sacrifice of marriage, but marriage had, in fact, opened the door to a greater personal independence than she had enjoyed as a single woman. Moreover, in marriage she preserved the southern social hierarchy that provided her with a fairly comfortable life.

18. Smith-Rosenberg, "The Female World of Love and Ritual" in *Disorderly Conduct.*

Safely ensconced in marriage, Louisa could venture into the public world through her essays. As a single woman, publication would have called her femininity into question and, again, threatened the hierarchy that dictated that a woman's position remain private and within the home. Even as a married woman, the charge could be leveled against her that she was neglecting her husband and children in order to pursue her own ambitions. Thus, she framed publication as another sacrifice. Because attacks by abolitionists and the women's movement were being taken seriously in the press, Louisa, as an American and as a woman, would have to sacrifice her own femininity and step outside of her domestic sphere in order to defend both the institution of slavery and women's subordinate position in society.

While these two sacrifices, marriage and publication, brought her greater independence and intellectual satisfaction, she soon learned that sacrifice and duty could also lead to great suffering and pain. First, in nursing her father as a dutiful woman and daughter, she observed his mental and physical decline and suffered much verbal and emotional abuse. Second, in supporting the Civil War, she lost her son, brother, and several nephews, as well as her home, land, and slaves to the conflict. She also operated a hospital where, on a daily basis, she dealt with material shortages and the physical agony caused by warfare. When the Confederacy fell and emancipation eliminated the institution on which she had based her entire notion of society, all her sacrifices seemed in vain. She did not live long enough to see the reestablishment of racial hierarchy in the New South under Jim Crow. By her death she had come to see life as a long chore with little reward. Her gravestone reflected all that she believed she had accomplished in life: "Louisa S. McCord, daughter of Langdon Cheves, wife of David J. McCord, Born Dec. 3, 1810, Died Nov. 23, 1879. At Rest."[19]

19. Gravestone of LSM, Magnolia Cemetery, Charleston, South Carolina. Significantly, though McCord is buried on the family plot at Lang Syne, Louisa is buried next to her father rather than her husband.

Bibliography

Primary Sources

Rare Book and Manuscript Collection, William R. Perkins Library, Duke University, Durham, N.C.
    Ann (Heatly) Reid Lovell Papers
    Langdon Cheves Papers
    Rachel Susan (Bee) Cheves Correspondence
Lancaster County Historical Society, Lancaster, Pa.
    Dr. John L. Farmer Abbeville Collection
Archives of American Art, Smithsonian Institution, Washington, D.C.
    Hiram Powers and Powers Family Papers
South Carolina Historical Society, Charleston
    Dulles-Cheves-McCord-Lovell Papers
    Langdon Cheves I Papers
    Langdon Cheves III Papers
    Smythe-Stoney-Adger Papers
South Caroliniana Library, University of South Carolina, Columbia
    McCord Family Bible
    Mrs. Augustine T. Smythe, "Recollections of Louisa Rebecca Hayne McCord"
Manuscripts Division, Southern Historical Collection, University of North Carolina–Chapel Hill
    Cheves-Wagner Family Papers
    William Lowndes Papers
    William Porcher Miles Papers

Writings of Louisa S. McCord

In *Louisa S. McCord: Political and Social Essays,* ed. Richard C. Lounsbury. Charlottesville: University Press of Virginia, 1995:
"British Philanthropy and American Slavery" (1853), 281–320.
"Diversity of the Races; Its Bearing upon Negro Slavery" (1851), 159–86.
"Enfranchisement of Woman" (1852), 105–24.
"Justice and Fraternity" (1849), 57–78.
"A Letter to the Duchess of Sutherland from a Lady of South Carolina" (1853), 350–60.
"Negro and White Slavery—Wherein Do They Differ?" (1851), 187–202.
"Negro-mania" (1852), 222–44.
"The Right to Labor" (1849), 79–102.
"Separate Secession" (1851), 203–21.
"Slavery and Political Economy" (1856), 422–69.
"Uncle Tom's Cabin" (1853), 245–80.
"Woman and Her Needs" (1852), 125–55.
In *Louisa S. McCord: Poems, Drama, Biography, Letters,* ed. Richard C. Lounsbury. Charlottesville: University Press of Virginia, 1996:
Caius Gracchus: A Tragedy in Five Acts (1851), 161–232.
"Langdon Cheves: Review of 'Reminiscences of Public Men'" (1870), 235–40.
My Dreams (1848), 41–145.
"Woman's Progress" (1853), 150–54.

Secondary Sources

Allen, Katherine R. *Single Women/Family Ties: Life Histories of Older Women.* Newbury Park, Calif.: Sage Publications, 1989.
Ascher, Carol, Louise DeSalvo, and Sara Ruddick, eds. *Between Women: Biographers, Novelists, Critics, Teachers, and Artists Write about Their Work on Women.* Boston: Beacon Press, 1984.
Ash, Stephen V. *When the Yankees Came: Conflict and Chaos in the Occupied South, 1861–1865.* Chapel Hill: University of North Carolina Press, 1995.

Bailey, Hugh C., and William Dale Pratt III. "Missus Alone in de Big House." *Alabama Review* 8:1 (January 1955): 43–54.

Baker, Paula. "The Domestication of Politics: Women and American Political Society, 1780–1920." In *Unequal Sisters: A Multi-Cultural Reader in U.S. Women's History*, 2d ed., ed. Vicki L. Ruiz and Ellen Carol DuBois, 85–110. New York: Routledge, 1994.

Barbre, Joy Webster, ed. *Interpreting Women's Lives: Feminist Theory and Personal Narratives*. Bloomington: Indiana University Press, 1989.

Bardaglio, Peter. *Reconstructing the Household: Families, Sex, and the Law in the Nineteenth-Century South*. Chapel Hill: University of North Carolina Press, 1995.

Basch, Norma. *In the Eyes of the Law: Woman, Marriage, and Property in Nineteenth-Century New York*. Ithaca, N.Y.: Cornell University Press, 1982.

Bass, Robert D. *Ninety Six: The Struggle for the South Carolina Back Country*. Lexington, S.C.: Sandlapper Publishing, 1978.

Bausman, Lottie M. "General Position of Lancaster County on Negro Slavery." *Journal of Lancaster County Historical Society* 25:1 (January 6, 1911): 5–21.

Baym, Nina. *Feminism and American Literary History*. New Brunswick, N.J.: Rutgers University Press, 1992.

———. *American Women Writers and the Work of History, 1790–1860*. New Brunswick, N.J.: Rutgers University Press, 1995.

Bennett, Susan Smythe. "The McCords of McCords' Ferry, South Carolina." *South Carolina Historical and Genealogical Magazine* 34:4 (October 1933): 117–93.

———. "The Cheves Family of South Carolina." *South Carolina Historical and Genealogical Magazine* 35:3 (July 1934): 79–95.

Bernhard, Virginia, Betty Brandon, Elizabeth Fox-Genovese, and Theda Purdue, eds. *Southern Women: Histories and Identities*. Columbia: University of Missouri Press, 1992.

Binney, Horace. *The Leaders of the Old Bar of Philadelphia*. Philadelphia: C. Sherman & Son, 1859.

Bleser, Carol, ed. *In Joy and In Sorrow: Women, Family, and Marriage in the Victorian South*. New York: Oxford University Press, 1991.

Bloch, Ruth H. "American Feminine Ideals in Transition: The Role of the Moral Mother, 1785–1815." *Feminist Studies* 4:2 (June 1978): 100–26.

Brittan, Arthur, and Mary Maynard. *Sexism, Racism, and Oppression.* London: Blackwell, 1984.

Brodie, Janet Farrell. *Contraception and Abortion in Nineteenth-Century America.* Ithaca: Cornell University Press, 1994.

Brubaker, Marianna G. "The Underground Railroad." *Journal of the Lancaster County Historical Society* 25:4 (April 7, 1911): 95–119.

Burton, Orville Vernon. *In My Father's House Are Many Mansions: Family and Community in Edgefield, South Carolina.* Chapel Hill: University of North Carolina Press, 1985.

Bynum, Victoria E. *Unruly Women: The Politics of Social and Sexual Control in the Old South.* Chapel Hill: University of North Carolina Press, 1992.

Carlyle, Thomas. "Occasional Discourse on the Nigger Question." In *Critical and Miscellaneous Essays,* 5 vols., 4:348–83. New York: Charles Scribner's Sons, 1899.

Carpenter, Jesse T. *The South as a Conscious Minority, 1789–1861.* New York: New York University Press, 1930.

Cashin, Joan E. *A Family Venture: Men and Women on the Southern Frontier.* New York: Oxford University Press, 1991.

Catterall, Helen Tunnicliff, and James J. Hayden, eds. *Judicial Cases Concerning American Slavery and the Negro.* 5 vols. 1929. Reprint, New York: Negro Universities Press, 1968.

Chambers-Schiller, Lee. "The Single Woman: Family and Vocation in Nineteenth Century America." Bunting Institute Working Paper, Radcliffe College, 1980.

Chessler, Ellen. *Woman of Valor: Margaret Sanger and the Birth Control Movement in America.* New York: Simon & Schuster, 1992.

Cheves, Langdon. *An Oration, Delivered at St. Philip's Church on the Fourth of July, 1810.* Charleston, S.C.: E. S. Thomas, 1810.

Chodorow, Nancy. "Mothering, Male Dominance, and Capitalism." In *Capitalist Patriarchy and the Case for Socialist Feminism,* ed. Zillah R. Eisenstein, 83–106. New York: Monthly Review Press, 1979.

Clarke, Erskine. *Our Southern Zion: A History of Calvinism in the South Carolina Low Country, 1690–1990.* Tuscaloosa: University of Alabama Press, 1996.

Clinton, Catherine. *The Plantation Mistress: Woman's World in the Old South*. New York: Pantheon Books, 1982.

Cogan, Frances B. *All-American Girl: The Ideal of Real Womanhood in Mid-Nineteenth-Century America*. Athens: University of Georgia Press, 1989.

Coleman, Peter J. *The Transformation of Rhode Island, 1790–1860*. Providence: Brown University Press, 1963.

Coryell, Janet L., Thomas H. Appelton Jr., Anastasia Sims, and Sandra Gioia Treadway. *Negotiating Boundaries of Southern Womanhood: Dealing with the Powers That Be*. Columbia: University of Missouri Press, 2000.

Cott, Nancy F. *The Bonds of Womanhood: "Woman's Sphere" in New England, 1780–1835*. New Haven: Yale University Press, 1977.

Cott, Nancy F., and Elizabeth H. Pleck, ed. *A Heritage of Her Own: Toward a New Social History of American Women*. New York: Simon & Schuster, 1979.

Culler, Daniel Marchant, et al., eds. *Orangeburgh District, 1768–1868: History and Records*. Spartanburg, S.C.: Reprint Company Publishers, 1995.

Cunliffe, Marcus. *Chattel Slavery and Wage Slavery: The Anglo-American Context, 1830–1860*. Athens: University of Georgia Press, 1979.

Davis, Susan G. "The Career of Colonel Pluck: Folk Drama and Popular Protest in Early Nineteenth-Century Philadelphia." In *Material Life in America, 1600–1860*, ed. Robert Blair St. George, 487–501. Boston: Northeastern University Press, 1988.

DeBeauvoir, Simone. *The Second Sex*. New York: Knopf, 1952.

Degler, Carl N. *At Odds: Women and the Family in America from the Revolution to the Present*. New York: Oxford University Press, 1980.

Demos, John. *Past, Present, and Personal: The Family and the Life Course in American History*. New York: Oxford University Press, 1986.

DePauw, Linda, and Conover Hunt. *"Remember the Ladies": Women in America, 1750–1815*. New York: Viking Press, 1976.

Diffenderffer, F. D. "Langdon Cheves." *Journal of the Lancaster County Historical Society* 11:2 (February 1, 1907): 45–58.

Dobson, Joanne. *Dickinson and the Strategies of Reticence: The Woman*

Writer in Nineteenth-Century America. Bloomington: Indiana University Press, 1989.

Domhoff, G. William. *The Higher Circles: Governing Class in America.* New York: Vintage Books, 1970.

Donovan, Josephine. *Feminist Theory: The Intellectual Traditions of American Feminism.* Rev. ed. New York: Continuum, 1994.

Douglass, Frederick. *Narrative of the Life of Frederick Douglass, an American Slave, Written by Himself.* Ed. John Blassingame. New Haven: Yale University Press, 2000.

Dudden, Faye E. *Serving Women: Household Service in Nineteenth-Century America.* Middletown, Conn.: Wesleyan University Press, 1983.

Duyckinck, Evert A., and George L. Duyckinck. *Cyclopaedia of American Literature,* 2 vols. 1856. Reprint, Detroit: Gale Research, 1965.

Eacker, Susan A. "A 'Dangerous Intimate' of the South: Louisa McCord on Gender and Slavery." In *Southern Writers and Their Worlds,* ed. Christopher Morris and Steven G. Reinhardt, 27–40. College Station: Texas A&M University Press, 1996.

Eaton, Clement. *Freedom of Thought in the Old South.* Durham, N.C.: Duke University Press, 1940.

Ehrenreich, Barbara, and Deirdre English. *For Her Own Good: 150 Years of the Experts' Advice to Women.* New York: Doubleday, 1978.

Eisenstein, Hester. *Contemporary Feminist Thought.* Boston: G. K. Hall, 1983.

Eisenstein, Zillah R. "Some Notes on the Relations of Capitalist Patriarchy." In *Capitalist Patriarchy and the Case for Socialist Feminism,* ed. Zillah R. Eisenstein, 41–55. New York: Monthly Review Press, 1979.

Elbert, Sarah. *A Hunger for Home: Louisa May Alcott and* Little Women. Philadelphia: Temple University Press, 1984.

Eshleman, H. Frank. "The Position of Lancaster County on the Missouri Compromise." *Journal of the Lancaster County Historical Society* 25:7 (September 1, 1911): 215–18.

Faragher, John Mack. *Women and Men on the Overland Trail.* New Haven: Yale University Press, 1979.

Farnham, Christie Anne. *The Education of the Southern Belle: Higher*

Education and Student Socialization in the Antebellum South. New York: New York University Press, 1994.

Faust, Drew Gilpin. *A Sacred Circle: The Dilemma of the Intellectual in the Old South, 1840–1860.* Baltimore: Johns Hopkins University Press, 1977.

———. *James Henry Hammond and the Old South: A Design for Mastery.* Baton Rouge: Louisiana State University Press, 1982.

———. "Altars of Sacrifice: Confederate Women and the Narratives of War." In *Divided Houses: Gender and the Civil War,* ed. Catherine Clinton and Nina Silber, 171–99. New York: Oxford University Press, 1992.

———. *Mothers of Invention: Women of the Slaveholding South in the American Civil War.* Chapel Hill: University of North Carolina, 1996.

Federal Writers' Project. *Rhode Island: A Guide to the Smallest State.* Boston: Houghton Mifflin, 1937.

Fields, Suzanne. *Like Father, Like Daughter: How Father Shapes the Woman His Daughter Becomes.* Boston: Little, Brown, 1983.

Fitzhugh, George. "Southern Thought." In *The Ideology of Slavery: Proslavery Thought in the Antebellum South, 1830–1860,* ed. Drew Gilpin Faust, 272–99. Baton Rouge: Louisiana State University Press, 1981.

Foner, Eric. *A Short History of Reconstruction, 1863–1877.* New York: Harper & Row, 1990.

———. *Free Soil, Free Labor, Free Men: The Ideology of the Republican Party Before the Civil War.* 2d ed. New York: Oxford University Press, 1995.

Forrest, Mary [Julia D. Freeman]. *Women of the South Distinguished in Literature.* New York: Derby & Jackson, 1861.

Foster, Gaines M. *Ghosts of the Confederacy: Defeat, the Lost Cause, and the Emergence of the New South, 1865 to 1913.* New York: Oxford University Press, 1987.

Fox-Genovese, Elizabeth. *Within the Plantation Household: Black and White Women of the Old South.* Chapel Hill: University of North Carolina Press, 1988.

Franklin, John Hope. *The Militant South, 1800–1861.* Cambridge: Harvard University Press, 1956.

Fraser, Jesse Melville. "Louisa C. McCord." M.A. thesis, University of South Carolina, 1919.

Fraser, Walter J., Jr. *Charleston! Charleston!: The History of a Southern City.* Columbia: University of South Carolina Press, 1989.

Frederickson, George M. "Masters and Mudsills: The Role of Race in the Planter Ideology of South Carolina." *South Atlantic Urban Studies* 2 (1978): 34–48.

Freehling, William W. *Prelude to Civil War: The Nullification Controversy in South Carolina, 1816–1836.* New York: Harper & Row, 1965.

Friedman, Jean E. *The Enclosed Garden: Woman and Community in the Evangelical South, 1830–1900.* Chapel Hill: University of North Carolina Press, 1985.

Gay, Dorothy Ann. "The Tangled Skein of Romanticism and Violence in the Old South: The Southern Response to Abolitionism and Feminism, 1830–1861." Ph.D. diss., University of North Carolina, 1975.

Genovese, Eugene D. *The Political Economy of Slavery: Studies in the Economy and Society of the Slave South.* New York: Random House, 1967.

———. *Roll, Jordan, Roll: The World the Slaves Made.* New York: Random House, 1976.

Gilbert, Sandra M., and Susan Gubar. *The Madwoman in the Attic: The Woman Writer and the Nineteenth-Century Literary Imagination.* New Haven: Yale University Press, 1979.

Gill, Christopher J. "A Year of Residence [1852] in the Household of a South Carolina Planter: Teacher, Daughters, Mistress, and Slaves." *South Carolina Historical Magazine* 97 (October 1996): 293–309.

Gillespie, Michele, and Catherine Clinton, eds. *Taking Off the White Gloves: Southern Women and Women Historians.* Columbia: University of Missouri Press, 1998.

Glatthaar, Joseph T. *The March to the Sea and Beyond: Sherman's Troops in the Savannah and Carolinas Campaigns.* New York: New York University Press, 1985.

Golden, Claudia Dale. *Urban Slavery in the American South, 1820–1860: A Quantitative History.* Chicago: University of Chicago Press, 1976.

Gordon, Linda. *Heroes of Their Own Lives: The Politics and History of Family Violence.* New York: Penguin Books, 1988.

Greven, Philip. *The Protestant Temperament: Patterns of Child-Rearing, Religious Experience, and the Self in Early America.* Chicago: University of Chicago Press, 1977.

Hale, Grace Elizabeth. *Making Whiteness: The Culture of Segregation in the South, 1890–1940.* New York: Pantheon Books, 1998.

Hale, Sarah Josepha. *Woman's Record; or, Sketches of All Distinguished Women, from the Creation to AD 1854.* 1855. Reprint, New York: Source Book Press, 1970.

Hart, John Seely. *The Female Prose Writers of America.* Philadelphia: E. H. Butler, 1852.

Hawks, Joanne V., and Sheila L. Skemp, eds. *Sex, Race, and the Role of Women in the South.* Jackson: University Press of Mississippi, 1983.

Heilbrun, Carolyn G. *Reinventing Womanhood.* New York: W. W. Norton, 1979.

———. *Writing a Woman's Life.* New York: Ballantine Books, 1988.

Hensel, W. U. "Reminiscences of Langdon Cheves." *Journal of the Lancaster County Historical Society* 25:4 (April 7, 1911): 120–22.

Herrick, Cheesman A. *White Servitude in Pennsylvania: Indentured and Redemption Labor in Colony and Commonwealth.* Philadelphia: John Joseph McVey, 1926.

Hershbert, Theodore. "Free Blacks in Antebellum Philadelphia: A Study of Ex-Slaves, Freeborn, and Socioeconomic Decline." In *African Americans in Pennsylvania: Shifting Historical Perspectives,* ed. Joe W. Trotter Jr. and Eric Ledell Smith, 123–47. University Park: Pennsylvania State University Press, 1997.

Higginson, Thomas Wentworth. *Black Rebellion: Five Slave Revolts.* New York: DaCapo Press, 1998.

Hodes, Martha. *White Women, Black Men: Illicit Sex in the Nineteenth-Century South.* New Haven: Yale University Press, 1997.

Hopkins, Leroy T. "No Balm in Gilead: Lancaster's African American Population and the Civil War Era." *Journal of the Lancaster County Historical Society* 95:2 (1991): 20–31.

Huff, Archie Vernon, Jr. *Langdon Cheves of South Carolina.* Columbia: University of South Carolina Press, 1977.

Jabour, Anya. *Marriage in the Early Republic: Elizabeth and William Wirt and the Companionate Ideal.* Baltimore: Johns Hopkins University Press, 1998.

Jacobs, Harriet [Linda Brent]. *Incidents in the Life of a Slave Girl; Written by Herself.* 1861. Reprint, ed. Jean Fagan Yellin, Cambridge: Harvard University Press, 1987.

Jennings, Thelma. *The Nashville Convention: Southern Movement for Unity, 1848–1851.* Memphis: Memphis State University Press, 1980.

Johnson, Michael P. "Denmark Vesey and His Co-Conspirators." *William and Mary Quarterly* 4:58 (October 2001): 915–76.

———. "Reading Evidence." *William and Mary Quarterly* 1:59 (January 2002): 193–202.

Johnson, Paul E. *A Shopkeeper's Millennium: Society and Revivals in Rochester, New York, 1815–1837.* New York: Hill & Wang, 1978.

Jones, Anne Goodwyn. *Tomorrow is Another Day: The Woman Writer in the South, 1859–1936.* Baton Rouge: Louisiana State University Press, 1981.

Jones, Anne Goodwyn, and Susan V. Donaldson. *Haunted Bodies: Gender and Southern Text.* Charlottesville: University Press of Virginia, 1997.

Jones, Jacqueline. *Labor of Love, Labor of Sorrow: Black Women, Work, and the Family from Slavery to the Present.* New York: Basic Books, 1985.

Kerber, Linda K. *Women of the Republic: Intellect and Ideology in Revolutionary America.* Chapel Hill: University of North Carolina Press, 1980.

———. *Toward an Intellectual History of Women.* Chapel Hill: University of North Carolina Press, 1997.

Klein, Rachel N. *Unification of a Slave State: The Rise of the Planter Class in the South Carolina Backcountry, 1760–1808.* Chapel Hill: University of North Carolina Press, 1990.

Lambert, Robert Stansbury. *South Carolina Loyalists in the American Revolution.* Columbia: University of South Carolina Press, 1987.

Lapansky, Emma Jones. "'Since They Got Those Separate Churches': Afro-Americans and Racism in Jacksonian Philadelphia." In *African Americans in Pennsylvania: Shifting Historical Per-*

spectives, ed. Joe W. Trotter Jr. and Eric Ledell Smith, 93–120. University Park: Pennsylvania State University Press, 1997.

Latrobe, Benjamin Henry. *The Journal of Latrobe: being the notes and sketches of an architect, naturalist, and traveler in the United States from 1796 to 1820.* New York: Burt Franklin, 1905.

Leavitt, Judith Walzer. *Brought to Bed: Childbearing in America, 1750–1950.* New York: Oxford University Press, 1986.

Lebsock, Suzanne. *The Free Women of Petersburg: Status and Culture in a Southern Town, 1784–1860.* New York: W. W. Norton, 1984.

Lerner, Gerda. *The Grimke Sisters from South Carolina: Pioneers for Women's Rights and Abolition.* 1967. Reprint, New York: Schocken Books, 1971.

———. *The Creation of Patriarchy.* New York: Oxford University Press, 1986.

———. *The Creation of Feminist Consciousness: From the Middle Ages to Eighteen-seventy.* New York: Oxford University Press, 1993.

Lewis, James, and Kenneth A. Lockridge. "'Sally Has Been Sick': Pregnancy and Family Limitation among Virginia Gentry Women." *Journal of Social History* 22 (1988): 5–19.

Litwack, Leon. *North of Slavery: The Negro in the Free States, 1790–1860.* Chicago: University of Chicago Press, 1961.

Loetscher, Lefferts A. *A Brief History of the Presbyterians.* 3d ed. Philadelphia: Westminster Press, 1978.

Lounsbury, Richard C. "*Ludibria Rerum Mortalium:* Charlestonian Intellectuals and Their Classics." In *Intellectual Life in Antebellum Charleston,* ed. Michael O'Brien and David Moltke-Hansen, 323–69. Knoxville: University of Tennessee Press, 1986.

———, ed. *Louisa S. McCord: Political and Social Essays.* Charlottesville: University Press of Virginia, 1995.

———. *Louisa S. McCord: Poems, Drama, Biography, Letters.* Charlottesville: University Press of Virginia, 1996,

Lucas, Marion Brunson. *Sherman and the Burning of Columbia.* College Station: Texas A&M University Press, 1976.

Martineau, Harriet. *Retrospect of Western Travels,* vol. 1. London: Saunders & Otley, 1838.

Mayer, Henry. *All on Fire: William Lloyd Garrison and the Abolition of Slavery.* New York: St. Martin's Press, 1998.

McCardell, John. *The Idea of a Southern Nation: Southern Nationalists and Southern Nationalism, 1830–1860.* New York: W. W. Norton, 1979.

McCurry, Stephanie. *Masters of Small Worlds: Yeoman Households, Gender Relations, and the Political Culture of the Antebellum South Carolina Low Country.* New York: Oxford University Press, 1995.

McMillen, Sally G. *Motherhood in the Old South: Pregnancy and Childbirth in America.* Baton Rouge: Louisiana State University Press, 1990.

McPherson, James M. *Battle Cry of Freedom: The Civil War Era.* New York: Oxford University Press, 1988.

Miers, Earl Schenck, ed. *When the World Ended: The Diary of Emma LeConte.* Lincoln: University of Nebraska Press, 1987.

Mintz, Steven. *Moralists and Modernizers: America's Pre–Civil War Reformers.* Baltimore: Johns Hopkins University Press, 1995.

———, ed. *African-American Voices: The Life Cycle of Slavery.* St. James, N.Y.: Brandywine Press, 1993.

Mintz, Steven, and Susan Kellogg. *Domestic Revolutions: A Social History of American Family Life.* New York: Free Press, 1988.

Moltke-Hansen, David. "The Expansion of Intellectual Life: A Prospectus." In *Intellectual Life in Antebellum Charleston,* ed. Michael O'Brien and David Moltke-Hansen, 3–42. Knoxville: University of Tennessee Press, 1986.

Moore, John Hammond. *Columbia and Richland County: A South Carolina Community, 1740–1990.* Columbia: University of South Carolina Press, 1993.

Morton, Patricia. *Discovering the Women in Slavery: Emancipating Perspectives on the American Past.* Athens: University of Georgia Press, 1996.

Mott, Wesley T., ed. *Encyclopedia of Transcendentalism.* Westport, Conn.: Greenwood Press, 1996.

Muhlenfeld, Elisabeth. *Mary Boykin Chesnut: A Biography.* Baton Rouge: Louisiana State University Press, 1981.

Nash, Gary B. *Forging Freedom: The Formation of Philadelphia's Black Community, 1720–1840.* Cambridge: Harvard University Press, 1988.

———. "Slaves and Slave Owners in Colonial Philadelphia." In *African Americans in Pennsylvania: Shifting Historical Perspectives,* ed.

Joe W. Trotter Jr. and Eric Ledell Smith, 43–72. University Park: Pennsylvania State University Press, 1997.

Oakes, James. *The Ruling Race: A History of American Slaveholders.* New York: Knopf, 1982.

———. *Slavery and Freedom: An Interpretation of the Old South.* New York: Knopf, 1990.

O'Brien, Michael, ed. *An Evening When Alone: Four Journals of Single Women in the South, 1827–1867.* Charlottesville: University Press of Virginia, 1993.

Olwell, Robert. *Masters, Slaves, and Subjects: The Culture of Power in the South Carolina Low Country, 1740–1790.* Ithaca, N.Y.: Cornell University Press, 1998.

Osagie, Iyunolu Folayan. *The Amistad Revolt: Memory, Slavery, and the Politics of Identity in the United States and Sierra Leone.* Athens: University of Georgia Press, 2000.

Osofsky, Gilbert, ed. *Puttin' On Ole Massa: The Slave Narratives of Henry Bibb, William Wells Brown, and Solomon Northrup.* New York: Harper & Row, 1969.

Painter, Nell Irvin. *Sojourner Truth: A Life, A Symbol.* New York: W. W. Norton, 1996.

Pease, Jane H., and William H. Pease. *Ladies, Women, and Wenches: Choice and Constraint in Antebellum Charleston and Boston.* Chapel Hill: University of North Carolina Press, 1990.

Poston, Carol H., ed. *A Vindication of the Rights of Woman: An Authoritative Text, Backgrounds, The Wollstonecraft Debate, Criticism.* 2d ed. New York: W. W. Norton, 1988.

Poston, Jonathan H. *The Buildings of Charleston: A Guide to the City's Architecture.* Columbia: University of South Carolina Press, 1997.

Rable, George C. *Civil Wars: Women and the Crisis of Southern Nationalism.* Urbana: University of Illinois Press, 1989.

———. *The Confederate Republic: A Revolution against Politics.* Chapel Hill: University of North Carolina Press, 1994.

Reed, James. *The Birth Control Movement and American Society: From Private Vice to Public Virtue.* Princeton: Princeton University Press, 1978.

Robertson, David. *Denmark Vesey.* New York: Knopf, 1999.

Rogers, Sherbrooke. *Sarah Josepha Hale: A New England Pioneer, 1788–1879.* Grantham, N.H.: Tompson & Rutter, 1985.

Ross, Kristie. "Arranging a Doll's House: Refined Women as Union Nurses." In *Divided Houses: Gender and the Civil War*, ed. Catherine Clinton and Nina Silber, 97–113. New York: Oxford University Press, 1992.

Rothman, David J. *The Discovery of the Asylum: Social Order and Disorder in the New Republic*. Rev. ed. Boston: Little, Brown, 1990.

Ryan, Mary P. *Womanhood in America: From Colonial Times to the Present*. New York: New Viewpoints, 1979.

———. *Cradle of the Middle Class: The Family in Oneida County, New York, 1790–1865*. New York: Cambridge University Press, 1981.

Salley, A. S., Jr. *The History of Orangeburg County, South Carolina, from its First Settlement to the Close of the Revolutionary War*. 1898. Reprint, Baltimore: Regional Publishing, 1969.

Salmon, Marylynn. "Women and Property in South Carolina: The Evidence from Marriage Settlements, 1730–1830." In *Material Life in America, 1600–1860*, ed. Robert Blair St. George, 291–309. Boston: Northeastern University Press, 1988.

Schwartz, Hillel. *Never Satisfied: A Cultural History of Diets, Fantasies, and Fat*. New York: Free Press, 1986.

Scott, Anne Firor. "Women's Perspective on the Patriarchy in the 1850s." In *Half-Sisters of History: Southern Women and the American Past*, ed. Catherine Clinton, 76–92. Durham, N.C.: Duke University Press, 1994.

———. *The Southern Lady: From Pedestal to Politics, 1830–1930*. 1970. Reprint, Charlottesville: University Press of Virginia, 1995.

Secunda, Victoria. *Women and Their Fathers: The Sexual and Romantic Impact of the First Man in Your Life*. New York: Dell Publishing, 1992.

Sellers, Charles. *The Market Revolution in Jacksonian America, 1815–1848*. New York: Oxford University Press, 1991.

Sklar, Kathryn Kish. *Catharine Beecher: A Study in American Domesticity*. New York: W. W. Norton, 1973.

Smith-Rosenberg, Carroll. *Disorderly Conduct: Visions of Gender in Victorian America*. New York: Oxford University Press, 1985.

Stone, Elizabeth. *Black Sheep and Kissing Cousins: How Our Family Stories Shape Us*. New York: Penguin Books, 1988.

Stoney, Samuel Gaillard. *The Dulles Family in South Carolina*. Columbia: R. L. Bryan, 1955.

Stowe, Harriet Beecher. *Uncle Tom's Cabin, or, Life among the Lowly.* 1852. Reprint, New York: Signet Classic, 1998.

Stowe, Steven M. *Intimacy and Power in the Old South: Ritual in the Lives of the Planters.* Baltimore: Johns Hopkins University Press, 1987.

Sutherland, Daniel. *Americans and Their Servants: Domestic Service in the United States from 1800 to 1920.* Baton Rouge: Louisiana State University Press, 1981.

Taylor, William R. *Cavalier and Yankee: The Old South and American National Character.* Cambridge: Harvard University Press, 1979.

Thorp, Margaret Farrand. *Female Persuasion: Six Strong-Minded Women.* New Haven: Yale University Press, 1949.

Trollope, Frances. *Domestic Manners of the Americans.* Ed. Donald Smalley. New York: Knopf, 1949.

Vipperman, Carl J. *William Lowndes and the Transition of Southern Politics, 1782–1822.* Chapel Hill: University of North Carolina Press, 1989.

Wade, Richard D. *Slavery in the Cities.* New York: Oxford University Press, 1964.

Wagner-Martin, Linda. *Telling Women's Lives: The New Biography.* New Brunswick, N.J.: Rutgers University Press, 1994.

Walther, Eric. *The Fire-Eaters.* Baton Rouge: Louisiana State University Press, 1992.

Washington, Margaret, ed. *Narrative of Sojourner Truth.* New York: Vintage Books, 1993.

Watson, Harry L. *Liberty and Power: The Politics of Jacksonian America.* New York: Hill & Wang, 1990.

Weiner, Marli F. *Mistresses and Slaves: Plantation Women in South Carolina, 1830–1880.* Chicago: University of Illinois Press, 1998.

———, ed. *A Heritage of Woe: The Civil War Diary of Grace Brown Elmore, 1861–1868.* Athens: University of Georgia Press, 1997.

Welter, Barbara. *Dimity Convictions: The American Woman in the Nineteenth Century.* Athens: Ohio University Press, 1976.

Wertz, Richard W., and Dorothy C. Wertz. *Lying-In: A History of Childbirth in America.* New York: Free Press, 1977.

Wharton, Anne Hollingsworth. *Salons Colonial and Republican.* Philadelphia: J. B. Lippincott, 1900.

White, Deborah Gray. *Ain't I a Woman?: Female Slaves in the Plantation South.* New York: W. W. Norton, 1985.

———. "Female Slaves: Sex Roles and Status in the Antebellum Plantation South." In *Unequal Sisters: A Multi-Cultural Reader in U.S. Women's History,* 2d ed., ed. Vicki L. Ruiz and Ellen Carol DuBois, 20–31. New York: Routledge, 1994.

Whites, Lee Ann. *The Civil War as a Crisis in Gender: Augusta, Georgia, 1860–1890.* Athens: University of Georgia Press, 1995.

Wiebe, Robert H. *The Opening of American Society: From the Adoption of the Constitution to the Eve of Disunion.* New York: Knopf, 1984.

Williams, Susan Millar. *A Devil and a Good Woman, Too: The Lives of Julia Peterkin.* Athens: University of Georgia Press, 1997.

Wilson, Edmund. *Patriotic Gore: Studies in the Literature of the American Civil War.* Boston: Northeastern University Press, 1962.

Wolfe, Margaret Ripley. *Daughters of Canaan: A Saga of Southern Women.* Lexington: University of Kentucky Press, 1995.

Woodward, C. Vann. *Reunion and Reaction: The Compromise of 1877 and the End of Reconstruction.* Rev. ed. Garden City, N.Y.: Doubleday, 1956.

———. *The Burden of Southern History.* 3d ed. Baton Rouge: Louisiana State University Press, 1993.

———, ed. *Mary Chesnut's Civil War.* New Haven: Yale University Press, 1981.

Wright, Frances. *Views of Society and Manners in America.* 1821. Reprint, ed. Paul R. Baker, Cambridge: Harvard University Press, 1963.

Wyatt-Brown, Bertram. *Southern Honor: Ethics and Behavior in the Old South.* New York: Oxford University Press, 1982.

Young, James Sterling. *The Washington Community, 1800–1828.* New York: Columbia University Press, 1966.

Index

LSM refers to Louisa S. McCord.

Abbeville plantation, S.C., 66, 70, 129, 175, 181
Abbeville plantation/farm, Pa., 8, 16, 20, 28, 143
Abolitionism: and American Colonization Society, 58, 60, 78; distribution of abolitionist materials, 79; in England, 150; and Grimke sisters, 19, 69, 114; and John Brown's raid, 149, 151; and Langdon Cheves, 80, 130; LSM's opposition to, 59–60, 75, 105, 108, 112, 113, 124; married women's support for, 69n7; in Pennsylvania, 53, 58; and Quakers, 53, 78; and Stowe's *Uncle Tom's Cabin*, 113, 150. *See also* Slavery
Africa, 58, 60, 78, 110, 111n28
African Americans. *See* Free blacks (before Civil War); Freedmen (during Reconstruction); Slavery
Alabama, 83, 89, 93, 153
Alcott, Bronson, 99
Alcott, Louisa May, 69, 75
Alzheimer's disease/dementia, 100, 114, 127, 129, 130–43, 148, 186
American Colonization Society, 58, 60, 78
American Indians. *See* Native Americans
American Revolution, 16–18, 53, 62, 67n3, 80, 83
Amistad revolt, 79
Anderson, Robert, 153, 154, 154n14
Anna (slave), 23
Apprenticeships, 44

Asia, 111, 111n28
Assassination of Lincoln, 176
Australia, 111, 111n28

Bank of South Carolina, 83
Bank of the United States, 2, 11, 26, 27, 30, 39
Bastiat, Frédéric, 36–37, 73, 101
Battery Wagner battle, 164
Bee, Rachel Susan. *See* Cheves, Rachel Susan Bee
Beecher, Catharine, 69, 75, 119
Ben (slave), 139
Bennett, Susan Smythe, 92–93
Betty (slave), 47–49, 47n11
Biddle, Nicholas, 26
Blacks. *See* Free blacks (before Civil War); Freedmen (during Reconstruction); Slavery
"Blood-Stained Rose" (McComb), 85–86, 122
Boyd (servant), 140, 142
Britain. *See* England
Brontë sisters, 122
Brown, John, 149, 150, 151
Buchanan, James, 26, 153, 154
Buist, Rev. George, 18, 19
Burns, Robert, 37
Byron, George Gordon Lord, 37, 72

Caius Gracchus: A Tragedy in Five Acts (McCord), 1, 72, 74, 81, 102, 108, 120–21
Calhoun, John C., 26, 77, 152
Canada, 2, 182

Capers and Heyward, 139
Caretaker role of women, 80–82
Carlyle, Thomas, 110n25
Catholicism. *See* Religion
Charleston, S.C.: and battle/surrender of Fort Sumter, 153, 154, 154n14; Cheves family in, 2, 14, 26, 30, 47; during Civil War, 153, 154, 154n14, 160, 166; and distribution of abolitionist materials, 79; Dulles family in, 22; elite class in, 14, 18–19; fear of slave revolts in, 54–56; imprisonment of black sailors in, 55–56; Langdon Cheves's work in, 18–19; LSM in, after Civil War, 181; LSM's birth in, 2, 14; Mary Dulles's birth in, 22; and Negro Seaman's Act, 55–56; schools in, 72; Smythe home in, 183; social life in, 66; Vesey plot in, 54–56, 54n27, 60, 79; workhouse in, 114, 139
Charleston Mercury, 155
Charlotte, N.C., 166
Chesnut, James, 158, 166
Chesnut, Mary: and battle/surrender of Fort Sumter, 154, 154n14; and childbearing, 95; on Civil War casualties, 162; and death of LSM's son, 164; and hospital duties by LSM during Civil War, 158; husband's warnings to, about end of Civil War, 166; and LSM on destruction of Columbia, S.C., 175; on LSM's intellect and character, 1, 2, 154–55, 163; on mulatto children, 113; in North Carolina during Civil War, 168; on Sherman, 167; on slaveholding, 5, 124; on southern women after Civil War, 149–50; on Union occupation of Columbia, S.C., 171n71
Chesnut family, 2
Chessler, Ellen, 33n16
Cheves, Alexander (father of Langdon Cheves), 16–20, 23, 150
Cheves, Alexander (son of Langdon Cheves), 30, 32n15
Cheves, Andrew Heatly, 30, 32
Cheves, Anna Maria. *See* Huger, Anna Maria Cheves

Cheves, Charles Manly, 32, 66n2, 70, 72, 96, 127–28, 145
Cheves, Charlotte "Lottie" Reynolds, 150, 159, 163–65, 164n48, 168
Cheves, Charlotte McCord, 83, 92, 93, 94, 133–34, 166
Cheves, David Johnson, 32, 70
Cheves, Edward, 96, 162
Cheves, Emma, 96, 166
Cheves, Harriott, 96
Cheves, Henry, 96, 96n70
Cheves, Isabella (daughter of Charles), 96
Cheves, Isabella Middleton, 66n2, 96
Cheves, John Richardson: birth of, 30; and brother Hayne's illness and death, 133, 143; children of, 96; in Civil War, 153–54; education of, 70, 76; lawsuit contesting father's will by, 144–47; marriage of, 22, 94n65; and mother's illness, 76; as tutor to younger siblings, 70
Cheves, Joseph, 23, 30, 32
Cheves, Langdon: and abolitionism, 80, 130; and American Revolution, 16–18; birth of, 16; childhood and youth of, 16–17; children of, 23, 26, 28, 30–32; commemorative statues of, after death, 143, 151, 183; courtship and marriage of, 15, 20; death and burial of, 18, 127, 143, 150, 186n19; deaths of children of, 30, 31, 32, 32n15, 70, 127, 143; dementia/Alzheimer's disease of, 100, 114, 127, 129, 130–43, 148, 186; education of, 18; in elite class, 23–24, 28; finances of, 10–11, 19, 28; freedom for slaves of, 114–15, 137–39; and Heatly family, 22–23; homes of, 26–28, 32, 71; as lawyer, 1, 15, 18–19, 27; LSM's relationship with, 1–2, 13, 37, 38–42, 67–68, 91, 94, 100, 129–40, 148, 177, 183, 185; marital relationship of, 29–30; as merchant's clerk in Charleston, 18; and mother's death, 16; papers of, 8; personality of, 40–41; as planter and slaveholder, 23, 28, 45–50, 53–55, 61, 64, 71, 72, 80, 114–15, 129–30, 144; political career

and accomplishments of, 1–2, 10–11, 19, 25–30, 38–39, 41–42, 68, 87, 130; property of, 19–20, 28, 61, 64, 66, 71, 88, 129–30, 132, 144–47; servants of, 12, 44–46, 51–52, 140, 142; stepmother of, 17, 20, 23, 94; and wife's death, 76; will of, 127, 130n7, 144–47; writings about, by LSM, 40, 41, 183

Cheves, Langdon (son of Charles), 96, 96n70

Cheves, Langdon, Jr.: birth of, 30; and brother's illness and death, 129; children of, 94, 96; in Civil War, 153; death of, 165; as executor of father's will, 144–48; and father's dementia/Alzheimer's disease, 132–34, 141; illness of, 133; and LSM as businesswoman, 89; and LSM as slaveholder, 114; and LSM's finances, 142; LSM's letters to, 9, 89, 114, 142; marriage of, 83, 92, 93; plantation and slaves of, 129, 133, 148

Cheves, Langdon III, 9, 96, 183

Cheves, Louisa. See McCord, Louisa S.

Cheves, Mary (daughter of Langdon Jr.), 96

Cheves, Mary Dulles: children of, and childbearing, 23, 26, 28, 30–32, 95, 96, 185; and children's education, 21, 31, 35; courtship and marriage of, 15, 20; death and burial of, 76; deaths of children of, 30, 31, 32, 32n15, 70; education of, 15, 20–21, 36; elite class of, 14, 16; family background of, 21–23; and father's death, 31; grave of, 143; homes of, 26–28, 32, 71; household duties of, 72; illness of, 75–76; marital relationship of, 29–30, 76; and mother's stroke, 31–32, 70–71; moves of, based on husband's career, 29–31, 32, 71; property of, 64; and religion, 76; servants of, 12, 44–46, 51–52; social graces of, 20, 41

Cheves, Mary Elizabeth (Langdon Cheves Jr.'s daughter), 166

Cheves, Mary Elizabeth (LSM's sister), 30, 31, 96, 96n70

Cheves, Mary Elizabeth "Minna" (John Cheves's daughter), 166, 168

Cheves, Mary Langdon, 16, 143

Cheves, Rachel Susan Bee: and Ann Richardson, 94n65; children of, 96; and Civil War, 166, 168, 170–71, 175; and death of Hayne Cheves, 143; marriage of, 22; and will of Ann Lovell, 64

Cheves, Robert Hayne: birth of, 32; childhood of, 128; death of, 143; education of, 70, 82; father's ignorance of illness and death of, 131, 143, 144–47; and father's will, 144–47; in Italy, 128–29, 133, 143; LSM's daughter named after, 94; LSM's relationship with, 70, 77, 128; personality of, 128; plantation for, 130; tuberculosis contracted by, 128–29, 131, 133, 143

Cheves, Sophia. See Haskell, Sophia Cheves

Cheves, Susannah, 17, 20, 23, 94

Cheves, William Dulles, 31

Cheves, William Lowndes, 31, 32

Cheves family genealogy, xi–xii, xiv

Cheves-McCord-Bee connection, xiv

Childbearing, 30–34, 33n16, 67, 70, 74–75, 95–97, 185. See also Marriage and family; Motherhood

Child rearing, 34, 74, 77, 95–97, 99. See also Marriage and family; Motherhood

Children's education. See Education

Christianity. See Religion

Churches. See Religion

Cilla (slave), 114–15, 136–40

Civil War: Battery Wagner battle of, 164; and battle/surrender of Fort Sumter, 153, 154, 154n14; burning of personal documents by LSM during, 8; casualties of, 2, 161–65, 176, 186; in Columbia, S.C., 2, 167–76; enlistments from LSM's family in, 153–54, 155; fall of Vicksburg in 1863, 165; fires in Columbia, S.C., during, 172–74, 174n78; food during, 161, 175; Gettysburg battle of, 164;

impact of generally, 149–50; and Lee's surrender, 175–76; LSM's hospital work during, 1, 2, 106, 156–59, 176, 186; LSM's patriotism during, 154–56, 158, 176; Second Manassas battle of, 162; Seven Days' battle of, 162; Sherman's total war during, 165–75, 178; and slavery, 168, 169, 178–79; Soldiers Aid Societies during, 155; supply shortages and inflation during, 158, 159, 160–61; Union blockade during, 158, 161; Union occupation of LSM's Columbia home during, 2, 170–71, 173, 174. *See also* Confederate States of America
Class. *See* Social class
Clay, Henry, 26
Clinton, Catherine, 4–5
Clothing, 71, 77, 119, 161
College of Charleston, 72, 103
Columbia, S.C.: bazaar in, during Civil War, 167–68; Cheves family in, 27; church in, 11; during Civil War, 2, 167–76; evacuation of, during Civil War, 168–69; fires in, during Civil War, 172–74, 174n78; Heatly family in, 30; hospital for Confederate troops in, 156–59, 169, 186; LSM's home in, 25; South Carolina Convention on secession (1860) in, 152; Union occupation of LSM's home in, 2, 170–71, 173, 174
"Comet" (McCord), 84
Communism, 59
Compromise of 1850, 130
Concord, Mass., 103
Confederate States of America, 153, 154–55, 178. *See also* Civil War
Congress, U.S., 26, 29, 53, 177–78
Cornelia, 1, 13
Cotton production, 22, 61, 70, 88
Courtonne, Marie Elise, 22, 61
Cousin marriage, 96n70
Covey, Edward, 114
Crime, 106, 107
Cult of domesticity, 81

"Daughters of Hope" (McCord), 81, 81n35
David Copperfield (Dickens), 141
Davis, Jefferson, 153, 154, 155
DeBow, James, 103
"Dedication: To My Father" (McCord), 39
De Leon, Dr., 76
Delta plantation, 93, 93n64, 94, 129
Dementia/Alzheimer's disease, 100, 114, 127, 129, 130–43, 148
Democracy, rhetoric of, 125, 184
Democratic party, 152, 182
Dickens, Charles, 141
Dickinson, Emily, 40n34
Dinah (Maum Di; slave), 97, 99, 168, 180
Dobson, Joanne, 40n34
Domesticity, cult of, 81
Domestic violence, 116, 117n39
Douglas, Stephen A., 152
Douglass, Frederick, 113, 114
Dred Scott case, 53, 112n31
Dulles, Joseph Heatly, 15–16, 22, 27, 31, 51, 64, 141
Dulles, Mary. *See* Cheves, Mary Dulles
Dulles, Sophia Heatly: childbearing by, 96; family background of, 61, 83; grandnieces of, 94n65; property and slaves of, 22, 63, 64; servants of, 51; stroke of, 31–32, 70–71; as widow, 27, 31–32
Dupin, Amandine-Aurore-Lucile, 122
DuPont, Eleuthera, 7, 8, 35, 36, 66
DuPont, Eleuthère Irénée, 36
DuPont, Sophia, 36

Eacker, Susan A., 117n39
Education: of boys and men, 12, 18, 21, 25, 28, 31, 36, 38, 70, 72, 82, 94, 98–99; experiential approach to, 98–99; of girls and women, 12, 13, 20–21, 25–26, 28, 31, 35–38, 70, 72, 98–99, 119; LSM's approach to, with her children, 97–99; mother's role in education of her children, 21, 31, 35, 77, 97–99; southern colleges compared with northern universities,

102–3; tutors for young children, 35, 70, 72, 77, 98

Egypt, 110n23

Elite class. *See* Social class

Elizabeth, Queen, 121

Elliot, George, 122

Elmore, Grace Brown, 167–69, 172, 173, 175

Emancipation of slaves. *See* Manumission of slaves

Emancipation Proclamation, 177

Emerson, Ralph Waldo, 99

"Enfranchisement of Woman" (McCord), 91

England, 106, 110n25, 111, 111n28, 148, 150, 151

Enlightenment, 119

Equality of women. *See* Women's rights movement

Evans, Mary Ann, 122

"Falling Star" (McCord), 84, 87, 122

Family. *See* Marriage and family

Female Persuasion: Six Strong-Minded Women (Thorp), 3–4

Femininity. *See* Womanhood

Feminism. *See* Women's rights movement

"Fire-fly" (McCord), 73

"First Star of the Evening" (McCord), 40

Fitzhugh, George, 104, 105

Florida, 153, 182

Food, 161, 175

Fort Moultrie, 153

Fort Sumter, 153, 154, 154n14

Fort Wagner, 153, 154

Fox-Genovese, Elizabeth, 4–6

France, 148, 151

Fraser, Jesse Melville, 1, 3, 3n2, 8

Free blacks (before Civil War): and churches, 57–58; imprisonment of black sailors, 55–56; LSM on, 56, 57, 59–60, 110; middle and elite classes of, in Philadelphia, 57; and Negro Seamen's Act, 55–56; in Pennsylvania, 56–61; poverty of, 43–44, 56–61, 111; relocation of, to Africa, 58, 60; as

servants, 50, 51–52; and workhouses, 114; working class of, 57–61. *See also* Freedmen (during Reconstruction)

Freedmen (during Reconstruction), 178–82

Freedom, 109, 111, 118

Freedom for slaves. *See* Abolitionism; Emancipation Proclamation; Manumission of slaves

Fugitive Slave Law, 112n31

Fugitive slaves, 51–54, 58, 112n31

Garrison, William Lloyd, 78

Gender. *See* Manhood; Womanhood; Women slaveholders

Georgia, 72, 93, 153, 158, 165–66, 167, 175

Germany, 151

Gettysburg battle, 164

Gilbert, Sandra M., 40n34

Glatthaar, Joseph T., 174n78

Godey's Ladies Book, 69

Goldsmith, Oliver, 37

Goodwyn, Thomas L., 167, 170

Government intervention, 107–8, 117

Grant, Ulysses S., 165

Gray, Thomas, 37

Great Britain. *See* England

Greek civilization, 102

Grimke, Angelina, 19, 114, 117n39, 185

Grimke, Sarah, 19, 69, 69n6, 75, 114, 117n39, 185

Grimke, Thomas, 19

Gubar, Susan, 40n34

Gulla Jack, 56

Haiti, 110, 110n25

Hale, Sarah Josepha, 69

Hall, Ainsley, 47n11, 83

Hammond, James Henry, 103–4, 114

Hampton, Wade, 169, 182

Harpers Ferry raid, 149, 151

Harry (slave), 23, 46–50, 47n11

Harvard, 103

Haskell, Alexander, 162, 164

Haskell, Charles (son of Sophia Haskell), 164

Haskell, Charles Thompson, 64, 66–67, 70, 129, 144–47

Haskell, Jennie, 160
Haskell, John, 162
Haskell, Langdon, 143
Haskell, Rebecca Singleton, 162
Haskell, Sophia Cheves: birth of, 30; and brothers' deaths, 127, 128; children of, 67, 74, 95, 96; and Civil War, 154; education of, 35–36; and father's dementia/Alzheimer's disease, 133; and father's will, 145, 146, 147; finances of, 11; and grandmother's death, 16; and housewifery training, 33, 34–35; on Langdon Cheves' youth, 16, 17, 18; letters of, 7, 8, 9; marriage of, 64, 66–67, 96n70; and marriage of grandparents, 15; siblings of, 30–33, 35, 128; on social life in South Carolina, 66; as tutor of siblings, 35
Haskell, Sophia Louisa, 159–60
Haskell, William, 164
Hawaii, 180
Hayes, Rutherford, 182
Hayne, Robert, 94, 94–95n67
Health reform for women, 119, 119n44
Heatly, Andrew, 63, 64
Heatly, Ann. See Lovell, Ann Heatly Reid
Heatly, Marie Elise Courtonne, 22, 61
Heatly, Rachel. See Richardson, Rachel Heatly
Heatly, Sophia. See Dulles, Sophia Heatly
Heatly, William, 22, 61, 83
Heatly-Dulles-Cheves family tree, xi
Heatly family, 20, 22–23
Heyward, Joseph Manigault, 129
Hierarchical relationships: and affluent blacks, 57; and LSM's conflict between desire for order versus individual fulfillment and independence, 9–10, 12–13, 65, 67, 75, 98, 99–100; of paternalism, 5, 12, 60–61, 65, 101–2; racial hierarchy in New South, 186; and separate spheres for men and women, 29, 68n4, 117–21; and slavery, 5, 12, 60–61, 103–6, 108, 112, 115, 118; in wage labor system, 45; and white superiority, 103–6, 108, 112; and

women's physical weakness versus men's physical strength, 86, 115–21, 124, 125; women's role in hierarchy, 25, 101–2, 115–26, 185, 186
Holland, 151
Hospital work during Civil War, 1, 2, 106, 156–59, 169, 176, 186
Household management, 33, 34–35, 45, 70–72, 76–77
Howard, Oliver O., 2, 166, 169, 171, 173
Huger, Anna Maria Cheves: birth of, 31; and childbearing, 95, 96; and Civil War, 166; education of, 35, 70, 72; and father's dementia/Alzheimer's disease, 133; and father's will, 147; marriage of, 11, 48, 66n2, 129; and McCord's courtship of LSM, 92; and mother's death, 76; slaves of, 48
Huger, Thomas Pinckney, 48, 66n2, 129, 143
Huger family, 2

Immigrants, 16, 22, 50, 57, 98, 106, 116
Incidents in the Life of a Slave Girl (Jacobs), 113
Indentured servitude, 44–45, 46, 51–54
Indians. See Native Americans
Industrialization, 44, 78, 80, 106, 116
Inferiority. See Hierarchical relationships
Intelligence of women, 115–16, 118–20, 124, 125
Ireland, 106, 111, 111n28
Irish immigrants, 22, 50, 57
Italy, 148, 151

Jackson, Stonewall, 155
Jacobs, Harriet, 113
Jamaica, 110
Jefferson, Thomas, 60, 104, 152
Johnson, Andrew, 177
Johnson, Michael P., 54n27
Jones, William, 47, 47n11
June (slave), 114–15, 137–40

Keats, John, 72
Kentucky Resolutions, 152
Ku Klux Klan, 181, 182

Labor: apprenticeships, 44; bargaining power of domestic servants, 51–52; black servants, 50, 51–52; black working class, 57–61; immigrants in Philadelphia, 57; indentured servitude, 44–45, 46, 51–54; laboring class as foundation of society, 103–4; paternalism of employer-employee relationships, 45; poverty of working class, 60–61, 106–9; resistance of servants, 50–54; servants of Cheves family, 12, 44–46, 51–52, 140, 142; servants of LSM, 175, 178; wage labor system, 12, 44–46, 48, 52, 78, 80, 104–9; working class versus slavery, 105–9, 184–85. *See also* Slavery

Lancaster, Pa., 28, 39, 44, 52–53, 58

Lancaster County Historical Society, 8

Land. *See* Property

Langdon, Patty, 16

Lang Syne plantation, 22, 64, 76, 82, 88–91, 98, 99, 141, 143, 151, 155–56, 179, 180, 180n8, 185

LeConte, Emma, 161, 167, 168, 169, 171–73

Lewis (slave), 23, 46, 49, 50, 51, 53–54

Liberator, 78–80

Liberty. *See* Freedom

Lieber, Francis, 2, 103

Lincoln, Abraham, 152, 154, 176, 177

Logan, John A., 171n71

Lost Cause, 180–81, 183

Louisiana, 153, 182

Lounsbury, Richard C., 1, 6–8, 7n5

Love. *See* Marriage and family; Romantic love

"Love, Wisdom and Folly" (McCord), 85

Lovell, Ann Heatly Reid: birth of, 61; children of, 62; and cotton production, 22, 61; family background of, 61; grave of, 76, 143; marriage of, 8, 62–64, 64n52, 91; in poetry by LSM, 85; as property owner and slaveholder, 22, 61–64; visitors of, 26, 66–67, 71, 83; will of, 64, 64n52

Lovell, James, 62–63, 64n52, 91

Lowndes, William, 8, 20, 38

Loyalty oath, 177, 180–81

Lucas, Marion Brunson, 174n78

Madison, James, 152

Manassas, Second battle of, 162

Manhood: and intelligence, 116, 118–19; and physical strength versus women's physical weakness, 86, 115–21, 124, 125; and property, 91; separate spheres for men and women, 29, 68n4, 117–21. *See also* Paternalism

Manumission of slaves, 46, 50, 53–55, 114–15, 137–38

Marianne (slave), 137, 168

Marriage and family: and childbearing, 30–34, 33n16, 67, 70, 74–75, 95–97, 185; and child rearing, 34, 74, 77, 95–97, 99; companionate marriage, 68, 68n4; cousin marriage, 96n70; and financial security for women, 61–62; household management role in, 33, 34–35, 45, 70–72, 76–77, 82; husband's/father's role in family, 40, 41–42, 45; marriage of migration, 29–30; marriage of separation, 29–30; and motherhood, 74, 80–82, 95–97, 123; mother's role in education of her children, 21, 31, 35, 77, 97–99; in nineteenth-century America generally, 15; number of children in families, 95–96; and romantic love, 84–86; separate spheres for men and women in, 29, 68n4, 117–21; slave families, 47–48, 114–15, 136–40; and southern womanhood, 9–10, 12–13, 185–86

Marshall, William, 18

Marx, Karl, 104

Maum Di (slave), 97, 99, 168, 180

Maum Lucy (slave), 137, 168

Maum Rache (slave), 168, 169

McCord, Ann, 83

McCord, Anna, 93

McCord, Charlotte, 83, 92, 93, 94, 96, 133–34

McCord, David (son of David James McCord), 93

McCord, David James: children of, 1, 2, 25, 83, 86, 88, 90, 92–95, 97,

135–37, 185, 186; as college trustee, 103; cousins of, 94n65; death, funeral, and burial of, 2, 89, 97, 100, 127, 148, 150, 186n19; deaths of children of, 93; family background of, 82–83, 88; first marriage of, 83, 88, 92–93; genealogy of, xiii; grandchild of, 93; as husband of LSM, 2, 10, 12–13; legal and political career of, 83, 87; life of, before marriage to LSM, 7, 83; marriage of, to LSM, 82, 83–95, 99–100, 185–86; as overseer of Lang Syne, 90; personality of, 86; physical appearance of, 86; and property, 87–91; and publication of LSM's writings, 3n2; and religion, 97; and Texas land, 130; will of, 90

McCord, Emma, 93, 94

McCord, Emmeline Wagner, 84, 88, 92, 93, 95

McCord, Hannah Cheves: birth of, 94, 95; childhood and education of, 97, 98, 136, 137, 150; and Civil War, 157, 168, 174; death of, 182; female friendships of, 150, 159, 160; and grandfather's illness, 136, 137; marriage of, 160, 181

McCord, Henry James, 93, 94

McCord, John, 82–83

McCord, Joseph, 83, 96n70

McCord, Julia, 93, 94

McCord, Langdon Cheves (son of LSM): birth of, 94, 95; childhood and education of, 90, 97, 98, 136, 137; in Civil War, 153–54, 155, 162–64; college education of, 153; death of, 164, 164n48; and grandfather's illness, 136, 137; marriage of, 159; and plantation life, 90; and trip to Europe, 147, 150–51; vision problems of, 150, 151

McCord, Langdon Cheves "Chev" (granddaughter of LSM), 96n70, 165, 168

McCord, Lorain, 93

McCord, Louisa Rebecca Hayne. See Smythe, Louisa "Lou" Rebecca Hayne McCord

McCord, Louisa S.: biographical sketch of, 1–3; birth of, 2, 14, 23, 186; in Charleston home of daughter Lou and Gus Smythe, 183–84; childhood and youth of, 2, 5–6, 12, 24–26, 32–35; children of and childbearing, 1, 2, 25, 90, 94–95, 97, 135–37, 185, 186; and Civil War, 1, 2, 22, 106, 153–76; Civil War hospital work by, 1, 22, 106, 156–59, 176, 186; death and gravesite of, 3, 184, 186, 186n19; deaths of brothers of, 127–29, 143, 144, 148, 165, 186; deaths of children of, 163–64, 164n48, 182, 186; depression of, after Civil War, 2, 176, 180–81; education and intellectual interests of, 12, 13, 21, 25, 26, 28, 35–38, 72, 98–100, 103, 185; education of children of, 97–99; in elite class, 14, 42; and father, 1–2, 13, 37, 38–42, 67–68, 91, 94, 100, 129–40, 148, 177, 183, 185; and father's death, 127, 143–44, 148, 150; and father's dementia/Alzheimer's disease, 100, 114, 127, 129, 130–43, 148, 186; finances of, 10, 142, 144; and freedmen after Civil War, 179; and freedom for father's slaves, 114–15, 137–39; genealogy of, xi–xiv; grandchildren of, 165, 182, 183–84; health problems and failing vision of, 3, 144, 147–48, 150, 151, 184; homes of, 26–28, 32, 71, 170–71, 184; household duties of, 70–72, 76–77, 82; and husband's children by first wife, 92–94; and husband's death, 97, 100, 127, 144, 148, 150; inheritance of, from father, 144–47; and Lang Syne plantation, 22, 64, 88–91, 98, 99, 141, 151, 155–56, 179, 185; and lawsuit contesting father's will, 144–47; and Lost Cause, 180–81, 183; and loyalty oath, 180–81; marriage of, 2, 3, 6, 9–10, 12–13, 25, 82, 83–95, 99–100, 185–86; and mother's final illness and death, 75–76; name used by, 3n2; nursing duties of, within family, 70–71, 72, 75–76, 77; papers of and documentation on, 6–9, 114; patriotism of, during Civil

War, 154–55, 158, 176; personality of, 1, 67; as plantation manager and slaveholder, 10, 64–65, 70, 89–91, 98, 99, 114–15, 136–41, 144, 148, 155–56, 168, 178, 185; property of, 2, 12, 13, 64–65, 87–91, 98, 99, 136–37, 185; and religion, 11, 25, 59, 97–98; scholarly work on, 3–8; sculpture of, by Hiram Powers, 151; siblings of, 30–33, 70, 128; significance of, 1–2, 184–86; single status of, 2, 6, 12, 64–65, 67–77, 82, 87, 92, 185; and son's injury and death, 162–64, 164n48, 186; trip to Canada by, 2, 182; trip to Europe by, 147, 148, 150–51; as tutor of siblings, 70, 72, 77; Union occupation of Columbia home of, during Civil War, 2, 170–71, 173, 174; as widow, 100

—views of: conflict between desire for order versus individual fulfillment and independence, 9–10, 12–13, 65, 67, 75, 98, 99–100; defense of slavery and paternalism, 2, 3, 6, 12, 43–44, 58–61, 65, 101–26, 176, 184–86; on equality of women, 118–21; on freedom, 109, 111, 118; on government intervention, 107–8, 117; on secession of southern states, 152–53, 176; on separate spheres for men and women, 117–21; on social reform, 107–8; on wage labor and working class, 105–9; on women's inferiority, 115–18, 124, 125–26; on women's rights movement, 121, 125–26

—writings by: book reviews, 99, 101; essays, 1, 2, 3, 11, 36, 37, 43, 73, 99, 101, 117, 119, 122–23, 186; LSM's gender identity in, 121–23; play *Caius Gracchus*, 1, 36, 37, 72, 74, 81, 102, 108, 120–21; poetry, 1, 3, 10, 11, 36, 37, 39–40, 72–73, 81, 84–87, 101, 122; publication of writings, 3, 3n2, 37, 73, 87, 99, 100, 119, 186; translation of Bastiat's *Sophismes Economiques*, 36–37, 73, 101

McCord, Mary Eliza, 93, 94
McCord, Mary Elizabeth "Bet," 64, 64n65

McCord, Russell (father of Russell Paul), 83
McCord, Russell Paul (brother of David James McCord), 83, 88, 89, 94
McCord, Russell Paul (son of David James McCord), 93, 94
McCord, Turquand, 93, 94
McCord's Reports, 83
Meriwether, R. L., 92–93
Middle class. *See* Social class
Middleton, Isabella, 66n2, 96
Middleton family, 2, 66, 66n2
Miles, William Porcher, 2, 72, 103, 162
"Mirage" (McCord), 73
Miscegenation, 113
Mississippi, 153
Missouri Compromise (1820), 78–79
Monroe, James, 26
Monument Association, 181, 183
Moore, John Hammond, 174n78
Motherhood, 74, 80–82, 95–97, 123. *See also* Childbearing; Child rearing
Motte, Elizabeth, 67, 67n3
Mulatto, 113
"My Dream Child" (McCord), 73
My Dreams (McCord), 37, 39–40, 73, 81

Nancy (slave), 23, 46, 49, 55
Napoleonic Wars, 26
Nashville Convention (1850), 130
Native Americans, 60, 111, 111n28
"Negro-mania" (McCord), 43
Negro Seaman's Act, 55–56
Newport, R.I., 28, 32
New York, 103
Nightingale, Florence, 156
North Carolina, 166, 168
Northwest Ordinance, 78
Nullification Crisis, 77–78, 80, 83, 95n67, 130, 152, 153
Nursing duties: in Civil War hospital, 156–59, 186; in families, 70–71, 72, 75–76, 77

O'Brien, Michael, 1

Panic of 1819, 10–11, 63, 88
Panic of late 1830s, 10

Paternalism: breakdown of, by northern working class, 60–61, 108, 125; breakdown of, during Civil War, 175; of employer-employee relationships, 45; LSM's defense of, 2, 3, 6, 65, 101–26, 176, 184–86; and slavery, 45, 48–50, 101–2, 104, 111–13; violence required for preservation of, 112, 113–14, 116, 117n39, 126; women's role in hierarchy, 25, 101–2, 185, 186
Patriarchal society. See Paternalism
Pease, Joseph, 19
Pendleton, S.C., 66, 71, 72, 79–80, 94, 129, 130
Pennsylvania: Abbeville plantation/farm in, 8, 16, 20, 28; Cheves family homes in, 26–28; Cheves family in, 2, 5–6, 8, 11, 16, 26–28, 30, 39, 44, 46, 49, 51–53; churches in, 11; free blacks in, 56–61; fugitive slaves and indentured servants in, 52–53, 58; Lewis's move to, as indentured servant, 46, 49, 53; and Lewis's suit for freedom, 53; literary and artistic movements in, 103; LSM's trip to Philadelphia in 1856, 141; race riots in Philadelphia, 57; schools in Philadelphia, 21, 36, 39, 72; servants of Cheves family in, 51–53
Peterkin, Julia, 10, 180n8
Peterkin, William G., 180n8
Philadelphia: Cheves family in, 26, 27–28, 30, 44, 49; free blacks in, 56–57; Lewis's move to, as indentured servant, 46, 49, 53; and Lewis's suit for freedom, 53; literary and artistic movements in, 103; LSM's trip to, in 1856, 141; race riots in, 57; runaway slaves and indentured servants in, 52; schools in, 21, 36, 39, 72; and Vesey plot in Charleston, 55. See also Pennsylvania
Phoebe (slave), 23
Physical weakness of women, 86, 115–21, 124, 125
Physick, Synge, 31
Pinckney family, 66, 66n2

Plantation Mistress (Clinton), 4–5
Pliny (slave), 23
Plutarch, 72
Poetry, 1, 3, 10, 11, 36, 37, 39–40, 72–73, 81, 84–87, 101, 122
Port Royal, S.C., 158
Potter, John, 27, 55, 56
Poverty: of free blacks, 43–44, 56–61, 111; of working class, 60–61, 106–9
Powell, John W., 129
Powers, Hiram, 143, 151, 183
Powers, Preston, 183
Pregnancy. See Childbearing; Motherhood
Presidential election of 1860, 152
Presidential election of 1876, 182
Preston family, 2
"Pretty Fanny" (McCord), 85, 86
Privilege, 42
Property: of Ann Lovell, 61–64; investment in western land, 89, 91; of Langdon Cheves, 19–20, 28, 61, 64, 66, 71, 88, 129–30, 132, 144–47; of LSM, 2, 12, 13, 64–65, 70, 87–91, 136–37, 185; and manhood, 91; slavery as institution of, 28, 61, 112n31; and will of Langdon Cheves, 144–47; women's ownership of, 2, 12, 13, 61–65, 70, 87–91. See also Slavery; Women slaveholders
Protestantism. See Religion
Pseudonyms of female authors, 122

Quakers, 53, 78

Race riots, 57
Racial amalgamation, 111, 113, 185
Rape of slaves, 112, 113
Reconstruction, 176–80, 182
Reid, William, 62
Religion, 11, 25, 59, 76, 97–98
Reproduction. See Childbearing; Motherhood
Republican Motherhood, 80–82, 123
Republican party, 105n14, 152, 177, 182
Reynolds, Charlotte "Lottie." See Cheves, Charlotte "Lottie" Reynolds
Reynolds, John, 159, 181

Rhett, Hannah Cheves McCord. *See* McCord, Hannah Cheves
Rhett, John Taylor, 160, 181
Rhode Island, 28, 32, 141
Rice production, 67
Richardson, Ann, 94, 94n65
Richardson, Edward, 62, 64
Richardson, Rachel Heatly, 22, 62, 63, 64
"Right to Labor" (McCord), 122
Rolla (slave), 56
Roman civilization, 1, 7n5, 13, 72, 74, 81, 102, 108, 120–21
Romantic love, 84–86
Romantic poets, 37, 72
Runaway slaves and indentured servants, 51–54, 58
Rutledge family, 66

Sacrifice and duty of women, 122, 123, 127, 148, 176, 184, 185, 186
St. Domingue, 54, 55
Sale of slaves, 114–15, 139–40
Sand, George, 122
Sanger, Margaret, 33n16
Savannah, Ga., 72, 93, 166
Scarlet Sister Mary (Peterkin), 180n8
Scotland, 150, 151
Scott, Anne Firor, 4
Scott, Dred, 53, 112n31
Scott, Sir Walter, 98
Sea Islands, Ga., 158, 165
Secession of southern states, 130, 149, 152–53, 176
Second Manassas battle, 162
Seneca Falls Convention (1848), 115
Separate spheres for men and women, 29, 68n4, 117–21
Servants: bargaining power of, 51–52; black servants, 50, 51–52; of Cheves family, 12, 44–46, 51–52, 140, 142; child rearing by, 96–97, 99; indentured servants, 46, 49, 53; of LSM, 175, 178; resistance of, 50–54. *See also* Labor; Slavery
Seven Days' battle, 162
Sewing of clothing, 71, 77
Sexual abuse of slaves, 112, 113

Sexuality, 33–34, 33n16, 113. *See also* Childbearing
Shakespeare, William, 37, 72, 98, 146
Sherman, William Tecumseh, 165–75, 178
Simms, William Gilmore, 2, 103
Single women, 67–77, 82, 87, 92, 185
Slaveholding women. *See* Women slaveholders
Slave revolts, 8, 11, 54–56, 60, 79, 109, 149
Slavery: Ann Lovell as slaveholder, 61–64; benevolence toward slaves, 46–50; British abolition of, 110n25; and Cheves family, 11–12, 23, 44, 45–50, 53–55, 61, 72, 114–15, 136–40, 144, 148; child-rearing duties of slaves, 74, 77, 97, 99; and Civil War, 168, 169, 178–79; as class system, 5; end of, in U.S., 177–78, 186; families of slaves, 47–48, 114–15, 136–40; Fitzhugh's defense of, 104, 105; household duties of slaves, 72, 77; income from hiring out slaves, 23; as institution of property, 28, 61, 112n31; LSM as slaveholder, 10, 12, 64–65, 70, 114–15, 136–40, 144, 148, 168, 178, 185; LSM's defense of, 2, 3, 6, 12, 43–44, 58–61, 65, 101–13, 118, 125, 176, 184–86; manumission of slaves, 46, 50, 53–55, 114–15, 137–38; and nature of blacks according to LSM, 56, 57, 59–60, 109–10; and paternalism, 45, 48–50, 101–2, 104, 111–13; in Pennsylvania, 44; plantation mistresses' relationship with generally, 4–5, 124, 140, 140n39; and religion, 98; resistance of and retaliation by slaves, 50–56, 139; and Roman civilization, 102; runaway slaves, 51–54, 58; sale of slaves, 114–15, 139–40; sexual abuse of slaves by masters, 112, 113; and slave revolts, 8, 11, 54–56, 60, 79, 109, 149; status of women compared with slaves, 116, 117; in territories, 78–79; violence against slaves by masters, 112, 113–14; and western civilization, 110–11, 112; white superiority as justification for,

103–6, 108, 112; and workhouses, 114, 139; working class versus, 105–9, 184–85. *See also* Abolitionism; Women slaveholders

Smyth, Thomas, 2, 9, 159, 159n29

Smythe, Augustine T. "Gus": children of, 183–84; in Civil War, 153, 159, 166, 166n56, 168; college education of, 153, 159; courtship and engagement of, 9, 159–60; father of, 9, 159, 159n29; home of, in Charleston, 183; and Lang Syne plantation, 179, 180; as lawyer, 183; and loyalty oath, 181; marriage of, 179, 180; spelling of last name of, 159n29

Smythe, Hannah, 183

Smythe, Louisa "Lou" Rebecca Hayne McCord: birth of, 94–95; and brother's injury and death, 163, 164, 164n48; childhood and education of, 97–99; children of, 183–84; and Civil War, 157, 161–62, 168–74; courtship and engagement of, 159–60; and father's death, 97; father's relationship with, 86; and freedmen after Civil War, 179–80; and grandfather's illness, 136, 136n26, 137; home of, in Charleston, 183; and Lang Syne plantation, 179, 180; on LSM's business dealings, 89; and LSM's final illness and death, 184; on LSM's hospital duties during Civil War, 156; LSM's life in home of, 183–84; and LSM's reaction to her father's dementia/Alzheimer's disease, 141; and loyalty oath, 181; marriage of, 179, 180; memoirs of, 7–8, 9, 10; and niece Chev, 165; romance between Augustus Smythe and, 9; on sculpture of LSM by Hiram Powers, 151; and secession of South Carolina, 152; on slaves during Civil War, 178; on Stowe's *Uncle Tom's Cabin*, 150; and trip to Europe, 147, 150–51

Smythe, Loula, 183–84

Smythe, Susie, 184

Social class: black working class, 57–61; and Cheves family, 14, 16, 23–24, 28; in Civil War hospital, 158; and class warfare, 108; elite class in Charleston, 14, 18–19; and family size, 95–96; free black middle and elite classes in Philadelphia, 57; immigrant working class in Philadelphia, 57; laboring class as foundation of society, 103–4; of LSM, 14, 42; Marx on working class, 104; and religion, 97–98; slavery as class system, 5; slavery versus working class, 105–9, 184–85; urban middle class, 80, 95

Socialism, 59, 108, 109, 185

Social reform, 106–8

Sophismes Economiques (Bastiat), 36–37, 73, 101

South America, 180

South Carolina. *See* Charleston, S.C.; Columbia, S.C.; and other specific cities and towns

South Carolina College, 1, 2, 103, 153, 156, 159, 161

South Carolina Convention on secession (1860), 152

South Carolina Historical Society, 7, 8, 9

South Carolina legislature, 19, 83

South Carolina Monument Association, 181, 183

South Carolina Zouaves, 155

Southern Lady (Scott), 4

Southern womanhood. *See* Womanhood; Women slaveholders

South Field plantation, 145, 147

Spinsterhood, 67–77, 82, 87, 92, 185

"Spirit of the Storm" (McCord), 73

States' rights, 83, 130

Stepney (slave), 23

Stowe, Harriet Beecher, 113, 150

"Sunbeam Sprite" (McCord), 73

Switzerland, 151

Tariffs, 77–78, 80

Texas, 89, 91, 129–30, 130n7, 153

Thirteenth Amendment, 178

Thoreau, Henry David, 99

Thorp, Margaret Farrand, 3–4
Tilden, Samuel, 182
Tilgham, William, 53
"'Tis but Thee, Love, Only Thee"
  (McCord), 84
"To a Fly" (McCord), 73
Tom (slave), 168
Treadwell, James D., 138
Truth, Sojourner, 119n44
Tuberculosis, 128–29, 131, 133, 143
Turner, Nat, 60, 79, 109

Uncle Tom's Cabin (Stowe), 113, 150
U.S. Congress, 26, 29, 53, 177–78
University of North Carolina, 8
University of South Carolina, 3,
  7, 92. See also South Carolina
  College
University of Virginia, 103
Unmarried state for women, 67–77, 82,
  87, 92, 185
Urbanization, 106–7, 116
Urban reformers, 106–8

Vesey, Denmark, 8, 11, 54–56, 54n27, 60,
  79, 109
Vicksburg, fall of, 165
"Village Churchyard" (McCord), 37
Violence: domestic violence, 116,
  117n39; and Ku Klux Klan, 181, 182;
  and preservation of paternalism, 112,
  113–14, 116, 117n39, 126; riots during
  elections of 1876, 182; slave revolts,
  8, 11, 54–56, 60, 79, 109, 149; against
  slaves, 112, 113–14
Virginia, 58, 60, 109, 162–64, 165
Virginia Resolutions, 152

Wage labor system, 12, 44–46, 48, 52,
  78, 80, 104–9. See also Labor
Wales, Prince of, 151
War of 1812, 26, 27, 29, 30, 38–39, 53
Washington, George, 62
Washington, D.C., 2, 26, 28, 29, 30, 38,
  41
West Indies, 110n25
Westminster Quarterly, 123
White superiority, 103–6, 108, 112

"Who Dares to Say They Died?"
  (McCord), 40
Whooping cough, 31
Widowhood, 69, 75, 100
Within the Plantation Household (Fox-
  Genovese), 4–6
Womanhood: caretaker role of women,
  80–82; and childbearing, 30–34,
  67, 70, 74–75, 95–97, 185; and
  child rearing, 34, 74, 77, 95–97, 99;
  compared with Roman matron, 7n5,
  13, 120–21; and cult of domesticity, 81;
  and education of girls and women, 12,
  13, 20–21, 25–26, 28, 31, 35–38, 98–99,
  119; and female authors disguising
  their gender, 121–22; and health
  reform for women, 119, 119n44; and
  hierarchical relationships, 25, 101–2,
  115–26; and household management,
  33, 34–35, 45, 70–72, 76–77, 82; and
  inferiority of women, 115–18, 124,
  125–26; and intelligence, 115–16,
  118–20, 124, 125; and marriage, 9–10,
  12–13, 185–86; and motherhood, 74,
  80–82, 95–97, 123; and mother's role
  in education of her children, 21, 31, 35,
  77, 97–99; and nursing duties during
  Civil War, 156–59; and nursing duties
  within family, 70–71, 72, 75–76, 77;
  and ownership of property, 2, 12, 13,
  61–65, 70, 87–91; physical weakness
  of women versus men's physical
  strength, 86, 115–21, 124, 125; private
  sphere for women, 80–82; role of,
  in hierarchy, 25, 101–2, 115–26, 185,
  186; and sacrifice and duty, 122, 123,
  127, 148, 176, 184, 185, 186; separate
  spheres for men and women, 29,
  68n4, 117–21; and sexuality, 33–34,
  33n16; single women's role and
  status, 67–77, 82, 87, 92, 185; and
  social graces, 20; status of slaves
  compared with women, 116, 117;
  and verbal abuse by men, 87; and
  widowhood, 69, 75, 100. See also
  Women slaveholders
"Woman's Progress" (McCord), 86–87,
  91

Women slaveholders: Ann Lovell as, 61–64; Chesnut as, 5, 124; LSM as, 10, 12, 64–65, 70, 99, 114–15, 136–40, 144, 148, 168, 178, 185; and miscegenation, 113; physical and supervisory labor of, 77n26; relationship between slaves and, 4–5, 124, 140, 140n39; Sophia Heatly Dulles as, 22, 64; and violence against slaves, 114

Women's rights movement, 69, 69nn6–7, 115, 116–19, 116n38, 121, 123, 125
Workhouses, 114, 139
Working class. *See* Labor; Social class
Wright, Fanny, 50

Yale, 103

Zimmerman, Daniel, 180

About the Author

 LEIGH FOUGHT is Associate Professor of History at Le Moyne College. She is the author of *Mystic, Connecticut: From Pequot Village to Tourist Town* and *Women in the World of Frederick Douglass*. She lives in Fayetteville, New York.

Living Well at Others' Expense

Stephan Lessenich

Living Well at Others' Expense

The Hidden Costs of Western Prosperity

Translated by Nick Somers
with the assistance of Stephan Lessenich

polity

First published in German as *Neben uns die Sintflut. Die Externalisierungsgesellschaft und ihr Preis* © Hanser Berlin im Carl Hanser Verlag, Munich, 2016

This English edition © Polity Press, 2019

The translation of this work was supported by a grant from the Goethe-Institut.

Polity Press
65 Bridge Street
Cambridge CB2 1UR, UK

Polity Press
101 Station Landing
Suite 300
Medford, MA 02155, USA

ISBN-13: 978-1-5095-2562-1

A catalogue record for this book is available from the British Library.

Library of Congress Cataloging-in-Publication Data

Names: Lessenich, Stephan, author.
Title: Living well at others' expense : the hidden costs of Western prosperity / Stephan Lessenich.
Other titles: Neben uns die Sintflut. English
Description: Medford, MA : polity, 2019. | "First published ... as Neben uns die Sintflut. Die Externalisierungsgesellschaft und ihr Preis." | Includes bibliographical references and index.
Identifiers: LCCN 2018041739 (print) | LCCN 2018043141 (ebook) | ISBN 9781509525652 (Epub) | ISBN 9781509525621 (hardback)
Subjects: LCSH: Social change–Economic aspects. | Globalization–Economic aspects. | Poverty–Social aspects–Developing countries. | Equality–Economic aspects. | Income distribution. | Environmental degradation–Developing countries.
Classification: LCC HM831 (ebook) | LCC HM831 .L4713 2019 (print) | DDC 339.22–dc23
LC record available at https://lccn.loc.gov/2018041739

Typeset in 11 on 13 Serif by Toppan Bestset

Printed and bound in Great Britain by CPI Group (UK) Ltd, Croydon

For further information on Polity, visit our website:
politybooks.com

It is a pervasive condition of empires that they affect great swathes of the planet without the empire's populace being aware of the impact – indeed, without being aware that many of the affected places even exist.

Rob Nixon, *Slow Violence and the Environmentalism of the Poor* (2011)

Contents

1 Next to Us, the Deluge   1

2 Externalization: A Relational Perspective
   on Social Inequality   19

3 Live and Let Die: Externalization as an
   Unequal Exchange   54

4 Within Versus Without: Externalization
   as a Monopoly on Mobility   92

5 We Have To Talk: We Can't Go On Like This   127

Acknowledgements   155

Notes   158

Bibliography   172

1
Next to Us, the Deluge

The division of labour among nations is that some
specialize in winning and others in losing.
Eduardo Galeano, *Open Veins of
Latin America* (1973)[1]

Chronicle of an accident foretold, or Rio Doce is everywhere[2]

Mariana, 5 November 2015 In this mining town in the
state of Minas Gerais, Brazil, the walls of two reservoirs
containing the waste water from an iron mine burst, causing
60 million cubic metres of heavy-metal-containing mud
– enough to fill 25,000 Olympic swimming pools – to
flood the neighbouring community of Bento Rodrigues
and enter the Rio Doce.[3] Caused by a minor earthquake,
according to the mine operator Samarco Mineração SA,
the mud flowing out of the reservoir engulfed surrounding
villages and some of their inhabitants. Three-quarters of
the 853-kilometre-long 'Sweet River' became a toxic mix
of iron, lead, mercury, zinc, arsenic and nickel residues,
abruptly cutting off some 250,000 people from access to

clean drinking water. After fourteen days, the tide of red mud reached the Atlantic coast and flowed out into the ocean, leaving behind a devastated ecosystem. At the Paris Climate Change Conference a few weeks later, the Brazilian President Dilma Rousseff described it as the worst environmental disaster in her country's history.

However striking the pictures may be of the mud-covered landscape and expired animals, of the dead river and its estuary, coloured a dirty red, the case of the Rio Doce is depressing not because of its uniqueness, but rather because of its perverse ordinariness. Rio Doce is everywhere. The causes of the 'accident', the way it was handled, its predictability and the reactions to it are typical of a state of affairs that exists worldwide. It is not only typical of an economic and ecological world order in which the opportunities and risks of social 'development' are systematically distributed in an uneven fashion. It amounts to a textbook example of the ideal type – the local, regional and global business-as-usual approach to the costs of the industrial-capitalist social model.

What happened at the Rio Doce was a perfectly normal catastrophe – and one that was waiting to happen. For many years, similar incidents have been occurring repeatedly, in Brazil and in other countries around the world with plentiful natural resources. Given the global division of labour, these countries are forced to exploit these resources as an economic strategy – and they do so in an intensive and sometimes reckless manner. The expression 'they do so', however, requires some qualification, because in many cases the business operations are contracted out to transnational corporations. In 2011, Brazil mined 400 million tons of iron ore, making it the third-largest producer after China and Australia. The formerly state-owned company Companhia Vale do Rio Doce was privatized in 1997 and renamed Vale SA. Alongside the British–Australian corporations Rio Tinto Group and BHP Billiton, it is one of the three largest mining companies in the world and the world's largest iron ore exporter, with a market share of

35 per cent.[4] Together with BHP Billiton, it is the co-owner of the mine in Mariana through its subsidiary Samarco.

Samarco initially announced that the sludge from the burst reservoirs was not toxic and consisted mainly of water and silica. This announcement soon turned out to be false, as did the claim that the accident had been caused by earth tremors. More likely, the causes are to be found in familiar features of the administrations of 'third-world countries', namely corruption, clientelism and lack of controls. And, indeed, all these appear readily evident at first glance: there had been security concerns about the safety of the tailings dam for a long time, noted by the public prosecutor's office as early as 2013. In their criticism, the authorities also mentioned the immediate risk for the village of Bento Rodrigues, pointing out that no preventive measures of any kind had been taken to protect its inhabitants. The safety reviews ordered by Minas Gerais, the state with the largest ore-mining area in Brazil, were carried out not by independent experts but by members of the company itself. Almost at the same time as the dam burst, a commission within the senate, the upper house in the Brazilian parliament – where the mining lobby can always count on political support – voted for 'more flexibility' in the regulation of mining operators by the authorities.

So, is it all a question of underdeveloped governance, failing institutions, a 'non–Western' political culture? Perhaps. The other side of the chronicle of this 'accident' foretold is that, only a short time before it occurred, the physical stress placed on the dams had been significantly increased. In spite (or because) of the recent decline in world market prices, the two major corporations had increased the output of the Samarco mine to 30.5 million tons, a rise of almost 40 per cent compared with the previous year. In the case of Mariana, this market-flooding strategy had led to a large increase in waste from the mine and, as a result of this, the subsequent flooding of the surrounding area. Incidentally, the third and largest iron mine retention basin in Mariana is also showing dangerous cracks in its walls. And these are only three of 450 dams that hold back mining and industrial waste water in Minas Gerais alone. Around a dozen of these toxic reservoirs threaten the Rio Paraíba do Sul and hence, indirectly, the supply of drinking water to the metropolitan region of Rio de Janeiro and its 10 million inhabitants.

What happened at the Rio Doce is a disaster for nature – and for the people living in and off it – yet it was not a natural disaster. The background to it is anything but 'natural'. Its causes are to be found in the structure of the world economic system: in the development models – which are influenced by this system – of countries rich in natural resources; in the global market strategies of transnational corporations; in the hunger for resources of rich industrial countries, and in the consumer habits and lifestyles of their inhabitants. What happened in Mariana, Minas Gerais, Brazil, and what is happening there every day, beyond the accidents and disasters reported by the media, is not caused by local conditions – at least not exclusively, and only peripherally, in the literal sense. What, from our perspective, happens at the 'periphery' of the world, at the outposts of global capitalism, is connected with the central hub – or, to be more precise, with the social conditions in those regions that believe themselves to be the centre of the world and that use their position of power in the global economic and political systems to dictate the rules that others must obey and whose consequences are felt elsewhere.

One of these rules – maybe even the most important one – says that, after 'incidents' such as the one that occurred in Mariana, life should return to normal as soon as possible. This does not apply only at the local level, where resistance to the mining industry is difficult to organize, for obvious reasons: whether they want to or not, the people of Minas Gerais depend on it. Four out of five households in Mariana rely on the mines for their existence. According to the mayor, Duarte Júnior, if they were to be closed, the entire village might as well be boarded up. In the wake of the 'disaster', people repeatedly took to the streets – not in protest against the mine's operators, but to demand that the mine start operating again as soon as possible. At the same time, there were, of course, 'experts', who sounded the all-clear or warned against unfounded environmental hysteria. Paulo Rosman, Professor of Coastal Engineering at the University of Rio de Janeiro and author of a hastily written report on behalf of the Brazilian Ministry of the Environment, declared that the Rio Doce was 'temporarily dead', but estimated that it would take only a year for nature to regenerate at the site of the burst dam and that the effects at the river estuary were 'negligible'. He said that the situation there would stabilize in a few months and that the expected heavy seasonal rainfall would 'wash out' the Rio Doce, an 'entirely natural process'.

The whitewashing of an ugly situation like this suits not only the multinational mining corporations operating in the area, but also the general public in the highly industrialized societies of Europe and North America. The people in these countries are deeply implicated in the causal chain leading up to the Brazilian disaster. They – in other words, 'we' – are partly responsible for the woes of Brazil and Latin America. They support the massive global depletion of natural resources and the environmental problems, as well as the working and living conditions in the countries where these resources are extracted.

Consider the case of the aluminium ore bauxite, which is found in many tropical countries.[5] According to 2008 figures, Brazil is the third-largest producer of bauxite, after Australia and China and ahead of Guinea. Over the last decade, extraction has risen considerably in all of the countries with significant deposits. Between 2006 and 2014, the mining company Rio Tinto, for example, increased global extraction from 16 to 42 million tons (and iron ore extraction during the same period from 133 to 234 million tons). Bauxite was discovered and mined in Europe as early as the nineteenth century, but the deposits in the southern regions of the world are incomparably larger and more valuable in terms of industrial production. Practically all of the bauxite is used for the production of aluminium, which in turn goes into the making of many goods for daily consumption and for other needs in the countries that use these natural resources – such as neatly portioned and easy-to-use coffee capsules.

A huge amount of energy is required to produce the aluminium that is used to make coffee capsules: it takes 14 kWh of energy to make 1 kg of aluminium from bauxite, releasing around 8 kg of carbon dioxide in the process. This is not the only reason why the success of the aluminium capsules, popularized in advertisements featuring a handsome and world-famous actor, is so monstrous.[6] In 2014, Germany alone consumed 2 billion of these coffee capsules, which only a few years earlier had been completely unknown. And the figure is still rising. According to the industry's estimates, the Nestlé subsidiary Nespresso sold 27 billion units worldwide in 2012. If each capsule weighs 1 g, this alone is equivalent to an annual mountain of aluminium waste weighing almost 30 million kilograms. And that is just one year, just coffee capsules, and just one manufacturer. Despite all this, Nespresso is even praised for using pure-grade capsules that are easier to recycle, while its competitors just put an aluminium lid on their much heavier plastic containers. The company's advertising slogan, 'Nespresso. What else?', is thus also backed by environmental claims.

But let's be honest – without sarcasm. Instead of savouring the 'extraordinary taste' ('Savour our Grand Cru varieties from three gourmet aromatic families', rapid delivery with the Nespresso mobile app), we should think about the bitter aftertaste of the actual production and consumption conditions. Our brief enjoyment of a cup of coffee at home comes at the cost of intensive bauxite mining in Brazil's rainforests. For our coffee at the end of an exquisite, but heavy, dinner, 'somewhere in Africa' resources are plundered, natural habitats destroyed, and toxic waste reservoirs and dumps filled. And executives consume coffee in the conference rooms of their globally operating firms as a quick-acting stimulant to help them keep the wheels of business turning – the wheels that produce our prosperity but that will unfortunately – and inevitably – run over other people in far-flung parts of the globe.

And yet this is only the tip of the iceberg as far as the European and North American coffee capsule hype is concerned. There is also the matter of the working conditions in the Brazilian mining industry; and then there is the fact that the toxic waste occurs not only as a result of mining the raw materials in the tropics but also through its re-export there from the richer parts of the world; and, finally, the social, economic and ecological aspects of coffee growing, harvesting and transport to the coffee-consuming centres of the world. Moreover, the coffee value chain, the parts of the world where these little capsules are produced and consumed, is itself just the tip of an even larger iceberg, a gigantic global process of perpetual redistribution of profits and losses.[7] Be it cotton production or soya bean cultivation, the ubiquitous SUV or smartphone mania: 'Rio Doce' is everywhere.

More precisely, the flooding of huge tracts of land with toxic waste water from the extraction of natural resources for the Global North could have taken place anywhere – anywhere, that is, in the Global South. There are countless 'Rio Doces' in the world, and it is no coincidence that most of them flow through southern regions. Or else they no longer flow there because their water has been cut off by the North – like the water of the Rio Doce, which has been transformed into a slow-moving, gelatinous red mass. Thus, to tell the story of the 'accident' at the Rio Doce, the narrator has to tell *two* stories: the intersecting and linked stories of misfortune for some and good fortune for others.

It is this dual story that will be discussed in this book. It will look at the context, interdependencies, global relations and interactions – the relationality of world affairs. It will also consider the other, 'dark' side of the modern Western world, its rootedness in the structures and mechanisms underpinning the colonial domination of the rest of the world.[8] It will be concerned with the production of wealth and the enjoyment of luxury at the expense of others, and with the relocation of the costs and burdens of 'progress' to other parts of the world. And there is a *third* story to be told – that of the reluctance to acknowledge this dual story, its suppression from our conscience, its omission in the social narratives of individual and collective 'success'. Whenever we speak about our prosperity, we should not remain silent about the associated, interwoven and causally connected hardship of other people elsewhere. And yet this is precisely what happens all the time.

The global wealth gap – or I wish I were a dog

We can also examine life at the expense of others from a different perspective: that of social statistics. Although the resulting view might appear at first glance to be more abstract, it turns out to be just as striking as the pictures from the hell of Brazil's red toxic waste. Just in time for the 2015 World Economic Forum in Davos, Oxfam, the international aid organization, presented impressive data on worldwide social inequality.[9] The study confirmed the continued widening in 2016 of the global wealth gap observed in recent years, whereby the wealthiest 1 per cent of the world population owned as much as the remaining 99 per cent. In other words, a small group of rich citizens had the same share in global wealth as the vast remainder of the world's population. In this way, the 2011 protest slogan 'We are the 99 per cent' coined by the Occupy Wall Street movement was given a statistical blessing on a global scale. An even more impressive Oxfam statistic, on the face of it, was the fact that the eighty richest people in the world had at their disposal the same amount of material resources as the entire bottom 50 per cent of the global population.

As absurd as this ratio may sound – 80 against 3½ billion – figures like these also run the risk of misleading an interested public, or rather of saying what they want to hear. They suggest that the problem of global social inequality is basically the fault of an extremely small group of super-rich citizens and that the solution is therefore to be found in a policy of properly taxing these few dozen multi-billionaires – if not in the hands of the world's largest earners themselves, as exemplified by generous magnates like Bill Gates or Mark Zuckerberg. It is true that the wealth polarity demonstrated by the Oxfam data is nothing short of scandalous. And there can be little objection to an internationally coordinated taxation policy for global financial transactions, for example – as Thomas Piketty, the rising star in the economics firmament, recently demanded – except for the unlikelihood that it could be enforced politically or managed administratively.[10]

But the heart of the problem – unfortunately, one might be inclined to say – lies much deeper. The social diagnosis 'wealth: having it all and wanting more', as the title of this Oxfam study so eloquently puts it, describes the way of life, interests and ambitions not only of the 'upper ten thousand' of this world. Having it all and wanting more is not just the pragmatic agenda of these happy few at the upper end of the social wealth distribution scale, the object of the righteous moral indignation of ordinary citizens urgently demanding a significant redistribution of wealth. Essentially, the description might apply equally well to the lifestyle, sentiments and wishes for the future of a vast majority in the societies of the world's affluent countries. The attitude of having everything and wanting more is not the prerogative of those 'up there'. Wanting to safeguard one's own prosperity by depriving others of theirs is the unspoken and unacknowledged motto of 'advanced' societies in the Global North – and their fundamental collective deceit is to deny the dominion of this distribution principle and the mechanisms for securing it. On a worldwide scale, the average citizens of the Global North are 'up here' when it comes to the national distribution of wealth – and we are quite happy to blithely ignore the situation of those 'down there'.

This is completely understandable – not only because there are massive and continuously growing inequalities, visible to us today quite literally 'on our doorstep', but also because, if we were to look beyond the national distribution of wealth, we would discover something quite monstrous. In fact, once we have become aware of the enormous differences in income between the richest and poorest regions of the world, if only in dry statistical terms and figures, we cannot really carry on as before.[11] The global inequality scale calculated for 2007 by the American sociologists Roberto Korzeniewicz and Timothy Moran shows that practically all income groups in European countries are among the wealthiest 20 per cent of the world population; in Norway, even the 10 per cent of the population with the lowest income are still among the wealthiest 10 per cent in the world. By contrast, a large part of southern Africa – 80 per cent of the almost 100 million people living in Ethiopia, for example – are among the poorest 10 per cent in the world.

To be clear, this is not about trivializing – much less denying – the social inequalities of varying degrees that exist in all countries. There is poverty in Germany and there are rich people in Ethiopia. A comparison of the situation in the generally affluent societies of the Global North – with, on average, a high standard of living, extensive options for shaping their lives and considerable consumption of resources – and the conditions in the, on average, much poorer societies in the Global South, which have fewer opportunities but which also consume less, does not mean that the internal inequalities on both sides should be overlooked. It should, nevertheless, make us aware that something like Piketty's much-acclaimed and widely discussed treatise *Capital in the Twenty-First Century* offers a very one-sided view. The French economist shows that there are rich people in the wealthiest countries of the world who are becoming even richer and who – in contrast to the prevailing idea of meritocracy in these societies – owe their position and its consolidation essentially not to their own efforts but to the exploitation of inherited capital. What his illuminating study fails to look at, however, is the fact that a similar structure has established itself on a global scale.

If, unlike Piketty,[12] we look not only at the dynamics of inequality *within* the societies of the United States, the United Kingdom and France – not to mention Japan and Germany – but expand our vision to consider a global structural pattern of inequality *between* societies, we will once again find the wealthiest 10 per cent becoming increasingly rich at the expense of the rest. This 10 per cent is effectively made up of the five countries mentioned taken together. Their collective position at the upper end of the global wealth distribution scale is not due – and certainly not solely due – to the 'industriousness' of their citizens or the 'productivity' of their economies, but to a large extent to their strategic position in the world economy and the historically inherited 'capital' that comes with it. On a global scale, the inequality between rich and poor countries is even greater than the inequality between the richest and poorest population groups in the most unequal countries of the world – in other words, even more glaring than in a country like Brazil. Likewise, the relative inequality of opportunity resulting from the good fortune of being born in Germany, compared with the misfortune of being born in Brazil, is more pronounced than the unequal distribution of opportunity that the lottery of life offers to new-born babies within German or within Brazilian society.[13]

One thing that we thus tend to ignore in our latitudes, and that is inevitably absent from a perspective focusing on the wealth of individuals and exclusively on inequalities within society, is the fact that the national distribution patterns are embedded in a wider global structure of inequality – one that, it seems, is invisible and meant to remain so. In their book *Unveiling Inequality*, Korzeniewicz and Moran play a statistical game, inventing a fictional society consisting solely of the dogs kept as pets in US homes.[14]

The average maintenance cost per household of these pets in 2008 becomes the 'per capita income' of this notional society. And guess what? This country, 'Dogland', ranks as a middle-income nation, above countries like Paraguay and Egypt, and better off than 40 per cent of the world's population. By this reckoning, it's better to be a dog – at least in the United States.

The authors use this small statistical game merely to illustrate the unsuspected scale of social inequality in the world. But the sudden wealth of the united pooches of America also illustrates the plausibility of the idea that we do not *wish* to know about these extreme inequalities – and much less about the fact that our wealth, reflected in the relative income ranking of the inhabitants of this virtual canine republic, not only stands in glaring contrast to the poverty in large areas of the world but also is connected with it – in other words, that our relative wealth can be understood only *in relation to* the lower income and more limited options and opportunities available to the vast majority of the world's population. The positions in the global inequality structure are a function of one another: some do 'well' or are better-off *because* others do 'badly' or are worse-off.

This is something that people appear to be simply unwilling to talk about, however. In public discussion in the affluent regions of the world, the connections between 'our' wealth – however unequally it might be distributed – on the one hand, and the working, living and survival conditions outside the world's economic and political centres, on the other, appear still to be a 'secret' to which only Marxist groups, development policy organizations and Pope Francis I are privy. And there are very good reasons – at least from a subjective point of view – why we want to hear nothing about these connections, between wealth and poverty, prosperity and deprivation, security and insecurity, opportunity and lack of prospects: as soon as we recognize and acknowledge these connections, we cannot but question the fairness of the resulting inequalities – or at least find it extremely difficult to justify our own privileged positions.

It is thus quite understandable that there should be resistance to such insights and also fear of the consequences that changes in global inequality would bring with them. We members of affluent societies have much more to lose than our chains.[15] The fact that we secretly fear giving up our privileges suggests that we are aware of the global conditions on which our lifestyle depends. Nor does it surprise social analysts that we prefer to suppress our dawning awareness of the facts, that we don't want to hear about our lives being led at the expense of others, or that we prefer to conveniently 'forget' any feelings of unease this might cause us. It is precisely the purpose of this book to confront this forgetting.

Externalization or the 'good life' – at the expense of others

The complex connection outlined – or at least, touched on – so far concerning the life of some at the expense of others will be examined in this book from the point of view of a single term, namely 'externalization'. To externalize means to move something from the inside to the outside. The accusation normally levelled at organizations or businesses that do not pay for the environmental damage they cause and benefit from, by passing on these costs to innocent third parties, can also be applied to larger social units. The rich, highly industrialized countries of this world transfer the negative effects of their actions to countries and people in poorer, less 'developed' regions of the world. The wealthy industrial nations not only systematically accept these negative effects but also count on them – the stakes are worth it for them. The entire socioeconomic development strategy of European and North American industrial society has always been based on the principle of development at the cost of others. In this sense, externalization means exploiting the resources of others, passing on costs to them, appropriating the profits, and promoting self-interest while obstructing or even preventing the progress of others.

Externalization is not merely an abstract 'social' strategy or the effect of a self-perpetuating and actor-less systemic logic. It is true that externalization describes the logic by which the global capitalist system works. But it is pursued by really existing social actors – not only large companies and political leaders, economic élites and powerful political stakeholders. Even if the wealthiest owners of capital and transnational companies pull the levers in the externaliza-tion society, the system is also shored up by the tacit agree-ment and active participation of large segments of society. 'We', citizens of the self-proclaimed 'Western' world, live in externalization societies – in fact, in the large external-ization society of the Global North. We live in an exter-nalization society, we live with it, and we are happy to accept it. Of course, the good life is also unevenly distributed here. The top fifth of rich societies have the greatest global opportunities. But in global terms, 'all of us', the wealthy citizens of the world, are better-off because others are worse-off. We are well-off because we live *off* others – off what they achieve and suffer, off what they do and put up with, off what they bear and have to accept. This is the inter-national division of labour, which the Uruguayan writer Eduardo Galeano described critically almost fifty years ago: we have specialized in winning, and the others in losing.[16]

We live in a society that by way of externalization – at the expense and cost of others – stabilizes and reproduces itself, and that can in fact stabilize and reproduce itself only in this way. This form of social organization, this mode of social development, is not at all new. 'Externaliza-tion society' is not a strictly modern diagnosis – like Ulrich Beck's diagnosis of a 'risk society', basically describing the new living conditions resulting from the rise of industrial technologies in the post-war world.[17] The externalization society is not something that has appeared only recently, and as such it is not simply the latest version of modern civilization. 'Externalization' is not a diagnosis of our times but rather an analytical structural formula. 'Externalization society' is a generic term rather than a contemporary concept. Modern capitalist society has always been an externalization society – even if it has never admitted it. Capitalist societies are externalization societies, albeit in historically changing forms, with evolving mechanisms and continuously shifting global constellations.

It is this constant mutation of the externalization society, the long history of the constitution and reproduction of Western and Northern affluent capitalism at the expense of the Global South, that also gives the term – coined today and applied to the present – a contemporary diagnostic note. The social structure and patterns of externalization have taken on a new form in the last quarter of a century with the implosion of state socialism and the global spread of the capitalist production and consumption, working and living model.[18] In principle, there is no longer an 'outside' in the global society to externalize to. The likelihood has risen that the social and environmental costs of industrial affluent capitalism are not simply offloaded elsewhere, far from the originators and beneficiaries, but rebound on to them – in other words, us. And it doesn't take much imagination, but merely observation and analysis, to anticipate a huge increase in these rebound effects in the near future.

It has thus been confirmed once again that the 'end of history' proclaimed after the global victory of capitalism has not taken place. The end of 'real socialism' has merely heralded a new phase in the historical development of global capitalism. The 'one world' is now becoming a reality – in the form of radicalized externalization, and in the form of the increasing difficulty in keeping the externalized costs outside, even if we are not yet ready to admit it. Affluent capitalism typically exacts its toll outside its own borders. Now, however, it looks as if the empire is beginning to strike back, and that the consequences of externalization are returning home. Germany has a 'rendezvous with the reality of globalization', as Wolfgang Schäuble said in November

2015 in the face of the 'refugee crisis' in the country at the time.[19] Most Germans hope that this rendezvous will not be too intense, and the then Minister of Finance is probably among those who still expect that the advantages of globalization can be exploited by the German economy and society and that the disadvantages can be kept at a distance. But this idea is likely to prove to be a misconception – a classic, and possibly tragic, case of wishful thinking.

It is quite understandable that large segments of the externalization societies fear losing their privileges, and so they hope that everything will stay as it is and that the others will stay where they are. For that reason, our awareness of the preconditions for the huge social privileges that we are now in danger of losing is swept under the carpet – or out the door. In other words, it is itself being externalized and left to scientists and experts, who are best able to deal with it without any social consequences resulting. For that same reason, we cling to the utopian idea of a global 'elevator effect', whereby the life of the poorest populations in the world would also improve without the relative privilege of affluent societies and their established way of life being seriously affected or questioned.[20] Or to the illusion of 'green' capitalism,[21] which would supposedly be capable of disconnecting growth from resource consumption and reconciling the collective lifestyle of an expanding modernity[22] with the limited natural resources of the planet Earth.

However tempting these visions of the future might be, a different scenario is much more likely, and many people in the affluent capitalist centres are beginning to sense this. They suspect that, in the long run and in general, global capitalism will not produce elevator effects but rather a massive zero-sum game, in which the benefits for some are matched by the losses for others. This is particularly true when account is taken not only of economic variables but also of the ecological balance of capitalist globalization, whose costs are distributed in an extremely one-sided fashion – and, curiously, with the same people always on the winning and losing sides.[23] Gradually, a few people are realizing – perhaps during an extended visit to the poorer regions of the world, or simply in a moment of reflection after the evening news – that there are finite limits to the 'good life' at the expense of others, to the fabulous wealth of a few and the wretched struggle for existence of the many, to an uninhibited consumption of natural resources and its destructive and sometimes lethal consequences for the rest of the planet, to the daily display of insouciance in the upper reaches of the global social hierarchy and the continuous fight for survival in the lower reaches.

This book reflects and highlights this as yet subliminal, but – so I believe – gradually increasing, concern about the externalization society and its cost. To avoid misunderstanding, it will not offer a 'comprehensive analysis' of the situation in the world. Externalization cannot explain 'everything', the entire chain of cause and effect that produces global inequalities. It offers, however, a *central dimension* in our understanding of the historical and contemporary economic and environmental inequalities in the capitalist world system.

It should also be stated at the outset that this discussion of an externalization society is not just yet another episode – on this occasion, in the form of a guilt-ridden and stage-managed act of self-criticism – in the long history of academic, intellectual Eurocentrism. This time, it is not, once again, the Euro-Atlantic modernists who are calling the tune – in terms of social analysis, moral responsibility or political agitation. On the contrary, the reference to the social reality of the externalization society merely confirms what has been said and thought, realized and proclaimed, questioned and protested about, for decades – if not centuries – in the Global South.[24] It is just that these diverse and many-voiced, multi-local and transnational, scientific and political counter-movements supported by many people in different places have not yet been recognized, or at least publicly acknowledged, in our latitudes. If this book can make a contribution to, and change, this awareness, it will have served its purpose.

'A rising tide lifts all boats.'[25] This slogan and comforting mantra for the affluent capitalist society, popularized in the early 1960s by John F. Kennedy, the USA's favourite president, is no longer realistic today. Affluent capitalism has not reduced social inequalities but tends to exacerbate them. On a global scale, it literally inundated world society in the twentieth century – with affluence for some, and flooding for others. This flooding doesn't come *after* us, it is right there *next* to us. Those who wish to can see it at Mariana and the Rio Doce. Or they can read about it here.

2

Externalization: A Relational Perspective on Social Inequality

This manner ... is what characterizes relative wellfare and, in the opposite case, relative illfare.

Johann Jakob Hottinger, *Theophrast's Characterschilderungen* (1821)[1]

Capitalistic dynamics – and its cost

The 'externalization society' is not a 21st-century phenomenon. Externalization has been practised in society as long as global capitalism has existed – and this in turn was not invented with the fall of the Berlin Wall and the end of the Soviet Union. When the era of globalization and the 'single' capitalist world was proclaimed in 1989, social scientists pointed out that globalized capitalism had already existed before the First World War,[2] and that in the decades between 1870 and 1914 the internationalization of commerce and capital had been even more pronounced than in the late twentieth century after the end of the Cold War and the rival-bloc system.

But even this historical perspective falls short when it comes to considering the history of global capitalism. Since its beginnings as an economic system, capitalism has been driven by expansion, extension of its scope and overcoming limitations[3] – and not only in the sense of its *abstract* inherent systemic logic, which calls for the continuous search for profits, which are then profitably reinvested to keep the circulation of capital going, to maintain the cycle of production and the reinvestment of profit in the following period and to continue it on a larger scale. This logic of economic reproduction on an ever-widening and enlarged basis also has a *concrete* material and territorial dimension. In order to survive in the long term, capitalism needs to extend its scope to new social spheres, fields and areas. The conducting of business on the principle of the profitable exploitation of capital has a built-in need to become more widespread and comprehensive: the 'whole world' becomes its hunting ground, and virtually 'everything' becomes an object of economic exploitation and is sucked into the capitalist world of commodities.

The market strategies of globally operating companies – and, as the other side of the coin, national competition policies as they are practised by individual states around the world and reported on every day in the business sections of the newspapers – are merely the present-day, albeit currently intensified, version of this systemic expansion tendency: industrial, commercial and service companies all regularly outgrow their domestic markets; segments of the value-added chain are outsourced all over the world as soon, and as long, as labour, in particular, is cheaper there than in domestic or previous locations. Global investors stream into these new 'emerging markets' – until more attractive investment opportunities suddenly appear elsewhere. First there was Taiwan, then Vietnam, and now it is the turn of Cuba. Even North Korea, despite its missile tests, will discover sooner or later that it will not be able to escape the (further) opening of its markets as an entrance ticket to the global capitalist system.

This global capitalist system is not new in itself.[4] It has existed in different historical forms for around 500 years.

It did not cover the entire world at the outset, nor even the entire known world. But it has always been a global economic system to the extent that it encompassed different world regions with diverse economic functions and linked them together: production regions with sales and consumer markets, areas where natural resources are extracted with those where they are processed and finished, industrial and agricultural regions, centres of capital ownership and of labour. Or, in the terminology used in world-system analyses to describe the functional and regional division of the 'single' world of modern capitalism, the 'centres' and the 'peripheries'. The systemic character of this arrangement results from the fact that the form and evolution of its different elements are based on a *reciprocal relationship*. The way in which the global capitalist system presents itself at its peripheries depends directly on its specific nature in the centres (and vice versa): changes in one place in the global system inevitably produce changes elsewhere.

Adam Smith, one of the founders of classical economics, was clear on the principle on which the 'wealth of nations' was based – namely, that of the strategic exploitation of relatively favourable circumstances.[5] Why do some regions prosper while others do not? Why do some progress economically while others lag behind? Smith's answer and the 'relatively favourable circumstances' refer not only to the simple fact that the basic conditions for the development of wealth might be better in one place than another – milder climate, absence of natural catastrophes, a more peaceful community but, above all, more industrious workers, more adventurous entrepreneurs, more imaginative inventors. However, the matter is not as simple as it is frequently presented. Smith's reference to the *relativity* of social wealth is to be understood more in terms of its *relationality*. The constellation that contributes to the production of wealth in one place is in a recognizable and describable relationship with a less wealth-producing constellation elsewhere, and the advantage enjoyed by one is related to the disadvantage suffered by the other. In our context, we might even go as far as to say that the rapid progress of one is only possible thanks to the much slower progress of the other.

Smith describes this relational character of social wealth not with regard to nations but to the early capitalist inter-action of urban and rural development.[6] In their commerce with the surrounding areas, urban dwellers took advantage systematically of their more favourable conditions for exchange – the advantageous *terms of trade*, as we would call them today. Among the economic conditions that favoured urban society was the difference in productivity between artisans and agricultural workers. With the same amount of work, the urban craftsman could produce far more valuable goods than the farm labourer, and, in the direct exchange of goods, the urban producers thus had a structural advantage. Smith's analysis already shows how unequal economic development can occur as a result of this asymmetrical relationship between inexpensive urban and expensive rural 'imports' (or more or less valuable 'exports') over time, and as a result of various social mecha-nisms. Urban dwellers are in a better position to close ranks and cut themselves off from the outside, to coordinate, regulate and protect their production activities from outside competition, to form economic interest groups and to trans-fer the competitive pressure to suppliers in rural areas – for example, by paying the lowest possible price for goods required for production. In the long run, these advantages stabilize and become more powerful, to produce a constel-lation that may be described as a balanced imbalance: the dynamic of the urban increase in wealth goes hand in hand with the socioeconomic stagnation of the rural area.

World-system analyses that have circulated since the 1970s typically extend this local relationship, the unequal exchange structure and the resultant inequality between the 'centre' (city) and the 'periphery' (country), to the global level – and trace this inequality over long historical periods. According to them, the modern capitalist system arose from the economic and political crisis of European feudalism in the 'long sixteenth century', extending from the crisis of the Northern Italian city republics of the late fifteenth century to the Treaty of Westphalia in 1648, which marked the end of the Thirty Years' War. The associated rise of Europe to become the political and economic centre of the world at the time can be understood only in the context of a geographical hierarchy arising thanks to the unequal exchange with the global periphery – as it was perceived from the centre. And it can be understood only if account is taken of a factor that Adam Smith – and, with him, classical and neoclassical economic liberalism as a whole – seems to have considered to be of secondary importance: namely, the emergence of the modern state and the deployment of state power.

In the early nineteenth century, the liberal British economist David Ricardo sought to replace the eventuality suggested by Smith – of a structural development imbalance resulting from a free exchange of goods – by his theory of 'comparative cost advantage'.[7] He argued that all of the countries and economies competing on the world markets could achieve the best market position for themselves through intelligent specialization in their most competitive production sectors and the effective division of labour that this would entail – thereby ensuring prosperity in every country. Ricardo's theoretical model of the mutually beneficial effects of free trade failed, however, to take into account the massive differences in political power within the international community. Even if the market analogy is plausible at all, not all states are equally well positioned on the market of economic strategies to offer 'their' national capital the best chances for profitability. Far from it: then, as now, there were states with varying degrees of influence (if any) on, and with varying degrees of access (if any) to, the shaping of global trade relations. Then, as now, some countries could be forced to orientate their economies towards certain production and value-creation models and towards certain export/import structures – by other countries whose economies benefitted from the corresponding position and orientation of others. From the Corn Laws

in nineteenth-century Britain to the present-day Transatlantic
Trade and Investment Partnership regulations, it has always
been possible for the most powerful states to shape the
world trade regime to their advantage – while systematically and fervently proclaiming their commitment to 'free
trade' and economic exchange 'among equals'.

Against this ideology – as it might be called – of globalized 'equal exchange', the world-system approach offers
an alternative interpretation of the capitalist dynamic on
a global scale. The modern world system has always pursued
a *dual* geoeconomic and geopolitical expansion logic. We
have already pointed to the continuously expanding and
globally oriented dynamic of capitalism.[8] Karl Marx summed
it up famously in his $M - C - M'$ formula: in the capitalist
economic process, goods are turned into commodities (C)
that only serve a mediating function within a system which
is designed to convert money (M) into more money (M').
The idea is to increase the capital invested for the production of commodities and then to use it to further develop
commodity production (which then, as C', is meant to
deliver more capital for investment, M'' – and so on). This
process of accumulation of economic capital, in which
centres and peripheries on a global scale are involved in a
division of labour, is only one side of the world-system
development dynamic. Apart from the accumulation of
capital, there is also the equally important dimension of
the accumulation of political power. Even at the local level,
but especially at the global level, neither Smith and Ricardo's
strategic advantage models nor Marx's concept of the reproduction of capital are conceivable as an ongoing process
without the permanent leverage of political power.

Unequal economic exchange does not come about – and
much less does it perpetuate itself – as a result of market
mechanisms. The possibility of implementing and maintaining unequal exchange relations on a global scale was based
historically on the rise of centralized state authority, the
extension of European powers to territories and populations in the rest of the world, and ultimately the use of

military might to secure the position of European states – and the prosperity of their nations – in the world system. This story is one of a cyclic sequence of global hegemonies, their rise and fall: from the Genoa city-state in the seventeenth century to the 'middle powers' of the Netherlands in the eighteenth, the United Kingdom in the nineteenth, and the continental power of the United States since the First World War – and possibly China in the twenty-first century.[9] From a global point of view, however, it is perhaps more interesting to consider the more complex stories of multipolar power structures – for example, between the various colonial powers in the nineteenth century or the nuclear powers in the twenty-first – or the rise of 'semi-peripheral' economies, such as the 'threshold countries' after the Second World War or the BRICS states today,[10] and the constant power shifts in the world system that cannot be artificially limited to particular centuries.

Whatever the case, the modern world system is defined by a logic of politically based economic expansion, whose 'power component' is historically evident and tangible to a greater extent (during the heyday of imperialism and European colonial dominion) or a lesser one (as in the mid-1990s in the regime of the World Trade Organization[11]). In this way, a variable but also extremely well-defined matrix of centre and periphery has become established, which for centuries – and still today – provides the geopolitical framework for the phenomena of interest to us here: the interlinked and relational structure of inequality, the structured processes to produce wealth and increase prosperity at the expense of others.

If this world system operates on the basis of a constant and linked accumulation of political and economic power, however, the question still arises of where global capitalism obtains its immense, unforeseen and apparently 'endless' dynamism – one that has always fascinated observers and interpreters of capitalism, regardless of whether they are supporters and defenders or critics and denigrators. There is probably no more impressive document celebrating

– however ambivalently – the expansive and sweeping power of capitalism than the *Communist Manifesto*, no more breathless and reverential description of its incessant rise and development, its continuous liberation from former shackles and its transcendence of new boundaries.[12] 'Meantime the markets kept ever growing, the demand ever rising', as Marx and Engels described capitalist expansion. One might ask how this works.

The social sciences do not have many satisfactory answers to this question. They content themselves mostly with referring to an 'inner' dynamism of capitalism, whose substantive mechanism remains unexplained. As a theoretical explanation of the system, this reference to the 'inherent logic' driving capitalist economics leads, for example, to the conclusion that capitalism reproduces itself through economic transactions or, more precisely, through continuous and reciprocal cycles of societal communication consisting of the demand and need for payments, on the one hand, and the willingness and ability to make payments, on the other.[13] From this perspective, the economic system of modern societies is driven by an 'autopoietic' impulse: capitalism is sustained 'by itself', develops 'from itself', and grows 'through itself'.

However appropriate this description of an inherent logic might be, it is misleading to assume – like an economic Baron Münchhausen – that it can pull itself by its own coat tails out of any crisis it might be mired in and lift itself on its own to new heights of economic development. Capitalism is not a *perpetuum mobile* that, once started, remains eternally in motion without any further impulse. Like every motor, the driving force behind capitalist accumulation needs to be continuously fuelled. The capitalist market system requires the constant supply of value of all kinds: labour, land and money; manual, intellectual and care work; biomass, natural resources and fuels. It is this that Max Weber, not known for his materialistic analysis, had in mind when he suggested in the early twentieth century that the driving force behind modern capitalism – the ascetic rational lifestyle of individuals emerging from monks' cells into the working world – would continue 'until the last ton of fossilized coal is burnt'.[14]

In reality, capitalism *cannot* survive of its own accord. It depends on the existence of an 'exterior' that it can appropriate; it draws on all possible material and immaterial forms of 'fuel' supplying it, without which its supposedly eternal flame would soon be extinguished. Social science analyses in the tradition of historical materialism basically assume that capitalism has to keep opening up 'fresh ground', as the *Communist Manifesto* puts it. More precisely, it requires fresh ground to be opened up for it. In the Manifesto, it is literally new territories that were opened up to the market – with the discovery and colonization of America, the conquest of the East Indian and Chinese markets, and the growing 'exchange with the colonies' in general. The ongoing process of the capitalist 'land grab' can also be understood in a metaphorical sense: new categories of people are repeatedly involved as labourers in market-like value-chain concepts (e.g. 170 million children worldwide,[15] and increasing numbers of senior citizens in Western Europe); more and more capabilities and characteristics of these labourers (their knowledge, conscience, feelings) are utilized for economic ends; new forms of life (human, animal and plant genetic material) are made available to the private economy; all conceivable – and seemingly inconceivable – goods become capitalized and traded on financial markets.

This has been going on, as mentioned, for several centuries. But the capitalist expansion logic also appears to be capable of further development, and appears itself to be subject historically to a persistent need for growth – one need only consider, in the context of the tendency to 'financialize' global capitalism,[16] the common and sometimes absurdly expanded derivative forms of capital investment, even after the crisis in 2008/9. Modern globalized capitalism knows no inherent limitations. It is like a permanent winter-sale of values, in which 'everything must go'. Everything must be exploited: natural resources from the earth, performance through labour, the future through money. Everything must go in order to incorporate it into the market mechanism and to exploit it economically. Seen this way, capitalism is a gigantic arrangement based on *incorporation* and the added value created by it – on the one hand, at least.

On the other hand, modern globalized capitalism also operates on the basis of an equally extensive *outsourcing* arrangement – of the immense cost of this same economic added value. A good deal of these costs are externalized, because wherever immense prosperity is created, it is accompanied everywhere by what the British writer and social critic John Ruskin called an 'evil'.[17] Ruskin had British industrial capitalism of the mid eighteenth century in mind when he compared Adam Smith's vision of the 'wealth of nations' with the social reality of 'evil' for much of the nation. He saw both of these phenomena, a good life for some and a bad life for others, as being inherently connected. And he was right: the much-vaunted capitalistic dynamism has its price, in two senses. For some, the price they pay gives them 'wealth'. The price that others pay, however, gives them 'illth'. In justifying this unorthodox neologism, Ruskin claimed that there was a need for this opposite expression to hold a mirror to the wealthy and to open their eyes to 'others'.

The ungainly term 'externalization' is also a coinage, but it aptly sums up what the wealth of nations corresponds to on a global scale and what its dark and all too often ignored side looks like: the illth of other nations.

Externalization – the sociological perspective: living at the expense of others

To speak of 'externalization' is to speak the language of economists – which is not necessarily a bad thing, given the continuing prevalence of economic arguments and economic rationality in public discourse on what is socially reasonable and possible, real and sensible. The principle of externalization is well established in economics and is dealt with under the headings of 'external effects' and 'externalities'.[18] The basic idea is simple: it concerns the effects of economic action that do not play a role in the actor's decision-making. The actors are typically corporations, the most important 'economic subjects' in a market economy. In principle, however, any market actor can produce external effects through its actions.

The classical example of *negative* external effects of corporate action stems from environmental economics. A large-scale printer, for example, not only makes a specific product – a book on the 'externalization society' with an *x*-thousand print run, perhaps – but also produces effects that are not included in its cost–benefit calculation and are therefore not contained in the market price of the product either. Environmental damage, for example: perhaps waste water is fed back untreated into the river running next to the plant, or gases are emitted unfiltered into the atmosphere. The costs for operating a water treatment plant or treating the respiratory diseases of local inhabitants are thus externalized – they are incurred elsewhere and must be paid by others, perhaps by the 'general public' or the 'state'. At all events, these externalized costs are not relevant to the manufacturer: it doesn't have to bear them itself or take account of them in its pricing. In our example, this product might be sold by the publishing company 'below its real value', in other words underneath the 'actual' production costs – which will be welcomed by readers, who effectively have in their hands a lot of 'externalization society' for a little money.

This notional company might also use large amounts of energy, whose production causes environmental damage, which is not factored in and is not therefore taken into account by the printer as a cost factor – likewise the environmental costs of manufacturing the paper and ink, or the transport of these materials to the manufacturing company or the products to the market. Without elaborating further, we are talking basically about an economic activity that, *apart* from the costs of the activity itself, can *ignore* those costs that do not have to be factored into the economic calculation but can be passed on to third parties, and that therefore have to be borne by other market participants.

Economists disagree whether this constellation is the fault of the market or of the state. Some would say that the market is defective and that the solution would lie in more transparency with regard to the 'real' price of goods and services; others point to the absence or inadequacy of government regulations that would force the perpetrator to calculate on the basis of the 'real' production costs. Whatever the case, it is evident that the negative external effects of economic activity have to be 'internalized' somewhere and by someone. They do not simply disappear or dissipate, and they cannot be erased, but must be absorbed somewhere and paid for by someone. The effective internalization of externalities would be equivalent to the enforcement of the 'polluter pays' principle. Those responsible for the external effects should include them in their calculations (or their utility function, as an economist might call it). Otherwise, the necessary internalization must inevitably be borne by others. The commonest way in which this is done is through the indirect assumption of the costs by a public institution, and hence the taxpayer.

However illuminating this strictly economic or market economic perspective might be for understanding the structure of the externalization (and, hence, the necessary internalization) processes, it does not go far enough – in terms of its microeconomic fixation on individual decision-making, but also, in a macroeconomic perspective, in terms of its concentration on a description of social processes based on the assumption that they always follow a market model – as if the social world functioned according to and was effectively guided by market principles. For our purposes, this approach needs to be enlarged and also transcended. When considering externalization (and internalization) structures and processes on a global social scale, a microeconomic analysis is of limited utility. And then the conventional reference to market metaphors, the concentration on market actors, mechanisms and relationships does not get us very far. We need an explicit and systematic in-depth historical analysis.

As already mentioned, the externalization society is a historical concomitant to a capitalist world system that has been continuously reproducing itself in changing forms for centuries. Its colonial past, whose effects are still being felt today, shows how this world system has always operated by outsourcing poverty and violence from the centre to the periphery – from the early 'civilizing' of indigenous populations on the American continent to the seemingly remote present-day 'Mexican' drug war, whose victims die to provide people in Europe and North America with narcotics. But this global externalization story, the global historical relationship between 'underdevelopment' on the one hand and – as the US sociologist C. Wright Mills aptly put it over fifty years ago – 'overdevelopment' on the other, cannot be adequately explained by economic models or market analyses alone, however sophisticated they might be.[19]

In order to understand the modern externalization society, its structural features and process dynamics, a *systematic sociologization* of the analysis is required. However, sociology, for all its 'natural' affinity to social life and affairs, is not known as a popular, and above all accessible and easily understood, discipline – a prejudice that a term like 'systematic sociologization of the analysis' probably does little to allay. And yet, by looking through the eyes of a sociologist at the phenomena represented by the term 'externalization society', we can recognize not only the structures and mechanisms of outsourcing and ignoring social costs that we are all 'somehow' familiar with, but also the fact that externalization has something to do with social behaviour, with the 'completely normal' life of 'average' people. Externalization is a question of social, and not just of economic, activity, and as such is a phenomenon that concerns all of us – not only because it is a matter of social costs that we ourselves produce every day, but also because externalization and the externalization society would not be conceivable without our collusion.[20]

What does 'sociologization' mean exactly? In our context, it means first of all emphasizing the *relation* between the capitalist dynamic and social inequality. We live in a world of relations on both a small and a large scale. We have various relations with others, sometimes close, sometimes distant. How we live and what we are is determined by these social relations and would not be conceivable without them. What we do – and what we fail to do – always has an effect on others, sometimes direct, sometimes indirect, and sometimes barely perceived. In short, the social world is a world of relations and reciprocity. The realization of this elementary fact and its serious consideration in observing society are part of the sociological perspective.

What does this perspective show us?[21] We see interdependencies and interactions; we see that social structures exist only *in the context* of their components; and we see that social developments take place only through the *interaction* of the various inherent processes. We can then see that power is relational. It is not a unilateral relationship – one party has power and the other doesn't; rather, different power positions are connected with one another. A person can exert power over another only inasmuch and as long as the other 'accepts' this specific power relationship, be it voluntarily, coercively or out of necessity.

In a similar fashion, a sociological view reveals that not only social structures but also social processes always have two sides. The capitalist dynamic, for example, arises out of the interaction between the processes involved in the production of wealth and of poverty: the two are connected. Rising prosperity and increasing poverty are opposing developments – which, as such, both belong to the reality of the capitalist world system. Seen from a sociological point of view, social structures are the relational fabric, and social developments the relational dynamic – and the one cannot be understood without the other. Sociological thinking therefore means no longer ignoring the other but always considering *both*, and the inner relationship *between* them: between the power of some and the powerlessness of others, the benefits for some and the disadvantages for others, the opportunities for some and the risks for others, our own lives and the lives of others.

All this still sounds abstract enough for it to be safely filed away with the rest of the stereotypes surrounding sociology, and left there. The purpose of this book is to refute the typical stereotypes. It will show how a sociological approach can bring things together that belong together. It will illustrate the relationship between different worlds – our own social world and the social worlds of others elsewhere. It will seek to show the *relationship* between the two, 'us' and 'the others'. This might sound like couple therapy – and, indeed, a certain sociotherapeutic impulse cannot be denied. The same applies to the recurrent moralizing tenor, which cannot be avoided in the light of the social facts. But the focus here is on analysis: a contemporary sociology of the externalization society. And a terminological framework is required so as to be able to paint a clear picture of these relationships, not with thick paint but with a fine brush. This will be our first task here – and the living sociology will have to wait a while.

Externalization structures, mechanisms and practices

Externalization is a structure, a mechanism and a practice. The last named is of particular significance since it is only through the social practice of people that social structures and mechanisms effectively come alive. Understanding externalization as a social practice is also important because this is the only way of preventing it from appearing abstract, alien or 'esoteric'. Focusing on social practice puts the emphasis on us as actors – and on our own externalization actions – without ignoring the fact that our actions take place within structures that are not immediately accessible or available to us, and by way of mechanisms that under normal circumstances we cannot directly influence.

By being aware of the structures and mechanisms that make externalization possible, the realization that we continuously externalize in our daily actions, and that ultimately it is us *ourselves* who keep the externalization society alive, becomes something more than a mere moralistic observation. It assumes an analytic quality: we are not active externalizers because we are all evil, selfish or remotely controlled (or maybe that as well, but that is the subject for other books by theologians, economists or neuroscientists). We externalize because we *can*, because social structures enable us to do so, because social mechanisms allow us to do so, because general practice confirms our doing so. To a certain extent, however, we also externalize because we *cannot do otherwise*, because social structures force us to do so, because social mechanisms drive us to do so, because the general practice in our social environment causes us to do so. We all externalize because we live in an externalization society, in a society in which opportunity invites theft, in which ineluctable forces prevail, and in which we are all accomplices. This interpretation is not intended either as an accusation or excuse for our actions, but rather to enable us to understand better why we externalize and what we actually do when we externalize, so as to be able to consider possible alternatives on that basis – more productive ones than if we were simply to label our actions immoral or pathological, driven by interests or impulses.

Structures, mechanisms and practices are the categories that we will be using here for our sociological explanation. The central terms in a sociology of the externalization society are therefore power, exploitation and habitus. Externalization can be understood first only on the basis of an *asymmetrical power* structure in the global society. Second, in this context, externalization is to be understood as a multidimensional globalized *exploitation mechanism*. Third, it operates on a daily basis in the form of a specific *externalization habitus*, which is a result of continuously reproduced power-structured exploitation relations. It is only by considering these three dimensions together that we can come closer to understanding the externalization society and our own contribution to its continued existence.

In the *structural dimension*, the concept of externalization breaks with the conventional understanding of social inequality in the sense of income and wealth hierarchies within a country's social framework, which is still deeply rooted and fixed not only in our heads but also in sociological analyses. It is true that sociological research on inequality has been enlarged in the last few decades to include numerous categories of 'horizontal' inequality (gender, ethnicity, age, etc.) and their overlap and mutual reinforcement,[22] bringing it in tune with today's more complicated social world. But, at the same time, the 'vertical' perspectives of 'higher' and 'lower' still dominate in the analysis of the social distribution structure. This is understandable because these inequalities still exist on a massive scale, and in the recent past have tended to become even more marked. In both cases – horizontal and vertical inequality – the conventional view of the distribution in individual societies unduly narrows the sociological field of vision. The criticism, over the last two decades at least, of 'methodological nationalism' in inequality research – in other words, of its focus on the situation within individual nation states and on 'local' inequality – remains completely valid today.[23]

The concept of the externalization society systematically widens this field of vision. The yardstick here is social inequality on a global scale. Here, too, there is a 'higher' and 'lower' hierarchy, coinciding roughly with the global North–South polarity.[24] Between these poles, inequality has developed to an extent that cannot be found in any national society in the world, and that is remarkably stable from a historical point of view.[25] Above all, however, it is 'horizontal' inequalities that dominate on a global scale, and on closer inspection the global 'higher' and 'lower' hierarchy turns out to be a complex worldwide structure consisting of mutually dependent components. Every component of the global inequality system is related to and connected with other corresponding components. And it is only *as such*, as a contextualized and relational structure, that the actual inequality situation can be understood at all.

In the German-speaking world, research on inequality led by, among others, the sociologist Reinhard Kreckel,[26] has also adopted the categories of 'centre' and 'periphery', even if they have not as yet become established termini. Using the analytical matrix of centre and periphery, the global 'higher' and 'lower' inequality structure turns into an asymmetrical force field, and the *positions* in the world social structure appear as unequal and interrelated *constellations*. The conditions of life and development, work and production, mobility and consumption at a 'locality' in the world social structure are linked to the entire set of conditions of life, development and the rest 'elsewhere'.

To that extent, the question of the *structural interlinking* of living conditions is vital for an analysis of global social inequalities, and hence for the sociology of an externalization society. This means one thing in particular: the more or less unequal 'internal affairs' of wealthy societies in Europe and North America cannot be understood without accounting for their external conditions – in other words, for the 'internal affairs' of the countries in poorer world regions. Even more strictly speaking, there are no longer any 'internal' or 'external' social relationships, if indeed they ever existed. All that exists are asymmetrical internal *global* relationships: a global world structured by way of interrelated inequalities, and local social arenas whose unequal structures are embedded in the global society.

From that perspective, the 'tip of the iceberg' – the world of wealthy societies – is precisely that: the visible part of an otherwise mostly invisible world social structure. In physical terms, the fact that the tip is above water because the much larger base is underneath is not at all a puzzle for us. From an analytical and political point of view, however, the reference to this structural connectedness still seems scandalous. Lenin's theory of imperialism, written more than a century ago, clearly showed that the relatively privileged life of wage labourers in the capitalist centres was a result, to a large extent, of the fabulous profits earned through colonial dominion outside Europe and funnelled back into the controlling European countries.[27]

But who reads Lenin today? Those who still speak of 'colonialization' at all are referring not to global domination and inequality but, like Habermas, to the economization of the life-world in the highly industrialized 'centres' of the globe.[28] And yet the 'good old' colonization is by no means a thing of the past, because its consequences can still be felt in, and have a marked impact on, today's externalization society. They do so not only in the sense of continuing socioeconomic inequality but also with respect to the socio-ecological inequalities that have evolved over the centuries out of the differing paths of economic development taken by colonizing and colonized countries.

This brings us to the second dimension of externalization, namely its *process dimension*. The terminology here comes mainly from the US sociologist and historian Charles Tilly, who, in his writing, repeatedly referred to the interactive moment of social inequality production.[29] Tilly defines inequality in general as a relationship between people or groups of people whose interaction produces greater advantages for one side than for the other. In material terms, just about anything can become the object of interaction: material or immaterial goods, work or leisure, money or love. In sociological terms, the most important thing is the fact that inequality occurs through people's interrelated actions – and that, over time, these social relations have developed an independent dynamic that reinforces those inequalities.

The asymmetry characteristic of unequal relations comes into play through the different social positions of the actors participating in the interaction: from the outset, one side has greater, and above all more powerful, resources than the other. This original asymmetry is further reinforced by the ongoing interaction, insofar as one side – always the one with more power – systematically accumulates the advantages. The inequality, which intensifies over time, is finally supported by social categorizations employed by the more powerful actor and established thanks to its existing or acquired power advantage. Typically, these are binary categorizations connected with the two sides of the social relationship and thus appearing to justify the continued reproduction of the unequal advantage structure: categorical differences such as that between civilized and uncivilized, white and black, hardworking and lazy. Such social constructions – from the Spanish conquistadors in South America and the European settlers in North America to the euro emissaries in Greece – which draw the lines between the advantaged and disadvantaged elements of a social relationship, are well known.

The same is true of the differentiation between men and women and the demarcations, power asymmetries and inequality dynamics of gender-specific division of labour. It is no coincidence that the feminist critique of the social division and opposition of production and reproduction, or 'productive' and 'reproductive' activities, may be cited as a central source for a sociological externalization concept.[30] And the practice, in the highly industrialized post-war capitalist world, of socializing work as wage labour in the form of the 'male breadwinner model' is a typical externalization constellation.[31] The feasibility of a 'standard employment relationship' – long-term full-time employment, typically in the 'productive' sector of industry – for most men was based on the social construct of 'reproductive work', in which rearing, care and household activities are provided free of charge as a supporting structure by women outside the labour market. The fact was that the father's traditional place during the working week in the office (and on Saturday in the public celebration of car-washing)[32] was due to his relationship, codified by marriage, with the traditional mother, who from Monday to Sunday was tied to the children and the kitchen (and thus, in some way, also to the father). Reproductive activity was assigned to the female sex, kept separate from the productive 'male' work. It was performed invisibly in the home, unpaid and therefore socially devalued and appropriated free of charge by businesses and those working in them. Put in a nutshell, this was a classic externalization relationship, functioning by way of the equally classic social mechanism of exploitation.

The concept of 'exploitation', which had otherwise unjustifiably disappeared from sociological discourse, was resurrected by Tilly in his relational interpretation of inequality in production processes.[33] Almost as discredited as Lenin's theory of imperialism, Marx's exploitation theory was considered to have been seen off, at the latest, by the end of state socialism and the ensuing general condemnation of the Marxist ideology. Tilly liberates the idea of exploitation from its original link with the theory of labour value and makes it a primary mechanism for producing social inequality: exploitation always occurs when people command resources or can dispose of them in a way that enables them to make other people produce added value whose benefits they are completely or partially deprived of. This added value does not have to consist of work or working time for which the worker is not paid but which is appropriated as profit by the entrepreneur – in other words, exploitation in the Marxist sense. It can also take other forms of one-sided, uncompensated advantage within a social relationship: the exploitation of the natural resources of other countries, the knowledge of other cultures, or the predicament of other people.

Complementing exploitation as an inequality mechanism, Tilly introduces the concept of 'opportunity hoarding'.[34] This consists of limiting the availability of a resource that presents the opportunity for exploitation or one-sided appropriation of added value to the members of a specific group. This is equivalent to what Max Weber described as 'social closure', which occurs whenever a group – however defined and distinct from another group – is in a position to reserve a particular resource, or has the opportunity to acquire or appropriate a specific resource, solely for the members of that group.[35] Social closure is thus a mechanism that enables group members to exclude non-members from the possibilities for exploitation, and to monopolize the profits of exploitation for themselves.

Exploitation and social closure together constitute the *modus operandi* of the externalization society. By removing the connection with the labour theory of value, the term 'exploitation' can now be understood not only in terms of the 'vertical' relationship between wage labour and capital, but also in terms of the 'horizontal' relationships of appropriation of, and exclusion from, resources – such as the gender-segregated relationship between productive and reproductive work, or the relationship between workers in different world regions.[36] In the era of European imperialism, for example, the workers at home were the effective beneficiaries of the exploitation strategies of European capital in the colonies. The organization of labour in the second half of the nineteenth century ensured that these workers, although themselves exploited, could improve their own working conditions at the expense not only of the non-unionized marginal segments of the workforce but, above all, at the cost of the wage and forced labour in the peripheries of the world economy to which the social reality of brutal 'naked exploitation' was consigned.[37]

Thus, even then, externalization was based on a dual principle: it is done because there is the possibility to do so, but also because there is no other possibility. The costs of one's actions were shifted to others because it was possible to do so, or because society made it possible to do so. Others were made to pay for prosperity at home because those at home were in a position that allowed them to let others pay. However, the example of externalization by European wage earners, who obviously were anything but the 'ruling class', in the age of imperialism is also indicative of the complementary phenomenon: people externalized because they had to. They found themselves in power structures that required, or even compelled, costs to be transferred to others. As wage-earners are today, they were also entangled in competitive mechanisms that normalized externalization effects and made externalization quite simply the norm of action.

This brings us to the third – and possibly decisive – dimension of the externalization society, the *practical dimension*, and to the idea of 'habitus' developed by the French sociologist Pierre Bourdieu.[38] According to him, habitus is a system of attitudes and orientations typically connected with the position of a person or group of people in a given structure of unequal social positions, and which typically influences the social actions of this person or group of people. Habitus provides the basis for conscious plans of action and their practical implementation, but at the same time the actors are unaware of it. Regardless of this absence of awareness, however, people's habitual actions still have a direct social impact.

For example, if a person is in a disadvantaged position in a structure of inequality, he or she will attempt to move to a better position, revealing a correspondingly ambitious habitus – unless the underprivileged position appears so permanent and a way out so difficult, the better-placed group so unattainable and untouchable, that a fatalistic habitus establishes itself and action is confined to obtaining at least the minimum required for survival. On the other hand, those in a better social position will want to retain their relatively privileged position, so that their habitus revolves around isolating themselves from those less well-off, while at the same time glancing covetously 'upwards' or to where life is considered to be (even) better or optimal. There, in the objectively and subjectively most privileged areas of the social structure, the *happy few* will adopt a habitus of ownership or superiority, possibly also exclusivity and arrogance, which will be reflected in their everyday behaviour: from a confident and 'natural' attitude to their own privilege to its arrogant flaunting or aggressive justification.

The crucial step now in a sociological analysis of the externalization society is to transfer Bourdieu's habitus concept for the 'inner world' of a (national) society to the social reality of global inequality structures. In this context, the societies of the Global North as a whole, regardless of the multiple differences in their internal social structures, are the ones in a particularly privileged position. And it is in relation to these positions that it is possible to speak of an externalization habitus, a habitual practice, at both individual and collective levels – by status groups and social milieus, national communities and, ultimately, entire world regions – of *externalizing* the costs of their way of life to others while at the same time *blanking out* this structural connection from their daily lives. This is one of the central assumptions of this book: what we are calling an externalization society draws on and literally lives from a specific habitus, which the members of the externalization society display quite naturally and which determines the practical aspects of their daily lives. This externalization habitus is linked to a specific individual and collective position in the global inequality structure. People have to be able to 'afford' it, in the literal sense, on the basis of their own positioning in the social space of global capitalism. It is a pre-conscious, practical and consequential expression of relative privilege in the capitalist world system.

This is the analytical toolbox for the sociological explanation of the externalization society: externalization is a question of power, exploitation and habitus. In the externalization society, power consists of the opportunity for transferring the costs of one's way of life to others – and this opportunity is distributed in a structurally unequal fashion, because certain social groups have managed to appropriate the opportunities for externalization and to prevent others from obtaining them. These others are exploited by those in the positions of power, insofar as they are the main bearers of the cost of externalization while being permanently excluded from enjoying its profits. The power inequality and exploitation dynamic are effectively implemented and stabilized by the specific habitus of the exploiters acting from positions of power. For them, externalization becomes a social practice that they perceive as possible, customary and legitimate, and that they therefore pursue as a matter of course.

To a certain extent – in a further inequality mechanism identified by Tilly – the practices thus adapt to the structures, and the actors to the conditions in which they act. For the externalization society, this produces a self-reinforcing dynamic. The global power structures allow a habitus of externalization, transfer and displacement of the social costs of prosperity from the centres to the periphery, and this habitus helps essentially to cement the social exploitation relationship in the long term, at the expense of the latter. Against this background, Joseph Schumpeter's economic theory of the capitalist development dynamic as 'creative destruction'[39] – the idea of displacement and destruction of 'old' structures in favour of 'new' ones – can be seen as a simple and effective narration legitimizing the social reality of externalization. The two movements – creation and destruction – happen to take place at different times and in different places. For some, the externalization society is creative and wealth-producing; for others, it is destructive and wealth-inhibiting.

Externalization – the psychoanalytical perspective: the veil of deliberate ignorance

One of the favourite clichés in what is conventionally called 'neoliberal' social discourse – although 'wealthy authoritarian' might be a better description – is that we have been living 'beyond our means'. Usually, this seemingly self-critical reproach by troubled economic experts and supposedly responsible financial politicians is directed at others, the general public, who are advised that their material demands have now become excessive and jeopardize the continued economic prosperity of the community. The instinctive inference from this diagnosis is then to urge the members of society to 'tighten their belts', as the customary euphemism for the political demand for workers to refrain from making wage demands and for welfare recipients to abstain from receiving benefits – in other words, for economies to be practised by others. The established liturgy follows up with the observation that tighter belts will make fatter stomachs possible in general in the future, and that the economic growth fostered by a reduction in demand by society will lead in the long term to an increase in prosperity again, and hence to more resources being available once more 'to everyone'.

However often this story has been churned out in the last three or four decades, it does not become any truer for being repeated. We do not live beyond *our* means. And this questioning of the 'we' idea refers not only to the situation in our national societies, in which the better-off typically call on everyone else to tighten their belts and economize. From the point of view of the global society, the questionable nature of this 'we' perspective formulated by the political and economic élites becomes even clearer. We do not live at all beyond *our* means but at the expense of *others*.

First of all, we actually live *beyond* the means of others. There are large swathes of people in the rich countries who in absolute terms are much better-off than large swathes of people on a global scale. They are more prosperous, and live longer and in greater security. But that's only one aspect. Such absolute measures are only a visible expression of a further, more basic relationship. Wealthy societies live in particular *through* the means of others. The emphasis might sound puzzling at first, but it is a good description of the externalization society. It lives through the means of others as determined by its relationship to others. The living conditions of the externalization society depend on the relationship with the living conditions of others. Its privileged position is due to the less privileged position of others in other parts of the world; and these privileges can be maintained only through this inequality. People in the externalization society are well-off because *others* tighten their belts, because forgoing is something that happens *elsewhere*

– continuously and permanently, so that the externalization society will be able to benefit from it not only today but also tomorrow and in the future.

But let's be honest: this situation is hardly a secret known only to sociologists. Every child knows that Western industrial societies are much more prosperous – sometimes embarrassingly so – than many other parts of the world. It is no coincidence that Germany regards itself as a 'donor country'.[40] Its citizens have the means, and are aware of the poverty around them. In 2015, Germany gave 7 billion euros, more than ever before, and the World Giving Index for that year put Germany in twentieth place overall – and even in ninth place among 145 countries in terms of the absolute number of donors: 35 million people. The USA was in second place after Myanmar and India, respectively. Philanthropy market analyses like the one on betterplace lab show that, in Germany, older people remain the most important donors, but that younger ones have caught up considerably in recent times and give larger amounts more frequently than they used to. So, is everything fine? And is the world at least on its way to becoming a better place, thanks to our charitable aid?

The opposite is more the case, and even the many committed donors should know better. At all events, they *could* know better. They could know not only that they are better-off than all the recipient nations in the world, but also that their own 'wellfare' is linked to the 'illfare' in these countries. But do they *want* to know? Who would want to know that the beautifully fitting donor pants we wear have been made by child labour at the other end of the world? Who would want to know why they are so well-off, as long as they are well-off? The externalization society has always lived off the labour and resources of others, from the offloading of social and environmental damage to others. Moreover, since the Second World War in particular, democratic societies in the West have lived on the basis of a broad-based 'implicit social contract', which Craig Calhoun, a US sociologist and director of the London

School of Economics, sums up as follows: 'Citizens tolerate inequality and the externalization of long-term costs in return for growth.'[41] Growth is the anchor that stabilizes the externalization society. It has to continue and, as long as it does, no one will ask how it is achieved – as long as electricity comes from the socket, salaries come from the wage negotiations, and the annual growth rate comes from entrepreneurial innovation. And at the end of the year, the heads of state or government announce on television that it will all continue in the new year – if everyone makes a little more effort.

But how is that possible? How can the externalization society be so confident of its conception of itself and so convinced of its self-image, while ignoring the logic of externalization so completely? How can the other side of the externalization society be overlooked and remain below the perception threshold? There are two possible interpretations. One has vaguely to do with the concept of the 'veil of ignorance' famously discussed by the US philosopher John Rawls in his book about the theory of justice.[42] In this thought experiment, people cannot have knowledge of their position as structural beneficiaries in the system of global distribution – and, in their ignorance, accept a national social contract by which economic growth brings maximum benefits even to the least well-off. A more plausible explanation than the assumption of widespread *inability* to know is provided, however, by the idea of *not wanting* to know. Under this premise, the externalization society functions essentially on the basis of individual or collective amnesia, not only of the past – how it came about that we are so well-off – but, above all, of the present – how it comes about that we remain so well-off.

The assertion that, in order to survive, the externalization society needs to be wrapped in a veil of ignorance – disregarding the living conditions around it – suggests that a psychoanalytical explanation is required alongside the sociological analysis of this form of society. As we have seen, the externalization society is associated with a certain habitus that makes both the individual and collective externalizing processes seem appropriate, self-evident and legitimate. This pre-conscious structure cannot be understood, however, without the individual and collective psychological structures with which it is inherently connected and to which it is functionally bound. Outsourcing and shifting, suppression and dissociation, discharging and diverting are not only social, but also psychological, practices of, and in, the externalization society.[43] These phenomena need to be looked at more closely before we can proceed, with a well-stocked analytical toolbox, to demystify the externalization society.

'Externalization' is an established term not only in economics but also in psychology, although in the latter case it is less common than the opposite, 'internalization', meaning the internal appropriation of social rules, norms and values (and also the moral perceptions of significant others) by the subject. Internalizing forms of psychological problem-solving are those in which the problems are projected onto the self. We turn on ourselves and look 'on our own doorstep' for explanations and solutions, which under certain circumstances can lead to social withdrawal and isolation. Externalization is then the opposite problem-solving mechanism, in which the oppressive weight or motive is shifted to the outside and attributed to a concrete or abstract other to enable us to maintain our internal balance. From a psychopathological point of view, externalizing behaviour leads to the shifting of originally internal conflicts to the outside world through the dissociation of unpleasant or insupportable parts of the self – a defence mechanism that frequently makes it difficult for targeted outsiders to protect and dissociate themselves from the psychodynamics of the person concerned.

So much for the psychology textbook definitions. If we consider them not only as a description of individual psychological mechanisms, motivations and disorders but in the context of the social phenomenon that concerns us here, we will once again perceive the reality of social

externalization practices from another, completely different angle. We can thus begin to discern a psychological
profile of the externalization society. Its specific mode of
problem-solving operates, not only in material terms but
also with regard to its psychodynamics, by the mechanisms of outsourcing, dissociation and diversion. On the
one hand, the social costs and environmental burdens of
our own collective way of life are shifted to a (supposedly)
'outer space', where they are to be borne by others. On
the other hand, in a complementary (and secondary) form
of externalization, the psychological burden of a general
awareness – or at least an inkling – of the hardship imposed
on other people and world regions is separated from the
collective sensitivity and shifted outside the realm of societal perception. This mechanism has a stabilizing 'internal'
effect and has psychofunctional significance in maintaining
the social contract of affluent capitalist societies. Those
on the receiving end of this dual externalization practice
have thus not only to confront the effects of the externalization society in the form of degrading working conditions and environmental damage, but also to deal with
symbolic exclusion processes and devaluation experiences.
The psychological relief mechanism goes hand in hand with
burden-shedding and guilt-shifting practices that project the
blame for the damage onto the victims themselves. Then,
claims for compensation by low-emission countries suffering from the effects of climate change are reinterpreted
as 'transparent' financial blackmail strategies, and young
male war refugees are advised to make themselves 'useful'
in their own countries by fighting for peace and democracy
instead of seeking shelter here. As for the psychological
processing of our own externalization actions, what we
split off and shove off doesn't 'go away'. It is not gone and
cleared up but reappears somewhere else, where it has to
be processed by others.

The social practice of giving mentioned above is a good
example of this connection. It is well known and evident
that the act of giving to people in need is also one of

reassurance regarding our own prosperity. This also applies to the spontaneous and situative practices of so-called 'social awareness' – for example, the whole spectrum of 'environmentally friendly' behaviour, which gives the 'friend of the environment' a good and 'green' conscience. But giving is not always just a question of subjective unburdening. It is also often a moment of self-congratulation. What should be a 'normal' practice of helping those who are suffering without really impacting one's own way of life is elevated to become a noteworthy act. This is particularly evident in the self-aggrandizement of Germany, one of the richest countries in the world, to a 'donor nation' – 'do good deeds and talk about them', appears to be the motto. Or, rather, don't mention that the donations require no material sacrifice at all, but emphasize instead that they testify to the human sympathy of the well-off. As the online organization betterplace lab pointed out in its Philanthropy Market Analysis for 2014, the online donation figures 'developed positively on the whole', and payments by PayPal and credit card were increasingly replacing the 'good old direct debit'.[44] As we can see, giving costs almost nothing – not even time. And yet it is apparently so valuable.

Donations to the 'Third World' – a concept born of the post-war US–Soviet clash of systems that persists today – are not only charitable acts, however. They are also to some extent a mental and emotional act of domination, even if it is a well-meaning one. Giving demonstrates helpfulness and generosity – and, alongside the money transfers and aid packages, it communicates an implicit demand for action by the beneficiary 'third parties', namely gratitude. Or – perhaps much more important from a psychoanalytical point of view – the act of charity offers the heroic, self-congratulating giver the possibility of perceiving the recipients' reaction as an indication of their ingratitude. We know this at the individual level, when the recipient of a present doesn't react as the giver expects: no gushing joy, no sparkling eyes, not even a polite 'thank you'. The projection of one's own position onto the reaction of others works the same way at the collective level. In the public perception, 'they' show no respect for the assistance they are receiving – and then, for example, the supposedly 'ungrateful' and 'insatiable' refugee becomes a negatively connoted social figure.

But the psychological coping mechanisms of transferring and devolving which are built into our externalizing actions go further. We have heard enough over the past decades about the effects of state 'development aid'. Standard arguments in this context, for example, include the belief that financial aid from the donor countries systematically 'trickles away' in the recipient countries. This is usually explained by a whole range of attributes that make it possible to understand the others not only as different but also as incompetent, evil or criminal. These countries 'over there' are ruled by 'corrupt élites' who enrich themselves at the expense of the poorest members of the population, an 'ineradicable administrative inefficiency' that cannot be overcome by donors – even with the best will in the world – and in general a 'mentality' that simply cannot be changed and makes all aid a mere waste of time. In this way, responsibility for the fact that everything remains the way it does is shifted to the other: do what you like, there's no helping them.

This is also a pattern for all discourse about 'underdevelopment' that has been narrated in the West for so long – by which we transfer our own ideas of how societies and institutions should be to those countries that are supposedly not as advanced as we are. A recent example is the academic and political discussion about 'failed states'.[45] This is never meant as a reference to European states, which are all too often incapable of protecting the life and limb of everyone living on their territory, including the non-citizens among them. The reference, of course, is to states (or, from this perspective, non-states) such as Syria, Afghanistan or Eritrea, whose home-made problems, inadequacies and incapacities Europe now has to deal with, while nothing is normally said about the background and historical reasons for the absence of a 'Western' institutional order in these countries. The social psychology of the externalization society also involves a feeling of superiority: that the others are basically incapable of doing better – or at least of doing as well as we can. According to this interpretation, there must, after all, be something to it if we manage to progress while the others permanently stand still and lag behind. First, they should become like us – and then we will see.

Dissociation and transfer, repression and sublimation, defence and projection: all these mechanisms form the psychosocial substrate for life in an externalization society – and for its survival. They are also linked with the psychological structure of modern capitalism and its apparently perpetual expansion logic.[46] The accumulation dynamic inherent to modern capitalism – unending, and somehow not meant to end – meets the deep-seated desire of mankind for an eternal future. With its endless 'more of the same' logic, capitalism binds the psychological energy of people – it ties them, in their fear of the end, to its compulsive idea of limitlessness, the idea that the life we live should go on forever. The fact that this existential desire cannot be fulfilled – at either the collective or the individual level – is repressed and dislodged from the collective and individual consciousness. So is the knowledge that our assured life comes at the expense of the livelihood of others – not that of future generations, our children and grandchildren, as a one-sided sustainability discourse focusing on the future of the affluent Western world would have it, but of the many billions of people already living today, who keep the externalization society alive by being part of its constructed 'outer world'.

The consequences of our way of life will be felt not *after* us but here and now, *parallel* to us. And it is not as if the repressed knowledge were not accessible to us. On the contrary: in September 2014, at a meeting of the Heads of State or Government of the NATO countries, the outgoing NATO Secretary General Anders Fogh Rasmussen, confronted by the war in Ukraine and the advance of Islamic

State in Iraq, gave an eloquent summary of what the rich
democracies stood to lose: 'Surrounded by an arc of crises,
our Alliance, our transatlantic community, represents an
island of security, stability and prosperity.'[47] An island of
security, stability and prosperity surrounded by a sea of
economic rivals, buffeted by the waves of terrorist militias
and violent conflicts, threatened – to extend the metaphor
– by a tide of poor migratory populations. This panorama
is a fairly accurate reflection of the sentiments of most of
the crisis-threatened majority populations of the core countries of the North Atlantic world. Among the 'islanders',
who fear for the future of their life in security, stability
and prosperity, ideas and attempts to maintain the status
quo are thus very popular. 'To the south we see violence,
insecurity, instability.' May it remain so, is how the words
of the former NATO Secretary General might be understood. He could have been echoing the thoughts of the
externalization society. May violence, insecurity and instability remain where the pepper grows, in the ex-centric
places on the global periphery – thanks to intensified transatlantic arms deliveries, a stricter control regime at the
outer limits of the European Union and the repeated invention of 'safe countries of origin' among the 'failed' neighbouring states.

As with all repression, however, it returns somehow as
a suppressed instance and, at some point, hits back as the
'abject' at even the most skilful suppression artist. The
collective psychological trick of the externalization society
– 'out of sight, out of mind' – doesn't function forever.
And there are many indications that this is precisely a
feature of the historical phase the world is currently in,
towards which the modern world system is rapidly progressing. It is the era of the 'boomerang effect' in world
society.[48] The externalization society comes at a cost – and
not only to others, but ultimately also to us. To a certain
extent it is fulfilling itself by being confronted by its own
effects. Under the radically new conditions that globalization has created – among other things, as a result of

information technology and mobility – the 'objects' of the externalization society – large populations in the countries of the Global South – are becoming 'subjects' or actors in the counter-movement, quite literally, since some of them are moving from the periphery to the centres and are demanding repayment for the cost of the externalization society.

The theoretical discourse above becomes tangible now: there is no social 'outer space' any more, even if we keep trying to recreate it from our islands of security, stability and prosperity. It is only against this background that we can understand the protectionist, repressive, racist reactions that Europe's confrontation with the consequences of its own externalization practice is currently provoking, from the closing-off of the continent to the violent attacks on refugees – in a literally reactionary attempt to deny the signs of the times and to continue to ignore the realities of the global society. The many small beneficiaries of externalization are feeling that 'if nothing happens' to keep things as they are, the good life could soon be over. Or at least a life beyond the means, and at the expense, of others.

3

Live and Let Die: Externalization as an Unequal Exchange

Somewhere bodies are being broken, so that I can live in my shit.

Heiner Müller, *Die Hamletmaschine* (1977/9)[1]

The categorical imperative in reverse

Europe is regarded as the birthplace of the Enlightenment and the stronghold of enlightened thinking – and this cultural heritage has remained until today an essential component of the European identity: from the primacy of reason to the rule of law, from protection of personal independence to the formation of a critical public. When sociologists look for similarities in the very different individual European societies, they regularly emphasize the shared set of values that has evolved historically beyond national boundaries and been developed in essentially similarly structured institutions. When 'Europe' is shaken by crises, as is the case at the moment, and the actors in Brussels and the capitals of the Member States wring their hands in search of a unifying thread in their political union, they like – at least in the western part of the continent – to appeal to the European community of values, to shared beliefs in what is 'good' and 'right', the rules by which society should be governed, and how individual and community welfare can be reconciled.

It was left to the Enlightenment philosopher Immanuel Kant to reduce the basic principles, which still hold today, of this set of European values to a few formulations that could be generally understood even by non-philosophers – or that were made to be generally understandable. The much-cited emergence 'from self-imposed immaturity'[2] is one of these formulations, which summarizes the objective content of enlightened modernism and, at the same time, is meant as an individual call to action. In modern societies, the inability of a person to use his or her own reason is, for Kant, no longer a question of obstacles due to legal constraints or personal dependence but a matter of will, a question of (lacking) determination and (lost) courage. Kant's second formulation identifying the 'spirit' of Enlightenment is the equally well-known 'categorical imperative':[3] 'Act only according to that maxim whereby you can, at the same time, will that it should become a universal law.' It is a moral imperative and hence a guarantee of peaceful coexistence that all others could be reasonably expected to observe in their general behaviour. If your own actions do not pass this test, they undermine the standards of enlightened morality.

Much has been said and written since then about the ambivalence of enlightened modernism. One of the classic lines of criticism, entitled *Dialectic of Enlightenment*[4] and formulated against the background of the rise of National Socialism by the social philosophers Max Horkheimer and Theodor W. Adorno, concentrates on the inherent contradictions in the Enlightenment idea and its perversion in an advanced stage of industrial capitalism. According to these two main representatives of the early critical theory of the Frankfurt School, towards the middle of the twentieth century self-interest finally replaced rational morality in the centres of the Western world, and enlightenment had degenerated into a myth and been transformed into an industrial culture of mass deception. The modern bourgeois capitalist society was producing the exact opposite of the Enlightenment impetus: domination and oppression, violence and destruction. For a long time, however, a more far-reaching global interpretation of this Western history of the Enlightenment, its preconditions and consequences, was overshadowed by this negative self-reflection. Even today, such an interpretation has still not become established, either in society's understanding of itself or in the reflective academic theories of European modernity.[5]

If, however, as in this book, the history and present of the affluent European societies is seen as a matter of externalization, a second no less fundamental dialectic of the Enlightenment emerges – a structural contradiction which questions the conventional 'internal cost calculation' of social progress. The externalization society functions in a diametrically opposed fashion to the Enlightenment ideal, operating to a certain extent as a mirror image of the categorical imperative: its mode of operation definitely does *not* follow maxims that could be regarded as 'universal laws' or that one could reasonably wish to be adopted as general rules of behaviour. On the contrary, externalization constitutes a fundamental violation of the idea of a universally acceptable rule. In externalization societies, social action is steered systematically in a direction that, characteristically, is *not* at all generalizable. Life in societies in the Global North is based precisely on the principle that not everyone can live this way – and that the negative effects of this life are to be borne by the societies of the Global South. Externalization is exactly the *opposite* of a way of life that its protagonists would wish to see as a universal law, since life in an externalization society stands and falls on its exclusivity.

The social reality of the externalization society is thus in glaring contrast to the normative ideas on which sociological modernization theories[6] and developmental modernization strategies have been based for decades, and which continue to characterize our daily discourse – namely that, with our aid, the 'underdeveloped' countries can 'catch up' and embark on the development path of affluent democratic capitalism; that the equalization of global living standards – however wearisome and difficult – is not only desirable but also feasible through the establishment of growth-promoting institutional arrangements in low-income countries;[7] that the ecological balance of the planet can still be maintained or restored through the development of intelligent, energy-efficient technologies and their worldwide dissemination. All these are familiar beliefs regarding modernization that we like only too well to hear and to adopt. However, none of them are credible, because the externalization society does not – or, to be more precise, cannot – tolerate societies equal to its own. It requires the construction of an 'externality' that is effectively 'different' from it. Steady improvement processes, substantial convergence tendencies and symmetrical-balance constellations have no place in the halved world of externalization. If they were to ensue and really materialize, they would mark the end of the externalization society, because it would lose its basis for doing business the way it does. Depending on who propagates them, such modernization fantasies are wishful thinking, cheap talk or simply a deliberate piss-take, if you will excuse the expression.

Let's not fool ourselves. In the externalization society, the 'golden rule' that Kant's categorical imperative became in its popularized form still applies, albeit in a perverted fashion. Its unabashed principle is rather 'inflict on others what you don't want to be done to you'. In this way, it deprives others of exactly what its members, as mature citizens, claim for themselves: the ability to live as free and self-determining subjects who are not being told what to do. This statement should not be misinterpreted as the brandishing of a moral club and an attempt to teach Kant to the ignorant. The sociology of the externalization society is an exercise not in moralizing, but in system critique. It looks critically at the social system that creates the very structure making externalization possible, the structure that in fact provokes and enforces it – and that, conversely, systematically prevents, obstructs and basically makes impossible a way of life that can be conducted according to universally applicable laws.

It is this context that will be illustrated in the following sections on the basis of the material flows of the externalization society, before the next chapter discusses its mobility regime. We will thus look first at the material cycles of production and consumption, waste and emission, focusing on the extractivist and agroindustrial value chains[8] and the socio-ecological destruction potential of products that we consume every day without considering the conditions and consequences of their production. The possible examples are legion and are all – as cynical as this might sound – basically the same, and therefore equally apt as illustrations of the structures, mechanisms and practices of externalization. Each of these 'random' examples reflects the price of our way of life – a price that we do not pay ourselves, but that has to be paid to a large extent by others.

The curse of soya or who gives a bean?

Let's stay for a moment in Germany and Europe. Like its European neighbours, after the Second World War at the latest, Germany ceased to be an agrarian society – and was somehow proud of the fact. 'Agrarian society' smells of tradition and pre-modernism, provinciality and backwardness, cow dung and yokels – times long gone for most of us. The proportion of workers in the agricultural sector has steadily dwindled in recent decades – in Germany, from around a quarter of workers in the early 1950s to just 1.6 per cent in 2012, and in the UK, for the first time in that year, under the 1 per cent mark.[9] The European agricultural sector is of marginal significance today in employment terms. At the same time, the supply of food to a growing population has improved incomparably. How can that be? Is it through increased productivity that has seen the yield per hectare of wheat triple from 2,730 kg in the early 1950s to 7,330 kg in 2012? Or through technical progress, which the German Farmers' Association sums up as 'precision agriculture, computer-controlled feeding, integrated food chains and automatic milking systems' as 'indicators of today's modern agriculture' (conveniently forgetting other indicators like factory farming and the use of pesticides)?

Things are a little more complicated. In some way, Germany, and any other country in Europe, is still an agrarian society – but an outsourced, externalized one. Farmland has decreased in Germany by almost a sixth, or around 3 million hectares, from the area it accounted for in the 1950s, and has continued to decrease since the reunification of Germany (from 17.3 million hectares in 1995 to 16.7 million in 2015). Against this, Germany, like all other supposed 'service societies' in the OECD world, manages huge amounts of cultivated land in other world regions. By importing a wide array of farm products, it 'exports' its farmland to 'genuine' agrarian societies, where this farmland is used to grow export products (and is thus no longer available for domestic use). By outsourcing this land, all economic, ecological and social consequences of 'modern agriculture' are also exported abroad: the effects of monoculture and agro-business, genetic engineering and agrochemicals – as in the case of soya bean cultivation in Latin America.

According to the 2014 *Living Planet Report* by the World Wildlife Fund (WWF),[10] through its agricultural business in the 2000s Germany continuously exploited over 5 million hectares of land outside the territory of the European Union. The EU as a whole used over 25 million hectares in that period, and at its peak even more than 35 million. A good deal of it was taken up by virtual land commerce through soya imports from South America. For Germany, the average 5.3 million tons of soya and soya equivalent imported between 2008 and 2010 was equivalent to the outsourcing of 2.2 million hectares – an area around the size of Slovenia. A further 1.1 million hectares of soya imports from the rest of the world required 0.4 million hectares of land. To produce these amounts domestically, the entire area of several German states would have to have been turned into farmland – which obviously didn't happen.

The story of soya cultivation can also be told by looking at Brazil and Paraguay, two of the large producer countries on the South American continent, as an externalization story linked to our own consumer habits, lifestyle and supposed farewell to the agrarian society. But in no other country has the mass cultivation of what critics also call 'killer beans' changed the economic structure to such an extent as in Argentina, and nowhere else is the soya syndrome so evidently tangible within society as a whole.[11] More than 20 million hectares of farmland – almost two-thirds of the fertile land in the country, an area the size of the United Kingdom or Romania – are covered with soya plants. After the USA and Brazil, Argentina is the third-largest producer of these pulses, and the world market leader in derivative products like soya meal, soya oil and soya diesel. Driven by the global increase in meat consumption and the quadrupling of world market prices in the last fifteen years, the soya bean has increasingly replaced the meat industry itself, turning the Argentinian pampas into a huge soya factory. Only 3 per cent of the country's export revenue is still accounted for by meat production, which used to be the mainstay of its balance of trade, a quarter of which is now attributable to soya. It earned US$23.2 billion in 2013, representing the most important source of Argentina's foreign exchange and making up 10 per cent of the country's tax revenues.

Around three-quarters of the more than 200 million tons of soya beans grown in the world are destined to become protein-rich feed for intensive livestock farming in Europe, North America and China. But soya bean components are present in practically all common food items, as well as technical products like paints and dyes. Most of the farmland cleared for bean cultivation in Argentina (in the last decade alone, the total area has increased by no fewer than 9 million hectares) is used exclusively for soya beans, with two harvests a year. This intensive cultivation calls for the massive use of chemicals, or a combination of this toxic mix with gene technology. In 1996, Argentina was the first country, under the presidency of Carlos Menem, to allow the cultivation of genetically engineered soya plants, marking the start of the ultimate boom, as the genetic bean quickly replaced conventional cultivation, which ended completely in 2010.

Soya bean growers are now also completely dependent on the agrochemical industry. In 1990, 34 million litres of herbicides, pesticides and fungicides were sprayed on Argentinian crops; by 2015, the figure had risen to 317 million litres. The favourite product is the broad-spectrum herbicide glyphosate[12] – sold since 1974 by Monsanto, one of the world's largest seed producers with headquarters in St Louis, Missouri, and now owned by the German Bayer group – as the active ingredient of the low-price Roundup. It is used principally to clear land of weeds before seeding. In 1995, the same company developed a soya bean that was resistant to the proprietary pesticide, enabling glyphosate to be used throughout the entire growth cycle. For Monsanto, this represented the perfect business model: seeds (Roundup Ready) and herbicide from a single source.

At the other end of the production chain, the farmers are at the mercy of the vagaries of the world market. The world market price of soya beans fluctuates a good deal and recently fell again following the boom of the 2000s. Dwindling agricultural yields have led to further concentrations, however, with small and medium-sized businesses being forced out of the market – in a sector that already has a highly asymmetrical ownership situation. More than half of the Argentinian land is controlled by just 3 per cent of the producers, and two-thirds of all land is let out by their owners for cultivation. Soya production in Argentina is a massive industry, in terms of the size both of the sector as a whole and of the companies. There is no place any more in the pampas for conventional farming and traditional agricultural structures. The field is occupied by major corporations, farming pools and investment funds. Changes of ownership are sometimes dubious affairs, with compliant judges, corrupt land registry officials and armed 'security services' to help things along. And the former small farmers flee to the cities. In Argentina, the eighth-largest country in the world, 38 out of its 40 million inhabitants now live in an urban environment. In metropolitan Buenos Aires alone, the population increased in the 2000s by more than a million people; but what is growing most is the poor slum districts surrounding the cosmopolitan Western-style centre of this conurbation of 13 million inhabitants.

The blessing that soya brings to some – the equity owners in the sector and the consumers in the export countries – has become a curse for others, because of the damage to health caused by the pesticides. Glyphosate is suspected of being carcinogenic. While this did not become an issue in Europe until traces of it were found in mothers' milk and – horror of horrors – in beer, the people in Argentina have had to deal with this chemical cudgel for decades. Other toxic sprays used in soya cultivation contain 2,4–dichlorophenoxyacetic acid – 2,4-D for short – known from the Vietnam War as one of the ingredients of the defoliant Agent Orange. In view of the increase in miscarriages, deformities and cancer cases, the 'madres de Ituzaingó', a soya-growing area close to the city of Córdoba, began in 2001 to document the illnesses among families in the neighbourhood.[13] In 2011, they won a lawsuit on account of the health-damaging consequences of the use of chemicals – although not against the 'big bosses', but against a local soya farmer and the pilot of the crop-spraying aircraft.

What does that mean for us? At least this much: in Ituzaingó, in large parts of Argentina and in the entire South American 'soya belt', a monocultural farming style that is highly dependent on pesticides has become established. It has led there to permanent ecological damage, the destruction of the traditional agrarian forms of life, danger to public health, a massive rural exodus and structural economic dependence

– and to criminal and, if necessary, violent agrocapitalism, which feeds off our hunger for resources but at the same time serves as an illustration of the rampant 'corruption' and 'modernization deficits' in the Global South. Bribery and threats, blackmail and coercion – and, however unwilling we are to accept it, murder and manslaughter – are the inevitable concomitants of a socioeconomic 'development model' serving the production interests and consumer needs of the Global North.

The planting of genetically modified soya plants is prohibited in many EU countries – but not the import of genetically manipulated beans. What we don't produce ourselves, but want nevertheless to consume, we simply have grown elsewhere: 'Genetic soya sates here – and devastates elsewhere.'[14] During the German glyphosate scandal, which became a scandal only when the toxin was detected among members of the externalization society themselves, consumers there were once again made briefly aware of the poisoned life they lead and of the fact that Western prosperity is built in large part on chemical poison. A bitter truth indeed – particularly for the people outside our affluent Western world.

Beyond soya – from the diary of the externalization society

As mentioned, the case of the 'soya republic' of Argentina is eloquent but also chosen at random. Wherever one looks at the periphery of the global capitalist system, a similar structure can be observed. The specific position of the many Argentinas of this world as suppliers of natural resources to the resource-poor, highly industrialized and densely populated countries at the centre of global capitalism has produced a syndrome of economic dependence, ecological devastation and social distortions that becomes more acute and more fixed with every cycle of economic booms, inevitably followed by economic crises. In every cycle, business magazines and political advisers spotlight new 'winners' among the countries of the Global South – be it the Asian Tigers or the Five Lions,[15] the emerging countries of Africa, which are supposedly 'on their way up'. But after the next collapse of raw material prices or the next financial crisis, the supposedly emerging countries suddenly find themselves no longer making great strides but back where they came from: sunk in the pit of 'unattractive investment conditions' and 'political mismanagement'. Brazil, highly acclaimed by everyone only a few years ago, is now experiencing what so many of the former 'granaries', 'gold mines' and 'green lungs' of this world – as the metaphors of the externalization society would have it – have already gone through: from 'boom land' to has-been. And the caravan moves on.

Perhaps to Indonesia?[16] But wait – it's already been there. Except that the soya bean there is called oil palm, whose pulp is used to make cheap palm oil. The same harvest yield requires only a sixth of the area needed for soya beans, making palm oil the most widely produced oil in the world, even more than soya oil. It is grown in the rainforest regions of the world to allow for the production of food (margarine and cooking fat), but also of cosmetics and fuels, in our hemisphere. Indonesia and Malaysia are the largest palm oil producers in the world. They cover four-fifths of the global demand, and the cultivation area in these two countries alone has increased tenfold in the last two decades. The necessary slash-and-burn farming – in Indonesia, 26 million hectares of forest were destroyed between 1990 and 2010 – produces immense amounts of carbon dioxide, both through its release from the cleared areas and through the forest fires themselves. The gigantic loss of forest land has produced 13 gigatons of carbon dioxide emissions. The effects on the regions concerned are well known: irreversible destruction of habitats and biodiversity; social uprooting of the native population; widespread health damage, particularly chronic respiratory diseases. And, as always, child labour, forced relocation, human rights violations – the usual local political economy of predatory exploitation established to meet the demand for resources here, at the expense of the people and the environment elsewhere.

And so we could – should we say happily? – go on. With cotton production in India, for example: 6.75 million tons in 2014, around a quarter of world production, which has increased by 20 per cent in the last three decades.[17] Here, too, the vast majority is genetically modified cotton; here, too, Monsanto, Roundup and glyphosate are involved – more than a tenth of the agrochemicals used worldwide are employed for cotton cultivation. For this and for the further processing in the textile value-added chain, untold amounts of water – ground, surface and rainwater – are consumed: 21.6 million litres in India for every ton of cotton. We might recall that the most prominent victim of this water demand in the world is the Aral Sea, which over the past half-century has almost dried up. In India, however, it is mostly water pollution that the population has to deal with – if we ignore the working conditions in the local clothing industry, which occasionally make the headlines in the media here, when a huge sewing factory catches fire and hundreds of people are burned to death. Before then, however, they provide the world market, particularly the countries of Europe, with cheap textiles.[18] More than 3 million tons of textiles were imported in 2012 to the European Union from Asia, outcompeting other supply regions – beyond the Eastern European non-EU states. Just 34,000 tons came from North America, for example. The wages in the Indian clothing industry are hardly worth mentioning, at least for the big Western trading companies: in 2011, the average wage amounted to only 23 per cent of the official subsistence level. This was just 3 percentage points more than ten years previously, but it could even be described as generous compared with Bangladesh, where wages in textile production have remained steady at 14 per cent of the average wage and where the risk of accidents and death is even higher.

More examples, perhaps? Let's take a look at the most widely used natural resource in the world, sand, a substance that you would think is not in short supply.[19] At all events, it is everywhere, in everything we need for our daily lives. Or at least everything we use. Sand is not only required for building. Obviously, it is a component of windowpanes, concrete and cement. But mineral sand is also found in lots of other products like toothpaste and face cream, in credit cards and mobile phones. In the course of the building boom in all highly industrialized societies, 'normal' sand has also become a rare commodity, and its extraction increasingly irresponsible: seacoasts and riverbanks erode, groundwater levels sink, biodiversity is reduced, habitats become uninhabitable. Singapore, the eighth-richest country in the world in terms of per-capita GDP (around US$55,000 in 2013) and one of the most important global financial centres, has imported well over 500 million tons of sand since 1989, making it the largest importer in the world. Its main supplier is neighbouring Indonesia (US$3,510 per-capita GDP in 2013, 116th position). The burgeoning city-state has intensive land-reclamation programmes on its coasts, the building boom is in full flow, illegal sand trading flourishes, the 'sand mafia' is cleaning up, the working conditions to obtain the sand are bad, the use of chemicals extensive – the same old story, in other words. The demand for sand has recently increased even further with the development of fracking technology, which requires large amounts of water, chemicals and sand,[20] to exploit unconventional sources of natural gas in the USA, for example. Here, the demand is for high-quality sand that cannot be found everywhere. In 2013, 30 million tons of sand were used in the USA for fracking, and the estimated demand for 2015 was put at 50 million tons. The market leader and fracking profiteer US Silica saw a 58 per cent rise in revenue in 2014, and investors have now set their sights on this 'otherwise boring sand industry' (*Börse Online*). Fracking is now being discussed fiercely in the USA and elsewhere, not because of fears of damage for man and the environment but because the production forecasts in the early years proved to be too optimistic. There is still growth though, and that's a good sign for the sand industry. Not necessarily for the sand-producing countries, however.

The same is true of shrimp production.[21] There too, the shrimp-farming industry benefits more than the people in the breeding nations. Germans love shrimps, and annual consumption there has almost tripled in the past decade to 1.2 kg per person (in the USA, it is as much as 2 kg per person per year). During this time, import prices have dropped by nearly half – an example of the real market economy in action. The import prices are relevant because 84 per cent of the shrimps eaten in Germany are not bred locally – most recently, 56,000 tons per year. For a long time, the only shrimps available in Germany came from the North Sea. Now they are factory-bred like pigs or chickens, a mode of production called 'aquafarming' or 'aquaculture' in the trade – both more appetizing than the idea of agroindustry or animal abuse. Whatever the case, no other food sector is growing so rapidly as mass production of shrimps in artificial ponds. For this purpose, mangrove forests are being cleared on a large scale: since 1980, the forest area has been reduced by a fifth. As you might imagine by now, the shrimps on our frozen pizza or in our healthy lunchtime salad come from some remote region, in this case frequently Thailand, the world's largest shrimp-exporting nation. As elsewhere in industrial animal breeding, chemicals and medicaments are used en masse. Monocultures are particularly susceptible to disease, and the use of antibiotics is therefore more or less obligatory. Thai shrimp breeders oversee the process from beginning to end or sell the young shrimps to breeders in China. The breeding farms generally employ immigrant workers from even poorer neighbouring Cambodia, Laos or Myanmar. In the cold light of day, the Thai shrimp industry is a living example of the existence of forced labour and wage slavery in the globalized modern world.[22]

What do you say? Stop? Enough? Because a recent article about shrimps in the press had the headline 'Children's hands in icy water'? And reported that these children's hands shelled shrimps in ice-cold water for sixteen hours a day, and that anyone who complained was mistreated? You're right – this really is intolerable. Let's stop our whistle-stop tour of the material cycle of the externalization society. But there is perhaps at least one more question to ask – namely, where do the waste products from the consumer goods used in the Global North end up?[23] In most cases, at all events, not in the Global North. In 2011 alone, the USA exported 300,000 tons of electronic scrap to Asia, and well over 100,000 tons (not including the unrecorded amounts) were dumped legally over the border – fenced off from the USA, closely guarded and impassable except by illegal immigrants – in Mexico. Above all, however, Africa's metropolitan regions are favourite dumping grounds for transatlantic waste. Rare earths in, surplus waste out – thus runs the import–export strategy of the externalization society.

Too much for the sensitivities of the citizens of affluent societies? Perhaps we should move on from this stark and vivid narrative and return to the sober explanations and analytical interpretations put forward by international sociology – unfortunately, in most cases, inaccessible to a wider public – to decipher the global phenomenon of an asymmetrical appropriation of nature. How is it that some world regions have to systematically destroy their natural environment and the livelihoods of their inhabitants so that the inhabitants of other world regions can consume without hindrance or limitation? What is behind the ability of modern capitalism again and again to create 'cheap nature', as the US sociologist and environmental historian Jason Moore puts it?[24] And why is it that this cheap nature is typically located in the Global South but is appropriated and exploited by the Global North?

The dirty will become clean: the global ecological paradox

The dynamics of uneven ecological exchange have been studied in detail by two other US sociologists, Andrew

Jorgenson and James Rice.[25] The starting point for their empirical research was the paradoxical discrepancy, on a global scale and in temporal, spatial and social terms, between the exploitation of resources and the harm to the environment. Whereas the 'developed' countries in the Global North typically have a large ecological footprint[26] through their consumption and the concomitant demand for biologically usable areas – agricultural and grazing land, forests and fishing grounds – the amount of environmental pollution within their borders is surprisingly small. In 'underdeveloped' countries of the Global South, the opposite is true: a generally much lower level of consumption and hence a lower demand for land, together with massive damage to the natural environment.

This seeming puzzle is quickly solved – though only satisfactorily for those in the Global North, however. According to Jorgensen and Rice, the ecological footprint / environmental degradation paradox is due basically to the fact that the rich industrial societies are in a position to transfer the prerequisites for and consequences of their excessive consumption systematically to other world regions – namely, the societies in the poorer, resource-exporting regions. In this way, they can keep their own environmental and social balance on an even keel while leaving the dirty business to others – except, of course, for the economic profit that they can obtain.

Jorgensen and Rice talk explicitly of an international dynamic of environmental externalization anchored in the historically evolved structures of the world economic and trading system. According to them, global commerce is always a question of the transfer and relocation, the export and import, of environmental burdens. The countries of the world with the highest revenues leave the largest ecological footprint – since the late 1960s, it has been calculated at over 5 'global hectares' (gha) per person, much more (currently three times higher) than the planet's available biocapacity,[27] which has dwindled in the last five decades from over 3 to just 1.7 gha per person. While the footprint of the poorest countries in the world has remained practically unchanged during this time at just over 1 gha, it has steadily grown since the new millennium in middle-income countries[28] such as Brazil and South Africa, Mexico and Malaysia, and is now slightly higher there than the biocapacity limit. In general, it may be said that for generations the rich industrial nations have lived well beyond the means of the planet – and at a much higher level than billions of people in the South, whose resource-sparing way of life is effectively protecting the Earth's biocapacity. In 2010, the Arab oil-producing countries had the highest per-capita resource consumption, followed by practically all OECD member states, with the USA (approx. 7 gha/person) in eighth position and Germany in position 25 (approx. 4.5 gha). Consumption in the seventy or so countries below position 85, including a huge country such as India (position 135, approx. 1 gha/person), was under the planetary limit.

And yet the citizens in the highest-consuming societies at the top of the resource demand scale can enjoy a much less polluted environment than those of poorer countries, whose consumption is of necessity much more restrained. Clean rivers where people live it up, stinking cesspools where people are kept down – all thanks to the unequal global ecological exchange. Among the ten countries of the world with the largest imported biodiversity deficit,[29] for example, are not only oil-producing economies like Kuwait and the United Arab Emirates and city-states like Singapore, but also the Benelux countries and New Zealand. Through their imports of natural resources and food, they all systematically and consistently consume the natural environment of other countries, while at the same time environmental protection is strongly advocated, at least in the European countries.

The relatively good performance of advanced industrial societies in terms of local environmental damage is thus by no means the result solely, as they would like to claim, of their particularly effective environmental policies. And hence the absence, which we take for granted, of the consequences of environmental pollution – such as increased child mortality or overburdened public infrastructures – is not due simply to our much-vaunted pioneering environmental protection activities. On the contrary, the blue skies above the consumer centres of this world are due to a significant extent to the externalization of the ecological costs to the peripheries. The rich countries tap the resources of the poor ones, importing the natural resources cultivated and extracted there, but not the burden to the environment and habitat that their production causes. They fleece the poor countries by systematically exploiting not only the economic but also the ecological and social benefits of the unequal exchange structures associated with international production and commerce.[30]

Moreover, while the poorer societies have to put up with irreversible environmental damage and problems of social cohesion caused – take your pick – by soya, palm oil, or tobacco growing,[31] the cotton, sand or shrimp industry, they are also systematically deprived of consumption opportunities. Ultimately, the rich societies benefit also from the smaller ecological footprint of poor nations resulting from the system of unequal exchange that they themselves command. The 'producing' companies in this system are usually located in the affluent societies of the Global North – but they outsource the environmentally harmful parts of their production, in the form of natural resource extraction, to the poorer countries, which in turn are dependent on the export of these resources. The goods they produce are delivered to 'developed' countries with high capital intensity and consumed there, just as the profits also end up where the international mining and agricultural businesses have their headquarters, thereby intensifying and increasing the structural asymmetry with regard to the 'underdeveloped' societies. These countries then import the waste from the affluent centres, which again causes new environmental, health and social problems – a truly vicious circle.

Citizens on the 'more fortunate' side of this unequal exchange might well think this to be an ingenious system and one that, if it did not already exist, would have to be invented. Well over a million people in the factories in South-East Asia and the Far East belonging to the electronic giant Foxconn[32] work for our digitally networked life – in conditions that give a contemporary feel to Karl Polanyi's classic description of early capitalist production as a 'satanic mill'.[33] All of the little comforts of our daily life start and end in the oil-producing deserts and the huge dumping grounds spreading in rural and urban West Africa – from the murder and destruction to gain access to 'black gold' to the computer scrap recycled by children at great risk to their health. While the affluent nations continue their gigantic worldwide land grab, ruining the local subsistence economy and shamelessly extracting the last natural resources, the landless and unpropertied classes stream to the cities of the South to scrape together some sort of existence.

So this is how it is. The political and economic power relations that support the world economic system permit the establishment and maintenance of structural exploitation at the expense of the Global South, which is not really desired, but nevertheless tolerated, by the populations in the Global North, who have long since 'assimilated' the convenient by-products in their daily lives. And the entire game becomes a problem for us, if at all, only if it is played on a large scale – as is the case with the land grabbing to safeguard territory and natural resources in Africa[34] – not just by the usual suspects in the West but also, all of a sudden, by others, most recently 'the Chinese'. When others want to have their share, things start to get serious.

The world in the Capitalocene: the ecological debt of the Global North

Is China a new global player reaching for world power? Perhaps. In the last 400–500 years, however, other powers have divided the global externalization cake among themselves. This epoch, dubbed Anthropocene, was for a long time, and until recently, dominated by people in the Global North. 'Anthropocene' was supposed to designate a new geological era closing the 12,000 years of the Holocene epoch. As the name suggests, the Anthropocene is the era in which human beings have finally become a force shaping irreversible geological changes. There is still disagreement among scientists not only as to whether a fundamental epochal change of this type can in fact be claimed, but also as to when this new global era might have commenced.[35] According to the French historian Christophe Bonneuil, there are different interpretations. 'Was it America's colonization and the ethnocide of Native Americans or the birth of industrial capitalism, founded on fossil fuels? The atomic bomb or the great acceleration in consumption after 1945?'[36]

Whatever the conclusion in terms of geoscience or historical periodization, in the twenty-first century the structure-changing intervention of man in world development has become a social fact that can no longer be reasonably disputed. And there is much to be said for the idea that the era of the anthropomorphic transformation of the Earth coincides with the era dominated by the accumulation of capital. The capital change that we are experiencing today is a change driven by capital. The logic of capital investment and return on investment, of growth and expansion, of business on a continuously expanding basis, is not just a symbol of this most recent geological epoch, which has brought forth such wide-ranging, profound and relentless developments as global climate change. It is, rather, at the root of it.

The Anthropocene was basically an 'Occidentocene' epoch, one shaped by the West. 'Four fifths of the greenhouse gases discharged into the atmosphere between 1750 and 1900', says Bonneuil, 'were produced in North America and Western Europe'. And their emission is the result of the form of capitalist globalization that predominated in this time: industrial fossilism or fossil industrialism – in other words, the model of industrial production and social consumption based on the burning of lignite and coal, oil and natural gas. Jason Moore, mentioned earlier, suggests that Capitalocene would be a better word to describe this epoch,[37] one in which the capitalist dynamic has basically changed nature and society, and society's relationship to nature. The history of this epoch is marked by changing economic hegemonies, in which the respective economic hegemon was, not by chance, also the driving force behind the greenhouse effect.[38] In the nineteenth century, the United Kingdom not only controlled half of the world but also produced half of the carbon dioxide emitted worldwide. A quarter of the accumulated carbon dioxide emissions since 1850 have been produced by the United States. And the European – and German – 'economic miracle' following the Second World War was accompanied by a massive increase in energy consumption. Never has the ecological footprint of the Western nations been as large as it was at the end of the post-war boom, directly before the start of the oil crisis in 1973.[39]

Moreover, in all historically 'leading' nations in the capitalist world system – be it the British Empire, later the USA, after the war also Japan and the EU, and now China as the latest emerging superpower – economic success at a certain stage of economic development, supported by growing geopolitical power, has been linked with easing the ecological burden on their territories. Although the dynamic economic growth in the Global North was still based at first on the heavy demand placed on the 'local' ecosystems – as graphically illustrated today by the typical consequences of industrialization in China, such as water and air pollution – the further growth dynamic of the early industrialized nations was accompanied by the outsourcing of their domestic ecological burdens. After the serious chemical accident in the north Italian town of Seveso in 1976, for example, the problem of finding political legitimation for hazardous industrial production, coupled with the possibility of ecological externalization, meant that gradually 'Seveso' was no longer 'everywhere', but usually somewhere outside Europe.

Unequal economic and ecological exchange has thus always been closely linked to global capitalism. All the legendary stories of economic success and geo-economic ascent have been stories of the outsourcing of ecological and social costs. If China is currently on the way towards the world of value creation established in the Global North, this process is typically accompanied at a certain point of development by the externalization of the dirtiest and most exploitative forms of production to other economies – in China's case, for instance, to Bangladesh. The financial debt owed by the countries of the Global South to those of the Global North corresponds to the 'ecological debt' owed by the advanced industrial countries to the peripheries of the capitalist world – a debt that can never be repaid by the rich nations and conversely cannot be 'cancelled' by anyone.

What makes this ecological mortgage so burdensome for the populations of the Global South – while easing the load for those of the Global North – is the fact that it frequently remains invisible for a long time. It is true that nothing good can be extracted from 'disasters' like the toxic flooding of the Rio Doce described at the start of this book – their only 'advantage' is in the fact that their news-worthiness means that they briefly make the headlines. Above all, they provide an opportunity, for a moment, to impress the striking pictures of burst dams, masses of red mud and dead fish on the collective conscience of the afflu-ent societies in the Global North, far remote from the events themselves. But even the pictures of the famous toxic gas leak in Bhopal in 1984,[40] when several thousand people died in the course of a few hours, were less striking, not only because there were no social media at the time, but also because, despite the images of the ruined factory, the poisonous gas was quite literally invisible. This applies even more to the longer-term indirect consequences of the incident and the estimated 15,000 people – at least – who died in subsequent years, let alone the long-term health damage to at least 2 million inhabitants of the capital of the state of Madhya Pradesh. Even today, one in four of

Bhopal's babies is stillborn – a blood toll that no amount of compensation can make good – not to mention the fact that Union Carbide, the US chemical company responsible, and its legal successor Dow Chemical, have long since stopped making payments. Thirty years after the accident, the human rights organization Amnesty International appealed to people in the West to send 'letters against oblivion' to the Indian Prime Minister Narendra Modi.

It is unlikely that they will be read, just as thousands of other 'disasters' in India and elsewhere at the peripheries of affluent capitalism are overlooked – not least because they don't start with burst dams and exploding factories but with perfectly normal forms of production and work organization in the countries of the Global South, for a 'world market' dominated by the Global North. Their destructive effect on the country concerned and its people, on human beings and their environment, on the born and unborn, is insidious and delayed. 'Slow violence' is how Rob Nixon, Professor of English and environmental researcher at Princeton University, describes this particular form – typical of the globalization era – of physical assault by the capitalist centres on the living conditions at their peripheries.[41] The accelerated 'turbo-capitalism' that has been talked about for the last two decades can also manifest itself at a much slower pace if one only looks long enough and in the right place.

Against this background, the Easterlin paradox,[42] which is often cited to relativize the differential in global life chances, takes on a different allure. In the early 1970s, the US economist Richard Easterlin concluded from his analysis of international surveys that, beyond a certain wealth threshold, there is no longer any correlation between income and 'happiness', between material prosperity and subjective satisfaction with life. This was a scientific version of the popular adage 'Money can't buy you happiness.' At all events, above a level at which basic needs are secured, greater wealth does not necessarily lead to greater wellbeing; and with the super-wealthy, the correlation could even work in the opposite direction. At a global level, this conclusion could be reversed to produce the comforting thought that it is possible to be poor and happy. And to this day, this argument is used to relativize the social significance of global inequalities.

Studies by the US sociologists Kyle Knight and Eugene Rosa offer a very different picture, however – one that correlates the subjective happiness of the inhabitants of a country with their ecological footprint. Their findings do indeed indicate that the level of happiness can be the same in rich and poor countries. In the second half of the 2000s, for example, Norway and Costa Rica had the same (average) level of life satisfaction, in spite of the fact that per-capita income in the former was eight times higher than in the latter. The same applies to the ecological footprint: there was no difference in life satisfaction between Costa Rica and the USA – although the USA's footprint was five times as large as that of its Central American neighbour. So, is it possible to be poor, environmentally friendly and happy at the same time? Possibly. But Knight and Rosa's data clearly show that this is not the case as a rule. Costa Rica, 68th in the wealth ranking,[43] is in fact an anomaly. None of the 118 countries behind it have a similar life-satisfaction rating, and none in the lower half of the world income list have anything like a 'level of happiness' consistently found in the Western industrial nations. The same applies to the environmental dimension: the level of life satisfaction in countries with a small ecological footprint is much lower on the whole than that in the OECD countries. Wealth, environmental pollution and happiness are thus a much commoner combination on a global scale than the distorted late colonial image of the noble savage whose necessarily exemplary ecological balance makes him happy.

The imperial mode of living: is there a real life in the wrong?

Let us state once again: the history of global capitalism is a history of externalization.[44] The ecological dumping

practices of the economically leading societies are embedded in a historically evolved power structure that not only
makes it possible for these societies to repeatedly reassert
the advantages of their privileged position but also allows
them to outsource the environmental costs of their economic
value-creation strategies to others. The citizens of the economically 'successful' and ecologically 'advanced' societies
do not control this process, which is imposed on them as
wage-earners by the companies that employ them, but the
structural potential for making a profit out of this constellation while at the same time externalizing the costs of
their way of life has been assimilated by them and become
a matter of course. Ulrich Brand and Markus Wissen, political scientists in Vienna and Berlin, speak of an 'imperial
mode of living',[45] a way of life in which the resources –
labour, land, the environment – of others are appropriated
and exploited, and which can be maintained only through
this unacknowledged appropriation practice. It is also a
lifestyle that is not, therefore, accessible to all, however
much the inhabitants of the peripheral countries under-
standably strive to have a share in it, and though the
immense demand for commodities in the new middle classes
of the Global South is already factored into the corporate
balance sheets of the transnational companies of the Global
North. But, logically, the externalization imperium of one
part of the world has to exclude from it the other part. If
everyone wished to externalize, then no one would be able
to. Those who are dominated by the imperial mode of
living elsewhere on this planet, and who make up the vast
majority of the world population, must therefore inevitably
remain on the outside – for the benefit of the wellbeing of
all of the dominated subjects here, whose way of life is
simply dependent on the enduring success of this exclusion
process.

    In this reference to the global economic *structuration* of
externalization, its *structural conditionality* that has evolved
through the establishment over an extended historical period
of the capitalist world system based on institutionalized

power, one thing is clear: this externalization structure cannot be smashed through individual action alone, whatever good intentions are behind it. There are, of course, notable and socially structured differences in the size of personal ecological footprints,[46] as demonstrated by a group of authors led by the statistician Hans Messinger for the case of Canada. Those with a lower income are almost automatically more careful with the consumption of resources – and to that extent less 'imperial' – than higher-earning households usually are. And it is notably the educated, critically enlightened milieu that is particularly extravagant in ecological terms. At the same time, the use of resources in poor and even extremely poor households in the Global North is still well over the average level of most of the inhabitants of the Global South. And the land requirement for their lifestyle – which, as has been shown, is mostly outsourced to other parts of the world – continues to grow statistically: the 'great acceleration' continues on its happy way.

This does not mean that consumption cannot be reduced at the individual level. On the contrary, the possibilities for it are legion. We saw it in action at the beginning of this book with German coffee-drinking habits.[47] Practically unknown in that country at the start of the new millennium, the coffee-to-go lifestyle has developed since then at breakneck speed across the entire country and all social classes. But takeaway coffee is also throwaway coffee. Every day, around 7.6 million paper cups end up in German dustbins: 320,000 cups per hour, 24 hours a day, 7 days a week. In the USA, the figure is put at 25 billion cups a year. Each cup has a fine coating of plastic so that the contents are not absorbed in the paper, and, because coffee should be drunk hot, the cups also have a paper handle to prevent the fingers from scalding, and sometimes they come with a paper tray for group consumption. And, naturally, a plastic lid so that, on the way to the office, home or to the next best coffee shop, the contents don't spill over while your head is down concentrating on your smartphone. Seen this way – from the perspective of the habits of the affluent society – there would be no insurmountable obstacles to a practice of 'ethical' consumption. It is easy and available for almost every individual, particularly higher earners, to drink and eat alternatively, to shop more sensibly and to consume more responsibly.

And this does in fact happen – and much more besides. I am not trying to give the impression that there is no 'environmental awareness' in externalization societies, no sense of fairness, no individuals who are not mindful and act accordingly, no alternative movements to the unequal economic and ecological exchange. There are indeed many thousands of activists, volunteers and pro-bono workers, groups and initiatives, civil society organizations and even state institutions mobilizing in one way or another against the externalization society – environmental and development NGOs, world stores and eco-seals, textile agreements with Bangladesh and alliances against industrial aquaculture. There is 'corporate social responsibility' as the new strategic business trend, and the ambitious Sustainable Development Goals of the United Nations, campaigns to prohibit paper cups and glyphosate, information on radio and television and occasional features in glossy magazines. There is even, believe it or not, the Institutional Investors Group on Climate Change (IIGCC),[48] a club of 120 pension funds and other major investors, including (joke!) ethically correct companies like the Axa insurance group or the US hedge fund Blackrock, which have united to make sure they have a front seat in saving the planet. Despite the fact that all – or at least some – of this is good and important, let us be in no doubt that it won't fix anything.

It's capitalism, stupid! Wanting to know or not wanting to know, that is the question

One possible reaction to the examples of unequal eco-social change – soya and palm oil, cotton and sand, shrimps and coffee – could be to say: 'Sure, we know all that. We've read it in the paper and heard it on the TV, on the radio, online and in social media.' That is, in fact, the most likely reaction as well: seen that, heard that – but then promptly to forget it again or pretend to do so, and to carry on happily as before. Well, almost. Let's say we refuse the plastic cover on the paper cup, stop eating meat (but just for a while – it tastes so good), shell out for natural cosmetics for a change – or, better still, order them in the online shop ('ships in 24 hours, express delivery possible!').

Sounds familiar? Nothing new under the sun for a critical and aware public? Maybe. But if that were the case, it would only prove precisely that it's not a question of the lack of knowledge[49] that keeps the externalization society going but – in an undefined mixture of convenience and unease, thoughtlessness and excessive demands, indifference and fear – a generalized *lack of desire* to know. On both a small and, in particular, a large scale. We don't want to know what our excessive lifestyle entails, what sacrifices have to be made, where the work is done, and who pays for it. Above all, however, we don't want to hear about the underlying causes, or questions about the system itself. Questioning the system sounds like revolution, hard work and delusions of grandeur, like the 1970s, Communist splinter groups and lots of dirty washing. And yet there is probably something to all of this, and we suspect that we will not be able to avoid it.

Mind you, everyone – even the most critical minds – does their utmost not to have to ask these questions. 'It's the economy, stupid!'[50] This now famous dictum was coined by James Carville, adviser to Bill Clinton during his presidential campaign, to fire up campaign workers in 1992 to focus on this all-important question worrying voters during the recession at the time. The economy, what else? What counts is the economic situation, economic growth, economic prosperity. Clinton was elected and the USA remained prosperous – today, it is still the country with by far the highest GDP in the world – because it has remained an externalization society. To Carville's other election slogan, 'Change or more of the same', Clinton and his supporters and all future election winners and race-winning nations, in Europe no less than in the USA, responded with a resounding 'Let's carry on!' Carry on as before, with more growth, more externalization, to make sure that everything remains as it is: the best contributing to our affluence, and the rest for other parts of the world to deal with. And no more questions, please.

Or useful comments on the background to it all – comments that can be basically summed up with the phrase 'It's capitalism, stupid!' The fact that some can externalize and that others pay the price for it, that some are comfortable at the expense of the discomfort of others, points to a veritable *system question*. Externalization is based on a system, the modern world system, otherwise known as global capitalism. It is at this point that the discussion usually ends, because who wants to go on and cut off the hand that feeds them? Small adjustments, maybe; tweaking here and there, naturally; relief of the greatest hardship in the poorhouses of the world, of course – but changing the system? Really?

The ongoing economization of the sustainability discussion is a graphic example of the failsafe strategy of continuity through renewal. Anything ecologically and socially sustainable, says Michael Opielka, sociologist from Jena and head of the Institute for Social Ecology in Siegburg, must pass the quality test of economic sustainability.[51] And this means the requirement that, in a capitalistic world economy, the functional imperatives of the economic system should not be endangered – in other words that, for all the concerns about the 'environment', the system of growth, return on investment and investor confidence should not be affected. It is precisely these features of the system, however, that make a world of ecological and social sustainability structurally impossible. Anyone who really wants all citizens of the world to have a materially assured existence, a minimum degree of control over their own fate and the opportunity for peaceful social coexistence must inevitably question the externalization society – and hence the principles on which capitalism in general, and global capitalism as a system of unequal exchange in particular, are based. It is precisely at this point, however, that our enthusiasm for change and our utopian energies regularly abandon us.[52] 'When climate change and capitalism come together', says Opielka, 'society turns a blind eye'. With a little bit of climate protection here and a little bit of development aid there, we delude ourselves that everything will be all right – at least, for us.

There are also plenty of examples of this attitude among those who are aware of the problem but at heart remain self-interested. Journalists, for example, are often critical enough of the agroindustrial complex, and their demands are quite clear, at least as far as the local situation is concerned: a change in the national agricultural policy is long 'overdue' and even 'unavoidable'. But then comes the next step in their argument – large perhaps for us affluent citizens, but small for the rest of mankind – and one that doesn't question the system after all. Ultimately, it's always about finding 'an economically viable way for conventional agriculture to achieve environmentally compatible and sustainable cultivation'. Everything has to change – so that 'the food produced remains affordable'. That is what radical thinking in the context of internalized capitalist rule looks like: environmentally sound, healthy and ethically correct production, but, please, with affordable products for the critical consumer. All good intentions as the world around us collapses – but in a manner that is economically viable, above all for us. Because for us to have affordable products, others elsewhere have to pay. That's how things go in global capitalism.

Evi Hartmann, industrial engineer and holder of the Chair of Supply Chain Management at the University of Erlangen-Nuremberg, is clearly aware of this.[53] In her book

Wie viele Sklaven halten Sie? [*How many slaves do you have?*], she openly criticizes globalization but opts for an ethical rather than a structural analysis of the world economic system. She castigates the globalized production and cost accounting system as a 'snowballing transfer of pressure' along the value-added chain from the strongest to the weakest links. Her conclusion: 'The system is failing morally. And the individual attempts to find a way out of the mess with his conscience at least halfway intact.' We might ask whether systems can be an ethical failure or be criticized on ethical grounds at all – or whether such ethical preaching, when applied to systemic processes, is not ultimately just a lot of hot air. Of course, critical analysts are quite at liberty to exonerate individuals from moral blame. Indeed, 'ordinary people' cannot do otherwise – they don't act with evil intentions but attempt to make the best of the living conditions and power relations in which they find themselves.

And yet the moral principle of taking a good look at ourselves and reflecting on our personal contribution to the effective maintenance of our privileged status should also apply to us members of the externalization society. But, above all, we should turn from a moral to a structural criticism of the system. Taking system critique seriously, we would no longer rely on market economy instruments to control the effects of the unequal capitalist exchange structure – or at least not regard the use of such instruments as the 'solution' to some problem, as Hartmann apparently does when she tells of a chance encounter with an anonymous member of the externalization society. 'Recently a well-styled boutique saleswoman, of all people, said to me: "Actually we should charge an additional 5 euros as redemption money for some items from Asia." Good idea.' True, it's a good idea to factor in these reparation payments in our market economy system – a good idea, above all, if you want to salve a bad conscience while ensuring that the structures of global capitalism remain untouched. A common-sense idea after all, reflecting not only the common sense of stylish boutique saleswomen or critical economists, ethical consumers or officiating popes, but also the well-understood self-interests of an externalization society that does not wish to vanish.

It should also slowly occur to our common sense, however, that we live in a time in which the limits of externalization have been reached. The externalization society is increasingly being caught out by its own effects and confronted by its own negative externalities. The chickens are coming home to roost, so to speak. As will be seen in the next chapter, we are not only feeling the outsiders beginning to breathe down our necks. The waste cycle that we have created to get rid at least of the most detestable, but also mostly environmentally polluting, remnants of our lifestyle is now increasingly hitting back at us, as well. The circle is closing, the noose tightening, the bombardment coming closer – regardless of our looking away, unaffected by our attempts at 'clean' consumption, unimpressed by the wealth of ideas coming from the marketing departments all over the externalization world.

These departments are now coming up with ideas such as hip jeans made of plastic waste, proposed by the Dutch fashion label G-Star, for which the popstar Pharrell Williams (biggest hits 'Happy' and 'Freedom') has designed the 'Raw for the Ocean' line, the first jeans collection made from recycled plastic from the Pacific.[54] The company wanted to fish 9 tons of plastic from the sea for a good consumer cause. All of 9 tons – almost a millionth of the more than 10 million tons of waste that are dumped every year in the oceans, three-quarters in the form of plastic. In the 1950s, the entire world produced 1.5 million tons of plastic a year. Today, it is almost 300 million tons. A significant portion ends up not in rubbish dumps in Nigeria or China but in the sea, as the ultimate dumping ground. Every year it takes the lives of countless aquatic mammals and seabirds. A square kilometre of the surface of the ocean contains anything up to 18,000 bits of plastic of various sizes. But the surface is just the tip of the iceberg: more than 70 per cent of the waste sinks to the bottom and remains hidden from us. Sometimes it accumulates through hydrographic turbulence to form huge visible carpets of waste, the most well-known being the Great Pacific Garbage Patch in the northern Pacific, which is now said to be the size of Central Europe.

As long as the plastic waste remains somewhere on or, better still, below the surface of the open sea, it will not worry the people of Central Europe overmuch. It will only become worrisome when it is clear that it is coming our way – in the form of microplastics, tiny particles created as the plastic waste disintegrates. Microplastics are used intentionally in toothpaste and shower gels, shampoos and peeling agents, to achieve mechanical cleaning effects. But these particles created (along with a wide range of other toxic agents) through the decomposition of the plastic waste also contaminate the aquatic food chain on their way to our own bodies through the food we eat. Plastic coming home to roost: a development that might even seem like poetic justice in view of the otherwise systematically unequal ecological exchange in the global society. For Central European households used to carefree externalization, on the other hand, it is quite obviously a cause for concern – one that is lapped up in its turn by the relevant consultancy industry. For those worried about microplastics, the Internet contains lists of the products to avoid, for example on www.utopia.de, 'Germany's number 1 website for sustainable consumption'. No joke: outwitting the plastics industry by online eco-shopping, making the world a better place by buying designer jeans. Utopia, millennium-style.

Design or disaster – or democracy after all?

This might all sound a little unkind and perhaps even unfair. But it's the principle that matters – or, in this case, two principles: consumer choice versus structural change. 'Concern is not enough', said the Swiss director and playwright Milo Rau in a noteworthy contribution to the 'refugee disaster', a topic that will be looked at in greater detail in the next chapter.[55] His dictum also applies to the context of unequal ecological exchange being considered here: concern, reparation supplements and ethical consumption are not sufficient to overcome the underlying structural problems of asymmetrical power distribution in the global capitalist system. Nor do 'intelligent' technologies provide a solution, as long as the fatal alliance between private profit, systematic growth imperatives and structural power asymmetries is not broken up.

There can be no material growth without growing resource and energy consumption – and hence further destruction of habitats and the natural environment. Above all, there can be no growth in the early industrialized societies of the Global North, inflated by the post-war economic boom into high-performance and extreme consuming economies, that is not at the expense – rising even further with every percentage point of increase in the GNP – of exploitation, and of nature and social habitats, in the Global South. The term 'green economy' frequently arises in discussion of the future of growth capitalism, suggesting that the power of an enlightened consumer society could combine with energy-efficient and eco-effective technological innovations to permit 'green growth'.[56] But, however understandable the vain desire to separate growth from exploitation of natural resources while retaining the living conditions and consumer habits of the externalization society might be in theory, in practice it must remain an illusion. It is not even necessary to make fun of the most absurd flowers of this unfettered lifestyle ecology – edible aircraft seat covers fitted in the first-class section of the long-haul Airbus A380[57] – to show up 'green capitalism' for what it is: the hoped-for sheet anchor for highly developed economies that are feeling the pinch after the latest cycle of capital accumulation, and the desperate reassurance for an externalization society doing its utmost to somehow salvage its exclusive lifestyle model in spite of all the signs that it has run out of steam.

Similar drives are at work when it is not only business lobbyists and financial analysts but also 'ordinary people' who get excited about, or make fun of, the discussion of 'peak oil', 'peak water' or 'peak everything'[58] that has been conducted recurrently in environmental policy circles and among critics of capitalism since the 1972 Club of Rome report about the 'limits to growth'[59] – the worry in these circles that the maximum amount of oil, the maximum worldwide availability of freshwater, or the maximum amount of practically any non-renewable resource has been reached or will soon be exceeded. Confronted by such prophecies of doom, 'experts' and non-experts alike point to the sinking oil prices, to new and 'unconventional' extraction methods or to progress in the extraction and development of renewable energy sources, so as to give the all-clear and to reassure the public – and possibly themselves. But this reassurance, if it does in fact have a social impact, is deceptive. The discussion of 'planetary limits'[60] is not the expression of individual or collective hysteria; nor is it far-fetched: in terms of biodiversity and the nitrogen cycle, these limits have already been exceeded today. And if not only the input side of disposable resources is considered but also the output side of the available sinks – in other words, the soil, forest and air capacities left for storing waste and binding carbon dioxide – the talk of 'peak soil', 'peak air' and 'peak biomass' must indeed be taken seriously.

Other parties involved in the discussion of the future are further along.[61] Bernd Sommer and Harald Welzer, social scientists at the Norbert Elias Centre for Transformation Design at the University of Flensburg, adopt the conclusion often drawn in critical debates on growth: that ecologically and socially exploitative growth capitalism will inevitably come to an end, be it by design or by disaster. With good reason, they opt for the constructive variant and collect ideas and approaches – as does the forward-looking Berlin foundation FuturZwei run by Welzer – for a societal shift towards what they call 'reductive modernity'.[62] However much of a break this might be with the externalization practices of the expansionist modern world, and however little the authors let themselves be carried away by any kind of technocratic control fantasy,[63] from a global perspective the alternative of design or disaster nevertheless reveals an all too self-centred view of the end, or possible ends, of the externalization society. It implies that a social transformation imposed on us 'from outside' would be equivalent to a calamity, a disastrous conclusion to the story. And it suggests, at least, that a strategy of 'internal' reversal would enable us to remain in the driving seat and keep control of our fortunes.

However, both of these scenarios appear unrealistic at the moment. The end of the global capitalist system of unequal ecological exchange on which the externalization society is based is likely to occur neither by design nor by disaster. These alternative choices once again fail to take other potential agents for change into account – namely, those who have always provided the affluent capitalism of the Global North with the resources required for it to produce and reproduce its wealth: cheap labour and fertile land, valuable natural resources and huge waste dumps, biomass and carbon sinks.

Let us imagine the transformation instead as one that is driven above all by the Global South, by the people off whose labour and land, water and air, natural resources and deposits we live, at whose expense we do business, and who are now finally demanding payment. The social movements that are doing exactly this have existed for some time; there are many of them already and many more are being created – from the Brazilian landless movement MST to the international peasant organization Via Campesina, from the Zapatistas in Mexico to the National Alliance of People's Movements in India. These and many others, many thousands of agents of change from the 'outside', are the ones initiating the transformation that 'threatens' the externalization society today and in the future – in the form not of disaster but of the demand for global democracy, a demand that calls for the empowerment of the historically disempowered and that thus eludes the design aspirations of the Global North. It is a demand for global democracy – but one that will not and cannot be a globalized growth democracy emulating the Western development model.

Democracy on a global scale is not a question of design or disaster. For beneficiaries of the externalization society, it augurs less a disaster than a fundamental loss of control – difficult enough to put up with for those who for centuries have been pulling the strings. For all others, however, it holds out the prospect for putting an end to the system of unequal exchange. Transformation by democracy:[64] according to the author and journalist Kathrin Hartmann, on the 'inside' of the externalization society this would mean not relying on the power of consumers and technological progress but on 'courage, solidarity, determination, free thinking and the unconditional belief that we are the ones who can bring about the changes we want' – in a word, relying on democratic politics. As for the 'outside', in a global perspective, democratization means what Milo Rau aptly describes as 'global realism':[65] the realization of the fact that continued externalization is reaching limits today that can be overcome only by brute force, and can be ignored only with recourse to the coping ideology of 'cynical humanism'. 'Let us therefore stop', says Rau, 'believing in the capitalist myth that it can go on like this forever – in a manner that is somehow less lethal for the losers of the system, somehow less embarrassing for the winners, somehow cleaner for the planet.' This narrative has, indeed, finally lost its credibility.

Postscript

The aphorism by Heiner Müller introducing this chapter reveals – *avant la lettre*, so to speak – the embarrassing secret of the externalization society.[66] Not, of course, in the candy-wrapped words that we would like to hear so that we can ingest them all and then shamefacedly excrete them again so as to be rid of them, but rather bluntly and unsparingly: 'Somewhere bodies are being broken so that I can live in my shit.' Admittedly, this is vulgar, disquieting, unashamed. But are we really unable to deal with the truth even when it is expressed in artful terms? The dramatist Müller hits the nail on the head. If his words appear to be too strong, then it is us who are too weak.

4

Within Versus Without: Externalization as a Monopoly on Mobility

There were musicians, there was Beauty, there was wine. All these and security were within. Without was the 'Red Death'.

Edgar Allan Poe, *The Mask of the Red Death* (1842)

Do not come to Europe. Do not risk your lives and your money. It is all for nothing.

Donald Tusk, President of the European Council, 3 March 2016[1]

Semi-globalization

No one will dispute that we are living in the age of globalization. We associate the fall of the Berlin Wall and the end of the bloc confrontation that defined post-war Europe with all kinds of lasting liberalization: the removal of border fences, globalized markets, the worldwide dissemination of Western values and the victory of liberal democracy. Until recently at least, barriers and passport controls appeared to be a thing of the past. For Germans or the Irish, there is no need any longer to change money for a summer holiday in Greece or a weekend in Madrid. And even beyond the borders of Europe, our freedom of movement has also expanded massively. The planet has become a global village, and we are all citizens of the world.

Driven additionally by the rapid developments of recent times in information, communication and transport technology, our lives today are almost unrecognizable from the way we lived in the late 1980s. Space and time are available to us in a completely new form. Karl Marx's dream of empowering members of society to do anything they want – 'one thing today and another tomorrow'[2] – appears to have come true for us, at least in part: eating an exotic fruit for breakfast, working for an international company during the day, skyping with friends on the other side of the globe in the evening. And then, as in the Marxist utopia, to 'criticize after dinner, just as I have a mind' – and to think about where to go for my next holiday, a city break or cruise, the Northern Lights or glacier calving in Patagonia.

The battle of the sexes – she wants a holiday in the mountains, he one by the sea (or vice versa) – that economic game theorists cite as a classic example of a difficult lifestyle decision turns out on closer inspection to be a game for the privileged, one that not everyone can play, and one posing decision-making problems that not everyone has. Sea or mountains, Rome or Paris, Togo or Fiji – or maybe all of them together. These are dilemmas that even in the era of globalization do not concern 'the whole world'. Even in the wealthy societies of the Global North, they don't concern everyone. Here, too, the possibility of living in grand style is unevenly distributed. For the vast majority of people living in the Global South, however, these alternatives – and countless others that we also take for granted – sound strange, absurd or even cynical.

Seen this way, globalization is not a fact of life, an undeniable reality. It is a reality for some, but an illusion for many others. To a certain extent, globalization is a chimaera, a phantom picture produced and disseminated in the Global North of the economic and social, material and cultural situation in the world. And the popular talk of the 'chances' offered by globalization, the opportunities, productive effects and ability to bring people and nations together, is quite often merely ideological – especially when it is claimed that these chances and opportunities are evenly distributed and available to all. The opposite is true in fact: while globalization no doubt opens up certain options, it also quite clearly closes down others. It creates restrictions as well as opportunities; it is a force of separation as much as of connection.

'Opening' and 'fluidity', 'hypermobility' and a 'borderless world' – all of these terms and ideas that have been heard since 1989 and are still current today, not only in public discussion of globalization but also more recently in academic papers, present a remarkably incomplete picture of 'one world'. The reverse side offers a completely different reality – a world surrounded by fences and full of restrictions. The era of globalization has indisputably produced newly won freedoms, but it has also undeniably created restrictions on freedom. And neither – freedom or constraints, benefits or losses – evens out or offsets the other, since they are both extremely unevenly distributed in the world. While the inhabitants of some world regions have seen the creation of new options through globalization, those on the other side of the world have seen their options cut back.

In a second attempt to define the structures, mechanisms and practices of the externalization society, the existence on a global scale of a systematically unequally distributed 'globalization yield' will now be looked at from the point of view of mobility. The externalization society is also characterized by consistently asymmetrical travel opportunities. In this area as well, the categorical imperative in reverse described in the previous chapter applies. The physical freedom of movement allowed to members of the externalization society is not granted in anything like the same way to the others, the 'outsiders'. On the contrary, an integral component of the lifestyle practised in the 'free democracies' of the Western world is the restriction of the freedom of others. The 'open society' advocated after the

Second World War by the philosopher Karl Popper, and repeatedly and eloquently proclaimed by politicians of every hue since then, has an uncomfortable secret: it lives with, and in the final analysis off, its effective closure to an 'outside' that is perceived or represented as intrusive, encroaching and threatening.[3]

The Israeli sociologist Ronen Shamir sums up the unequal inclusive/exclusive mobility of the supposedly 'global' era as a two-edged movement towards guarded borders on the one hand and gated communities on the other – in other words, a double movement towards selectively restricted movement.[4] The gated communities – exclusive, fenced-in and guarded residential complexes where the wealthy can live happily and safely – have their transnational counterpart in the form of guarded borders, the frontiers of rich nations with technical, police and military controls designed to keep out non-citizens seeking access to the affluent regions of this world. On both a small and large scale, social spaces are created to keep 'outsiders' at bay, secured zones of prosperity seeking to seal themselves off from the impositions of social reality. And above it all hovers what Shamir calls the 'paradigm of suspicion': those who rattle the fences surrounding the affluent islands of this world are troublemakers at the very least, and are actually perceived as criminals; those who enter the home of the prosperous without authorization disrupt the lifestyle of the privileged and violate the integrity of their world.

The current 'refugee crisis', which will be dealt with at the end of this chapter, brings to mind a story by Edgar Allan Poe – a gloomy one, needless to say – that reads like a metaphor for the current dissociation of the affluent societies from the outside world. The main character in *The Mask of the Red Death*, a prince with the apt name of Prospero, barricades himself along with thousands of courtiers in a fortress and hosts a masquerade ball while a deadly epidemic is raging outside. 'A strong and lofty wall girdled it in. This wall had gates of iron.' The courtiers 'resolved to leave means neither of ingress or egress to the sudden impulses of despair or of frenzy from within'. The contrast between the two worlds, between the glittering celebrations within and the wretched misery without, is vividly described by the master storyteller: 'There were buffoons, there were improvisatori, there were ballet dancers, there were musicians, there was Beauty, there was wine. All these and security were within. Without was the "Red Death".'

'The external world could take care of itself.' Poe's story can be read as an allegory of the externalization society, one that in real life even manages to communicate news of the 'frenzy from within' to the outside world. Its members repeatedly leave the fortress to pass on the tidings of their prosperity and, having done so, return to the safety of their own walls – walls that are then made even higher so as to continue to ward off outsiders attracted by the affluence within. Freedom of movement is highly valued by the externalization society, but it is an asset that cannot be made universally available. Mobility is a monopolized resource exploited by the chosen few but denied to the rest. Physical regulation of movement – mobility for some, lack of mobility for others – is an essential element of the Western lifestyle. It is a constitutive component of a supposedly 'globalized' world, which the Prosperos of affluent capitalism want to keep to themselves.

In Poe's story, the Red Death nevertheless manages eventually to penetrate into the festive society, with devastating results. And the externalization society is less and less in a position – or only with even more misanthropic measures – to keep the fortress open for its own population but closed to uninvited guests. The mobility regime established by the societies of the Global North is in crisis, as its jittery reaction to the current migration situation clearly shows.

Hey ho, hey ho: away we go from the externalization society ...

Spatial mobility means travelling. Kant is reputed to have said that 'travel broadens the mind'. If that is the case, the citizens of the Global North are avid to have their minds broadened. For decades, the Germans have been regarded as the 'world champion travellers'.[5] In 2015, at least, they flew abroad more than ever before: 81.6 million passengers left German airports for journeys of various lengths, continuing a growth trend of previous years. In purely mathematical terms, the entire population of Germany was abroad once during the year. Only one in ten Germans has never flown. According to statistics, men fly more often than women. Three-quarters of the flights were to other European countries, but a good 20 million were intercontinental flights, almost 6 million of them to the USA, followed closely by North Africa, South-East Asia and the Far East.

The Germans are not the only ones to travel, however. The members of all rich societies have become globetrotters. The route from London to New York is the most popular in the world: in 2015 alone, 4.2 million passengers made the journey between the two cities. Organized tourism has become a global phenomenon that has now also captured the new Chinese middle classes. The annual holiday in sunny climes has become the social norm, and the generalized wanderlust has remained unaffected by financial crises and the increasing number of trouble spots around the globe. There are enough destinations on offer: if bombs explode in Turkey, Tunisia or Bali, tsunamis rage in Thailand, or hurricanes wreak havoc in the Caribbean, the holiday portfolio just has to be diversified, with vacations in neighbouring countries or on other sun-drenched islands or – if all else fails – in good old Spain. In 2016, it received 76 million visitors (compared with 68 million in 2015), making it the greatest beneficiary of European tourists' fear of terrorism. Instead of flying to the Mediterranean or the Dominican Republic, those who prefer an individual experience can seek out remote and as yet supposedly 'undiscovered' spots or opt for some kind of global aid tourism, which has recently become a flourishing market niche – in the form, for example, of volunteer work in Costa Rica, where young Europeans dig out tortoise eggs from the beach at night for transport to safer incubation sites.[6] 'Thanks to your assistance, a few more tortoises can be safely deposited in the sea', animal-loving travellers are promised by the tour organizer, which feathers its own nest with the aid of the generous and not inconsiderable contributions from the loving parents of its clientele.

This is not the place to ponder on the well-known *ecological* consequences of the widespread and growing enthusiasm for travel – for example, the paradox of an intercontinental flight to help tortoises give birth. According to the United Nations World Tourism Organization (UNWTO), international tourist arrivals increased from 50 million in 1950 to 684 million in 2000, picking up once again to over 922 million in 2008 and almost 1.1 billion in 2013.[7] Surveys ('Have you travelled at least once on holiday in the past year?') reveal that the proportion of adult Germans going on holidays increased from 49 per cent in 1972 to 76 per cent in 2008 and has probably not decreased since then. The questionable *social* consequences of a monocultural touristification of the most popular holiday destinations in this new global recreational colonialism will not be discussed here either. However, a few comments on both of these aspects may be appropriate.

When stressed or dissatisfied affluent citizens travel to distant fields to take part in 'work & travel abroad'[8] or to recharge their proverbial batteries, they inevitably consume energy elsewhere and demand the labour of others. Anyone coming from Germany who wishes to know more about their climate footprint as a tourist can consult the World Wildlife Fund (WWF), which predicts the resources typically exploited by leisure travel.[9] Apart from the price of the holiday, for example, two weeks' all-inclusive holiday on the Caribbean beaches of Cancún, Mexico, cost the rest of the world 7,218 kg of carbon dioxide per person – 90 per cent for the flight and the rest for the air-conditioned hotel, the immense grounds with green lawns (which are not found anywhere else in the region) and the odd hour or two on jet-skies, not to mention the ice-cold bottled water (unlike the locals, travellers in these regions cannot be expected to drink the tap water) and the bite-size plastic-wrapped pieces of fruit. By comparison, the impact of a seven-day cruise in the western Mediterranean is almost negligible: just 1,224 kg of carbon dioxide per person, which no doubt makes the wellness oasis on board and the stress-ful lightning coach trip through the streets of one of the ports the ship fleetingly stops at easier to reconcile. Could the less dramatic eco-balance explain why the number of German passengers on ocean cruises has increased sixfold since 1998, from 300,000 to over 1.8 million in 2015?[10] Who knows? At all events, 'sustainable flying' is one of the advertising slogans of the German tourist giant TUI.[11] The marketing departments of the major cruise companies could well have done with a slogan like that.

But let's leave that aside. Nor should we spend too much time considering the consequences for the friendly locals of the structural over-exploitation of natural resources at the global destinations headed to by the travel-hungry masses of the affluent countries: the enormous use of land through the building boom in coastal regions; the immense consumption of water by visitors at the expense of the local population; the problem of disposing of the sewage and waste of the succession of new groups of holidaymakers; the misuse of natural resources to satisfy the craving for souvenirs by rich leisure-seekers and do-gooders; the shifts in the structure of local economies towards the sole production of tourist-related services, with the associated destruction of traditional work and lifestyles; the vital reliance of entire economies on the constant and unending stream of visitors from the centres of global wealth.[12] The business sectors in the Global North that channel these streams like to talk of 'tourism as a development factor',[13] but as a rule it merely reinforces the unequal development in the world regions sought out by the millions of 'development aiders'. Faced by the dilemma of having to live off the destructive wanderlust of the Global North, the destination countries in the Global South even welcome the predicted further growth of global tourism – which is expected to entail the doubling of water consumption and tripling of the requirement for land by 2050.[14] There are no corresponding estimates for the further growth of South-East Asian sex tourism or the Western orphanage tourism in Africa, Asia or Central America. Here too, however, the 'development' is likely to continue merrily.

Nevertheless, none of these side effects and collateral damage caused by Western travel habits will be the focus of our discussion here, but rather the *unequal entitlement structures* within this global mobility system. While some can visit other countries and peoples more freely, more often and more intensively – added comfort is now a major factor in both holiday and business travel – billions of others are faced by restrictive mobility policies. The freedom of movement taken advantage of as a matter of course and valued as a fundamental feature of their lifestyle by citizens of the affluent democracies in the Global North is in glaring contrast to the limited and withheld opportunities for most of the world's population. Their lack of mobility is determined not only by their much lower, if not completely absent, material opportunities for international travel – they simply cannot afford the globe-trotting habits of consumers in the Global North. What is more, their possibilities for entering other countries are restricted by law, and their desire for travel is systematically suppressed or thwarted from the outset by formal obstacles, obstructions and prohibitions.

The externalization society is based on a globally split mobility regime. 'Hey, let's see what's going on out there' is the battle call of the modern cosmopolitan – who asks the rest of the world to kindly stay where they are. Just as Donald Tusk, President of the European Council and representative of 338 million EU citizens, responded to the latest surge in refugee migration from the Middle East and North Africa. In his official public discouragement of potential refugees, he did not fail to mention not just the physical dangers but also the material costs of a desperate and ultimately hopeless land or sea journey to the borders of the European Union: 'Do not risk [...] your money.'[15] The affluent European knows what counts in life.

... and into the externalization society? The value of a passport

Border controls and the visa policies in rich democracies that specifically structure the inequality of mobility provide graphic evidence of the chasm separating the Global North from the countries of the Global South. A working group led by the Berlin sociologist Steffen Mau has studied this 'global mobility divide'.[16] The results illustrate the difference in status between rich and poor countries, which is constantly reproduced by granting visa-free travel for the ones and imposing compulsory visas on the others. While the citizens of rich nations can set off at will on their voyages of discovery or business trips, the legal travel opportunities for citizens of many poor countries are extremely limited and subject to extensive, wearisome and expensive checks. The democratic societies of the Global North have erected a sturdy legal wall around themselves for (or against) travel at short notice by undesirable or unattractive visitors – while they are in a position, conversely, to make full use of their documented right to freedom of travel. Like so many things, the value of a passport is unequally distributed in the world. The door-opening power of the wine-red EU and the dark-blue North American passport reflects the economic clout, geopolitical status and global authority of the countries that its passport holders are fortunate enough to be citizens of – in contrast to the misfortune of those who do not possess such passports.

The asymmetry of global freedom of movement is striking.[17] Those who can decide spontaneously to go to the airport and fly 'somewhere' are usually no longer aware of this power differential. Citizens of the United States, for example, can travel without a visa to ninety countries, while citizens of only thirty-six countries have the right to enter the USA in this way. The visa-freedom index established by Mau and colleagues shows that this non-reciprocal mobility entitlement is by no means only a North American phenomenon, but that in general there is a clear bias in recognition of freedom of movement in favour of the Western nations. In 2010, for example, ninety-five countries allowed Irish citizens to enter without a visa, ninety-four did so for Danish citizens and ninety-three for Germans – while citizens of Iran could travel without problem to a mere six, Pakistanis to four and the citizens of Iraq, Somalia and Afghanistan to two. This radically unequal freedom of movement correlates statistically with the wealth of the countries concerned: the higher the GDP – i.e., the economic per capita value added in a country – the more freely the people of those countries could travel the world. Wealth gives mobility – this dictum applies both locally and globally, not least because rich countries and the wealthy in other countries are not seen as a direct threat to our own wealth or its safe enjoyment.

Above all, however, it is evident that the international mobility gap has widened markedly in the age of globalization. From a long-term historical perspective, we can see that mobility in the years between 1969, before the most recent globalization boom, and 2010 has become polarized on a global scale. In this period, the rich countries have introduced an asymmetrical mobility regime to their taste: free movement of goods and persons from the Global North and simultaneous restrictions on the movement of goods and, in particular, of persons from the South. In the mid-2000s, half of the world population could travel without a visa to fewer than twenty-five countries, and two-thirds could do so to fewer than thirty-five. In the supposed 'global epoch', only people from the OECD world, whose economic privileges translate directly into preferential legal treatment and social advantages, have true global freedom of movement. The affluent capitalist societies have thus created a global mobility monopoly, a one-sided maximization of their mobility opportunities. Citizens of the European Union can travel to practically any country in the world without a visa, or else – so they cannot be accused of anything beyond their status as privileged citizens of the world – obtain a tourist visa without difficulty.

The citizens of the less affluent nations in turn can only dream of this practically unlimited freedom of spontaneous movement at short notice throughout the world. Or most of them, at least. A further feature of the divided mobility regime is its social structure: there are also first- and second-class citizens (and many more classes besides) within poorer countries with limited and controlled mobility. To be more precise, by way of their visa policies, the rich countries have created a selective system for issuing entry and residence permits, based not only on the applicants' nationality but also on their economic and social status. A number of conditions have to be fulfilled for a visa to be issued: financial resources and insurance protection, an address in the country being visited, and a return ticket or intention to return. The visa-based mobility regime thus proves to be a highly complex system with different speeds and structural probabilities. Within it, citizens of the capitalist democratic centres can travel in and out of countries practically at will, whereas those living on the periphery of the supposed 'global village' can do so only if they meet the harsh and self-interested criteria of the affluent capitalist nations' border gatekeepers, and even then usually only for a limited time.

So here we have the border regime of the externalization society. If we think of visa policy as an instrument of mobility monopolization, two 'border issues' are of particular significance. The first is the question of reciprocity and the functional connection between opening and closing. While we children of affluent societies can go out into the world, the world 'out there' cannot come into ours, or at least not in the flesh-and-blood form of people. Borrowing a term from biology, the mobility regime tailored to the centres of the global society could be described as 'semi-permeable'.[18]

Like a cell membrane, the prevailing visa policy allows border traffic in one direction but prevents it in the other. The borders of the externalization society have exit gates but are not permeable from the outside, or are designed at least so as to keep out undesirable elements. In terms of mobility, this means not only that the costs of our own freedom of travel are imposed on the destination societies but also that any attempt by these societies to gain access to the affluent world is repulsed.

The second 'border question' about the visa system that is raised – and, in a certain sense, deported – concerns where border management actually takes place. And here once again we encounter a manifest – at first, seemingly just administrative, but in fact quite material – externalization effect. The politics of visa application, issuance or refusal is a means of outsourcing the borders of the externalization society to distant countries and regions of the world. 'Pushing the border out' beyond one's own world is the way Steffen Mau and his colleagues describe this shift: the access control points are extraterritorialized: they are transferred from the territory of rich countries to the social no-man's-land of the consulates and consular departments of their embassies in the poorer world regions.[19] What we have come to know as the Dublin Regulation in refugee policies, which makes the first state where a refugee arrives responsible for examining an asylum request, has long been a feature of visa policy. The visa application is made and examined in the country of origin so that the person wishing to move does not even get to his or her desired destination and does not appear before those who don't want him or her in the first place. If 'Dublin' is meant to protect us from unwanted immigration and to turn back asylum seekers far from our own doors (thereby sparing us the unpleasant business of deporting them), the discreet visa policy may be seen as 'Dublin for all' or a 'permanent Dublin': in some office out there in the world, immigration, transit and residence applications are submitted, but we never hear about their rejection and we never see the faces of the applicants – thanks to the political authority and bureaucratic rationality of the externalization society.

On the subject of authority, extraterritorializing borders, externalizing them, also means externalizing the force and coercion inevitably connected with border demarcation and controls, border security and maintenance. Force and coercion are exercised at and beyond the borders in order to maintain 'social peace' within them. The development sociologist and economist Ernst Neumayer from the London School of Economics describes the visa policy and its restrictive application with regard to citizens of poor nations as the 'first line of defence' against undesired access. It is the legal outpost that preserves our world and lifestyle from potential intruders. German statesmen are fond of saying that the country's security is (also) defended in the Hindukush.[20] But Germany's prosperity is defended, for the time being mainly by the police and military of other states, not only at the borders of Macedonia and in the refugee camps on Chios, but also unobtrusively on a daily basis by German administrative offices round the globe. If the military actions at the outer borders of the European Union and the visa policy of European embassies in the rest of the world are regarded as two sides of the same coin – and this is the only realistic way of seeing them – it becomes evident that the externalization of mobility control is a shared responsibility. At the border posts, the shielding forces of the externalization society show their brutal face; at the office desk, a more subtle mode of smart borders, 'intelligent' access control using information technology, is at work.[21]

Both forms of outsourced protection of the externalization society from the outside have their violent side, even if we children of affluence have successfully erased it from our conscious perception and eliminated it from our everyday life. Pushing the borders out is to be understood not only in a physical sense; it also means removing the border regime of the externalization society from our field of vision and our sensibilities. It would appear that our constant experience of being able to travel at will and without complication has made us blind to the fact that this experience is not granted to many other people in the world, and even that – in our name and to foster our wellbeing – they are legally denied the right, if necessary by force.[22] It is only since the Schengen crisis, with the potential – and, in some cases, actual – restriction on the hitherto unlimited freedom of movement within Europe, that we have become aware of the reverse side of this mobility. Otherwise, we have simply grown accustomed to the asymmetrical, selective, exclusive freedom of movement enjoyed by us; it has become an unquestioned and self-evident everyday practice.

Against this background, it is quite understandable that the Turkish government should have agreed in early 2016 to act as the first line of defence against refugees coming to Europe from the Middle East only on the condition that Turkish citizens would not require visas to enter the European Union.[23] This political request and the direct reaction to it provide an eloquent illustration of the divided global mobility regime and are indicative of an externalization practice that has become second nature to us: the Turkish state was required to satisfy no fewer than seventy-two criteria for its citizens to be able to travel freely in Europe. Turkey's progress towards visa liberalization was to be continuously verified by the EU Commission, and a 'safety mechanism' was to be established that would allow the EU, if need be, to put on an 'emergency brake' and reverse the liberal visa regulation.

In spite of all these delaying tactics and self-defence mechanisms, the attempt by Turkey as a threshold country to gain access to the mobility monopoly of the European centre provoked great uproar and indignation – particularly among 'Christian Social' politicians in Germany. CSU Chairman and then Bavarian Minister President Horst Seehofer publicly stated that he could 'only warn' against the planned visa liberalization for Turks in Europe, as there was a great risk that 'domestic Turkish' problems would be imported.[24] This statement summed up the conventional logic of problematization as well as the typical problem-solving method of the externalization society: as always, the import/export balance needed to be tilted in our favour – thus preventing the import and encouraging the export of problems, while enjoying the best of both worlds.

Citizenship rights and carbon democracy: the boat is full

The gains in freedom as a result of globalization and the right to transnational mobility are thus evidently two-tiered: some have such rights and freedoms – and use them at the expense of others who are excluded from them. Who is on which side of the 'mobility divide' depends first of all on nationality – basically where one was born: in Europe or the Middle East, in the USA or West Africa. The Israeli legal and political science scholar Ayelet Shachar describes this luck of the draw, which gives some a privileged status on account of their birth and puts others at a disadvantage from their earliest days, as a 'birthright lottery': those who were born in the right place and at the right time are the winners in the lottery of life.

Such arbitrary disadvantages are typically condemned in modern societies: at least, in keeping with the normative aspirations of these societies, the inherent inequalities of gender, race or class call for political measures to achieve more equality. This approach does not apply, however, to the equally arbitrary inequality of nationality. In fact, the opposite is the case: right or wrong citizenship (or non-citizenship) is a recognized and potent reason for legal or social advantage or disadvantage. In the global mobility lottery, a citizen of the Netherlands or New Zealand has a winning ticket for that reason – and for that reason alone – while someone from Armenia or Ethiopia draws a blank – unless they are among the wealthiest citizens with the means to purchase a more attractive nationality. Malta, for example, sells citizenship of its country, and hence of the EU, for a fixed price of 650,000 euros (plus 500,000 euros investment within a year).[25] Even after the birthright lottery,[26] some people are more equal than others.

Citizenship rights, that much-vaunted institution offering participation in society, whose civilizing content is of central importance to the way democratic civil societies depict themselves, are thus evidently a two-edged sword. Right after the Second World War and as a reaction to the disruption of all standards of civilization by the Nazis, the British sociologist Thomas H. Marshall, the most important analyst and interpreter of modern citizenship rights and the status of citizenship entailed by them, emphasized – and by today's standards possibly over-emphasized – their enabling and inclusive side.[27] According to him, modern democratic societies are exceptional in that they guarantee their members – the citizens – a comprehensive set of rights, including freedom of opinion and the right to conclude contracts, freedom of assembly and the right to vote, and not least the right to education, health and social security.

What Marshall saw but failed to analyse systematically was the other side of the coin: access to citizenship and its rights necessarily involves the exclusion of non–citizens. In economic terms, citizenship is a classic 'club good':[28] members of the club – here, citizens and those with an equivalent legal status – enjoy certain benefits, while non-members can be, and are in fact, generally excluded from them. In terms of citizenship, 'welcome to the club' then applies only to those born on the club premises or accepted by the club management as members even without this birth certificate. In Germany, for example, even the fact of having been born in the country did not for a long time guarantee membership – a situation that a whole generation of children of Turkish 'guest workers' are only too familiar with.

Whatever the case, for 'insiders' the constitutional and welfare state in democratic capitalist societies worked, at least in the decades after the Second World War, as an institutional arrangement to increase the opportunities of large population strata. More than ever today, however, it has revealed itself to be in fact what it has always been – namely, an effective instrument for the exclusion of 'outsiders' from society. From the beginning of modern capitalism, it was the citizens of Western democracies themselves – the vast majority of whom were members of a dispossessed class in a society of private ownership – who waged political and social battles for recognition and the progressive extension of their rights, but also for the exclusion of others from these self-same rights. The US sociologist Immanuel Wallerstein, the main protagonist of the world-systems analyses introduced in Chapter 2, has compared this constant social struggle of disadvantaged groups for greater access to citizenship rights and their parallel effort to restrict this access for other groups with the squabbling of shipwrecked passengers for a place in the lifeboat: 'They tended to act as though they wished to secure a place on a lifeboat called citizenship, but feared that adding others after them would overload it.'[29]

'The boat is full': the fear that the space in the 'lifeboat called citizenship' was limited, and that a place in the radiated warmth of relative entitlement was a rare commodity in a democratizing capitalist society, has always been translated into a political move by the occupants of HMS *Welfare State* to pull up the gangplank of rights to access as soon as they were on board. In the history of citizenship rights, the fear of the large number, of a mass of additional entitlement holders, has regularly given rise to demands for limits to access: those 'inside' wanted to remain among themselves; those who had managed to join the citizenship club no longer wanted to make a fuss about its exclusivity. Wallerstein shows how in the history of democratic capitalism workers originally campaigned against citizenship rights for women – and then the two together agitated against 'foreigners'. The more vehemently the disadvantaged appealed to 'equality' as the guiding principle of social transformation and political reform, the greater the obstacles erected to prevent the assertion of rights by 'all-comers' – a dynamic driven not only by the ruling classes but also on the initiative of those who already enjoyed a certain set of rights. The recurrent emergence of binary social categorizations – bourgeois and proletariat, man and woman, black and white, native and foreign, civilized and barbarian – bears witness to the constant endeavour in the political community to limit legal entitlements for others or to completely prevent these groups from gaining access to citizenship.

If, in the German case, former East Germans – though not only them – revolt against the supposed 'Islamification' of the community of citizens that they themselves joined only a generation ago, this defence mechanism is merely another instance of a historically familiar citizenship pattern of 'exclusive inclusion'. It would seem that little worries large groups of citizens and their political representatives today more than the imagined danger of an 'immigration into the social system', and nowhere in civil society is 'zero tolerance' practised so absolutely as in the denial of legal rights to 'foreigners'. Marshall had already pointed out that recognition of others as equals and therefore as citizens with equal rights depended on the perceived belonging to a shared 'culture' – meaning above all the respective national identity of European societies. It would appear today that national reservations regarding the recognition of citizenship rights are becoming more rather than less important. Citizenship rights, whose protection and guarantee are a basic constituent of 'advanced' democracies' self-conception, are regarded as a precious commodity and pre-empt, if the going gets tough, even those human rights that common sense would normally accord priority to. In externalization societies, this prioritization is evidently absent: when it comes to pledging mobility and access rights, citizenship trumps human rights and non-citizens are reduced to second-class humans.

It might also be mentioned that the denial of citizenship rights in Western capitalist democracies is directly linked with the material and ecological externalization practices discussed in the previous chapter. In this regard, the US political scientist and historian Timothy Mitchell has come up with the telling concept of 'carbon democracy'.[30] The history of citizenship rights and the corresponding dual externalization dynamic – protection from claims from the outside accompanied by the shifting of costs to third parties – can be properly understood only when the political economies of the 'developed' world are seen in the interplay with their specific political ecology. The social entitlements achieved by citizens in the Global North are essentially an effect of the material wealth accumulated over a long period of time. In European societies, however, this wealth – and with it the growing scope for distribution and the structural possibilities for integrating the have-nots in the community of citizens – was closely connected with their specific energy regimes, established since the eighteenth century.

It is no coincidence that 'Kohle', the German word for coal, is also a slang word for money, assets, prosperity. The expansion and intensification of coal mining in this part of the world in the mid nineteenth century also in some way marked the birth of features that still define the modern externalization society today: continuous economic growth; the rise of industry and factory work; workers' struggles for social rights and their increasing organization and unionization; growing material prosperity, also for the non-propertied classes; the dual movement of mass production and mass consumption; and the spread in all classes of a lifestyle with intensive resource utilization and emissions. This social dynamic was impelled to an even higher and more expanded level, perhaps reaching its peak, in the shift in the twentieth century from coal to oil as the economic, political and social lubricant of the Western way of life: the seemingly unlimited availability of 'black gold' as a cheap and mobile resource, whose extraction sites could be much more easily decoupled from the sites where it was consumed than was the case with coal, revolutionized societies in the Global North and the lifestyles of most of their citizens.

In this way, by the end of the Second World War at the latest, a society had evolved that in practically every respect was dependent on drilling rigs and pipelines – with respect to its prosperity, its everyday life, its powerful position in the world system. What may be called 'fossilist' capitalism,[31] in other words an economic system based on the massive use of fossil fuels – coal, lignite, oil and natural gas – was ingrained in all institutions and penetrated all areas of social life. Carbon capitalism seeped far into the heads, bodies and hearts of the people in the Global North, for the simple reason that their social reproduction – their earnings, their material upkeep, their entire daily lifestyle – was now directly linked to a certain form of resource exploitation, energy generation and production organization. The basic, and without any doubt justified, interest of the vast majority of wage-earning citizens in a better – perhaps even a good – life, participation in political and social life, social advancement and 'a bit of a life of their own'[32] made an essential contribution to Western industrial capitalism's transformation into a 'carbon democracy'. This specific type of democracy was supported ultimately by a great social coalition: those who wished to benefit from growing prosperity now inevitably developed the same interest in the perpetuation of the new social reproduction model as those who called in their election manifestos for the long-term stabilization of economic prosperity and, preferably, its unlimited growth.

Industrial capitalism and carbon democracy thus became the driving forces of a society whose production and consumption patterns, work and lifestyles, common perceptions and everyday practices were based on the steady supply of cheap resources and the effective externalization of the economic, ecological and social costs of this entire arrangement. To put it more simply, the confident and persuasive 'more of the same' became the overarching political project throughout the entire Global North – exploit nature, use cheap labour, sell goods and overload ecological sinks elsewhere, while increasing prosperity, promoting mass consumption, manufacturing 'intelligently' and 'cleanly' and granting social rights at home. This was the remarkably simple equation of the externalization society that proved progressively to be working out. So much so that at some point it developed into a constellation that fostered a broad consensus in favour of the whole arrangement, a constellation in which the economy was buzzing, more democracy was dared *and* the sky above the Ruhr industrial region became blue again[33] – a veritable social miracle. An advanced capitalist win-win situation, but one which also included giving access to the outside world while preventing the outside from encroaching upon the inner world.

Who can blame the externalization society for its ambition to maintain this ingenious structure and advantageous global status quo? It is an ambition held above all by the main beneficiaries, the large corporations and capital owners in the rich societies of the world – but one that also inevitably animates 'ordinary people' in the externalization society. The carbon democracy did not solve capitalism's structural problem of systematically allotting unequal social positions to the owners of capital on the one hand and wage-earners on the other, and essentially made no difference to the fact that the rich in a particular country had greater opportunities in life than the poor. But it definitely raised the standard of living of society as a whole and boosted the level of consumption in the rich, and increasingly richer, industrial capitalist countries to hitherto unseen heights, from where they could look down on the 'underdeveloped' nations in the rest of the world – and have a look at the ecological devastation no longer happening on their doorstep but somewhere 'on the other side of the world', a sight they could ultimately choose not to look at.

Since then, we have all been sitting somehow in the same boat, even if some are on the bridge and others manning the oars – in a carbon-driven, luxury, representative democratic steamer by the name of *Externalization Society*. And as we cruise merrily along, we are suddenly finding our progress blocked by rubber dinghies and people smugglers.

Nothing to lose but our value-added chains?[34]
Working at externalization

The externalization society has two standards of measurement: what it allows for itself, it doesn't necessarily allow to others. It therefore comes as a surprise to the externalization society if others begin to question this double standard, while it reacts to the demands of the excluded with a vehemence and aggression that speak volumes. The externalization society had not expected the losers to fight back – but they are obviously on their way to doing so.

At the end of 2016, the United Nations High Commissioner for Refugees (UNHCR) estimated that there were 65.6 million people in the world who had had to abandon their homes to flee from violence and war, persecution and human rights violations – more than ever before, at least since the Second World War.[35] Those who claim that we Europeans now have this misery directly on our doorstep and are particularly 'threatened' or 'burdened' are clearly ignorant of the figures, as apparently are those who state without any factual evidence that Germany cannot absorb 'all the world's refugees'.[36] As if this were anything like the case. According to the UNHCR, in absolute numbers, the countries taking in by far the most refugees in mid-2015 were all outside the European Union and, in most cases, at a safe distance: Turkey, Pakistan, Lebanon, Iran and Ethiopia head the list, and the first ten places are all occupied by countries in Asia and Africa.

Even more interesting, however, were the UNHCR's calculations regarding the relative number of refugees and the economic challenges for the host countries. In Lebanon in 2015, for example, there were no fewer than 209 refugees registered by the United Nations for every 1,000 inhabitants of the country; in other words, 1 in 5 people living in the country had had to flee their homeland. In Jordan, the ratio was 90 to 1,000, almost 1 in 10. How would Germany and the rest of Europe have dealt with anything approaching those proportions? In spite of the dramatic public discourse surrounding the 'refugee crisis', this completely hypothetical question becomes even more critical when the number of refugees is seen in relationship to the economic performance of the recipient countries. This shows that the economic burden caused by the current migration worldwide is extremely unequally distributed – to the disadvantage of the countries of the Global South. Per 1 US$ GDP per capita (purchasing power parity), as a benchmark for the real performance of a national economy, Ethiopia has 469 refugees, Pakistan 322, Uganda 216, Congo 208 and Chad 193.[37] Turkey, the new bulwark of European national security, has 94 refugees. And Germany? Under 20. The actual economic burden through the assistance and integration of refugees is thus an incredible twenty-five times higher in African countries than it is in Germany. And yet, while the 'Alternative for Germany' arose rapidly as an anti-immigration party, nobody has ever heard of the formation of an 'Alternative for Ethiopia',[38] perhaps because access to international media from the periphery of global capitalism is more difficult than from the heart of Europe. Or perhaps because the people there have different concerns.

Different at least from those of the rich economies of the North. The UNHCR also lists the number of internally displaced persons (IDPs) – more than 40 million people worldwide, a sevenfold increase over the number ten years ago. In the first half of 2015 alone, there were 4.2 million new IDPs, people who had been forced to move because of the violent conflicts in their own country. Altogether they included almost 1 million in Yemen, over half a million in the Democratic Republic of the Congo, 7.6 million in Syria, 6.5 million in Colombia, 4 million in Iraq, 2.3 million in Sudan (and a further 1.5 million in South Sudan). These figures relativize the social feat of the century by our standards – namely, the reunification of Germany. Even at the highpoint of the east–west migration within Germany in the early 1990s, the number never exceeded 300,000 per

year.[39] In two decades, between 1991 and 2012, the population of the former East Germany dropped by 1.1 million
as a result of internal migration – about the same as the
number migrating recently in six months in Yemen, a country
whose population is less than a third that of Germany.

There are 65 million refugees in the world, equivalent
to the population of France – and that is just the official
figure. The world is on the move. But not all refugees head
for the Global North, and not all of them are on the move
in search of a better economic future. Even if public opinion
would have it that entire countries are only too eager to
get to the promised land of Europe first, the reality is quite
different. And to judge by the differences in prosperity, one
might even wonder why this isn't the case – why the people
in the Global South aren't packing their bags and heading
north. A careful study of the data, however, points to the
fact that migration, particularly migration across borders,
is an extremely serious and far-reaching, life-changing decision. No one moves for fun – migration is not a form of
tourism. Anyone leaving his or her home or homeland
permanently or for a long time has important reasons for
doing so, and the incredible, even absurd, extent of social
inequality in the world is without doubt a persuasive one.

The US sociologists Roberto Korzeniewicz and Timothy
Moran compared the income level in US dollars, and its
distribution, in eighty-five rich and poor countries in 2007.
The result is astonishing and the global and regional differences in prosperity striking: the income levels of the
poorest and richest income groups in the populations of
countries in the Global South (not counting the super-rich
who are not included in income statistics) were *all* below
that of the poorest groups in the rich countries of the Global
North. For example, the earners at the tip of the income
pyramid in Bolivia earn less than those at the base of the
pyramid in the USA, and the entire income pyramid of
India is below that of South Korea. The richest 10 per cent
in Guatemala have a lower average income than the poorest
10 per cent in the USA, and 90 per cent of Mexicans have

a lower income than the bottom 10 per cent in Sweden. The top 10 per cent in Zimbabwe would be among the poorest in Argentina, and yet the richest 10 per cent in Argentina would be somewhere in the lower-middle section of the earnings table in the USA.

At this point, these relative discrepancies are merely statistical artefacts.[40] They might nevertheless give an inkling of what drives 'economic refugees' to turn their backs on their homeland. Korzeniewicz and Moran cite examples of real labour migration, such as that existing between Central and North America. Members of the middle class, whether lower or upper, in Guatemala will find themselves in the bottom 20 per cent of income distribution in Mexico, so that even a poorly paid job in their new country will almost certainly earn them more money. The same situation applies to Mexicans heading for the USA – provided they can get past the closely guarded southern border unscathed – to an even more striking degree. Practically every Mexican citizen outside the upper class can expect a massive increase in earnings when moving to the USA. The same applies to Bolivia and Argentina, and to Argentina and Spain – or to Ukraine and Romania, or Romania and Germany. The increased earnings to be expected through migration are always so great that in purely economic terms it would be unrealistic for inhabitants to hope for anything like such a far-reaching social advancement in their homeland. Those in Mexico or Bolivia, in Romania or Ukraine, who speculate on being able to benefit in their own lifetime from continued economic growth or their individual investments in education, from the advantages of EU membership or international development aid programmes, to the same extent as from migrating to one of the centres of global capitalism have lost before they even start. No 'internal' advancement strategy can produce anything like the improved situation that the bold venture onto the labour markets of the richest societies in the world will bring.

It borders on a miracle that flight and movement, global labour and poverty migration, can be held in check. But there are explanations for it. One of them is the divided mobility regime successfully established by the externalization society. The Global North attempts, through visa regulations and immigration quotas, green cards and seasonal labour permits, border security and deterrent legislation, to recruit 'skilled' labour and keep away 'unskilled' migrants, to attract 'high potential' for their economies and to block entrance for 'unproductive' elements. At least officially, because the mobility regime of the externalization society also includes the establishment of unofficial labour markets on which 'simple' services can be provided – for low wages, with little or no social security, without guaranteed residence status, not uncommonly with direct dependence on the employer. The global care chains[41] that have become increasingly widespread in the last two decades fit this pattern perfectly – and tend to develop in line with the international income gap, which then takes on more than just a statistical significance: Romanian women in Germany, Bolivian women in Spain or Filipino women in Hong Kong provide the care activities on 'grey' or 'black' labour markets for service provider companies or private households that can no longer be covered sufficiently, if at all, in richer societies by either the public or the private sector.

Global care chains are a paradigmatic example of externalization and the mobility regime of the externalization society. As discussed in Chapter 2, in a capitalist economy, private activities in education, childcare and care for the elderly – the whole *care economy* sphere of work, performed for the most part by women – are embedded in a structure of externalization. The continued existence in society of full-time productive work in a corporate context as an accepted way of earning a livelihood is directly contingent on the fact that all 'additional work' in support of the wage-earning situation, from cooking and washing to looking after children and the aged, is 'outsourced' within the household in the form of unpaid services – in a gender arrangement that appears 'classic' to us today but in fact became established only as a concomitant of the rise of capitalism:[42]

the man as the bread-winner, the woman as the partner who looks after everything else. In the progressive, flexible capitalism of the twenty-first century, in which female labour has been discovered – or rediscovered – and is no longer relegated to supposedly economically unproductive house-work, the balance in this gender arrangement is gradually shifting. More and more women are becoming wage-earners – and as a result responsibility for the household and family, the aged, children and kitchen is being delegated to third parties.[43]

This is certainly true for the upper and upper middle classes. Personal services, from cooking lunch and cleaning the home to taking the dog for a walk and looking after the mother-in-law during vacations, are being performed more and more frequently by domestics who are not part of the household or family and who are typically not citizens of the country where they work. Global care chains are created insofar as the work that the Mexican nanny in New York or the Ukrainian geriatric carer in Munich can no longer perform in their countries of origin is taken over by other women: mothers or sisters, aunts or nieces of the service providers working in affluent countries. In the Philippines, for example, where practically half of the economy is based on this form of 'global division of labour' and female carers have become the official number one export item, this has resulted in a massive strain on the local social networks, which presents daunting challenges to thousands of families.[44]

As if by magic, this once again means that the externalization society can enjoy the best of all worlds: the domestic labour market potential of well-educated women is exploited, the care work is carried out by cheap and reliable workers from abroad. In the meantime, the social consequences of making full use of a global care-industry reserve army are ignored, and it is even assumed that the 'treasure' who performs these services, as well as the economy of her own country, are being helped in this way. In reality, the benefits are enjoyed principally by the centre rather than the periphery. Geriatric care in rich countries, for example, would break down completely without an externalized service economy – up to round-the-clock care – supported by informal migrant workers.[45] And you don't have to be a socio-political conspiracy theorist to realize that the statutory care insurance in Germany has effectively factored this in to its catalogue of benefits, which do not come close to covering the real care requirements of private households.

Workers from the periphery of global capitalism are welcomed within the externalization society – unofficially and temporarily, as required and without any further residence entitlement, of course. The semi-permeable mobility rules in affluent societies are flexible enough to permit the entry of those who are useful to the production and reproduction economy – in the building trade or for the harvest season, for cleaning and care – while at the same time keeping out those who are not useful to this economy, or even using their biological reproduction capability at a distance, for example in the form of surrogate mother tourism.[46] Now that India, the long-standing leader in transnational reproduction services, allows surrogate motherhood only for married heterosexual couples, business is booming in Mexico. Cancún on the Yucatán peninsula – the Mallorca of the USA, so to speak – has become the capital of surrogate motherhood. This artificial city, which emerged from nowhere in the 1970s, is now also seeing new babies borne by surrogate mothers. For US$49,000, fertility clinics and surrogate mother agencies offer all-inclusive packages: ovary donation and in-vitro fertilization, surrogate pregnancy and Caesarean, legal and notarial costs, and the agency commission. And as soon as the child is born and shipped to the USA, the surrogate mother's sister can migrate to the happy young couple's household as an illegal immigrant to wash the nappies and take care of everything else that parenthood involves: all-inclusive in the truest sense of the word.

Thus, the externalization society's mobility regime comes a full circle: new forms of exploitation are continuously being discovered for the externalized world of affluent societies – going as far as the externalization of biological services, commissioned during a flying visit, collected on completion and brought back home safely. A form of exploitation by which the externalization society can reproduce itself – in the truest meaning of the word.

Curtain up: the externalization society exposed?

The great Polish sociologist Zygmunt Bauman succinctly describes the double standard set by the externalization society and its global mobility divide: 'Travelling for profit is encouraged; travelling for survival is condemned.'[47] The prevailing mobility regime is profitable – in the narrow and the broad sense – for companies and citizens in the Global North, or simply enables them to enjoy themselves. Anyone in the Global South wishing to move to seek a better life, or having to move for the sake of survival, however, is seen as a burden and even a scrounger and is caught in the net of mobility controls. Profits for the chosen ones, parasites the rest: the dangerous classes in the externalization society are 'those over there', the people on the peripheries of global capitalism. As Ronen Shamir puts it, echoing the Italian philosopher Giorgio Agamben, 'humanity itself has become a dangerous class'.[48]

The much-cited 'refugee crisis', which is turning out increasingly to be more a crisis of humanity in European societies, gives this statement a deeper and shocking meaning. Confronted by transborder mobility, as a reaction to the exclusive mobility regime of affluent societies and at the same time intersecting with it, the externalization society appears to be losing its grip – and its control. Words like 'waves', 'floods', 'flows' – language that has never been heard to describe any of the tourism emanating from the Global North and invading the Global South – are frequently used by politicians to describe the manageable number of war and crisis refugees who have arrived temporarily on the European mainland. The first drops of the deluges that have engulfed people and countries next to us, on the margins of the democratic capitalist world, are now splashing back on us – and we have nothing better or more pressing to do than to build barrages or increase the height of those that already exist.

The social coalitions that stand behind these defensive reactions in Europe are considerable – from German 'border-control' philosophers like Peter Sloterdijk,[49] who in the same breath invent and criticize a 'moral duty to self-destruction', and heads of government such as the Hungarian Prime Minister Viktor Orbán, who, in defiance of the laws of physics, would like to 'hermetically seal' their countries' borders, to the 'national fronts' present in various European countries under diverse party names, who ultimately all want just one thing: namely, to continue to keep the social reality of poverty, need and violence 'over there' hidden and out of their lives. And, in some way, 'normal', respectable and apolitical citizens are also involved in this great externalizing, excluding and suppressing enterprise, preparing themselves for the time when the law of the capitalist jungle no longer works and the 'outside' no longer wishes to remain outside.

Those who can afford it and are man enough or in pronounced need of security arm themselves with an SUV for the purpose of personal crisis management.[50] In 2001, some 100,000 sport utility vehicles were sold in Germany; in 2012 it was half a million, and the Federal Statistics Office is predicting sales of 900,000 vehicles in 2020. These huge vehicles driven by the externalization élite are not only the material symbol of a denial of climate change. They also represent the desire to be equipped against the possibility, after all, of a deluge – be it through heavy rain and flooding, or refugee flows and immigration waves. SUV drivers in our cities give the impression of being ready to defend the country's borders. And perhaps they are – pre-consciously, of course. Perhaps they suspect subliminally that those 'over there' are fighting back – in the form of climate change, which is perhaps after all something more than the reprise of the externalized 'dying forests' of the 1980s, generally ridiculed today; and in the form of migratory movements, which are being countered with asylum laws and military might, but which are not likely to end merely because we want them to.

Climate change and migration pose a particular challenge to the externalization society and foster such vegetative reactions by its defenders because both developments give a new quality – or better a new materiality – to the contact by this society with its 'outside world'. We are dealing with 'natural forces' that can no longer be ignored or forcefully stopped. The same applies to the human bodies that have suddenly materialized physically – at least those that have not drowned in the Mediterranean: 'bodies that matter' as the US philosopher Judith Butler puts it, that will not disappear into thin air and that, if need be, can react to violence by hitting back.[51]

Climate change and migration are the expression of a new form of materiality, tangibility and visibility of the externalization society – and its price. It's time to accept what we sense and to take note of what we see. 'Concern is not enough', says Milo Rau, cited earlier, in his urgent call for 'global realism'.[52] The migration we are currently experiencing in an as yet mild and restrained form in Europe is 'merely the outermost and most delicate offshoot of what billions of people experience every day. [...] The wall of mist that has protected us to date from seeing the consequences of our economic policy in the Middle East and Central Africa has dissipated.' Now that we have a clear view of what is going on in the global society, something more and different is required than the policy of either organized sympathy or reliance on other countries currently held to ransom to keep the misery of the world at arm's length.

And yet we tend still to keep our eyes closed, hoping that the increasingly evident crisis of the externalization society will ultimately be just a temporary irritation, after all. There are understandable reasons for this hope and also for the underlying concern. We have more to lose than our value-added and care chains and the advantages and profits that we have obtained from them for so long. With the rule of the externalization society, the imperial mode of living of the inhabitants of the Global North, a life at the expense of others, would also collapse. Most people in the Western world know about the decline of empires only through history books or hearsay.[53] But the end of empires is reliably accompanied by all of the psychosocial reactions that can currently be observed in 'fortress Europe' or Trump's America: crumbling certainties and defiant 'business-as-usual' slogans, vocal self-reassurance and withdrawal into the private sphere, collective whistling in the dark and sudden eruptions of violence.

In this externalization society crisis, a politico-economic consequence is becoming ever more evident, which the Viennese political scientist Ingolfur Blühdorn calls 'simulative democracy',[54] describing in an extremely illuminating manner the social mechanisms of the 'politics of unsustainability', as he puts it. His analysis spotlights a fundamental contradiction that affects and concerns both politicians and citizens of the rich democracies and that fosters the formation of an informal grand coalition between them: 'the contradiction between the rational realization of the fundamental unsustainability of the existing situation and the firm determination to defend it'. We can't go on like this – so let's go on like this. This is the tacit agreement between political élites and the people, both of whom are caught up in their own way in the conditions of the externalization society. 'Green capitalism' and 'intelligent growth' are responses to climate change on which both sides can agree – and which both sides know or suspect to be media-compatible forms of collective self-deception, but not a solution to the structural dilemma. The same is true of the popular slogans referring to the refugee policy, with the eloquent assurance of a 'new European security architecture' and a strategy of 'controlled immigration'. Anyone hearing these messages for solving the 'refugee problem' must rely on hope or belief rather than experience or reason.

And this is exactly what happens. The interaction of simulative discourse from 'above' and 'below' seems still to function in the carbon and border-security democracy of the twenty-first century – without the two sides necessarily being aware of this functional mechanism or of its underlying driving force, namely fear, the collective fear of the end of the 'good life' at the expense of others. Of course, there are quite a few corporate interests and political entrepreneurs who profit directly from the exploitation of nature and global misery and therefore deliberately and intentionally work on the continuation of the history of capitalism as a history of externalization. But most actors 'above' and 'below' make the necessity of their personal dilemma – namely, the need to justify to themselves their more or less active participation in an unjustifiable society model – into the negative virtue of a simulative and suggestive pact: to deceive themselves and to allow themselves to be deceived.[55]

What follows? What can be done in this constellation? It would be a huge step in the right direction if Milo Rau were right in his diagnosis that the exacerbation of the situation has an enlightening effect – if the assumption were correct that pictures of bodies floating ashore on Greek beaches and tear gas attacks at the border of Macedonia, and the experience of people removed from schools and businesses and deported on the next aeroplane, right next to the gate we are waiting at to go on holiday,[56] were to reveal 'even to the last of us the truth of the system' in which we live.[57] The truth about a system known as the externalization society.

Postscript

It is perhaps time to disclose the end of Poe's story *The Mask of the Red Death*.[58] At midnight an uninvited guest joins Prince Prospero's riotous celebration, behind a mask 'which had arrested the attention of no single individual before' – one with 'the countenance of a stiffened corpse' and dressed in a shroud stiff with blood. The company is gripped with a feeling 'of terror, of horror, of disgust', but the host is more angry and outraged at this unwanted disruption of the entertainment. He confronts the intruder, whose disguise has been identified as that of the Red Death raging outside, but when the shocked guests attempt to seize him, they gasp 'in unutterable horror at finding the grave cerements and corpse-like mask, which they handled with so violent a rudeness, untenanted by any tangible form'. Behind the Mask of the Red Death is – nothing. Or perhaps ourselves?

5

We Have To Talk: We Can't Go On Like This

Structural violence is silent, it does not show – it is essentially static, it *is* the tranquil waters.
John Galtung, 'Violence, Peace, and Peace Research' (1969)

Ordinary citizens will have to change their lifestyles to avert disaster, but disaster appears abstract and faraway – until it actually happens.
Michael Mann, 'The End May Be Nigh, But For Whom?' (2013)

Inequality! What inequality?

In the last few years, inequality has once again become a social issue. It began in summer 2013 with Thomas Piketty's monumental opus *Capital in the Twenty-First Century*, in which the French economist identified an ironclad development law of modern capitalism.[1] Without political intervention, a capitalist normality becomes established in which the rate of return on capital will tend to outstrip the rate of growth of the economy as a whole. The profits from capital assets absorb the distributable wealth then, and a disproportionate amount of the increased prosperity will be enjoyed by those who are already rich, while lower-income households will remain out in the cold. Left to its own logic, capitalism will produce a steadily growing income and asset disparity – a trend that Piketty describes in detail for the affluent societies of Europe and North America, particularly in the 'neoliberal' era since the 1970s.

While Piketty's study raised considerable dust, and the question of inequality was covered by editorial writers all over the world, particularly after the publication of the English translation in early 2014, the author also attracted a good deal of criticism from less social-democratically inclined colleagues. However, his findings were officially confirmed in May 2015, at least as far as the assessment of the most recent distribution trends are concerned. 'Never before in the history of the OECD has inequality in our countries been as great as it is today', said Angel Gurría, Secretary General of the organization that brings together the 'developed' industrial nations, in his presentation of the OECD social report.[2] The aid organization Oxfam went a step further when in early 2016 – as every year in the run-up to the World Economic Forum in Davos – it contrasted the unequal distribution of wealth in the OECD states with social inequality on a global scale.[3] According to the Swiss financial services provider Credit Suisse, the wealthiest 1 per cent of the world's population possess almost as much as the rest; and half of the global increase in prosperity since the start of the millennium has been enjoyed by this 1 per cent of mankind. Oxfam attracted even more attention a year later, when it pointed out demonstratively that in 2016 the fortunes of the 8 wealthiest people in the world were equivalent to the total 'wealth' of the poorer half of humanity – in other words, the material possessions of 3.5 billion people. Two years earlier, the 80 wealthiest persons would have had to pool their resources to achieve this figure, and in 2010 as many as 388 of them.

Along with the obligatory public outcry – so few! so much! – the academic experts immediately responded by pointing to the inadmissibility of comparing apples (private fortunes) with pears (national income) and hence of Oxfam's startling figures.[4] Instead of a couple of handfuls or a few dozen, they still insisted that it was several hundred wealthy households, as in earlier years, who shared half of the global economic prosperity. German economic wise men in particular took up arms to provide scholarly arguments to counter the uncontrolled talk of growing global inequality and to give a voice to economic reason.

For example, Clemens Fuest, former Professor of Economics at Oxford University and now President of the respected Institute for Economic Research in Munich, stated that global inequality was no longer such a big issue.[5] According to World Bank standards, only just under 13 per cent of the world population in 2012 lived in extreme poverty – in other words, with insufficient income to survive – compared with 44 per cent in 1981 and 37 per cent only twenty years earlier. Now there were no more than 720 million people living (or not) below the absolute minimum for existence: 'That is still too many, but enormous progress has been made.' Progress had been enormous, according to Fuest, not only at the bottom end of the scale but also with regard to the mean: 'In 1980, the average per capita income in threshold and developing countries was around 14 per cent that of the industrial countries. Today it is around 23 per cent.' Even if, for the sake of simplicity, the richer poor are combined with the really poor: with one-fifth of the average income in the affluent countries, one-tenth of the income disparity made good in three decades – should the upcoming nations of this world consider themselves to be on the right road to prosperity and general wellbeing?

This at least is what is suggested by a new economic master narrative that has received such great public acclaim in the last few years. The new élite consensus that the global prosperity gap is progressively narrowing was fuelled by Piketty himself, when he spoke in his international best-seller of the steady process of catching up by late industri-alized societies: 'The world clearly seems to have entered a phase in which rich and poor countries are converging in income.'[6] At around the same time, Piketty's French colleague François Bourguignon, former Chief Economist at the World Bank, came to a similar conclusion, pointing to a 'historical turning point' in global inequality that would do nothing less than 'effectively re-equilibrating standards of living between countries'.[7]

The main protagonist and most important coiner of catchwords in the 'convergence' discussion, however, was a second leading World Bank economist, Branko Milanović. Now at City University of New York, he has become the – perhaps reluctant – spokesman for those who would like to sugar-coat the notion of global inequality. In his extensive quantitative studies on the dynamics of global social inequal-ity, he concludes, amongst other things, that the era of globalization heralded by the fall of the Berlin Wall brought the first reduction in global inequality since the industrial revolution.[8] According to his data, after steadily increasing since the beginning of the nineteenth century, the Gini index of world income distribution dropped from 72 to 67 between 1988 and 2008. In the Gini index, 0 represents completely equal income distribution, and 100 maximum inequality – in other words, the concentration of all income in the hands of one person.

Thus, on a scale of 0 to 10, global inequality after two decades of 'convergence' is still at 7. As such, it still exceeds all national levels of inequality, a fact that professional global inequality experts themselves point out. Milanović is not the only one to state the obvious in his publications – namely, that the inequalities between societies are still enormous. For Bourguignon as well, regardless of how global inequality is measured, it 'is probably above the level of what a national community could bear without risking a major crisis'.[9] Germany, for example, scores 3 in the Gini index, and anything like the kind of inequality that has existed for decades on a global scale would be absolutely inconceivable there. Although the gap has narrowed slightly in the last quarter-century, the wealthiest 10 per cent of the world population are still ninety times richer than the poorest 10 per cent. The world as a whole is therefore more unequal than the societies of Brazil or South Africa, the nations with the most marked differences in income.

And yet the interested – or self-interested – public of the affluent societies claims with utter conviction that global wealth is converging and that the 'losers' of the most recent world economic trends are to be found in the wealthy industrial nations. The World Bank economist Milanović is also to be blamed for this remarkable interpretation of global inequality. His 'elephant curve' is a godsend for public relations workers seeking to relativize global inequalities.[10] This appealing graph, whose silhouette recalls the shape of an elephant, shows the real percentage increase in income for different global income groups between 1988 and 2008. The greatest relative increases are achieved by those between the fiftieth and sixtieth percentiles – in other words, the upper-middle classes in the emerging 'threshold countries', who form the 'head' of the 'elephant' (or its 'ears'). The least – or even zero – growth according to the graph is to be found among the lower-middle classes of affluent societies around the eightieth percentile of world income distribution, who form the bottom of the elephant's 'trunk', as it were, which then points in triumph almost vertically upwards to designate the highest global income groups and particularly the wealthiest 1 per cent of the world's population.

For convergence theoreticians of all academic and political hues, the 'elephant curve' symbolizes the gradual and ultimately unstoppable rise of the Global South. They confidently ignore the fact that, for the period from 1988 to 2008, Milanović demonstrated not only the relative shift in distribution positions in favour of the 'global middle class' outside the advanced industrial nations but also the continued absolute rise in middle-class income in the

Global North.[11] Nor do publicity-seeking interpretations take account of the fact that he described the supposed rise of the former 'Third World' explicitly as a phenomenon of the most highly populated countries of Asia alone – led by China – while large parts of the globe, not least practically the entire African continent, were effectively excluded from this development. And his precise indication that the urban Chinese middle classes were not comparable with those of the Global North in terms of income, material lifestyle or the actual level of consumption did not stop talk of the impending or even already complete 'downward mobility' of the middle classes from dominating the political stage in Europe and the USA.[12] At the same time, the discussion of global social inequality and its dynamics clearly suffers from what might be called its 'under-sociologization' and its statistical concentration on income variables, be it in the simple form of GDP per-capita income of entire nations or of a complex calculation of the world's income distribution. By contrast, a suitable and acceptable sociological analysis of world prosperity and changes in it should take into account the specific working and living conditions of the many hundreds of millions of people, particularly in China, who have recently risen above the statistical threshold of absolute poverty.[13] It should also consider factors such as the existence (or absence) of social welfare systems and the access to (or unavailability of) public infrastructures, the forced migration of rural populations, the ecological living conditions, the violence encountered in everyday life and much more besides. Only by widening the perspective in this way would it be possible to obtain anything like a realistic picture of absolute and relative prosperity outside the industrial capitalist centres of the world. But, as the inequality economist Bourguignon points out, 'such non-economic dimensions are more difficult to capture'[14] – particularly with a single statistical marker or in the form of some animal silhouette. It is for that reason that most analyses, or at least those that gain public attention, do not even attempt to take account of such non-economic factors.

Behind this is the impulse, by no means confined to economists, to sugar-coat the global capitalist situation. The 'great escape', as the British-American Nobel Laureate in Economics Angus Deaton described it in his Eurocentric review of the twentieth century,[15] is now being imagined as actually a global development path: the industrial route out of social poverty, the individual and collective ambition to improve, the self-liberation from existential hardship and material limitations. We happily attest the good health of the global capitalist world because we ourselves are happy and healthy and have prescribed for others the medicine that has worked for our own rise, and because we are in a position to condone the global prosperity situation – and to blithely state that 'the globalized world has never been as well-off as it is today.'[16]

The battlefields of global capitalism

This one-sided narrative needs to be set off against a different one, the story of the externalization society – and of its reverse. This narrative is not – or at least not only – one of the past, but still applies today: a counter-narrative to our wonderful story of progress; a counter-narrative in which the motto of modern affluence capitalism – 'internalizing profits and externalizing risks'[17] – plays a key role, and which involves the social fact of unequal – and, on a global scale, radically unequal – life expectancy.

Individual life expectancy is the prime indicator of social prosperity.[18] There is no more fundamental inequality: those who die younger are dead longer. And, guess what? It is usually the 'others' who are longer dead. This already applies to the inequality in death in Germany and Europe. Data to this effect is in sharp contrast to the opinion sometimes expressed that we should 'not get carried away' with the discussion of inequality.[19] In Germany, for example, 70 per cent of men from poorer households – but almost 90 per cent of those from the wealthiest milieu – live to be

65. While the mean life expectancy at birth in the rich households is 81 years, boys born in poor households can expect statistically to live only 70 years. In other words, rich men can envisage an average life dividend of 11 years. In terms of 'healthy life expectancy' – in other words the number of years spent in good health – the gap widens to 14 years. For women the situation is less dramatic, but the trend is similar. This discrepancy can also be found in Europe between the richer and poorer nations: a man in Germany, for example, has a life expectancy 10 years longer than one in Lithuania.

If we take the average EU life expectancy in 2013 of 80.6 years (men 77.8 years, women 83.3 years) as a yardstick, we can understand what Göran Therborn means by 'the killing fields of inequality'.[20] In the extremely unequal societies of the Global South, it is much easier on average to die than in the wealthy and – with all the reservations mentioned above – more egalitarian societies of the North, in spite of the undeniable social improvements in many regions of the southern hemisphere in the last two decades. In countries such as Chad, Afghanistan or Somalia, the life expectancy at birth today is still around 50 years – 30 years less than in Europe. Countries as diverse as Laos, Haiti and Eritrea have one thing in common: an average life expectancy of 63 years. And even the so-called 'threshold countries' or the BRICS group of countries, whose economic progress is often heralded, are nowhere near the level of a society with high longevity. The average life expectancy is still under 50 years in South Africa, 67 years in India, 70 in Russia, 73 in Brazil and 75 in China – 100th in the world longevity table.

This is the world of what Therborn terms 'vital inequality', the world of unequally distributed life expectancy and survival. When, at the age of 60, we look forward to a new chapter in life, one in two people in India have already died. However depressing the underlying social reality, this indicator is illuminating because it cannot be relativized even by the most radical believers in progress – as is done, for example, with measures like 'relative poverty', the low income of some households measured against the respective national average, which is often said to over-dramatize things and is not apparently 'real' poverty. Death, by contrast, cannot be relativized. It can, however, be conceived of as a relational category. It doesn't occur haphazardly: the Grim Reaper doesn't just visit some people sooner and others later, as the traditional image might suggest. On the contrary, the higher life expectancy of some is structurally linked with the lower life expectancy of others; worse living conditions at both the national and global levels are to be seen in their shared structural context. On a global scale, for example, the development strategies, driven by the world market, of countries rich in raw materials, the working conditions for large sections of the population in 'extractivist' economies and the unequal ecological exchange between resource economies and 'knowledge economies' effectively contribute to the structurally unequal life expectancies.[21] Ultimately, the globally wealthy live, quite literally, at the expense of the less well-off – until the early death of the latter.

This is the central argument of this book: we live at the expense of others – and in the last analysis, they die for us. Whatever economic liberalism might tell us and the others, productivity is not a miracle, progress is not universal, the narrower prospects at the peripheries of affluent capitalism are not coincidental. The remarkable, and remarkably ever-increasing, productivity of our economy is based essentially on the systematic exploitation of the material resources and physical labour – of human beings and nature – in other parts of the world. The prosperity dividend that this unequal structure has produced for many decades, if not centuries, is enjoyed for the most part by 'developed' societies – us, in other words – and further cements the global social inequalities. Progress thus takes place at the expense of those who make it possible for us to advance – while leaving them behind. By exploiting, we advance,[22] without asking afterwards how we have become prosperous – and why it is us and not others who benefit.

Imperial provincialism and the power of not having to know

It would obviously be unrealistic to claim that the global capitalist system of unequal prosperity dividends is historically fixed or that the structure of externalization winners and losers is chiselled in stone. The gradual and recently accelerating rise of China, which is forcefully elbowing its way into the hitherto exclusive Western club of externalization societies, is the most striking example of a geo-economic dynamic that is also of significance in an analysis of the externalization constellation.

China's accelerated project of state capitalist 'modernization' entails not only economic and political, but also ecological and possibly military, power shifts in the global system.[23] These in turn change China's position in the externalization structure of global society: the Chinese route to industrial capitalism is also marked by the principle of outsourcing costs – through a rapidly rising level of material consumption and the production of gigantic environmental damage, through the organization of contract manufacturing in poorer neighbouring economies, and through the strategic acquisition of land and natural resources in Africa. And, as with the European middle classes, the process of increasing material prosperity also puts the Chinese in an ambivalent social position. However precarious their relative prosperity might be, because it is not secured in the same way by the structures of the welfare state familiar to us, and however 'sub–imperial' their lifestyle might be compared with our resource consumption, by being entangled with the capitalist development strategies of the country's political and economic élite, at least the upper-middle classes in China increasingly mutate from mere objects to active subjects of externalization.

This constellation points to the complex system of overlapping and intertwined structures of externalization on a global scale. In his day, the sociologist Georg Simmel, referring to the process of European social development in the late eighteenth and early nineteenth centuries, saw the individuality of modern man as being derived from the 'intersection of social circles'.[24] Similarly, the specific positions within the social structures of the capitalist world system are derived from an 'intersection of externalizing circles'. According to Simmel, in complex and heterogeneous societies, the individuality that distinguishes every single person arises from their position at the intersection of numerous and diverse social identities. The same may be said of the features of the different positions within the complex structure of global externalization. The specific status of individual national economies, population groups and social milieus results from intersecting 'externalization circles', from their particular location at the interface of multiple, interconnected exploitation, appropriation and outsourcing processes.

Thus, it is only by looking at the complex intersection and interaction of local and regional, national and transnational externalization structures that the relative position of the German and Chinese middle classes, of the economic élites or simple wage-earners in the Global North and South, can be more precisely determined. Such a perspective casts doubt on a clear positioning of winners and losers along the North–South axis and across historical periods. At the same time, it also shows that in the last 200 years, despite wide-ranging changes in global society and even two world wars, the world has become clearly divided into countries with relatively little, and those with extremely great, inequality – a division that has remained remarkably stable to this day – and that strikingly lines up with the global North–South divide.[25] The manifold positive and statistically well-documented by-products of a more egalitarian distribution of income are therefore enjoyed unilaterally by the citizens of the wealthier societies in the world.[26]

On the whole, it therefore seems to be appropriate to frame a differentiated picture of global social inequalities within the more general externalization pattern as a basic principle of modern capitalism and its structural dynamic. The ways of the Lord may be unknowable – but the ways to the wonderfully prosperous world of the societies in the Global North from which large sections of their populations systematically benefit are not. They have been delineated here using two approaches. The first has shown how the entire individual and collective lifestyle in the wealthy societies of the Global North is based on a longstanding and extensive system of unequal exchange: work is performed, resources extracted, toxic substances set free, waste stored, land ravaged, social habitats destroyed and people killed far away at the many peripheries of the capitalist world economy – for us, for the people in the centres of prosperity, to enable and maintain our standard of living, prospects and lifestyle. The second approach showed how these centres of prosperity shut themselves off from the outside world that nourishes and unburdens them, or rather how these centres turn 'alien' living environments into an 'outside', which they can access to safeguard their way of life without their integrity being touched by them. The relationship between centres and peripheries is one of semi-permeability: while much goes 'out', little comes 'in'. The global mobility gap favouring the North is a pertinent example: one half of the world travels collectively to the other, but allows it only highly selective access to its own economic and social space. Like life prospects, mobility is obviously divisible – and effectively divided. What is possible for some is impossible for others. And yet we persist in talking about an era of 'globalization'.

Rob Nixon, an American environmental researcher teaching, like Angus Deaton, at Princeton, describes this global constellation as a result of combined outsizing and outsourcing originating in the highly industrialized countries of the world.[27] Driven by its internal growth imperative, Western affluence capitalism ruthlessly resorts to new natural and human resources on a global scale and offloads the follow-up costs of this expansion onto its external world. The fact that it succeeds again and again is due to its dominant position in the world system and the combination of economic and political power. This enables the societies of the Global North to demonstrate a structural indifference, in the form of an unquestioning assumption of the availability of the resources they need to continue their expansive and externalizing dynamic. The imperial lifestyle of the 'over-developed' societies is based on the power of ignorance, a collective attitude that Nixon calls 'imperial provincialism' (or, in the case of the USA, 'superpower parochialism'): the power not only not to deal with the consequences of their actions but also not even to take them into account, the right to claim ignorance.[28]

Indifference and ignorance, active passivity in the face of the global situation, are a great privilege. They are the living proof of a world in which the rulers themselves can externalize, mask, abstract the knowledge of their dominance and thus make it invisible. For a long time, the externalization society was extremely successful at this concealment: the question of security management at the outer limits of our prosperous world could be hidden behind a veil of not knowing or not having to know, and the practice of resource over-exploitation and environmental pollution could be tucked away somewhere beyond our own experience. The private activities and public agencies working to make the externalization process invisible are legion. And this invisibility has been gradually perfected, from the export of material waste to the other end of the world to the outsourcing of virtual waste disposal to the lower end of the global social structure.

Indeed, 'waste disposal on the Internet'[29] is also part of the externalization society in its present form, driven by 'digital cleaning crews' in the cheap-labour countries of the Global South – armies of screen workers every day sifting through millions of images to check their ethical suitability on behalf of the Internet companies we trust. As Till Briegleb describes in an impressive report on the hidden parallel world of our social network universe, round the clock they ensure 'that there are not any profile pictures on Facebook showing a decapitated head, no videos on YouTube showing child abuse, and no shredded chickens and skinned dogs on Instagram Grumpy Cat'. What, these horror pictures are not automatically deleted? The evil side of the power of virtual reality does not dissolve on its own, or at least with the aid of automatic search algorithms? No, our 'psycho-trash' is dumped in remote countries, mostly in South-East Asia, where the dirty work of disposing of it – euphemistically called 'commercial content moderation' (CCM) – is carried out manually by real people, who not only work for a pittance but also bear the psychological consequences: 'The suffering caused by the unspoken reten-tion of the horror images in their own heads extends from loss of libido, sleep disorders and depression to alcoholism and paranoid mistrust of other people.' Everything hunky-dory in the beautiful new media world of the Global North? Of course – as long as the rest of the world plays along.

The externalization society strikes back – on itself

But the world is changing.[30] The cost of the externalization society is becoming increasingly visible, and the collateral damage from our social model of progress and development is more and more difficult to overlook – however remote it might seem to us: dirty work in the factories of the Global South, mountains of waste in the metropolitan regions of Africa and Asia, refugee camps at the borders of third and fourth countries, melting polar ice caps and rising sea levels at the other end of the world.

Far away – and so near: the hidden reality can no longer be ignored. The enduring and until recently intact '"normal-ity" of externalization', as Immanuel Wallerstein, the doyen of sociological world-system research puts it, 'is a distant memory'.[31] It is becoming increasingly rare and difficult for costs to be passed on, profits to be pocketed, damage to be outsourced and the benefits to be claimed – and at the same time to pretend that all this is not the case. It wasn't all better before, but certainly things were easier – be it to make the economic recovery of Western Europe after the Second World War into a 'miracle', or to promise the countries of the 'Third World' steady development towards becoming affluent societies, provided they behaved and were friendly to the West. Today, we know that the train of progress doesn't stop everywhere. We cannot avoid the realization that, for many people and large parts of the world, it departed without them. And we can no longer avoid the increasingly glaring and merciless confrontation with their lives. We have only to put two and two together: to connect the living standards of others with our own production, consumption, work and living standards.

This confrontation will inevitably be made easier for us in the future – or at least it will be harder not to call the realities of global inequality by their name, and to simply carry on as before. The pendulum has swung back, and externalization is coming home to roost – already today in the form of the 'refugee flows' that we are attempting to stem at the borders of Europe with all the means available to us, including the use of armed force;[32] or in the guise of 'international terrorism' that brings into our cities, albeit on a reduced scale, the wars that have long been raging elsewhere and that until recently were known to us only by hearsay, if at all; and in a not-too-distant future, which is in fact already with us today, in the form of climate change, which for some time has been making itself clearly felt in the form of unusual droughts, storms and floods. And to a certain extent the continued, absolutely degrading disciplining of Greece within the euro crisis has also brought the time-honoured practice of imposing structural adaptation programmes, in the past applied only to 'developing countries', back to Europe, to our world of 'advanced' societies.

The pendulum has swung back, and the 'outside' is returning to the 'inside'. We will be inevitably confronted by the consequences of our own externalization activities. 'Playing ignorant', as the economist Hans Achinger put it a long time ago in a different context, is simply no longer an option.[33] It is true that systematically ignoring the preconditions and consequences of the externalization society is still common in public discourse – and still a sure way to win votes. But even that will become more and more difficult. Outside of politics at all events, in the field of academic analysis it is impossible today to continue to ignore the realities. The empirical evidence of our life at the expense of others is simply too strong. And the theoretical voices – some of them have been referred to in this book – that offer convincing arguments for reversing our view of the world have also become too numerous, pointing to the fact of *interdependent* inequalities,[34] the fact of a conditional relationship between great wealth and great poverty, bright or gloomy prospects in the global society.

Behind the continued political impulse to ignore what is happening globally is clearly the sheer anxiety that it could sometime affect our untroubled prosperity. This anxiety is understandable – and it is not just a question of 'German angst',[35] but a phenomenon that rightly affects all of Europe, and in fact the entire Global North. Throughout the wealthy countries of the Global North, the unacknowledged basis for their traditional prosperity model is beginning to crumble. Questions are being asked about the growth contract that gave them, and only them, the 'best of all worlds' in the second half of the twentieth century: a world of material security and widespread social advancement, a protected environment and pacified class relations; a life that is not available equally to every citizen in these societies, but one that, as such, is unimaginable for those in other parts of the world. For the globally better-off, in turn, the unspoken social contract contained the decisive additional clause that the worst 'collateral growth damage' should be passed on to others and kept at a distance.[36]

A sociological analysis like this one could further fuel the fear of loss in prosperous capitalist societies and would probably be counterproductive as a result, in terms of identifying the necessary transformations of the externaliza-tion society. By conveying an awareness of the social reali-ties, however, it could also assuage fears for the future. For the prosperous capitalist centres, the future will not suddenly become as gloomy as it is at present for hundreds of mil-lions of people at the peripheries of the capitalist world system.

Whatever the case, sociology is not social therapy, nor is it a lesson in morality. If this book has been read this way, it is probably a demand rather than supply effect, a self-questioning reflex by readers rather than the instructive effect intended by the author. It was not the intention to accuse the system or people of moral bankruptcy, to read the riot act to the externalization society. That is the job of ethics philosophers and business ethics specialists. Criti-cal social science takes a different approach. It uses its finger to point and not to warn. It points at power and domination and not at morality and conscience; it names structural conditions and not ethical principles; it reveals the self-evidence of everyday practices and does not ques-tion the moral integrity of those involved.

The analysis presented in this book lays bare the struc-tures of domination in the capitalist world, the structures that dominate globalized capitalism. The externalization by the wealthy societies of the world is embedded in a historical power structure that enables those in power to benefit again and again from the material advantages of their position. And this well-practised custom of outsourc-ing costs and pocketing the profits has become second nature to the externalizers, a 'normal' and no longer questioned way of behaving. Externalization is revealed to us as a self-evident habit suggested, fostered and even demanded by the structure in which we operate. Externalization as a social practice has assumed the form of a necessary act of complicity with the prevailing circumstances: those living in externalization societies who desire the 'good life' are obliged to live at the expense of others – even against their own will. That having been said, for the average citizen the question of will does not even arise, since affluence capitalism has established itself as a collective habitus whose consequences have remained hidden and could easily be ignored – but are now becoming increasingly visible.

In this context, the concept of 'structural violence' is useful in understanding the externalization society.[37] Coined in the 1960s by the Norwegian sociologist and peace researcher Johan Galtung, it describes the specific form of domination that the 'First World' of rich industrial nations imposes on the poor regions of the 'Third World'. It is true that the externalization society also exerts structural violence on itself: the 'imperial lifestyle' established in the Global North at the expense of others not only dominates global social structures but has also quietly taken charge of the lifestyles and thought processes in the societies of the 'First World'. Galtung connected this unobtrusive and subtle method of domination with the 'structural' aspect of the violent regime in the capitalist centres. Structural violence works almost imperceptibly, operating as a silent constraint and is as unnoticeable for the observer as 'still waters'.

But times have changed. The structural patterns and by-products of the externalization society are becoming increasingly evident. The smooth outer surface has been ruffled, and the once-still waters have turned rough. The deluge that we have continuously reproduced is no longer just somewhere else.

Living in the eye of the storm: nothing will happen unless you make it happen

People are fine with the externalization society – but for how long? The boomerang effect of our externalization activities is making itself felt with increasing clarity.[38] However, it does not result on its own in a heightened awareness of the connections between unequal opportunities on either side of the globe or between the options on one side and the limitations on the other. The political handling of the increasingly apparent consequences of externalization is still dominated by a policy of self-interested sugar-coating and cosmetic corrections, delaying tactics and screening reflexes. Be it at international climate conferences or in public initiatives to improve working conditions – for example in the textile and clothing industry – in refugee policies or world trade, the taxation of fuel-guzzling high-performance vehicles, or the seemingly unstoppable increase in air traffic or Internet shopping – governments and businesses, administrations and citizens are equally reluctant to allow the costs of their own actions to be calculated, or to be persuaded to assume or avoid these costs, or to offer some kind of compensation. With the success of externalization for as long as anyone can remember, why abandon it now and turn things around? Why do anything to change the externalization society? And anyway, how can it be done?

The 'why' is relatively easy to explain, without appealing to the morality of Christianity, civil society or human rights. If nothing else, it is our own informed self-interest that should make us call into question the principle of externalization and should prompt us to abandon it. There is no 'outside' in global society where we can outsource the prerequisites for and residues of our way of life forever and without consequences: land-grabbing and dirty work to the South, carbon dioxide emissions into the atmosphere or the ground, refugees from environmental disasters and conflicts over resources into camps throughout the world. Our prosperous societies have never had this 'outside', but merely the convenient and effective idea of having one, the naïve idea that outsourcing will solve all problems, as it indeed appeared to do for many years, in the highly effective form of suppression here and destruction there. But now it is also time for us, who have lived in the eye of the storm for so long, to look at the realities around us: the development of energy sources is becoming increasingly costly, the carbon dioxide sinks are reaching capacity, the refuse tips of the world are overflowing, the blood toll of our way of life is becoming greater, violent social conflicts around the world are multiplying, the poor and desperate can no longer be fobbed off with UN Development Goals – the most mobile among them are moving, and the life of others is coming closer to our everyday experience. The externalization society has reached a tipping point beyond which its effects will no longer be controllable and its self-destructive consequences no longer held at bay.

But this realization – even if it is a self-interested one – of the need for a change of direction in social reproduction does not automatically mean that one will take place. Knowledge on its own is by no means enough. Changing the externalization society creates a major dilemma because of the overlaying of national and global inequality structures, the 'intersection of externalization circles' mentioned earlier. Even if the entire population of Germany, including the most under-privileged household, is better off in material terms than around 85 per cent of the people in the world, obviously there are still massive inequalities in the country. We all live in an affluent society, but in very different ways. Strictly speaking, there is no 'we' in this affluent society. This creates a complicated constellation of interests and a fundamental political strategy problem: how to fight for more global equality without ignoring the justified claims to equality – for example, an equal life expectancy – in the national context? How to appeal to the disadvantaged in wealthy societies as structural beneficiaries of the externalization society while taking seriously their concerns about further social disadvantages compared with those who are better-off?

The same applies in principle to the other side of the global inequality structure: the counterparts of the externalization society are by no means homogeneous either. If the 'internal' social inequalities are great in our societies, they are much greater in the countries of the Global South. In Germany, the Gini index of income concentration, as mentioned earlier, is 30. As a reminder once again: a score of 100 would mean that the entire income of a society is in the hands of one person, and a score of 0 would mean that income is completely equally distributed. African and Latin American countries have a much higher inequality score: 48 for Mexico, 53 for Brazil, 61 for Botswana, and 65 for South Africa.[39] In other words, there are very rich people in the Global South who profit from the convoluted externalization situation and who no doubt live in extremely comfortable circumstances, even by European standards. Moreover, there are also large emerging middle classes on a global scale who are eager to attain 'Western' living standards – and, indeed, do so – and may also themselves be seen to a certain extent as beneficiaries of the global inequality system. Although Gini scores of over 50, or even 60, mean that large sections of the population in these countries live on the threshold of extreme poverty or even below, it is clear that in the societies of the Global South there is no undivided, mobilizable poor 'we' either.

The structural problem in politicizing global inequalities is that an extended global view of the situation necessarily complicates matters. First, there are the complex interests that have to be taken into account as a result of the fact that the costs of the externalization society are just as unequally distributed in the Global South as their benefits are in the Global North. Then there are the difficulties in politicizing this overlapping inequality situation and devising a suitable form of transnational solidarity. Reinhard Kreckel, who introduced the centre–periphery concept in sociological inequality research, himself points out that with the rejection of a concept of 'above' and 'below' applied merely to national societies, 'the ability to differentiate increases while the ability to communicate decreases'.[40] In other words, the more precise and comprehensive the scientific analysis of social inequalities, the more difficult and inappropriate simple political messages become.

In this complicated situation, the concept of the externalization society represents an attempt to bring up a painful subject that we don't usually consider worth talking about. Poverty and wealth, participating in society or being denied the right to do so have long been subjects of political discussion in capitalist democracies. They are the objects of election campaigns and trade union congresses, talk shows and government reports, and, as we have seen, with Piketty's great public success they have also become the subject of public debate in the societies of Europe and North America. By contrast, destitution and poverty, denial of benefits and restricted prospects *elsewhere*, outside our own lives, at the peripheries of the global capitalist system, are maintained quite literally in a shadow existence. They are mentioned occasionally in media reports, only to disappear again and to be confined otherwise to the Christmas collection in church. Above all, however, it is the *connections* between the two, between 'over-development' with limited inequality on the one hand and 'underdevelopment' with extreme inequality on the other, that have generally failed to arouse any political or media interest.[41] The one is commended as a manifestation of a 'social market economy' and the other, at best, deplored as an unfortunate destiny and left to its own devices. But that the two are connected? Not our business, not in our mental horizon, out of our control.

Talk of the externalization society breaks with the spiral of silence of affluence capitalism. Without denying its own internal inequality structure – it is capitalism, after all – the externalization diagnosis turns our attention, as the renowned sociologist Max Weber puts it, in a 'one-sided accentuation of one point of view', to its external effects.[42] In doing so, it focuses on advanced capitalism's *functional mechanisms* – the structural logic of the modern global system that means no wealth without poverty, no productivity on the one hand without destruction on the other. But it also focuses critically on how it is *legitimized*. It points out that our individual and collective prosperity is based not merely on hard work, clever economizing and the fortune of the brave, but at least as much on structural power, systematic exploitation and an active contribution to the misfortune of other countries and people. If we lift the lid off the externalization society, we discover that the enormous wealth benefits here are no longer a miracle but a function of the effective outsourcing of 'development costs' to others; then the environmental audits of Western service societies can be read as a result of the outsourcing of dirty industries; and then civil rights achievements inevitably must be seen in the light (or shadow) of their exclusiveness, defended if necessary by armed force.

'Externalization society': this is the answer to the question of why it is so often the same people who are on the winning and losing sides of global capitalism.[43] But the concept itself gives no indication of how another world beyond externalization might be possible. It does nothing more than to increase visibility – as a response to the dominant forces that still work on diverting attention and obscuring the background to and the by-products of affluence capitalism. At best, it can help to break the simulation cycle within society that allows the externalization wheel to keep turning according to the principle 'If you don't mention it, neither will I' – the tacit agreement by politicians and their constituents and among citizens themselves not to ask questions about the social realities behind the façade of their prosperous lives.[44]

Bringing the invisible out in the open, saying the unspeakable, revealing what is hidden – a seemingly modest result for sociological discussion of the externalization society. But it could become more: talk and knowledge of our externalization practices could be crucially helpful in politicizing public debate on their conditions and consequences. Politicization is the vital prerequisite for real change and an effective transformation of society. There can be no doubt that this will not be possible without changes in everyday behaviour, and all existing forms of a practical critique of externalization today, from a reduction in personal consumption to voluntary service at the peripheries of the affluent world, are important components of a future change.[45] But more is required to do something about the externalization society, something more than individual effort. Global problems, as Rob Nixon aptly points out, 'cannot simply be resolved by the aggregated actions of responsible individuals'.[46] There is a need not only for many individual responses but also, and above all, for a real collective effort.

This calls first for the *collective acceptance* of a number – mind you, much fewer for us than for many others – of unpleasant truths: that our affluence capitalist way of life is not available to everyone and that it is based on absurdly bad living conditions elsewhere and can only be maintained on this basis; that the shift to a policy of equal opportunities on a global scale will make massive changes to our lives in society. It calls in addition for *collective empowerment*, joint action to create these equal opportunities – based on the formation of regional and transnational alliances between the many thousands of initiatives and organizations, networks and movements that already exist in both the Global South and Global North, fighting for a world in which everyone can live with equal rights and entitlements.

Politicization requires collective action, and collective action is politicizing: this is the simple equation for the transformation of the externalization society, which at the same time calls for the replacement of the moral register of 'Indignez-vous!' ['Be outraged'] by 'Do something!'[47] But this also means that the aim of transformative action should be a sustainable change not only of social behaviour but also, and in particular, of social institutions – which is the only way to make this changed social behaviour permanent. Some basic elements of a radical institutional reform of the externalization society are perfectly obvious: a revision of the world trade regime breaking with the privileges of the most powerful economies, effective taxation of worldwide financial transactions, and the transformation of the rich nations into post-growth societies,[48] right up to a global social contract on limiting climate change and the egalitarian control of its consequences, and a transnational rights policy that supports entitlement struggles worldwide and effectively safeguards global social rights.

In brief, a reform of this type would call for a consistent policy of *dual redistribution* on a national and on a global scale, from the top down and from the inside out. This mammoth task cannot be completed alone by way of supportive economic niche projects or avant-garde consumer ethics – and will not be performed for us by technological change, digitization and the knowledge economy, as post-capitalism theoreticians who place their faith in technology, such as Jeremy Rifkin or Paul Mason, repeatedly suggest.[49] Ultimately, there is no alternative to the real difficult core project that Mathias Greffrath aptly names 'occupy political institutions'.[50] Only if we manage to restructure the national and transnational institutional framework of the externalization society as part of a democratic egalitarian global reform project will the life prospects of the large majority of the world's population experience a perceptible and sustained improvement.

It is impossible to say whether this will actually come about. But the spectres of the externalization society can no longer be banished, and its destructive effect 'somewhere else' can no longer be kept out of our collective social consciousness. The crises and wars around us give notice that the externalization society is now beginning to demand payback from us as well. We could react to the disquieting return of what we have concealed from ourselves with defensive reflexes and a denial of reality – exactly in the manner of the current 'crisis politics'.[51] An alternative would be no longer to have any illusions, to face up to realities and to set about radical changes.[52] Another alternative would be to take account of the connection between prosperity here and evil elsewhere – and in the knowledge of this connection to show solidarity. Indifference to the living conditions of others is always a form of social disconnectedness.[53] Overcoming social indifference means taking an interest in others, recognizing the structural dependence of our own living conditions on the living conditions of others – and hence espousing the social principle of relationality, the interconnectivity of different social living environments and opportunities.

Sociology can make a modest contribution to such a transformation.[54] Or, if the great French sociologist Pierre Bourdieu is anything to go by, a truly immodest one – namely 'organizing the return of the repressed and saying out loud to everyone what no one wants to know'.[55] What no one has wanted to know so far: we are living not beyond our own means but at the expense of others – and at the same time without making full use of our potential to change this situation.

Epilogue: the Rio Doce in the face of disaster

This book began in Brazil and on the banks of the Rio Doce. Let us return there briefly at the end. Its waters were coloured with reddish sludge months after the walls of two reservoirs of the Samarco iron ore mine burst. A court order banning fishing in the river delta on the Atlantic revealed that the hastily pronounced expert opinions stating that the ecological damage was limited and would clear up of its own accord were outright lies. Fishing was prohibited in the Rio Doce valley after the accident in November 2015. Thousands of fishermen were out of work, and the Brazilian government has meanwhile agreed that the mine operating company should pay the equivalent of 5.7 billion euros in compensation over fifteen years. According to press reports, at the shareholders' meeting of the British–Australian mineral group BHP Billiton, part-owners of the mine, Chairman of the Board Andrew Mackenzie 'fought back tears' when reporting on the disaster – possibly also because he had to announce to the company's shareholders that considerable write-offs had had to be made in the financial statements and that dividends were to be capped for the first time since 1988. After the accident, the price of the company's shares on the Sydney stock exchange dropped from 25 to 15 Australian dollars, but rose again rapidly when the compensation agreement was announced.

There are only two things wrong with the public statement by the Brazilian President Dilma Rousseff that the agreement with the international mining group would help to manage 'a tragedy without parallel': that the accident on the Rio Doce was a tragedy – because the defining feature of a tragedy is that it is fated; and that the tragedy was without parallel – because it is anything but, and is typical rather of countless similar events in Brazil and other countries of the South.[56] These 'disasters' are corporate business-as-usual not only for multinationals, which pocket huge profits for years and write off the odd loss now and then. For us privileged citizens of the world, whether shareholders or not, the same is also true, when we take advantage of the benefits of global production and occasionally regret a 'tragedy without parallel' in a post on Facebook, complete with sad-face emoji. For the people where the tragedy occurs, however, be they fishermen or farmers, exactly the opposite is true. Admittedly, the destruction of their way of life is in some way also business as usual – but they cannot simply write off their losses or return to the agenda for the day after the event, nor to any agenda item other than simply getting through the day in some way.

This is something that Maximilian Prinz zu Wied-Neuwied could not have imagined in his worst nightmare.[57] This aristocratic naturalist visited Brazil from 1815 to 1817 and was overwhelmed by the sight of the Rio Doce: 'On this river, so rich in magnificent natural scenery and unusual natural history features, the researcher will find plenty of work and the most diverse pleasures.' If the prince were alive today, 200 years later, he would have to console himself with other activities and pleasures. 'In the area of the Brazilian coastal rainforest visited by him, barely 5 per cent of the original fauna and flora have survived', writes Michaela Metz in her review of the reissue of Wied-Neuwied's travel reports, published to coincide with the latest destruction of local fauna and flora. The 'Rhenish

Humboldt' could not have imagined what was to happen
since then in Brazil and all the other sweet rivers of the
world. At all events, he was wrong about the indestructi-
bility of the overwhelming tropical environment: 'The animal
kingdom, the plant kingdom, and even the natural sur-
roundings without life are immune to the influence of Europeans and will retain their originality; their richness will
never end even if Brazil's foundations are scoured for gold
and precious stones.'

Today, we know that Brazil's foundations have indeed
been scoured and that the influence of the Europeans has
left its mark. The natural riches have not disappeared; they
have been shipped to Europe and other centres of prosperity – with poverty and exploitation, violence and destruction
as the generous return payment. One side wins, the other
loses, and both sides in this game remain the same. That's
the way it is in the externalization society. But it doesn't
have to stay that way.

Acknowledgements

I should like to thank all of the many individuals and institutions who have been involved and assisted in the writing of this book. First is the Post-Growth Societies research group at the University of Jena, funded by the German Research Foundation (DFG), within which I was first prompted to investigate the subject of this book and from which I constantly received intellectual stimulus to develop the concept of 'externalization'. Within this group of colleagues and fellows, I should like to mention in particular Barbara Muraca and Adelheid Biesecker, Uli Brand, Dennis Eversberg, Tine Haubner, Urs Lindner, Joan Martinez Alier, Nivedita Menon, Philippe van Parijs, Göran Therborn and Uta von Winterfeld. After my transfer to the University of Munich, I was able to pursue the subject practically without interruption in the form of a thematic network ('Global Capitalism and the Dynamics of Inequality') at the University's Centre for Advanced Studies (CAS_LMU). My particular thanks go to Annette Meyer and Julia Schreiner.

Two master's seminars at the University of Munich ('Global Social Inequalities') and the University of St Gallen ('Externalization Society') were of particular importance in preparing this book, discussing the relevant topics and

identifying various lines of criticism. My explicit thanks
go to the extraordinary students at these two institutions.
Discussion of a first version of the central argument during
a Higher Seminar by my Munich colleague Armin Nassehi,
and the presentation of a later version in the context of a
guest lectureship at the University of Antwerp, thanks to
Gert Verschraegen, were also helpful. I thank Jens Luedtke
for important comments regarding the argumentation and,
above all, the concept of 'externalization habitus', and look
forward to continuing our discussions.

It was due to an initiative by Harald Welzer and the
openness of Andrian Kreye that the first article on the
subject, entitled 'Neben uns die Sintflut', was published in
the *Süddeutsche Zeitung* – and to the German Sociological
Association and the organizers of the Trier Sociology Congress headed by Martin Endress that the thesis was initially
formulated. I thank, in particular, Thomas Barth and Eva
Fleischmann for their many and inestimably valuable comments on the entire manuscript and the large amount of
background research carried out by them. Without their
assistance the book would certainly have been inferior.
Laura Späth helped to revise the text for the paperback
version. Finally, I should like to thank Daniel Graf for his
constant encouragement and important critical comments,
and Felicitas Feilhauer, Karsten Kredel and, in particular,
Ludger Ikas for their support at Hanser in Munich and
Berlin, and for their constructive editing. At Polity, I should
like to thank John Thompson and Paul Young for making
possible and supervising the English translation – and particularly, of course, Nick Somers for the translation of the
text into English.

This revised and expanded version of the book has benefitted from countless contributing discussions and sources
of information, which have provided valuable suggestions
for refining and honing my arguments during what will
soon be a one-year reading tour in and around Munich.
Without any claim to completion, I should like at least to
mention Jens Bisky, Ingolfur Blühdorn, Uli Brand, Josef

Brüderl, Franz Garnreiter, Mathias Greffrath, Kathrin Hartmann, Ulrich Kühn, Bascha Mika, Martin Mlinaric, Timothy Moran, Sighard Neckel, Sebastian Schief, Sebastian Schoepp, Bernd Sommer, Wolfgang Storz, Philipp Stürzenberger, Thomas Straubhaar and Markus Wissen. Please excuse me for anyone I have omitted from this list.

Finally, I should like to dedicate this book to Ulrich Beck, my predecessor in the Department of Sociology at the University of Munich, with whom I would like to have discussed the externalization diagnosis, which follows up much of his work on risk society and his thoughts on emancipatory disasters. I wrote *Living Well at Others' Expense*, however, for everyone whose circumstances prevent them from enjoying what Philippe van Parijs describes as *real freedom*: the possibility of living their own lives and making decisions of concern to them. I hope that they will not put up with these circumstances any longer, and I also hope those who have already stopped doing so remain on the ball.

Munich, summer 2017

Notes

1 Next to us, the Deluge

1 This is the English translation of the celebrated opening sentence of the much-read work by the Uruguayan journalist and writer Eduardo Galeano (2015, p. 15): 'La division internacional del trabajo consiste en que unos países se especializan en ganar y otros en perder.'

2 Reference to the title of the novel *Crónica de una muerte anunciada* (1981) by the Colombian writer Gabriel García Marquéz.

3 For the events on the Rio Doce reconstructed on the next pages, the background to the 'accident' and the subsequent developments, see, in particular, wsj.com, 5 November 2015; theguardian.com, 13, 16, 22–28 November 2015 and 15 October 2016; brasilienexkursion.wordpress.com, 15 November 2015; greenpeace.org, 17 November 2015; jungewelt.de, 19 October 2015; scientificamerican.com, 25 October 2015; sueddeutsche. de, 26 November and 1 and 11 December 2015; latina-press. com, 28 November 2015; taz.de, 3 and 16 December 2015; nzz. ch, 16 December 2015.

4 For a list of the largest iron ore mining companies in the world and the mining companies mentioned here, see the

corresponding entries in wikipedia.org and the companies' websites.

5 For the sources, mining and use of this ore, see the corresponding entry in wikipedia.org; for bauxite and iron ore mining by the Rio Tinto company, see the data at statista.com.

6 For German consumer data and the worldwide sales figures of Nestlé, see welt.de, 8 January 2014, and theguardian.com, 27 May 2015; the company's advertising slogan can be found at nespresso.com.

7 See Bertelsmann Stiftung & Sustainable Development Solutions Network (SDSN) 2017 (Annex).

8 See Mignolo 2011.

9 See Oxfam 2015, also at oxfam.org.

10 See Piketty 2014.

11 See Korzeniewicz & Moran 2009 (esp. ch. 5).

12 For this criticism, see Moran 2015.

13 See Shachar 2009.

14 For this thought experiment, see the introductory chapter in Korzeniewicz & Moran 2009.

15 Unlike the 'workers of the world', according to the closing section of the *Communist Manifesto*, in the context of the revolutionizing of social conditions in the mid nineteenth century: see Marx & Engels 1959 and 2016.

16 See quote at the beginning of this chapter, Galeano 1973.

17 See Beck 1992.

18 See Brand & Wissen 2017.

19 See spiegel.de of 12 November 2015.

20 The phrase was coined by Ulrich Beck to describe the general increase in prosperity in post-war European societies, see Beck 1992, ch. 3.

21 For example, the idea of 'intelligent growth' in Fücks 2013.

22 For this term and the opposing concept of a 'reductive modernity', see Sommer & Welzer 2014.

23 For this pattern, see Boltanski 2008.

24 Recently, for example, see Quijano 2010 or Sanyal 2007, and also Boatcă 2015 for a systematic summary of 'decolonizing' perspectives.

25 Said by John F. Kennedy in a speech in September 1960 before he became president; see the text at presidency.uscb.edu.

2 Externalization: A Relational Perspective on Social Inequality

1 See Hottinger 1821, p. 82 – a rendering of the character typology of the Greek philosopher Theophrastus of Eresos in 300 BCE; see also Bennett & Hammond 1902.

2 See Hirst & Thompson 1996.

3 See the 'appropriation' ('Landnahme') theorem developed in Dörre 2009, drawing on Rosa Luxemburg, Hannah Arendt, Burkart Lutz and David Harvey, in particular.

4 For an introduction to the concept, see Wallerstein 2004.

5 See Smith 2003.

6 See also Korzeniewicz & Moran 2009, pp. 79–81.

7 See Ricardo 1975.

8 For an instructive and readable discussion, see Fulcher 2015.

9 See Arrighi 1994.

10 This acronym stands for the 'emerging threshold countries' Brazil, Russia, India, China and South Africa; for the recent rise of China in the global system, see Schmalz 2016.

11 The WTO, with headquarters in Geneva, was founded in 1995 as the successor to the General Agreement on Tariffs and Trade (GATT).

12 See Marx & Engels 2016.

13 See Nassehi 2012.

14 Weber's well-known phrase regarding the limitless capitalist rationalization of the world can be found at the end of *The Protestant Ethic* written in 1904 (see Weber 2002).

15 According to a joint estimate by the United Nations Children's Fund (UNICEF), the International Labour Organization (ILO) and the World Bank, around 11 per cent of children and juveniles between the ages of 5 and 17 years are involved worldwide in child labour; see unicef.org.

16 For a summary, see Kornick & Hicks 2015.

17 The British writer John Ruskin coined the term 'illth' in his socially critical essay 'Unto this Last'; see Calhoun 2013, p. 147.

18 For microeconomic background, see e.g. McConnell et al. 2009, ch. 16.

19 Mills spoke as early as 1959 of the 'overdeveloped world'; see Mills 1959, p. 4.

20 For the use of this term in system theory, see Luhmann 1990, ch. 5.

21 For fundamental discussion of this perspective, see Elias 1978.

22 This refers to the wide field of intersectionality research; for an introduction, see Siltanen & Doucet 2008.

23 For discussion of the concept, see Wimmer & Glick Schiller 2002; for inequality research, see Beck & Poferl 2010.

24 For a relational understanding of the notions of the 'Global North' and the 'Global South', see Comaroff & Comaroff 2012.

25 See Korzeniewicz 2001; for a historical perspective on moderate and great inequality in the Global North and Global South, see Korzeniewicz & Moran 2009, ch. 2.

26 For background, see Kreckel 2004, esp. ch. 1.

27 See Lenin 2010; also Kreckel 2004, pp. 36–7.

28 The *locus classicus* of Habermas's theory of 'inner colonialization' of the life-world is volume II, 'A critique of functionalist reason', of his *Theory of Communicative Action*: Habermas 1987.

29 For following discussion, see Tilly 2001.

30 Biesecker & von Winterfeld 2014 link this perspective explicitly with the concept of externalization; see also Biesecker et al. 2013, Federici 2012.

31 On the concept of the 'male breadwinner model', see, e.g., Lewis 2001.

32 Reference to the slogan 'Samstags gehört Vati mir' ['On Saturdays, Daddy belongs to me'], with which the German trade unions celebrated the Day of Labour in 1956 and fought for a work-free Saturday.

33 See Tilly 1998, ch. 4.

34 See ibid., ch. 5.

35 For further thoughts on Weber's concept, see Parkin 1983.

36 See Haubner 2017, esp. ch. 5, who connects exploitation more generally with the one-sided use of situations of social vulnerability.

37 See Kreckel 2004, p. 28.

38 I thank Jens Luedtke for this valuable insight, including the term 'externalization habitus'; for details of the 'habitus' concept, see Bourdieu 1984, ch. 3.

39 For further details, see Deutschmann 1996.

40 See focus.de of 14 March 2013; on the World Giving Index of the Charities Aid Foundation (CAF), see cafonline.org; for a donation market analysis, see betterplace-lab.org.

41 See Calhoun 2013, p. 149.
42 See Rawls 1971, section 24.
43 For an introduction, see the corresponding entry in wikipedia.org.
44 See betterplace-lab.org.
45 For details of the concept, see Rotberg 2003.
46 See, e.g., Vinnai 2013, Welzer 2011.
47 See nato.int of 4 September 2014.
48 For discussion of this term, see Beck 1992, p. 37.

3 Live and Let Die: Externalization as an Unequal Exchange

1 See Müller 2001, pp. 552–3.
2 From the introductory sentence of Kant's essay on the question 'What is Enlightenment?'; see Kant 1995, p. 1.
3 One of the many variants is quoted, which Kant developed in his *Groundwork of the Metaphysic of Morals* in 1785; see plato.stanford.edu.
4 See Horkheimer & Adorno 2002.
5 It is posited, above all, in arguments under the general heading of 'post-colonialism'; see, e.g., main contributions by Said 1978, Chakrabarty 2000 and Bhambra 2007.
6 See Knöbl 2001.
7 This is a classification category used by the World Bank: in 2014, countries with a GDP per-capita income of US$1,045 or less qualified as 'low-income'; see data.worldbank.org.
8 See Sommer 2017 for the corresponding considerations for industrial production (vehicles and textiles).
9 For German data, see bpb.de, bauernverband.de (also the source of 'indicators of modern agriculture' further below) and statista.com; for UK data, see independent.co.uk, 5 June 2013.
10 See WWF Deutschland 2014, figs. 5 and 6.
11 For the following description of the situation in Argentina, see, especially, Suchanek 2013, Fink 2015 and Burghardt 2014; also land-grabbing.de, klimawandel.eu, grain.org and, most recently, Burghardt 2016 and Turzi 2017.
12 See corresponding entry in wikipedia.org and the presentation by the European Glyphosate Task Force (GTF) at glyphosate.eu.

13 For the 'mothers of Ituzaingó', see globalagriculture.org.

14 See Burghardt 2014, p. 12, and sueddeutsche.de, 16 March 2016 ('Glyphosat ist nur ein Symptom – und nicht das Problem' ['Glyphosate is just a symptom – and not the problem']).

15 See Kröhnert et al. 2012.

16 For information on oil palm cultivation and the production of 'green oil', see wikipedia.org, wwf.panda.org, worldagroforestry.org, pro-regenwald.de, faszination-regenwald.de, forumpalmoel.org, and zeit.de of 5 November 2015.

17 See fr-online.de, 22 January 2010, and worldwildlife.org, organiccotton.org, oeko-fair.de, nabu.de, umweltinstitut.org and virtuelles-wasser.de.

18 For the following discussion, see Jensen 2015.

19 See Pereira 2015 and ejolg.org; for details of the GDP per capita of Indonesia and Singapore, see wikipedia.org.

20 See Pereira 2015; financialpost.com, 2 June 2017; thebalance.com, 24 September 2016; jungle-world.com, 8 January 2015; and boerse-online.de, 20 October 2014 ('US Silica-Aktie: Warum Anleger auf den Fracking-Profiteur setzen können' ['US Silica shares: why investors may bet on the fracking profiteer']).

21 See wikipedia.org, greenpeace.de and zeit.de of 11 November 2010, wiwo.de of 13 June 2014, theguardian.com of 14 September 2015, and sueddeutsche.de of 15 December 2015 ('Kinderhände in Eiswasser' ['Children's hands in icy water']); for US consumer data, see undercurrentnews.com, 30 October 2015.

22 According to the Global Slavery Index, 46 million people lived in slavery in 2016, more than half in China, India, Pakistan, Bangladesh and Uzbekistan; see globalslaveryindex.org, also Bales 2005, for further details.

23 On the problem of electronic scrap, see e.g. Dannoritzer 2015, greenpeace.org and theguardian.com of 14 December 2015.

24 For further details, see Moore 2015.

25 For basic information, see Hornborg 1998, 2011.

26 For a more precise explanation of the concept and the 'global hectare' virtual unit of measurement, see WWF Deutschland 2014; for estimate of environmental resource requirements, see footprintnetwork.org; for the following paradox, see Jorgenson & Rice 2005.

27 For explanation of the concept of available biocapacity, see footprintnetwork.org.

28 According to the World Bank classification, these are countries with a per-capita GDP of between US$1,025 and US$12,736 (2014); see dataworldbank.org.

29 For this and other indicators of global ecological transfer effects, see Bertelsmann Stiftung & SDSN 2017 (Annex, here p. 28); Switzerland had the highest average spillover score worldwide in 2015, illustrating a close connection between economic prosperity and the outsourcing of ecological costs (see ibid., p. 14).

30 An emblematic example is the production of antibiotics in India, see theguardian.com, 25 October 2016, and sueddeutsche.de, 4 and 6 May 2017.

31 On the situation in Malawi, see Zick 2016, and theguardian.com, 14 September 2011 and 31 July 2015.

32 See wikipedia.org.

33 See Polanyi 1957, pt 2, section 1.

34 Such land-grabbing practices are, of course, not confined to the Global South; see Herre 2015.

35 For the following quotations, see Bonneuil 2015.

36 This refers to the rapid increase in the exploitation of nature by humans in the second half of the twentieth century; see McNeill & Engelke 2014 and, with many relevant statistics, igbp.net.

37 See Moore 2015.

38 See Bonneuil 2015 and, in detail, Bonneuil & Fressoz 2017.

39 See WWF International 2014 and wwf.panda.org.

40 For a description, see wikipedia.org, bhopal.com and bhopal.net; for the thirtieth anniversary, see amnesty.org.

41 See Nixon 2011.

42 See wikipedia.org and the subsequent discussion of the findings in Knight & Rosa 2011.

43 See list of countries by per-capita GNP at wikipedia.org.

44 For recent developments, see Dörre 2015, pp. 261ff.

45 See Brand & Wissen 2012, 2017.

46 See Mackenzie et al. 2008.

47 See the data published by Deutsche Umwelthilfe on duh.de, and spiegel.de of 31 August 2015; the estimate for the USA comes from carryyourcups.org.

48 See iigcc.org.

49 For recent data on environmental awareness and behaviour in Germany, see Bundesministerium für Umwelt, Naturschutz, Bau und Reaktorsicherheit 2017.

50 See entry in wikipedia.org.

51 See Opielka 2016; for follow-up, see Opielka 2017.

52 The classic text on this diagnosis is Habermas 1986.

53 See Hartmann 2016a; the following quotes are from Hartmann 2016b, p 49.

54 See Hartmann 2015 and, in greater detail, Hartmann 2009; for dumping waste in the sea and micro-plastic, see also nationalgeographic.com of 11 January 2015, nabu.de, greenpeace.de, wwf.de and utopia.de.

55 See Rau 2016.

56 See Brand 2015.

57 See Hartmann 2015.

58 See Mahnkopf 2014 and 2015 and Moore 2011.

59 See Meadows et al. 1972 and, as follow-up, Randers 2012.

60 See Rockström & Klum 2012.

61 See Sommer & Welzer 2014, also for the concept of 'reductive modernity'; for discussion of 'design vs. disaster', see also degrowth.org and postwachstum.de.

62 See futur.org.

63 This is common prejudice by authors critical of transformation, e.g. Nassehi 2015, ch. 2.

64 For the following quote, see Hartmann 2015.

65 The following quotes are from Rau 2016.

66 For his writings on a critique of capitalism, see Müller 2017.

4 Within Versus Without: Externalization as a Monopoly on Mobility

1 See Poe 1984; text online at xroads.virginia.edu, and theguardian.com of 3 March 2016.

2 This is the famous vision of daily life in a truly free society in *The German Ideology*; see Marx & Engels 1969, p. 33 (extracts on marxists.org).

3 See Popper 2013.

4 See Shamir 2005.

5 See, e.g., blog.lastminute.de, 27 August 2015 ('Deutschland hat den Titel "Reiseweltmeister" redlich verdient' ['Germany honestly earned the award of "world champion travellers"']); data on statista.com, tourismusanalyse.de and wikipedia.org; and tagesspiegel.de, 13 January 2016, and spanienlive.com, 1 February 2017.

6 See travelworks.de, also for the quote.

7 For details, see Mau et al. 2012, ch. 3, here pp. 31–2, and unwto.org; for German holiday travel activity, see tourismusanalyse.de.

8 'Arbeit & Reisen im Ausland' is the slogan of travelworks. de. With apologies to Klara Herrmann.

9 See WWF Deutschland 2009.

10 See statista.com.

11 See the travel operator's presentation of sustainability targets at tuireisebuero.de.

12 For detailed discussion, see, e.g., tourism-watch.de.

13 As does, for example, the Bundesverband der Deutschen Tourismuswirtschaft [German Association of the Tourism Industry]; see Bundesverband der Deutschen Tourismuswirtschaft 2015.

14 See statista.com and tourism-watch.de.

15 See the quote at the start of this chapter.

16 See Mau et al. 2012, esp. ch. 4, & 2015.

17 See Mau et al. 2015 and Neumayer 2006, also passportindex. org.

18 See Hess 2001, p. 201.

19 See Mau et al. 2012, ch. 5.2.

20 Said, unforgettably, by Peter Struck (SPD), then Federal Minister of Defence: see afghanistan–connection.de.

21 The 'smart borders' concept is an official EU border security strategy; see under this heading at ec.europa.eu and statewatch. org.

22 See the conclusions of Mau et al., 2012, ch. 8.2.

23 See Neumayer 2006, p. 9, and Torpey 1997.

24 See, e.g., sueddeutsche.de, 25 April (also for talk of the potential import of 'domestic Turkish problems'), 28 April and 4 May 2016, and theguardian.com, 3 May 2016.

25 See zeit.de, 13 May 2015 ('Pässe für Millionen' ['Passports for millions']), and ft.com, 29 June 2016; see also the Visa Restrictions Index of the consultancy company Henley & Partners with headquarters in Zurich, self-proclaimed 'global leader in residence and citizenship planning': henleyglobal.com.

26 See Shachar 2009.

27 See Marshall 1963.

28 For discussion of this concept, see the corresponding wikipedia.org entry; for nation states as clubs, see Straubhaar 2002, ch. 7.

29　See Wallerstein 2003, quote p. 657.

30　See Mitchell 2011, also Wissen 2016.

31　As, e.g., Bieling & Brand 2015, p. 197, do; see also zeit.de, 20 January 2017 ('Der neue Ölmensch' ['The new oil man']), where, on his inauguration, the US President Donald Trump is described as the embodiment of 'the ideology of fossil capitalism'.

32　This classic formulation comes from Beck-Gernsheim 2013.

33　This was an election slogan by Willi Brandt in the 1961 Bundestag election; see the corresponding entry in wikipedia. org.

34　The idea, loosely based on the analogous formulation in the *Communist Manifesto*, suggests that global production networks from which we ultimately benefit also chain us to the prevailing economic and social order; see Marx & Engels 2016.

35　See unhcr.org, 19 June 2017, and UNHCR 2015.

36　A horror scenario painted by all parties; see 'Fakten gegen Vorurteile' ['Facts versus prejudice'] at proasyl.de.

37　In other words, on the basis of an internationally comparable 'economic performance unit', Ethiopia has almost 500 refugees, while European countries have only a fraction of that number.

38　Reference to the radical right-wing party Alternative für Deutschland, which has recently scored considerable election success.

39　See timeline of German internal migration at statistica.com and bib-demografie.de.

40　The figures do not take into account locally divergent US dollar buying power and to that extent are skewed, but the authors' argument also points essentially to the potential signal effect of extremely different nominal income; see Korzeniewicz & Moran 2009, esp. chs. 4 and 5; for a long-term historical perspective, see also the impressive data in Maddison 2001.

41　See, e.g., Ehrenreich & Hochschild 2002.

42　See Lewis 2001.

43　For discussion of irregular employment in German private households, see the study by Gottschall & Schwarzkopf 2010; for the international situation, see Ambrosini 2013.

44　See Encinas-Franco 2010.

45　See Lutz & Palenga-Möllenbeck 2015.

46 See, e.g., Schurr 2014 and deine–korrespondentin.de ('Auf Umwegen zum Wunschbaby' ['Indirect routes to a planned child']), and nytimes.com of 5 July 2014.

47 For a highly instructive discussion, see Bauman 2002, esp. ch. 2 – here p. 84.

48 See Shamir 2005, quote p. 211, and Agamben 2008.

49 See Mau 2016; for Orbán's world of 'hermetically sealed' borders, see huffingtonpost.de, 4 March 2016, and politico.eu, 13 February 2017.

50 On 'imperial automobility', see Wissen 2016, p. 59, and in detail Brand & Wissen 2017, ch. 6.

51 See Butler 1993.

52 For following quotes, see Rau 2016.

53 See Prisching 1986, pp. 27–8; for the 'imperial mode of living', see Brand & Wissen 2012 and 2017.

54 See Blühdorn 2013, quotes on pp. 251–2.

55 See ibid., p. 183.

56 See Oulios 2015, Schlüter 2016.

57 See Rau 2016.

58 See Poe 1984 (text online at xroads.virginia.edu).

5 We have To Talk: We Can't Go On Like This

1 See Piketty 2014.

2 For the OECD Social Report and official explanation, see oecd.org.

3 For the Oxfam poverty report and following data, see oxfam. org and Oxfam 2016 and 2017.

4 See sueddeutsche.de, 19 January 2016 ('Besitzen 62 Menschen soviel wie die halbe Welt?' ['Do 62 people own as much as half of the world?']).

5 See Fuest 2016.

6 See Piketty 2014 (quote p. 89).

7 See Bourguignon 2015, quotes pp. 3 and 7.

8 See Milanović 2016, ch. 3.

9 See Bourguignon 2015, p. 20; also ibid., pp. 20ff and Moran 2015, p. 869 ('the world is more unequal than even Brazil or South Africa').

10 See Milanović 2016, ch. 1, who divides global income distribution into percentiles, the poorest 1 per cent of the world

population forming the first percentile and the richest the last (or 99th); for a graphic illustration and interpretation, see also sueddeutsche.de, 7 October 2016 ('Ein Elefant erklärt die Weltwirtschaft' ['An elephant explains the world economy']).

11 See Milanović 2016, chs. 1 and 4.

12 See, e.g., huffingtonpost.de, 8 October 2016, where, under the eloquent title 'Diese Kurve zeigt, warum wir Angst vor dem Abstieg haben müssen' ['This curve shows why we should be afraid of descent'], the German reader is told that 'the heavy-weight pachyderm is becoming the ultimate symbol of injustice and relative poverty'; the huge success of 'Abstiegsgesellschaft' ('Downward Mobility': Nachtwey 2016) in German feature articles and bookshops can be explained only in the context of this reinterpretation of relative poverty.

13 On the structure and development of absolute poverty on a global scale, see the outstanding entry on 'Global Extreme Poverty' on ourworldindata.org.

14 See Bourguignon 2013, p. 19, n. 6.

15 See Deaton 2013.

16 As recently stated by my Munich colleague Armin Nassehi; see zeit.de of 13 July 2017 ('Eine Linke braucht es nicht mehr' ['There is no need any more for the Left']).

17 See Nixon 2011, p. 35.

18 For the following data, see Kroh et al. 2012 for Germany, and laenderdaten.de and statista.com for the global situation; see also UNDP 2016.

19 'die Kirche im Dorf lassen', see Hank 2016.

20 See Therborn 2013, esp. chs. 1 and 6, in which the concept of 'vital inequality' is also discussed.

21 For the 'extractivist' development model, see e.g. Bartelt 2017, Veltmeyer & Petras 2016.

22 An admittedly weak pun on the Zapatista slogan 'preguntando caminamos' ['asking we walk'].

23 See Schmid 2010 and Schmalz 2016; for the 'sub-imperial' lifestyle of the Chinese middle classes, see Brand & Wissen 2017, ch. 5, quote p. 115, and Ming 2015.

24 See Simmel 2009, vol. II, ch. 6.

25 See Korzeniewicz & Moran 2009, ch. 2.

26 See Wilkinson & Pickett 2009.

27 See Nixon 2011, esp. the introduction, here pp. 33ff.; for 'imperial provincialism', see also the Nixon quote at the beginning of this book.

28 See Wehling 2006.

29 See Briegleb 2016; also wired.com, 23 October 2014 ('The Laborers Who Keep Dick Pics and Beheadings Out of Your Facebook Feed'); the Internet cleaners now also carry out their soul-destroying work in Europe, an indication that externalization 'is coming home to roost'; see 'Inside Facebook', sueddeutsche. de, 15 December 2016.

30 A remote paraphrase in a different context of the line from Bert Brecht's *Threepenny Opera* ('Doch die Verhältnisse, sie bleiben nicht so'), written in 1928.

31 See Wallerstein 2013, here p. 23.

32 Recent discussion in Austria has focused on shifting the outer borders to the heart of Europe, of reducing the threshold for the official use of force, and even of militarizing the border with 'refugee-ridden' Italy, seconded – as one would expect – by the Free State of Bavaria; see 'Seehofer bietet Österreich Hilfe bei Grenzsicherung am Brenner an' ['Seehofer offers help to Austria for securing the border at the Brenner'] and 'Kleingeist vom Walserberg' ['Small-mindedness in Walserberg'], sueddeutsche.de, 15 May 2016 and 3 May 2017.

33 See Achinger 1971, p. 38.

34 For this perspective, see Kreckel 2004, esp. ch. 1, and Costa 2011.

35 See corresponding entry in wikipedia.org.

36 See Calhoun 2014, p. 183.

37 See Galtung 1969 and the quote at the start of this chapter.

38 See again Beck 1992, p. 37.

39 See list of countries by income distribution on wikipedia.org.

40 See Kreckel 2004, p. 50.

41 For the term 'over-development', see again Mills 1967, p. 4.

42 See Weber 2012.

43 See again Boltanski 2008.

44 See Blühdorn's 'unspoken new social contract', 2013, p. 183.

45 The problems with this kind of commitment are pointed out in Kontzi 2015.

46 See Nixon 2011, p. 39.

47 See Hessel 2010, who also called for political action, adding an emphatic 'engagez-vous!' ('be committed!').

48 See Jackson 2009, Latouche 2009, Schmelzer & Passadakis 2011.

49 See Mason 2015, Rifkin 2014.

50 See Greffrath 2015, p. 13.
51 For this notion, see the classic psychoanalytical theories of Freud 2003.
52 See Rilling 2014, Wright 2006.
53 See Wesche 2017.
54 See Opielka 2016, p. 43, who rightly calls on sociologists to thrust themselves 'into the centre of future discourse where they can modestly assert their strengths'.
55 See Bourdieu 2002, p. 126.
56 For discussion of the 'disaster', see the list of sources in Chapter 1; for the Chairman of the Board fighting back tears, see sueddeutsche.de, 23 February 2016 ('Der Schotte muss sparen' ['The Scotsman has to save']), for the President's talk of a 'tragedy without parallel'; see ft.com, 12 November 2015.
57 For details including the quotes, see Metz 2015.

Bibliography

Achinger, Hans (1971): *Sozialpolitik als Gesellschaftspolitik: Von der Arbeiterfrage zum Wohlfahrtsstaat*, 2nd enlarged edn, Frankfurt am Main.

Agamben, Giorgio (2008): 'No to Biopolitical Tattooing', *Communication and Critical/Cultural Studies* 5 (2), pp. 201–2.

Ambrosini, Maurizio (2013): *Irregular Migration and Invisible Welfare*, Basingstoke.

Arrighi, Giovanni (1994): *The Long Twentieth Century: Money, Power, and the Origins of Our Times*, London.

Bales, Kevin (2005): *Understanding Global Slavery: a Reader*, Berkeley.

Bartelt, Dawid Danilo (2017): *Konflikt Natur: Ressourcenausbeutung in Lateinamerika*, Berlin.

Bauman, Zygmunt (2002): *Society Under Siege*, Cambridge.

Beck, Ulrich (1992): *Risk Society: Towards a New Modernity*, London.

Beck, Ulrich & Poferl, Angelika (eds.) (2010): *Grosse Armut, grosser Reichtum: Zur Transnationalisierung sozialer Ungleichheit*, Berlin.

Beck-Gernsheim, Elisabeth (1983): 'Vom "Dasein für andere" zum Anspruch auf ein Stück "eigenes Leben": Individualisierungsprozesse im weiblichen Lebenszusammenhang', *Soziale Welt* 34 (3), pp. 307–40.

Bennett, Charles & Hammond, William (1902): *The Characters of Theophrastus*, Cambridge.

Bertelsmann Stiftung & Sustainable Development Solutions Network, SDSN (2017): *Global Responsibilities: International Spillovers in Achieving the Goals – SDG Index and Dashboards Report 2017*, Gütersloh.

Bhambra, Gurminder K. (2007): *Rethinking Modernity: Postcolonialism and the Sociological Imagination*, Basingstoke.

Bieling, Hans-Jürgen & Brand, Ulrich (2015): 'Competitiveness or Emancipation? Rethinking Regulation and (Counter-)hegemony in times of capitalist crisis', pp. 184–204 in Richard Westra, Dennis Badeen & Robert Albritton (eds.), *The Future of Capitalism after the Financial Crisis: the Varieties of Capitalism Debate in the Age of Austerity*, London / New York.

Biesecker, Adelheid, Hofmeister, Sabine & von Winterfeld, Uta (2013): 'Draussen? Zur Dialektik von Enteignung und Aneignung und zu deren aktuellen Erscheinungsformen', *Das Argument* 55 (4), pp. 522–38.

Biesecker, Adelheid & von Winterfeld, Uta (2014): *Extern? Weshalb und inwiefern moderne Gesellschaften Externalisierung brauchen und erzeugen*, Working Paper 2/2014, KollegforscherInnengruppe Postwachstumsgesellschaften, Jena.

Blühdorn, Ingolfur (2013): *Simulative Demokratie: Neue Politik nach der postdemokratischen Wende*, Berlin.

Boatcă, Manuela (2015): *Global Inequalities Beyond Occidentalism*, Farnham/Burlington.

Boltanski, Luc (2008): 'Individualismus ohne Freiheit: Ein pragmatischer Zugang zur Herrschaft', *WestEnd: Neue Zeitschrift für Sozialforschung* 5 (2), pp. 133–49.

Bonneuil, Christophe (2015): 'Tous responsables?' *Le Monde diplomatique*, November 2015, pp. 16–17.

Bonneuil, Christophe & Fressoz, Jean-Baptiste (2017): *The Shock of the Anthropocene: the Earth, History and Us*, New York.

Bourdieu, Pierre (1984) [French original. 1979]: *Distinction: a Social Critique of the Judgement of Taste*, London.

Bourdieu, Pierre (2002): *Ein soziologischer Selbstversuch*, Frankfurt am Main.

Bourguignon, François (2015): *The Globalization of Inequality*, Princeton.

Brand, Ulrich (2015): 'Die Illusion vom sauberen Wachstum', pp. 52–3 in *Le Monde diplomatique* & Kolleg

Postwachstumsgesellschaften (eds.), *Atlas der Globalisierung: Weniger wird mehr*, Berlin.

Brand, Ulrich & Wissen, Markus (2012): 'Global Environmental Politics and the Imperial Mode of Living: Articulations of State–Capital Relations in the Multiple Crisis', *Globalizations* 9 (4), pp. 547–60.

Brand, Ulrich & Wissen, Markus (2017): *Imperiale Lebensweise: Zur Ausbeutung von Mensch und Natur im globalen Kapitalismus*, Munich.

Briegleb, Till (2016): 'Zensur als Geschäft', *Süddeutsche Zeitung*, 28 April 2016, p. 11.

Bundesministerium für Umwelt, Naturschutz, Bau und Reaktorsicherheit, BMUB (2017): *Umweltbewusstsein in Deutschland 2016: Ergebnisse einer repräsentativen Bevölkerungsumfrage*, Berlin.

Bundesverband der Deutschen Tourismuswirtschaft, BTW (ed.) (2015): *Entwicklungsfaktor Tourismus: Der Beitrag des Tourismus zur regionalen Entwicklung und lokalen Wertschöpfung in Entwicklungs- und Schwellenländern*, Langfassung, Berlin.

Burghardt, Peter (2014): 'Der Tod kommt mit dem Wind', *Süddeutsche Zeitung Magazin* 47, 21 November 2014, pp. 10–18.

Burghardt, Peter (2016): 'In der Erde, im Menschen', *Süddeutsche Zeitung*, 21/22 May 2016, p. 29.

Butler, Judith (1993): *Bodies That Matter: On the Discursive Limits of 'Sex'*, New York.

Calhoun, Craig (2013): 'What Threatens Capitalism Now?', pp. 131–61 in Immanuel Wallerstein, Randall Collins, Michael Mann, Georgi Derluguian & Craig Calhoun, *Does Capitalism Have a Future?* New York.

Chakrabarty, Dipesh (2000): *Provincializing Europe: Postcolonial Thought and Historical Difference*, Princeton.

Comaroff, Jean & Comaroff, John L. (2012): 'Theory from the South: Or, how Euro-America is Evolving Toward Africa', in: *Anthropological Forum* 22 (2), pp. 113–31.

Costa, Sérgio (2011): *Researching Entangled Inequalities in Latin America: The Role of Historical, Social, and Transregional Interdependencies*, desigualdades.net Working Paper Series No. 9, Berlin.

Dannoritzer, Cosima (2015): 'Giftige Geschäfte mit alten Geräten', pp. 86–9 in Le Monde diplomatique & Kolleg

Postwachstumsgesellschaften (eds.), *Atlas der Globalisierung: Weniger wird mehr*, Berlin.

Deaton, Angus (2013): *The Great Escape: Health, Wealth, and the Origins of Inequality*, Princeton.

Deutschmann, Christoph (1996): 'Marx, Schumpeter und Mythen ökonomischer Rationalität', *Leviathan* 24 (3), pp. 323–38.

Dörre, Klaus (2009): 'Die neue Landnahme: Dynamiken und Grenzen des Finanzmarktkapitalismus', pp. 21–86 in Klaus Dörre, Stephan Lessenich & Hartmut Rosa, *Soziologie – Kapitalismus – Kritik: Eine Debatte*, Frankfurt am Main.

Dörre, Klaus (2015): 'Social Capitalism and Crisis: From the Internal to the External *Landnahme*', pp. 247–79 in Klaus Dörre, Stephan Lessenich & Hartmut Rosa, *Sociology, Capitalism, Critique*, London.

Ehrenreich, Barbara & Hochschild, Arlie (2002): *Global Woman: Nannies, Maids, and Sex Workers in the New Economy*, New York.

Elias, Norbert (1978) [German original 1970]: *What is Sociology?* New York.

Encinas-Franco, Jean (2010): 'The State and the Globalisation of Care: the Philippines and the Export of Nurses', pp. 289–308 in Kirsten Scheiwe & Johanna Krawietz (eds.), *Transnationale Sorgearbeit: Rechtliche Rahmenbedingungen und gesellschaftliche Praxis*, Wiesbaden.

Federici, Silvia (2012): *Revolution at Point Zero: Housework, Reproduction, and Feminist Struggle*, Oakland.

Fink, Andreas (2015): 'Die Killerbohne', *Terra Mater* 4, pp. 76–98.

Freud, Sigmund (2003 [German original 1919]): 'The Uncanny', pp. 121–62 in Sigmund Freud, *Complete Psychological Works of Sigmund Freud*, vol. XVII, London.

Fücks, Ralf (2013): *Intelligent wachsen: Die grüne Revolution*, Munich.

Fuest, Clemens (2016): 'Zehn Thesen zur Ungleichheitsdebatte', *Frankfurter Allgemeine Zeitung*, 12 February 2016, p. 16.

Fulcher, James (2015): *Capitalism: a Very Short Introduction*, 2nd edn, New York.

Galeano, Eduardo (1973): *Open Veins of Latin America: Five Centuries of the Pillage of a Continent*, New York.

Galeano, Eduardo (2015) [original 1971]: *Las venas abiertas de América Latina*, Buenos Aires.

Galtung, Johan (1969): 'Violence, Peace, and Peace Research', *Journal of Peace Research* 6 (3), pp. 167–91.

Gottschall, Karin & Schwarzkopf, Manuela (2010): *Irreguläre Arbeit in Privathaushalten*, Arbeitspapier 217, Hans-Böckler-Stiftung, Düsseldorf.

Greffrath, Mathias (2015): 'Wider die globale Unvernunft', pp. 11–13 in Le Monde diplomatique & Kolleg Postwachstumsgesellschaften (eds.), *Atlas der Globalisierung: Weniger wird mehr*, Berlin.

Habermas, Jürgen (1986): 'The New Obscurity: the Crisis of the Welfare State and the Exhaustion of Utopian Energies', *Philosophy and Social Criticism* 11 (2), pp. 1–18.

Habermas, Jürgen (1987) [German original 1981]: *The Theory of Communicative Action*, vol. II, Boston.

Hartmann, Evi (2016a): *Wie viele Sklaven halten Sie? Über Globalisierung und Moral*, Frankfurt am Main / New York.

Hartmann, Evi (2016b): 'Wir Sklavenhalter: Warum die Globalisierung keine Moral kennt', *Blätter für deutsche und internationale Politik* 61 (3), pp. 41–9.

Hartmann, Kathrin (2009): *Ende der Märchenstunde: Wie die Industrie die Lohas und Lifestyle-Ökos vereinnahmt*, Munich.

Hartmann, Kathrin (2015): 'Grüne Märchen', *Süddeutsche Zeitung*, 29/30 August 2015, p. 45.

Haubner, Tine (2017): *Die Ausbeutung der sorgenden Gemeinschaft: Laienpflege in Deutschland*, Frankfurt am Main / New York.

Herre, Roman (2015): 'Landgrabbing in Europa', pp. 94–5 in Le Monde diplomatique & Kolleg Postwachstumsgesellschaften (eds.), *Atlas der Globalisierung: Weniger wird mehr*, Berlin.

Hess, Sabine (2001): 'Transnationale Überlebensstrategien von Frauen – Geschlecht und neuere Konzepte der Transkulturalität', pp. 197–225 in Steffi Hobuss, Christina Schües, Nina Zimnik, Birgit Hartmann and Iulia Pätrut, (eds.), *Die andere Hälfte der Globalisierung: Menschenrechte, Ökonomie und Medialität aus feministischer Sicht*, Frankfurt am Main / New York.

Hessel, Stéphane (2010): *Indignez-vous!*, Montpellier.

Hirst, Paul & Thompson, Grahame (1996): *Globalization in Question: the International Economy and the Possibilities of Governance*, Cambridge.

Horkheimer, Max & Adorno, Theodor W. (2002) [German original 1947]: *Dialectic of Enlightenment: Philosophical Fragments*, Stanford.

Hornborg, Alf (1998): 'Towards an Ecological Theory of Unequal Exchange: Articulating World System Theory and Ecological Economics', *Ecological Economics* 25, pp. 127–36.

Hornborg, Alf (2011): *Global Ecology and Unequal Exchange: Fetishism in a Zero-Sum World*, London.

Hottinger, Johann Jakob (1821): *Theophrast's Characterschilderungen*, Munich.

Jackson, Tim (2009): *Prosperity without Growth? Economics for a Finite Planet*, London.

Jensen, Annette (2015): 'Textilien für die Welt', pp. 63–7 in Le Monde diplomatique & Kolleg Postwachstumsgesellschaften (eds.), *Atlas der Globalisierung: Weniger wird mehr*, Berlin.

Jorgenson, Andrew K. & Rice, James (2005): 'Structural Dynamics of International Trade and Material Consumption: a Cross-National Study of the Ecological Footprints of Less-Developed Countries', *Journal of World-Systems Research* 11 (1), pp. 57–77.

Kant, Immanuel (1995) [German original 1784]: *Kant's Foundations of Ethics*, Millis.

Knight, Kyle W. & Rosa, Eugene A. (2011): 'The Environmental Efficiency of Well-being: a Cross-national Analysis', *Social Science Research* 40 (3), pp. 931–49.

Knöbl, Wolfgang (2001): *Spielräume der Modernisierung: Das Ende der Eindeutigkeit*, Weilerswist.

Kontzi, Kristina (2015): *Postkoloniale Perspektiven auf 'weltwärts': Ein Freiwilligendienst in weltbürgerlicher Absicht*, Baden-Baden.

Kornick, Sabino & Hicks, Alex (2015): The Rise of Finance: Causes and Consequences of Financialization, *Socio-Economic Review* 13 (3), special issue, Oxford.

Korzeniewicz, Roberto Patricio (2011): *Inequality: On Some of the Implications of a World-Historical Perspective*, desigualdades.net Working Paper Series No. 3, Berlin.

Korzeniewicz, Roberto Patricio & Moran, Timothy Patrick (2009): *Unveiling Inequality: a World-Historical Perspective*, New York.

Kreckel, Reinhard (2004): *Politische Soziologie der sozialen Ungleichheit*, 3rd edn, Frankfurt am Main / New York.

Kroh, Martin; Neiss, Hannes; Kroll, Lars & Lampert, Thomas (2012): 'Menschen mit hohen Einkommen leben länger', *DIW Wochenbericht* 38/2012, pp. 3–15.

Kröhnert, Steffen; Müller, Simon; Sievers, Florian & Klingholz, Reiner (2012): *Fünf Löwen auf dem Sprung? Wirtschaftliche und demografische Potenziale der aufstrebenden Länder Afrikas*, Berlin-Institut für Bevölkerung und Entwicklung, Berlin.

Latouche, Serge (2009): *Farewell to Growth*, Cambridge.

Lenin, V. I. (1962) [Russian original 1917]: *Der Imperialismus als höchstes Stadium des Kapitalismus: Gemeinverständlicher Abriss*, 6th edn, Berlin (East Germany).

Lenin, V. I. (2010) [Russian original 1917]: *Imperialism: The Highest Stage of Capitalism. A Popular Outline*, London.

Lewis, Jane (2001): 'The Decline of the Male Breadwinner Model: Implications for Work and Care', *Social Politics* 8 (2), pp. 152–69.

Luhmann, Niklas 1990 [German original 1981]: *Political Theory in the Welfare State*, Berlin.

Lutz, Helma & Palenga-Möllenbeck, Ewa (2015): 'Care-Arbeit, Gender und Migration: Überlegungen zu einer Theorie der transnationalen Migration im Haushaltsarbeitssektor in Europa', pp. 181–200 in Uta Meier-Gräwe (ed.), *Die Arbeit des Alltags: Gesellschaftliche Organisation und Umverteilung*, Wiesbaden.

Mackenzie, Hugh; Messinger, Hans & Smith, Rick (2008): *Size Matters: Canada's Ecological Footprint, By Income*, Toronto.

Maddison, Angus (2001): *The World Economy: a Millennial Perspective*, Paris.

Mahnkopf, Birgit (2014): '"Peak Capitalism"? Wachstumsgrenzen als Grenzen des Kapitalismus', *WSI-Mitteilungen* 67 (7), pp. 505–12.

Mahnkopf, Birgit (2015): '"Peak Everything", das gefährliche Maximum', pp. 62–3 in Le Monde diplomatique & Kolleg Postwachstumsgesellschaften (eds.), *Atlas der Globalisierung: Weniger wird mehr*, Berlin.

Mann, Michael (2013): 'The End May Be Nigh, But For Whom?', pp. 71–97 in Immanuel Wallerstein, Randall Collins, Michael Mann, Georgi Derluguian & Craig Calhoun, *Does Capitalism Have a Future?* New York.

Marshall, Thomas H. (1963) [original 1949]: 'Citizenship and Social Class', pp. 67–127 in Thomas H. Marshall, *Sociology at the Crossroads and Other Essays*, London.

Marx, Karl & Engels, Friedrich (1959) [original 1848]: 'Manifest der Kommunistischen Partei', pp. 459–93 in Karl Marx & Friedrich Engels, *Werke*, vol. IV, Berlin (East Germany).

Marx, Karl & Engels, Friedrich (1969) [original 1845/6]: *Werke*, vol. III, Berlin (East Germany).

Marx, Karl & Engels, Friedrich (2010) [German original 1848]: *The Communist Manifesto*, New York.

Mason, Paul (2015): *Postcapitalism: a Guide to Our Future*, London.

Mau, Steffen (2016): 'Alte Grenzen, neue Grenzen', *Süddeutsche Zeitung*, 9 May 2016, p. 2.

Mau, Steffen; Brabandt, Heike; Laube, Lena & Roos, Christof (2012): *Liberal States and the Freedom of Movement: Selective Borders, Unequal Mobility*, Basingstoke.

Mau, Steffen; Gülzau, Fabian; Laube, Lena & Zaun, Natascha (2015): 'The Global Mobility Divide: How Visa Policies Have Evolved over Time', *Journal of Ethnic and Migration Studies* 41 (8), pp. 1192–1213.

McConnell, Campbell R.; Brue, Stanley L. & Flynn, Sean M. (2009): *Economics: Principles, Problems, and Policies*, 18th edn, Boston.

McNeill, John R. & Engelke, P. (2014): *The Great Acceleration: an Environmental History of the Anthropocene since 1945*, Cambridge.

Meadows, Donella H.; Meadows, Dennis L.; Randers, Jørgen & Behrens III, William W. (1972): *The Limits to Growth: a Report to the Club of Rome's Project on the Predicament of Mankind*, New York.

Metz, Michaela (2015): 'Der Süsse Fluss vor der Katastrophe', *Süddeutsche Zeitung*, 23 December 2015, p. 14.

Mignolo, Walter D. (2011): *The Darker Side of Western Modernity: Global Futures, Decolonial Options*, Durham.

Milanović, Branko (2016): *Global Inequality: a New Approach for the Age of Globalization*, Cambridge.

Mills, Charles Wright (1967) [original 1959]: *The Sociological Imagination*, London.

Ming, Shi (2015): 'Chinas neue Mittelschichten', pp. 32–5 in Le Monde diplomatique & Kolleg Postwachstumsgesellschaften (eds.), *Atlas der Globalisierung: Weniger wird mehr*, Berlin.

Mitchell, Timothy (2011): *Carbon Democracy: Political Power in the Age of Oil*, London.

Moore, Jason (2011): 'Ecology, Capital, and the Nature of our Times: Accumulation and Crisis in the Capitalist World-Ecology', *Journal of World-Systems Research* 17 (1), pp. 109–47.

Moore, Jason (2015): *Capitalism in the Web of Life: Ecology and the Accumulation of Capital*, London.

Moran, Timothy Patrick (2015): 'It's Good to Be Rich: Piketty's *Capital in the Twenty-First Century*', *Sociological Forum* 30 (3), pp. 865–9.

Müller, Heiner (2001) [original 1977/9]: Die Hamletmaschine, pp. 543–54 in Heiner Müller, *Werke*, vol. IV: Die Stücke 2, Frankfurt am Main.

Müller, Heiner (2017): *'Für alle reicht es nicht': Texte zum Kapitalismus*, ed. Helen Müller and Clemens Pornschlegel, Berlin.

Nachtwey, Oliver (2016): *Die Abstiegsgesellschaft: Über das Aufbegehren in der regressiven Moderne*, Berlin.

Nassehi, Armin (2012): 'Ökonomisierung als Optionssteigerung: Eine differenzierungstheoretische Perspektive', *Soziale Welt* 63 (4), pp. 401–18.

Nassehi, Armin (2015): *Die letzte Stunde der Wahrheit: Warum rechts und links keine Alternativen mehr sind und Gesellschaft ganz anders beschrieben werden muss*, Hamburg.

Neumayer, Eric (2006): *Unequal Access to Foreign Spaces: How States Use Visa Restrictions to Regulate Mobility in a Globalized World*, LSE Research Online, London.

Nixon, Rob (2011): *Slow Violence and the Environmentalism of the Poor*, Cambridge.

Opielka, Michael (2016): 'Soziale Nachhaltigkeit aus soziologischer Sicht', *Soziologie* 45 (1), pp. 33–46.

Opielka, Michael (2017): *Soziale Nachhaltigkeit: Auf dem Weg zur Internalisierungsgesellschaft*, Munich.

Oulios, Miltiadis (2015): *Blackbox Abschiebung: Geschichte, Theorie und Praxis der deutschen Migrationspolitik*, Berlin.

Oxfam (2015): *Wealth: Having It All and Wanting More*, Oxfam Issue Briefing, January 2015, Oxford.

Oxfam (2016): *Ein Wirtschaftssystem für die Superreichen: Wie ein unfaires Steuersystem und Steueroasen die soziale Ungleichheit verschärfen*, Berlin.

Oxfam (2017): *An Economy for the 99%*, Oxfam Briefing Paper, January 2017, Oxford.

Parkin, Frank (1983): 'Strategien sozialer Schließung und Klassenbildung', pp. 121–35 in Reinhard Kreckel (ed.), *Soziale Ungleichheiten*, Soziale Welt – Sonderband 2, Göttingen.

Pereira, Kiran (2015): 'Sand, ein knappes Gut', pp. 72–5 in Le Monde diplomatique & Kolleg Postwachstumsgesellschaften (eds.), *Atlas der Globalisierung: Weniger wird mehr*, Berlin.

Piketty, Thomas (2014) [French original 2013]: *Capital in the Twenty-First Century*, Cambridge.

Poe, Edgar Allan (1984) [original 1842]: *Complete Stories and Poems of Edgar Allan Poe*, New York.

Polanyi, Karl (1957) [original 1944]: *The Great Transformation: the Political and Economic Origins of Our Time*, Boston.

Popper, Karl (2013) [English original 1945]: *The Open Society and Its Enemies*, Princeton.

Prisching, Manfred (1986): *Krisen: Eine soziologische Untersuchung*, Vienna.

Quijano, Aníbal (2010): 'Coloniality and Modernity/Rationality', pp. 22–32 in Walter D. Mignolo & Arturo Escobar (eds.), *Globalization and the Decolonial Option*, London / New York.

Randers, Jørgen (2012): *2052: A Global Forecast for the Next Forty Years*, White River Junction.

Rau, Milo (2016): 'Betroffenheit reicht nicht', *DIE ZEIT* 2, 7 January 2016, p. 41.

Rawls, John (1971): *A Theory of Justice*, Cambridge.

Ricardo, David (1975) [original 1817]: *On the Principles of Political Economy and Taxation*, Cambridge.

Rifkin, Jeremy (2014): *The Zero Marginal Cost Society: the Internet of Things, the Collaborative Commons, and the Eclipse of Capitalism*, New York.

Rilling, Rainer (2014): 'Transformation als Futuring', pp. 12–48 in Michael Brie (ed.), *Futuring: Perspektiven der Transformation im Kapitalismus über ihn hinaus*, Münster.

Rockström, Johan & Klum, Mattias (2012): *The Human Quest: Prospering Within Planetary Boundaries*, Stockholm.

Rotberg, Robert I. (ed.) (2003): *When States Fail: Causes and Consequences*, Princeton.

Said, Edward W. (1978): *Orientalism*, New York.

Sanyal, Kalyan (2007): *Rethinking Capitalist Development: Primitive Accumulation, Governmentality & Post-colonial Capitalism*, New Delhi.

Schlüter, Nadja (2016): 'Und nebenan wird abgeschoben', *jetzt* 2/16, pp. 8–13.

Schmalz, Stefan (2016): *Machtverschiebungen im Weltsystem: Der Aufstieg Chinas und die grosse Krise*, Frankfurt / New York.

Schmelzer, Matthias & Passadakis, Alexis (2011): *Postwachstum*, AttacBasisTexte 36, Hamburg.

Schmid, Fred (2010): *China: Krise als Chance? Aufstieg zur ökonomischen Weltmacht*, isw report 83/84, Munich.

Schurr, Carolin (2014): 'Retortenbabys aus der Retortenstadt', *Die Wochenzeitung* 35, 28 August 2014, www.woz.ch.

Shachar, Ayelet (2009): *The Birthright Lottery: Citizenship and Global Inequality*, Cambridge.

Shamir, Ronen (2005): 'Without Borders? Notes on Globalization as a Mobility Regime', *Sociological Theory* 23 (2), pp. 197–217.

Siltanen, Janet & Doucet, Andrea (2008): *Gender Relations: Intersectionality and Beyond*, Oxford.

Simmel, Georg (2009) [German original 1908]: *Sociology: Inquiries into the Construction of Social Forms*, vol. II, Leiden/Boston.

Smith, Adam (2003) [original 1776]: *The Wealth of Nations*, New York.

Sommer, Bernd (2017): 'Externalisation, Globalised Value Chains and the Invisible Consequences of Social Actions', *Historical Social Research* 42 (4), pp. 114–32.

Sommer, Bernd & Welzer, Harald (2014): *Transformationsdesign: Wege in eine zukunftsfähige Moderne*, Munich.

Straubhaar, Thomas (2002): *Migration im 21. Jahrhundert: Von der Bedrohung zur Rettung sozialer Marktwirtschaften?* Tübingen.

Suchanek, Norbert (2013): *Argentinien im Soja-Fieber: Dossier*, Forum Umwelt und Entwicklung, www.forumue.de.

Therborn, Göran (2013): *The Killing Fields of Inequality*, Cambridge.

Tilly, Charles (1998): *Durable Inequality*, Berkeley.

Tilly, Charles (2001): 'Relational Origins of Inequality', *Anthropological Theory* 1 (3), pp. 355–72.

Torpey, John (1997): 'Coming and Going: On the State Monopolization of the Legitimate "Means of Movement"', *Sociological Theory* 16 (3), pp. 239–59.

Turzi, Mariano (2017): *The Political Economy of Agricultural Booms: Managing Soybean Production in Argentina, Brazil, and Paraguay*, Cham.

UNDP (2016): *Human Development Report 2016: Human Development for Everyone*, United Nations Development Programme, New York.

UNHCR (2015): *UNHCR Mid-Year Trends 2015*, United Nations High Commissioner for Refugees, Geneva.

Veltmeyer, Henry & Petras, James (eds.) (2016): *The New Extractivism: a Post-Neoliberal Development Model or Imperialism of the Twenty-First Century?* London / New York.

Vinnai, Gerhard (2013): 'Geldsubjekt und Psychoanalyse', *psychosozial* 36 (2), no. 132, pp. 107–20.

Wallerstein, Immanuel (2003): 'Citizens All? Citizens Some! The Making of the Citizen', *Comparative Studies in Society and History* 45 (4), pp. 650–79.

Wallerstein, Immanuel (2004): *World-Systems Analysis: an Introduction*, Durham.

Wallerstein, Immanuel (2013): 'Structural crisis, or why capitalists may no longer find capitalism rewarding', pp. 9–35 in Immanuel Wallerstein, Randall Collins, Michael Mann, Georgi Derluguian & Craig Calhoun, *Does Capitalism Have a Future?* New York.

Weber, Max (2002): *The Protestant Ethic and the 'Spirit' of Capitalism and Other Writings*, New York.

Weber, Max (2012) [German original 1904]: 'The "objectivity" of knowledge in social sciences and social policy', pp. 100–38 in Hans Hendrick Bruun & Sam Whimster (eds.), *Collected Methodological Writings*, New York.

Wehling, Peter (2006): *Im Schatten des Wissens? Perspektiven der Soziologie des Nichtwissens*, Konstanz.

Welzer, Harald (2011): *Mentale Infrastrukturen: Wie das Wachstum in die Welt und in die Seelen kam*, Schriften zur Ökologie 14, Berlin.

Wesche, Tilo (2017): 'Gleichgültigkeit: Eine Sozialphilosophie der Selbsttäuschung', pp. 179–222 in Emil Angehrn & Joachim Küchenhoff (eds.), *Selbsttäuschung: Eine Herausforderung für Philosophie und Psychoanalyse*, Weilerswist.

Wilkinson, Richard G. & Pickett, Kate (2009): *The Spirit Level: Why Equality is Better for Everyone*, London.

Wimmer, Andreas & Glick Schiller, Nina (2002): 'Methodological Nationalism and Beyond: Nation-state Building, Migration and the Social Sciences', *Global Networks* 2 (4), pp. 301–34.

Wissen, Markus (2016): 'Jenseits der *carbon democracy*: Zur Demokratisierung der gesellschaftlichen Naturverhältnisse', pp. 48–66 in Alex Demirović (ed.), *Transformation der Demokratie – demokratische Transformation*, Münster.

Wright, Erik Olin (2006): 'Compass Points: Towards a Socialist Alternative', *New Left Review* 41, pp. 93–124.

WWF Deutschland (2009): *Der touristische Klima-Fussabdruck: WWF-Bericht über die Umweltauswirkungen von Urlaub und Reisen*, Frankfurt am Main.

WWF Deutschland (2014): *Living Planet Report 2014: Kurzfassung*, Berlin.

WWF International (2014): *Living Planet Report 2014*, Gland.

Zick, Tobias (2016): 'Sklaven des Gifts', *Süddeutsche Zeitung*, 18/19 June 2016, p. 38.